Leopold von Ranke

History of the Latin and Teutonic Nations from 1494 to 1514

Leopold von Ranke

History of the Latin and Teutonic Nations from 1494 to 1514

ISBN/EAN: 9783337326340

Printed in Europe, USA, Canada, Australia, Japan

Cover: Foto ©Thomas Meinert / pixelio.de

More available books at **www.hansebooks.com**

BOHN'S STANDARD LIBRARY.

RANKE'S LATIN AND TEUTONIC NATIONS.

1494-1514.

HISTORY OF THE
LATIN AND TEUTONIC NATIONS

FROM 1494 TO 1514.

BY LEOPOLD VON RANKE.

TRANSLATED FROM THE GERMAN

BY

PHILIP A. ASHWORTH,

OF THE INNER TEMPLE, BARRISTER-AT-LAW.

Translator of Gneist's Constitutional History of England.

LONDON: GEORGE BELL AND SONS, YORK STREET,
COVENT GARDEN.
1887.

[*Authorized translation.*]

CHISWICK PRESS :—C. WHITTINGHAM AND CO., TOOKS COURT,
CHANCERY LANE.

PREFACE.

IT has been my privilege, not only to have been entrusted by the world-renowned historian with the task of translating this work, but also, in personal interviews, to have been instructed by him how to proceed, in order to meet his views and wishes.

His demand, that I should adhere literally to the text, could not be disregarded. Therefore, in presenting this translation to the public, I have confidence that the sacrifice of literary style to scrupulous fidelity will not be imputed to me as a fault.

For myself, I modestly claim that my rendering of this work into English is, with all its blemishes, a fairly faithful reproduction of the author's words and meaning.

Few men, and still fewer historians, have been permitted to draw the space of seventy years within the range of their practical experience; Leopold von Ranke was allowed to see his nation, whose life and struggles at the commencement of the sixteenth century he has so vividly and realistically depicted, raise itself from abasement to a first and foremost position among the Latino-Teutonic nations. Possibly it was the resuscitation of the feeling of German unity, after the close of the Napoleonic wars, which awoke in him the desire to show how the energy and independence of the German national character asserted themselves in the middle ages.

The third edition of the original (1885) lacks any special introduction by the author; but I cannot omit reproducing here a sentence contained in the preface to the first edition (1824), which clearly shows the historian's feeling as to the treatment of history :—

"A strict representation of facts, be it ever so narrow and unpoetical, is, beyond doubt, the first law."

During an interview I had the pleasure to have with him a few weeks previous to his death, the historian made some observations of such interest that I should be unwilling to withhold them from publication. The conversation turned upon the sources of his historical information, when Professor von Ranke, in effect, said as follows:—"Great as is the respect and veneration in which I hold Sir Walter Scott, I cannot help regretting that he was not more available for the purposes of a historian than he is. If fiction must be built upon facts, facts should never be contorted to meet the ends of the novelist. What valuable lessons were not to be drawn from facts to which the great English novelist had the key; yet, by reason of the fault to which I have referred, I have been unable to illustrate many of my assertions by reference to him."

This statement, read together with the passage from the preface to the first edition of the original, shows the fears entertained by Professor von Ranke, that history might suffer at the hands of the novelist, and, at the same time, contains an expression of hope that it may be *seriously* used by posterity as a valuable storehouse for practical advantage, and *never* treated as fictitious matter.

It were presumptuous in me to attempt any comment upon the work now set before the English public. I shall be content if I have been able to make plain the meaning of the most distinguished historian of our era.

P. A. ASHWORTH.

TEMPLE,
    November, 1886.

CONTENTS.

	PAGE
Introduction.—Outlines of a treatise upon the Unity of the Latin and German Nations, and their common development	1

BOOK I.

Chapter I.—The relations of France and Italy.—Expedition of Charles VIII. to Naples	20
Chapter II.—Spain and Liga in war with Charles VIII.	61
Chapter III.—Maximilian of Austria and the Empire	93
Chapter IV.—The fall of the House of Sforza and Aragon	132

BOOK II.

Introduction	182
Chapter I.—The War in Naples and Romagna	187
Chapter II.—Variances between the Houses of Spain and Austria	214
Chapter III.—Of Venice and Julius II.	248
Chapter IV.—The rise of the Austro-Spanish House to almost the highest power in Europe	316

LATIN AND TEUTONIC NATIONS.

INTRODUCTION.

OUTLINES OF A TREATISE UPON THE UNITY OF THE LATIN AND GERMAN NATIONS, AND THEIR COMMON DEVELOPMENT.

AT the beginning of his fortune, and not long after the migration of nations had commenced, Ataülf, King of the Visigoths, conceived the idea of gothicising the Roman world, and making himself the Cæsar of all; he would maintain the Roman laws.[1] If we understand him aright, he first intended to combine the Romans of the West in a new unity with the German races, though they were sprung of many and diverse tribes, but had, after a union that had lasted for centuries, at length become one realm and one people.

He later despaired of being able to effect this; but the collective German nations at last brought it about, and in a still wider sense than he had dreamt of. No long time elapsed, and Lugdunesian Gaul did not, it is true, become a Gothland, but a Lugdunesian Germania.[2] Eventually the purple of a Cæsar passed to the German houses in the person of Charlemagne. At length these likewise adopted the Roman law. In this combination six great nations were formed—three in which the Latin element predominated, viz., the French, the Spanish, and the Italian; and three in

[1] Orosius, vii. 34. Cf. Mascow. Geschichte der Deutschen bis zur fränkischen Monarchie.
[2] Sidonius Apollinaris in Mascow, 480.

which the Teutonic element was conspicuous, viz., the German, the English, and the Scandinavian.

Wherein can the unity of these six nationalities be manifested and perceived? Each is again resolvable into various units, which never constituted a separate nation, and which were almost always in feud with each other. They are all sprung from the same or a closely allied stock; are alike in manners, and similar in many of their institutions: their internal histories precisely coincide, and certain great enterprises are common to all.

The following historical work, which is based upon this conception, would be unintelligible, were not the latter explained by a short survey of those external enterprises which, arising as they do from the same mental reason, form a progressive development of the Latin and Teutonic life from the first beginning until now. Such are the migration of nations, the Crusades, and the colonization of foreign countries.

1.

The migration of nations originated the unity of which we speak. The actual event, the movement itself, proceeded from the Germans; but the Latin countries were not merely passive. In exchange for the arms and the new public life which they received, they communicated to the victors their religion and their language. Reccared had, indeed, to become a Catholic before mutual intermarriage between the Visigoths and the Latin peoples could be legally permitted in Spain.[1] But, after this, the races and their languages became completely blended. In Italy the communities of Lombard and Roman extraction, in spite of their original separation, became so closely intertwined that it is almost impossible to distinguish the component elements of each. It is clear what great influence the bishops exercised upon the founding of France; and yet they were at first purely of Latin origin. It is not until the

---

[1] Lex Flavii Reccaredi Regis, ut tam Romano, etc., in Leges Visigothorum, iii. 1, 1 Hispan. Illustr. iii. 88. Also in Mascow and Montesquieu, de l'Esprit des Lois, xxviii. 27.

year 566 A.D. that we meet with a Frankish bishop in Paris.¹

Now, although in these nations we find that both elements in a short time became welded and blended together, the case was very different with the Anglo-Saxons, the implacable foes of the Britons, from whom they adopted neither religion nor language, as well as with the other Teutons in their German and Scandinavian home. Yet even these were not finally able to resist the Latin Christianity and a great part of the Latin culture. Between both divisions of this conglomeration of peoples there became formed a close community of kindred blood, kindred religion, institutions, manners, and modes of thought. They successfully resisted the influence of foreign races. Among those nations which besides them had taken part in the migration of peoples, it was chiefly the Arabs, Hungarians, and Slavs that threatened to disturb, if not to annihilate them. But the Arabs were averted by the complete incompatibility of their religion; the Hungarians were beaten back within their own borders, and the neighbouring Slavs were at last annihilated or subjected.

What can knit together individuals or nations into closer relationship than a participation in the same destiny, and a common history? Among the internal and external occurrences of these earliest times, the unity of one single event can be almost perceived. The Teutonic nations, possessors from time immemorial of a great country, take the field, conquer the Roman empire of the West, and, more than this, keep what they have gotten. About the year 530 we find them in possession of all the countries, extending from the cataracts of the Danube to the mouth of the Rhine and even to the Tweed, as well as of all the high country from Heligoland to that Bætica, from which the Vandals take their name, and across the sea, until where the Atlas range sinks down into the desert. As long as they were united, no one was able to wrest these territories from them; but the dismemberment of the Vandals, and the contrasts of Arian and Catholic doctrines, was the first beginning of their ruin. The loss that was

¹ Plank. Gesellschafts-verfassung der christlichen Kische, ii. 96.

caused by the fall of the Ostrogothic empire was to a certain extent retrieved by the Lombards when they occupied Italy—yet not entirely, for never at any time were they complete masters of Italy, to say nothing of Sicily or Illyria,[1] as the Goths were; but it was owing to these Lombards, who at first destroyed Herulei and Gepidæ, but thereupon left their hereditary and their conquered settlements to a Sarmatian people,[2] that the Danube was lost almost up to its sources. A fresh loss was the destruction of the Thuringian empire. The irruption of the Slavs far into the country lying to the west of the Elbe is probably not unconnected with this. But the greatest danger was threatened by the Arabs. They took Spain at a dash; invaded France and Italy; and, had they won a single battle more, at least the Latin portion of our nations might have been doomed. What could be expected when Franks and Lombards, Franks and Saxons, Angles and Danes lived in deadly enmity? Let us not forget that the founding of the Papacy and the Empire warded off this danger.

If I may be allowed to state my own convictions, the real power of the Papacy—that which was really durable—was not established before the seventh century. It was not until then that the Anglo-Saxons recognized in the Pope, from whom their conversion immediately proceeded, their true patriarch, took to them a primate of his appointment, and paid him tribute.[3] It was from England, that Boniface, the apostle to the Germans, went forth. Not only on being raised to the episcopal chair at Mayence, did he swear allegiance, sincere devotion, and assistance to St. Peter and his successors, but the other bishops also swore to remain until death subject to the Roman Church, and to keep the ordinances of Peter's successors. He did yet more. For a hundred years before his day not a single letter can be found from the Pope of Rome, addressed to the Frankish clergy, so independent were the latter. Boniface, on Pipin's incentive, brought them also into subjection; and the metropolitan bishops whom he instituted took the Pallium

---

[1] Manso. Geschichte der Ostgothen in Italien, v. 321.
[2] Paulus Diaconus, de rebus Gestis Longobardorum, ii. c. 7.
[3] Schröckh. Kirchengeschichte, xix. i. 35.

from Rome.[1] Those were the three nations in which, with the Lombards, Christendom consisted in the West after the Spanish disaster. Charlemagne also freed the Pope from the enmity of the Lombards; he made him the Frankish Patricius, so that he ceased dating his bulls by the years of the reigns of the Greek emperors, and drew him completely into the sphere of the newly founded world. Thus did the Pope become the ecclesiastical head of the Latino-Teutonic nations. He became so in those very days in which the Arabs became powerful and advanced; his new dignity assuaged the enmity of the hostile races, and effected a material reconciliation between them. But they were only able to cope with the enemy, when relying on the power of the Pepins and the empire of Charlemagne.

Merit is due to Charlemagne for having united all the Latino-Germanic nations of the Continent, in so far as they were Christians, or were becoming so. Egbert, moreover, who made the heptarchy of the Angles a single monarchy, was his disciple—for having given them a constitution suited alike for war and peace, and for having taught them to advance again against their enemies along the Danube, to the east of the Saale and Elbe, and across the Pyrenees. But all had not yet been done. There appeared on one side the Hungarians, irresistible at all points, with their fleet horses and their arrows; and simultaneously on the other, on all coasts, the Normans, Vikings, and Askemans, alike daring by sea and land. But at this very time the sovereign rule of Charlemagne perished through the mistakes made by his successors, who only received nicknames for their follies, so that the danger was renewed. It may be said that the migration of nations did not cease before these movements calmed down. The Hungarians were driven back, and became Christians; and at the same time the contiguous Slavish nations became Christian also. One and other of them long vacillated between the Romish and the Greek form of worship before—and this is doubtlessly due to the influence of the German emperors—they decided for the former. It will not be said that these peoples belong also to the unity of our nations; their manners and their constitution have ever severed them from it. At

[1] Notes in Plank, vol. ii. 680 *seq.*

that time they never exercised any independent influences, they only appear either subservient or antagonistic; the waves of the general movements sometimes reach them, and, so to say, die away there. But the Normans of German origin were drawn into the circle of the other nations, and established themselves in France and England. They retaliated by carrying German life in the eleventh century across to Naples and Sicily. Their kindred at home had also meantime become Christians, and, saving an insignificant remnant, completely entered into the circle to which they naturally belonged.

Here, then, in the middle of the eleventh century, the movements of the migration of nations ended. The future development of the European languages, an intellectual fruit of these stormy centuries, had now been laid in all its unity and diversity. If we glance at the French form of oath prescribed at Strasburg, we fancy we find therein traces of the Italian, French, and Spanish dialects all at once. As this points to the unity of the Latin dialects, so does the fact that they have been recently combined in a single grammar bear still greater testimony to the unity of the Germanic dialects. The foundations of all modern kingdoms and their constitutions had been laid. Empire and Papacy were held in universal regard; the former represented the Teutonic, the latter the Latin principle of the great union of nations; the one supported the other.

2.

After this, the original migratory impulse took a different turn, owing to the fact that it coalesced with a complete devotion to Christianity. The Crusades may almost be regarded as a continuation of the migration of nations. The same people that had concluded it, viz., the Normans, took, of all concerned, a most vigorous part in the first Crusade. In this they were not only led by three eminent princes, namely, Robert of Normandy, whom the old chroniclers place above the supreme commander in point of nobility, wealth, and even intellectual excellence,[1] Bohe-

---

[1] Passage from Radulfus Cadomensis in Wilken Kreuzzüge, i. 80.

INTRODUCTION. 7

mund of Tarento, whose participation contemporaries rightly connected with his operations against the Greeks and Tancred, but by so many more,[1] that a war, that was then being waged, had to be brought to a close, owing to dearth of warriors. It may perchance be a Norwegian, St. Olaf, who was the first to adopt the cross both for himself and his army, when engaging in war.[2]

The great armed pilgrimages to Jerusalem in the eleventh century appear to have originated with the Normans; the successful issue of them is at all events ascribed to them before all others by Roger Hoveden.[3] All the Latino-Germanic nations shared in this new enthusiasm. In the first expedition we find Spaniards, the counts of Cerdan and Caret.[4] Lopez de Vega has left us a grand poem, immortalizing the meritorious services of the Castilians in the Holy Land. As early as the year 1121, Sigurd of Norway earned the name of Jörsalafar (pilgrim to Jerusalem); of the other nations it is known that they also took part in it. Never did a foreign nation, and only on one occasion did a foreign prince, Andrew of Hungary, participate therein, and he only did so as being the leader of an upper German expedition, and he was, besides, the son of a French mother. The Crusades are in the main entirely and solely undertakings of the Latin and German nations.

Now let us observe how these Crusades caused our nations to extend on all sides and in all directions. Their goal was, it is true, the Holy Land, yet they went to the coast of the Mediterranean besides, and not to that land alone. The Latin Empire at Constantinople would, had it longer existed, have turned the whole Greek Empire into a Latino-German one.

Had it not been for St. Louis' ill-luck, Egypt would have become a colony of France; and there appeared at that time a sensible, and beyond all doubt instructive book upon the relations between the East and the West,

[1] Ganfredus Monachus de acquisitione Siciliæ, iv. 24.
[2] Gebhardi. Geschichte von Norwegen und Dänemark, i. 380.
[3] In Hugo Grotius. Prolegomena ad histor. Gothorum, p. 60.
[4] Mariana, Hist. Hisp. x. c. 3. Capmany, antiqua Marina de Cataluna, i. 124.

written with the express intention of inciting to renewed operations against Egypt.¹ In the year 1150 King Roger of Sicily—known as Rogier Jarl the Rich among his old countrymen—had possession of the coasts of Africa from Tunis to Tripolis, and occupied Mahadia.² But the most important and permanent achievements in the southern world were, without doubt, due to the Spaniards. Their Campeador, the Cid, lived to see the Crusades. In those selfsame times they first succeeded in holding Toledo and the valley of the Tagus, which Aldefons imperator had just conquered, against the violent attack of the Almoravides, and then advanced under Alonso Ramon and took the valley of the Guadiana; (at the extreme limit of his actual conquests, for all the rest were again lost, under a widespreading oak upon the Muratal Mountains, Alonso breathed his last). In the same period they gained under Alonso the Noble the great battle of Navas de Tolosa, and set foot on the Guadalquivir.³ And finally, at that very time, shortly before the first Crusade of St. Louis, St. Ferdinand subdued Jaen, Cordova, and Seville, and as Granada paid him tribute, the whole of Andalusia also, whilst, shortly before the second Crusade, Alonso the Wise subjected Murcia. In these days Portugal was founded and established as a kingdom. The union of Aragon and Catalonia, the conquest of Valencia, and the exploits of the Conquistador Jayme fall also into this period.

And all this is closely connected with the expeditions to the Holy Land. The Archbishop Richard of Toledo, who came to Rome with a host of Crusaders, was sent back again by the Pope, because both he and they were more indispensable at home; and instead of leading them against Jerusalem he now led them against Alcala.⁴ We know that it was chiefly Low-Germans, English, and Flemish, who, proceeding on a Crusade, conquered his capital for the prince, who first called himself King of Portugal;⁵ and that seventy years later Alfonso II.'s most brilliant

---
¹ Marini Sanuti liber Secretorum fidelium Crucis in Bongars.
² Raumer, Geschichte der Hohenstaufen, i. 557.
³ All taken from Rodericus Toletanus, de rebus Hispaniæ.
⁴ Rodericus, vi. 26.
⁵ Dodechini Appendix ad Marianum Scotum. Pistor. i. 676.

conquest was only effected by the same assistance.[1] In short, the conquest of the peninsula was only achieved by the co-operation of kindred races. Out of the plunder of Almeria, Alonso Ramon gave a splendid jewel to the Genoese as a thankoffering for their services. In the battle of Navas de Tolosa many thousands from beyond the Pyrenees [2] fought in the army of Alonso the Noble.

Concurrently with these operations and progressive advances of our nations on the coasts of the Mediterranean and in the South generally, there were others being carried on in the North which were prompted by the same spirit. Sigur Jörsalafar, whom we have referred to, made it his first business, after his return, to land at Calmar and to coerce the Smalandic heathen, man by man, to embrace Christianity. With the same object in view Eric the Holy led the Swedes against the Finns. He shed tears on seeing the battle, but did not stay his hand until he had baptized the Finns in the springs of Lupisala. On the occasion of the second Crusade, on the receipt of a bull from Pope Eugene, the Danes, Saxons, and Westphalians leagued together to make a common expedition against the neighbouring Slavs, resolved either to convert them to Christianity, or else to exterminate them.[3] Not long after this, Bishop Meinhard came with traders and artisans from Wisby to Estonia to preach there. These three undertakings led, if not immediately, at all events by degrees, to a brilliant success. On our side of the Oder the Slavs were, by the times of the Crusades, as good as perfectly exterminated. German nobility, German citizens and peasants were the real stock of the new inhabitants of Mecklenburg, Pomerania, Brandenburg and Silesia. Since that time the Eastern Pomeranians have not been called by the Western aught else than Saxons.[4]

At last, in the year 1248, after long struggles, Finnland became entirely Christian and Swedish.[5] Since that date

[1] Gotefridi Monachi Annales, 284.
[2] Epistola Alfonsi VIII. ad pontificem de belis, etc. in. Continuat. belii sancti, Basle, 1549, p. 246.
[3] Anselrri Gemblacensis Abbatis Chronicon. Pistor, i. 965.
[4] Kanzow. Pomerania, i. 216.
[5] Schöning in Schlözers Allgem. nord, Geschichte, 474.

Swedes dwell along the whole coast, and in the strongholds there. Proceeding from the unpretentious colony, Yxkull, the German rule extended over all Estonia, Livonia, and Courland; nay, when the "Knights of the Sword," who had been established there, despaired of being able to defend a certain fortress against the Prussians,[1] in spite of a great display of bravery, they were instrumental in bringing the "German Knights" to their assistance, who then made the land of the Letti a German country. A short time longer, and the joint possessions of both orders extended from Danzig to Narva. Here they met the Pomeranians, who were now either entirely germanized or partially so, owing to their subjection under Emperor and Empire. Here, on the Gulf of Finland, they became neighbours of the Swedes. The German name embraced the whole Belt.

To the sphere of these events belong the operations of Henry Plantagenet in Ireland. He brought it to pass that thenceforth two nations co-existed in Ireland—the native Irish, the subjected, and the Anglo-Germanic, the dominant, which latter, if it was not actually planted, was yet settled and established there by him.[2] At that time Venice taught the Dalmatians to speak Italian. This event must also be comprehended in our survey, for it is a new extension of our nations; and the Pope likewise instigated the attack upon Ireland, because that land would never obey him.

Yet, in order not to depart from the principle we have laid down, both those undertakings must be principally kept in view, viz., the Northern and the Southern, both which were sprung of the same tendency, and were carried out by the same arms, under the same symbols, and often with the assistance of the same men. They show the unity of our nations in idea, in action, and in development.

But this principle is most clearly visible in the Crusades of the South and the North. This stirring energy, the result of an intellectual impulse, expanding in all directions, found a fitting expression in those noble institutions

---

[1] Dusburg in Script. rer. Pruss. i. 35.
[2] Hume's Hist. of England, i. c. ix. p. 281.

INTRODUCTION. 11

and creations which belong to it, and belong to it exclusively.

Two alone we will dwell on. War may arouse every brutal passion in our nature, but it is the province of chivalry to save the true man, to soften force by manners, and the elevating influence of women, and to refine strength by pointing it to what is divine. Its origin, in this sense, is coeval with the formation of the two first ecclesiastical orders of knighthood, and the zenith of its bloom coincides beyond doubt with the foundation of the third. After the Crusades had passed by, it did not die out, but took another development which was different in different lands. It never spread to other nations. Even the Johannites and Templars never owned a province in any other nation, at most a few possessions. The "German Knights" stood in constant contrast to the Letti and the Slavs. One noble blossom of chivalry is the poetry of these times. If it is true, as seems to be the case, that the story of Bechadas, by Godfrey de Bouillon, was the first novel,[1] and if the cycle of tales of Charlemagne and Arthur are, as appears very probable, immediately connected therewith, it is evident what a great share the Crusades have had in the foundation of modern poetry. It binds all our nations exclusively together. The prefaces to the "Wilkina," and the Niflungasaga, confess that these were fashioned in Iceland after German models.[2] No other people had any share in it.

But war was not waged by knights alone, the freedom of the towns was also warlike. Their origin, in the case of all our nations, dates from the same,—that is this time. The first consuls of the Italian communities, chosen by themselves, and upon the selection of whom their whole freedom depended, appear contemporaneously with the first Crusade, in the year 1100. Beyond all question, we meet with them first in Genoa on the occasion of an expedition to the Holy Land.

In the course of our period they procured for themselves

---

[1] Passage from Gottfried de Bigeois by Eichhorn, Gesch. der Cultur und Literatur d. neuern Europa, i. p. 82.

[2] Proemium, quoted in Eichhorn. Geschichte der Cultur. Erläuterungen, p. 125.

the full powers of the old royal counts.[1] As early as the year 1112, we meet with the same institutions in France, free communities under magistrates and majores of their own election. In the same way as the king under the oriflamb, the standard of St. Denis—a device which appears to be the true origin of this imperial banner—so do all the communes, each under the standard of its local saint, take the field with him.[2] The cities in Castilia, because of their martial ardour, were, in the year 1169, given a seat in the Cortes; and in the battle of Navas their assistance does not appear to have been the most insignificant. The German cities, in the course of the same period, by freeing themselves from their bailiffs, developed to independent unions.[3] During the reign of Henry III. the English towns were summoned to Parliament.[4] It was in Gottland, upon Swedish soil, that Wisby flourished. Enough; hand in hand with chivalry and the crusades, cities developed both in freedom and importance throughout the Latin-Germanic nations from north to south. In the same way as the peculiarities of our poetry are due to chivalry, so does our peculiar architectural style appear to be due to the cities. In this self-same period it developed from the flat roof and the semi-circle to those beautiful symmetrical proportions we admire in the façade of the cathedral at Strasburg, in the choir at Cologne, in the spire of Freiburg, and in the whole edifice at Marburg—of the year 1235—as well as in the cathedrals of Sienna, Rouen, and Burgos.

Neither in chivalry nor yet in the development of the cities have other nations had a share. As late as the year 1501, the Russians of Moscow begged that a knight,—an iron man, as they expressed it,—should be sent them, and marvelled at him as a wonder. The gates of the cathedral at Novgorod are the work of Magdeburg craftsmen.

Let us dwell yet upon another phenomenon. In the same way that the migration of nations was accompanied by the establishment of the Empire and the Papacy, did the struggle

[1] Savigny, Geschichte des Römischen Rechts im Mittelalter, iii. 100-121. Sismondi, Histoire des républ. ital. i. 373, from Caffaro.
[2] Ordericus Vitalis in Du Cange, sub Commune. Velli, Hist. de France, iii. 93.
[3] Document of the year 1255 in Vogt's Rheinische Geschichte, i. 426.
[4] Woltmann, Englische Geschichte, ii. 121.

between these twain forces arise out of the Crusades. It is not merely a struggle between the Emperor and the Pope; its relations to all those confessing the Roman faith are patent and evident. The quarrel between Henry II. of England and Thomas à Becket is quite analogous to it, both in respect of the interests the combatants had at stake, as well as in the kind of weapons they employed. The two princes and the two ecclesiastics were allied; this quarrel concerns moreover all our nations. Frederick I. had Swedes in the army with which he invaded Italy in 1158;[1] it was mainly English gold that supported the popes in their struggles at Naples. The internal affairs of Castile act and react upon the history of Conradin.[2] Charles of Anjou, who brought these wars to a close, was the brother of the French king. It could not but be that internal dissensions influenced external. It was natural that in the midst of his Italian wars he should sigh for Asia, where the strength and energy he lavished upon them would have guaranteed him more genuine glory and more perfect happiness.[3] But also the internal forces destroyed themselves. The Papacy was in error in believing that it had gained in strength by the fall of the Hohenstaufen. Conradin had not yet been forty years dead, when it fell into the captivity of the French kings. Since that time it has never again been the old Papacy. Which of our nations could say that it has not been unaffected by this?

We may distinguish two periods, in respect of these external enterprises; the first is that, when they begin in all their first freshness and when they fill all thoughts and hearts. The second period is that of their continuation, their effects and results. If this strikes the professional eye at the first glance in the migration of nations, it is almost even more striking in the case of the Crusades.
After the decay and fall of the two great powers, and when the universal interest in external operations had, in the fourteenth and fifteenth centuries, gradually cooled

[1] Dalin, Schwedische Geschichte, ii. 88.
[2] Raumer, Hohenstaufen, iv. 586.
[3] Raumer from Ricobald, ii. 411.

down, there arose in the heart of our nations, so to say, a universal war of all against all. It was those that belonged most closely together that quarrelled most violently. The Provençals and Catalan are of one stock; but, owing to the pretentious claims of their princes,—the houses of Anjou and Barcelona,—to Naples, they at that time fell into an enmity that lasted for centuries. It was in this struggle that Naples and Sicily became sundered. Portugal was originally a fief of the crown of Castile. After this feudal bond had become severed, the pride of both nations caused a deadly hatred to take root in them.

Moreover, the party of the Nuñez and Gamboa pervaded the whole of Spain. Civil wars were only now and again interrupted by a campaign against the Moors, at other times it was the reverse. In Italy Guelphs and Gibellines, whose names scarcely existed before the commencement of the thirteenth century,[1] nursed and fostered a feud that divided up the whole land, town from town, and almost house from house. Owing to the strife between their royal houses, not, as was formerly the case, for a few fiefs, but for the crown itself, France and England became locked in deadly wars. At first it was France that was convulsed by English arms and a great English party; and then England itself was torn by the wars of the white and the red rose. In Germany, races and families fought together no less; Suabians and Swiss are both Alemans, but they now fell into deadly feud. Austrians and Bavarians are the same race; the battle of Mühldorf shows how little they regarded it. Franconia became split up into the opposing factors of knightly and ecclesiastical possessions. Wars of succession, wars of children against their fathers, and wars between brothers, laid waste Thuringia and Meissen. Brandenburg and Pomerania were both peopled by Saxon colonists; but the pretentious claims of the Brandenburg princes to the country of the Pomeranians became a great offence between them, and in Pomeranian chronicles the people of the Mark are always mentioned with dislike. Besides this, we have the rising of princes against the sovereign power, and of freeholders against the

[1] Muratori de Guelfis et Gibellinis, Antiquitat. Ital. iv. 607, 608.

princes; and, in cases where they were immediate subjects of the Empire, a rising of the knights against the cities; whilst in the cities the guilds rose against the families. Frequently, also, the crown was the object of contention. And it is not alone nations and races, states and cabinets, that regulate public affairs, but families, corporations, and individuals, everyone in each matter for himself as best as he may.

In this state of things it might be thought it were scarcely possible that the unity of an empire, let alone the collective body of our nations, could have been preserved. The party divides, but it also unites. It is mainly the Anglo-French wars that act and re-act upon the rest of the European complications, and bind them all together. What could appear to be wider apart than the rebellion of oppressed Scots against the English, and the struggle of Albert and Adolph for the crown of Germany? The battle of Cambus Kennet, in which the English were defeated, and that of Hasenbühel, in which Adolphus fell, both in the year 1298, are all the same intimately connected. Albert was allied with the French, and through them with the Scots, Adolph ·with the English. The English party in Europe was defeated in both battles. The quarrel between Louis of Bavaria and Charles of Luxemburg for the same crown of Germany was decided not so much in Germany, as by the battle of Cressy. Shortly before it took place, Charles had been raised with all pomp to the regal chair by four Electors; immediately after it—his party, the French, had lost—we see him hurrying back to Bohemia reft of dignity and power; but Louis sends and solemnly receives English embassies.[1]

In the interest of these two parties, and mainly with their assistance, Peter the Cruel and Henry of Trastamar waged their war for the crown of Castile. Peter's avarice having driven the Black Prince, who had assisted him, to the "Foagium," and the "Foagium" having goaded the latter's vassals to discontent,[2] which resulted in the decay of the English power in France, while Henry, on the

[1] Albertus Argentinensis apud Urstisium, ii. 139.
[2] Le premier volume de Messire Jehan Froissart, f. 136.

other hand, conquered with the French in Spain, it may be said that the English power had begun to wane in Spain. Other threads connect these events with affairs in Holland and Guelders, in Aragon and Sardinia, and in Venice and Genoa; hence, not much credence can be placed in the assertion, so often made, that the nations in the Middle Ages were isolated from each other. Even great intellectual movements pass through them all, and testify to their internal unity. About the year 1350 we find, almost as in these times in which we live, a general tendency to regenerate constitutions. Let us remark that it was then (1347) that Cola Rienzi, the Italian zealot, actually restored the good old state of things, as he called it—that is, a kind of republican form of government at Rome; further, that in those times (1356) plebeians and doge of Venice leagued together against the nobles, in order, in one murderous night, to restore their old rights; and that, at the same time (1355), in France, a first assembly of estates of the realm promised both to live and to die with the king, but did not a little curtail his rights; a second demanded reforms and presented a list of twenty-two high persons who were to be deposed from office; whilst a third finally ushered in a complete revolution, and forced the dauphin to don their red and green cap.[1] These movements were illegal and transitory. Others, at the self-same time, confined themselves within narrower limits and had more durable results. In Aragon, in 1348, in the place of the violent power of the union, the lawful influence of a Justicia became established.[2] For the first time in their history (under Edward III.) the Commons of England insisted upon the responsibility of the King's council; and, perhaps in Germany also, it was similar intellectual movements which, in 1356, caused Charles IV. to grant the "Golden Bull," that fundamental law of the German Empire for centuries to come. At all events, the first union of the provinces into estates, in Brunswick, in Saxony (1350) and in other countries, took place at the same time.[3] Is it possible that this coincidence is acci-

---

[1] Villaret, Histoire de France, vol. ix. from page 147 on.
[2] Hieronymi Blancæ rerum Aragon Commentarii, p. 810.
[3] Eichhorn, Deutsche Staats-und Rechtsgeschichte, iii. sec. 424 note.

dental? The common development of our nations will necessarily have produced the same ideas in all.

In the midst of these movements, in the same way as the after effects of the old feud between Emperor and Pope made themselves occasionally felt, the minds of men turned ever and anon towards the East and a common expedition against the Infidels. The Pope frequently encouraged the enterprise. In novels, tales, and popular books, the general tendency was at once ventilated and nourished. In the fourteenth century the Pastoureaux in France and in England believed that the conquest of the Holy Land was to be the work of the shepherds and peasants, and set out with this end in view.[1] As late as the end of the fifteenth century, in the year 1480, many of the citizens of Parma fastened a red cross upon their shoulder, and pledged themselves to fight against the Infidels.[2] It was chiefly in Spain and Portugal, where the Moorish campaign was continued at intervals, and finally led to an attack upon Africa, that the crusading spirit was kept alive.

3.

It was this crusading spirit that gave birth to colonisation. The following book will show us how the first discoveries and colonies are in a twofold manner connected with the Moorish war; firstly, by expeditions against Africa, whence proceeded the scheme for the conquest of India, and secondly, by the idea of defending and extending Christendom.

The intentions of the Portuguese were immediately directed at the heart of the Arabian faith. They desired to avenge Jerusalem upon Mecca. Their victories are once again fought and won in the enthusiasm of Crusaders.[3] The Spanish operations, on the other hand, being directed, as they were, against heathen, and not against Mohammedans, renewed rather the idea of the Northern Crusades. A gift of the Pope, a proclamation that "the enemy must be converted to Christianity or utterly destroyed," con-

---

[1] This work, p. 43.
[2] Diarium Parmense in Muratori Scrip. Rerum Ital. xxii. 349.
[3] Chronicon Monspeliense in Du Cange sub Pastorelli.

C

tains all the right to this proceeding.[1] The peasants too, whom Bartholomew de Las Casas intended to lead upon a more peaceful expedition to Cumana, wore each a red cross.[2]

As a fact, in both Spain and Portugal, migration of peoples, crusades, and colonisation form only one single and connected event. The "poblaciones," which moved from the Asturian hills to the coasts of Andalusia and Africa, and which were established as early as 1507 in Almeria, and in 1512 in Oran, now begin on the other shore of the Atlantic Ocean.[3] The Spaniards pride themselves on nothing so much as that they planted there, instead of barbarian peoples, as they say, the sons and descendants of illustrious Castilian families.[4] The five million white men, who are to be found there, are real Spaniards. A million Portuguese dwell in Brazil. An almost equal number, although degenerated, may be distinguished on the coasts of Africa, and in the East Indies. Colonisation on such a great scale may be regarded as migrations. Another idea that animates colonisations, and which they have in common with the Crusades, is the propagation of Christianity. A third that is peculiar to and characteristic of them, is the idea of the discovery of the world,—of itself one of the greatest—a scheme embracing the human race and the whole earth. It was promoted and fostered by greed for the spices of India, for the gold of America, and for the pearls of the unknown seas, as well as by the interests of trade.[5]

It is not necessary to describe the gradual participation of our peoples in these events (at least the share the Italians had in these discoveries); and it is unnecessary to prove at length, that they are exclusively peculiar to them. Other nations now and again took part in these movements, but, as a matter of fact, pursued other aims. The unity of a people cannot be better seen than in a

[1] Hoieda's proclamation in Robertson's Hist. of America, i. p. 516.
[2] Oviedo, dell' historie dell' Indie, vol. xix.
[3] Oviedo, Historia de la Conquista y poblacion de Venezuela. Cf. Schäffer, Brasilien, p. 32.
[4] Sandoval, Historia del Emperador Carlos I. 189.
[5] Sandoval, Historia del Emperador Carlos I. 189.

common undertaking; and wherein can the unity and the cohesion of several nations, like ours, be better demonstrated? The undertakings which we have here referred to, although continued through many centuries, are common to them all. They connect both the times and the peoples. They are, if I may so say, three great respirations of this incomparable union.

BOOK I.

FIRST CHAPTER.

THE RELATIONS OF FRANCE AND ITALY.—EXPEDITION OF
CHARLES VIII. TO NAPLES.

1. *France and Charles VIII.*

TWICE during the Middle Ages did the Capets conquer France. They went forth from their dukedom France, encountered the Eudons of Blois and the Plantagenets of Anjou, and were once cut off on all sides from the sea-coast. But Philip Augustus possessed himself of the provinces of North France, and St. Louis of Provence, whilst Philip the Fair subjected the Pope to his crown. This is the first conquest: by the direct line of Hugo Capet. After his line had become extinct, the kingdom was the bone of contention between his male descendants, the Valois, and the female line, the kings of England. King Edward III. of England once held half France; on another occasion, one of his successors, Henry V., was in possession of Paris, and even of the crown. It may be described as being a second conquest, when Charles VII. of Valois again got the upper hand of the English. It was the Maid of Orleans that opened him the gate to victory. She restored to him the Champagne province; but he owes the recovery of his capital, of Normandy, Guyenne, and the complete mastery over the country to the Dukes of Burgundy and Bretagne.

Yet the assistance rendered by the great vassals entailed the consequence, that the king was after all not completely sovereign. Louis XI., who was made to feel this—he had one day to come and implore peace of the armed barons,— determined to put himself into full possession of the sovereign power. He was very suspicious, very shrewd, and discerning enough besides. Yet these qualities would not have enabled him to attain his object, had not, as though by a providential intervention, the Dukes of Berry, Burgundy, Anjou, and Bretagne all deceased without leaving sons. The first-named, his brother, he succeeded without any opposition. In the case of the heiress of the second, her husband, Maximilian of Austria, failed to uphold her claim to Burgundy and the cities on the Somme. In order to have peace, he was besides obliged to consent to the marriage of his daughter, Margaret, with the Dauphin, and to assign to the French Artois and the free county as her dowry. The third, however, René of Anjou, who styled himself king of three kingdoms, duke of three duchies, and count of three counties,[1] might have made over the countries that he actually possessed, and his rights to the rest, to his grandson, René of Lorraine; but he himself was not in favour of such a course. He had hoped one day to be able to bring Lorraine to Anjou; and only because he had been taken prisoner had he acquiesced in that marriage of his daughter, of which his grandson was the issue. Should he, then, now go so far as to allow his hereditary lands to pass to Lorraine? The young prince would not even agree to exchange his arms of Lorraine for those of Anjou.[2] Ill-pleased at this, René appointed his nephew Charles, bearing the name and the arms of Anjou, as his heir.[3] The latter, who was also not blessed with issue, seven years later doth, as the chronicle says, for the sake of God, and the love which he bears King Louis, the son of his father's sister, assign to him the inheritance of all his kingdoms, possessions, and rights:[4] thus the territories of Provence and Anjou came directly to the Crown.

It may be regarded as an historical event, that the great feudal countries in the South and East, in contrast to the neighbouring princes who belonged to the German Empire,

[1] Pasquier, Recherches de la France, vi. p. 557.
[2] Garnier, Histoire de France, vol. 18, p. 462, from Le Grand MS.
[3] Testament in the Preuvres to Comines, ii. 118.
[4] Extraits du Testament, in the same, 182.

were united with the French Crown. Bretagne alone remained; but Louis had already purchased for his family the rights of the Penthièvre in the country, rights that had already once partly caused a great English war.[1]

But, in order to defend this last bulwark of the vassal-power, Louis of Orleans, the nearest agnate of King Charles, who was still a minor, leagued himself with the Bretons and all the King's domestic and external foes. But at St. Aubin he lost the day, and now sat in captivity at Bourges. Things were now in this position. The rebellion was hushed, yet not suppressed. Bretagne was, it is true, conquered, but yet ever ready to appeal afresh to arms, and was besides allied with the three most powerful neighbours of the French, England, the Netherlands, and Spain, when Charles attained the age of nineteen years (1491), and began to take heart, and to be desirous of becoming his own master. He signalized his assumption of the reins of government by a grand and unexpected action. One evening he rode off from Plessis to the tower of Bourges. He went to release the imprisoned duke, regardless of the fact that he had waged war upon him. He took him away with him.[2] They conversed and laughed together at table, and slept the night in the same bed.[3] He had well considered this, "He would be called a good prince, and would have faithful servants." And by this act he put an end to the old feud between the barons and the Crown. Immediately thereafter, Orleans, the Connétable, and many notables banded together, no longer, as was formerly the case, for the public, that is, the well-being of the vassals, but to obey and serve the King. That opened the way for Charles to effect the conquest of Bretagne. Dunois and other friends of the released Louis went to Orleans, and addressed themselves to Anna, the heiress of Bretagne, who was betrothed to Maximilian, and already called herself Queen of the Romans.[4]

They represented to her that "Since Maximilian's first

[1] Garnier, from Le Grand MS., xviii. 452.
[2] Extrait d'une histoire de France up to 1510, by Th. Godefroy, Charles VIII., p. 165.
[3] Extrait d'une histoire de Louys, by Godefroy, p. 375.
[4] MS. of Brienne in Daniel, H. d. F. iv. 478.

marriage with Marie of Burgundy her country had not enjoyed a single day's peace; that its wealth had become the prey of the Germans; and that a still greater disaster was in store for Bretagne, because of the distance at which it lay." They brought it about, that Anna came to Charles' court at Langeais, and signed the document by which, for the preservation of an eternal alliance and peace between Crown and Duchy, she assigned to him all her rights in the latter, and he all his to her.

By her marriage with the King she became Queen of France.[1] The day on which this took place, and before it was known abroad, it is told how Margaret, hitherto Charles' affianced bride, was seen walking sadly in the garden at Amboise. She told her attendant maidens she had dreamt she had lost a very brilliant and large jewel;[2] and it was certainly her great misfortune, when it turned out that the jewel imported the crown of France. But what cared the Council of France for this, when it found that it was upon Charles' marriage, not with her, but with Anna, that the domestic peace of the realm depended? Personal obligations retired when the consolidation of the French realm and its unity was at stake. The injured neighbours took no steps against it.[3] The renewed idea of the unity of France was even in a certain way favourable to them. Maximilian concluded his peace at Senlis, recovering Artois and the free county, together with his daughter. Henry VII., satisfied with a sum of money, returned to England. When too King Ferdinand of Spain had got back Rousillion out of pledge,—for Charles, mindful, probably, of St. Louis, would not be burthened with foreign property—and had thereupon promised neither to ally his house with Henry, nor with Maximilian, nor yet with the Neapolitans,[4] and in nowise reserving the rights of the Church, to lend the latter his support; when the old alliance between Castile and France had become renewed, king

[1] Contrat du mariage in the Preuves of Comines.
[2] Pasquier, Recherches, p. 586.
[3] The political relations, as they obtained in the summer of 1492, have been sketched in the oldest Venetian story of Zaccaria Contarini. Cf. S. W. vol. xii. p. 34 (note of the new edition).
[4] Zurita, Historia del Rey Don Hernando, f. 6, 13, 18.

with king, country with country, and man with man;[1]—then, and then only did the French again enjoy perfect peace. It may be said that only now had the second conquest of the whole land by the Valois been accomplished.

Then did Charles journey in joy through the villages, which rose out of desolated places, to the towns, that now once more dared extend beyond their walls. During the next thirty years after Louis XI., almost a third of the houses in the realm were rebuilt and fitted with contrivances for trade.[2] The poor peasant, who in the midst of such great fertility could not obtain high prices for his produce, could scarcely, it is true, when the tax-gatherer came, find the money at which he was assessed;[3] yet he needed no longer, as formerly, to fear either the English or the armed French, to hurry his goods and chattels into the church, and to leave his village. The King vouchsafed to them law and right. He himself lived with the nobles in his service, the heads of the great houses, who had been brought up at Court.[4] With them frequently were associated the second sons of the lower nobility, such as had neither inherited property nor had wished to enter the Church,[5] and who had learnt in a more illustrious house than their own,—perhaps with a trusty knight whom they had themselves chosen, or with a captain, to whom they had been assigned by the King —not the sciences that they did not esteem, but how to run, wrestle, throw, ride, and shoot with the bow,—in one word, the use of arms.[6] In them this free chivalry became developed into a regular, quasi military service. We find them mainly in the frontier towns, in corps of thirty, fifty, and a hundred men, under a prince or lord who could afford the expense, and who, although he received some pay, devoted as a rule his whole fortune to the service. Each had two archers, a young lad, who was trained up under him,

[1] Comines, Mémoires ann. 1682, i. p. 581. Corio, Hist. of Milan, p. 899.
[2] Claude Seyssel. Louanges du bon Roy Louys XII., p. 128.
[3] Continuation of the Monstrelet, iii. p. 249. Macchiavell, Ritratti della Francia, p. 161.
[4] Tremouille's instance in the Memoirs, p. 121.
[5] Bayard's instance in the loyal serviteur, ch. 2.
[6] Chartier l'Espérance, p. 316. Notes to Trem. Mémoires, p. 265, and Castiglione Cortegiano, ed. Venet. 1587, i. 81.

and a servant. They all went together on the campaign.[1] They were called Hommes d'Armes. In times of peace one of them, in honour of his lady, would often institute a prize and invite all his neighbours to a tournament. In these they preferred to engage in masses rather than singly. Umpires sat, and after the dance in the evening, and the mass the next morning, the prize was awarded. Others wandered through Spain and Portugal, through England and Scotland, to try the prowess of their neighbours. They imagined themselves a Lancelot or a Tristran—with whom they were well acquainted; their king was to them an Arthur, or the great Charles of story.[2] This intellectual and vigorous movement gave new life to the French nobility. With them their King rode from tournament to tournament. To humour them he called his son Roland; and when they all had inclination for fresh enterprises and he with them, an expedition to Naples began to be talked of.[3]

Now Charles had from his youth up both heard and believed that Naples, which through the adoption of both Johannas had become an hereditary portion of the House of Anjou, had devolved legally upon him with Provence. At the time of which we speak, all doubt upon this point was removed by the will of the younger Johanna, which a Genoese of the name of Calvo, a servant of the Queen, brought to his Court, having found it, as he alleged, among the papers of his deceased father.[4] Several members of Parliament and several doctors of laws appeared before a full assembly of the princes of the blood royal and notables of the realm, and confirmed its validity.[5] The bastard of the Conqueror of Aragon, who occupied the throne of Naples, was declared an usurper. Prince Antonello of Salerno, a fugitive from Naples, had for a long time been the mouthpiece of many other fugitives at the Court of France; did he now but tell the truth, how cruel and detested the

[1] Principal passages in Marineus Siculus, vol. 13, p. 428, and in Monstrelet, iii. 32.
[2] Instances in Bayard and Expilly's Supplément à l'histoire du Chevalier, p. 443.
[3] Histoire de Charles VIII., by Godefroy, 172.
[4] Senarega, Annales Genuenses in Muratori, xxiv. p. 537.
[5] Carl Balbiano to Lodovico in Rosmini. Vita di Gian Giacomo Trivulzio, 1815, vol. ii. Monumenti inediti, p. 194.

Aragon was, that was sure to move the young King to pity and to rouse his hopes. For some time past, the Cardinal Julian Rovere, who had fled from the Pope and the Aragons, and who had still fortresses and adherents in the States of the Church, also resided at the court. He likewise urged the young King to undertake an expedition against Naples. The messengers and letters of Lodovico the Moor, Administrator of Milan, decided the matter. "How long wilt thou," he wrote,[1] "leave the inheritance of thy Crown a booty in a foreign land, and the name of France in contempt? Thy people at Naples are oppressed and appeal to thee; I will assist thee with money and arms, with man and horse. Half Italy is with thee, and God himself. Gird thyself, delay is ever hurtful. And thinkest thou never, Charles, on thy great forefather, who advised that a war against the Turks should be begun from this kingdom? Sail from Brindisi to Avlona; and thou crushest the Turks, who are at present engaging in battle against the Hungarians, before they are aware of thy coming. Thou wilt conquer the holy lands, where thy forefathers were once triumphant, and restore Jerusalem itself to Christendom and thy realm. Thou fillest the earth and the sea, yea, and heaven also with thy name."

What Charles of Anjou had, in the thirteenth century, undertaken with no small prospects of success, appeared capable of being carried out by his successor, who had at his disposal the martial forces of France, and was animated by the like chivalrous spirit. The throne of Naples, to which the title and right of Jerusalem belonged, once taken, and Charles VIII. would by the course of these events, the excitement of men's minds, as well as by right and power, become the chosen champion of Christianity against the common foe. André de la Vigne wrote a poem; in it Christianity came flying across Mont Cenis into the garden of honour, where she found Charles and his nobles, complained to him of her sufferings, and renewed the prophecy of a young Charles, who had been crowned in his thirteenth year, and who again would crown her with

[1] Literæ Ludovici in Corso, 891.

everlasting praise.[1] To the same effect were the visions of the monk Spagnuoli and the physician Jean Michel.[2] Master Guilloche, of Bordeaux, went still further. In his twenty-fourth year, Charles would have subjected Naples, and, in his thirty-third, the whole of Italy; he would then cross the sea, be called King of Greece, and at last enter Jerusalem, and ascend the Mount of Olives.[3] The old dreams of Christianity, of an Eastern and a Western potentate, who should make all the world believers, had not yet been forgotten—those dreams which the Germans interpreted as applying to the last Roman king: after his victory over the enemies of the faith, he would lay down his crown on Golgotha before the crucifix there appearing to him, and would die; whereupon, with the advent of the Antichrist and Enoch and Elijah, the end of all things would be accomplished.[4] The Italians referred that prophecy to the King of France; in Jerusalem he would lay down his crown, and in death ascend up to Heaven.[5]

Charles was susceptible by nature to such ideas. In quite early years, when he was received in Troyes with the mystery of Goliath and David, he saw therein typified his war against the Turks; he adopted the titles of Naples and Jerusalem—" especially the latter appeared to him the fairest prognosticon;"[6] and forthwith, as though he meant to establish the Latin kingdom in the East, he had all the

---

[1] André de la Vigne in the Vergier d'honneur; after Foncemagne's extract.
[2] Foncemagne in Histoire de l'Academie des inscriptions, xvi. p. 246, and Mémoirs, xvii. 548. This prophecy is also given, though in an incomplete form, by Pilorgerie, Campagne et bulletins de la grande armée d'Italie, commandée par Charles huit, p. 431; la vision divine révélée à Jehan Michiel très-humble prophète de la prosperité du très-crestien roy de France, Charles VIII., de la nouvelle réformation du siècle et la récupération de Hierusaleme à lui destinée, et qu'il sera de tous les roys de terre le souverain et dominateur sur tous les dominants et unique monarchie du monde.
[3] Foncemagne in the Memoirs of the Academie, xvii. 845.
[4] Sebastianus Brandt, Revelatio Methodii, Basle, 1516. Preface of 1497.
[5] Alexandro Benedetto. Diarium Expeditionis by Eckardus. vol. Script. Medii Aevi, ii. p. 1579.
[6] Balbian to Lodovico in Rosmini, ii. 194.

rights of the Paleologers to Constantinople and Trapezunt ceded to him.[1] Tidings of the approaching expedition, for which all France was preparing, reached the Italian courts and cities. The army that Charles VIII. equipped did not consist alone of his French and the Italian refugees, but many comrades from other countries also joined the expedition. Robert d'Aubigny, the brother of Matthew Stuart, who had shortly before taken part in the war against James IV. of Scotland,[2] and Scotch archers also arrived. The Höks from the Netherlands, Philip of Ravenstein, who had just lost Sluys, and Engelbert of Cleve, who had lost Utrecht to Maximilian,[3] brought Flemish gunners[4] and German infantry.[5] The bailiff of Dijon brought Rudolph Schwend of Zurich[6] and several thousand Swiss with him. At the foot of the Pyrenees the Gascons collected in their numbers, whilst horses came from the coasts of Bretagne and from Portugal.[7] Ships were turned out of the dockyards of Marseilles and Genoa, and mounted guns, which, as was said of the Charlotte, "sung accord out of hell."[8] The King meantime amused himself in Lyons. Good and generous towards everyone; pious to the extent that only in trivial matters[9] would he take an oath upon himself, he lived entirely in youthful dreams of great exploits, and of eternal fame won in the battle field. Whenever he busied himself with these plans, his forehead appeared high, his eye large and fiery, and his brows lifted.[10] But showing himself ignorant of the complications of the world, many attribute what he resolved and achieved to his servants.[11] In personal appearance he was thin and malformed,[12] but

---

[1] Tractat in Foncemagne, Mémoirs de l'Academie, xvii. 572-578.
[2] Buchananus Rerum Scoticarum hist. lib. 13, p. 457, ed. of 1624.
[3] Wagenaar, allgem. Geschichte der Niederlande, ii. 265.
[4] Willeneufve, Memoirs, vol. xvi.
[5] Ferronus, Rerum Gallicarum, lib. i. p. 20.
[6] Stumpf-Schweizer Chronik, iii. 256.
[7] Corio, p. 899.
[8] Vergier d'honneur in Foncemagne, p. 588. Georgius Florus.
[9] Bayard, p. 14. Symphorian Champier in Godefroy, p. 314.
[10] Prophétie du Roi Charles in Foncemagne, Hist. xvi. 245. Brantôme after the testimony of a lady, Eloge, p. 22.
[11] Comines, Guicciardini, André.
[12] Passero, Giornale, p. 72.

was at the same time very keen for all sorts of knightly games and military duties. Sometimes he hunted with his sparrow-hawk;[1] and then it might happen that he saw a stripling exercising himself in a meadow, who was thereupon brought into his service. He made presents to the knights, who on their side again were liberal, and took part in the martial games which were held in the streets; whilst at the corners the women sat upon benches and stages, exactly like what is told in knights' tales of King Arthur at Caerleon.[2]

In Italy, meanwhile, many did vows and prayers for his coming;[3] they loved to call him the most Christian Monarch, and said, "Blessed be he that cometh in the name of the Lord!"

2. *The Situation in Italy.*

For about the last fifty years, two houses, which, owing to intermarriage, were almost one, had ruled over the greater part of Italy—to wit, the Sforza at Milan and the Aragon at Naples. Alfonso of Aragon and Francis Sforza had both simultaneously risen to fame in Italy. The first-named had not been long in possession of Naples when the latter seized Milan. Since that event their families had become allied, and spread in manifold affinities throughout Italy. The Este at Ferrara, the Gonzaga at Mantua,[4] the brothers Bentivogli, the princes of Urbino, Pesaro, Forli, almost all the heads of the States of the Church, and even some Neapolitan barons,[5] were among their connections. The power of the Aragons, which had been founded by Alfonso I., was shrewdly and rigorously swayed by his natural son, Ferrante. Once, when the great barons called in John of Anjou, and delivered to him the whole country, save the capital, the House of

---

[1] Zurita, Historia del Rey Hernando, f. 90.
[2] St. Gelais, Louis XII., p. 79. Histoire de Charles in Godefroy, p. 172.
[3] Benedictus in Eckardus, ii. p. 1579.
[4] Diario Ferrarese in Muratori, xxiv. p. 253, 279.
[5] Porzio, Congiura dei Baroni di Napoli, p. 29.

Aragon seemed to be lost. At that time the Queen once found herself compelled to sit with her little children at the convent of St. Piero at Naples with an alms-box before her, and to beg the labourers to do her voluntary work, and implore of other citizens a loan.[1] The dynasty and throne were only saved by the great barons again returning to their allegiance. The most distinguished of them was Ferrante's brother-in-law, Count Marsico Sanseverino, whom the King in his compact styled the illustrious, the most powerful, and his saviour from the deepest misery; he made over to him Salerno, with all the rights of the fiscus and coinage.[2] Sanseverino's example was followed by the others, but they in no wise succeeded in gaining the King's favour. Of some of his confidantes, who were instrumental in beginning the rebellion, as, for instance, his brother-in-law, Balzo of Tarento, he ridded himself by force.[3]

King Ferrante, once more firmly on his throne, thought to secure it mainly by foreign alliances. His son Alfonso he married to the daughter of Francis Sforza; the Popes Pius and Sixtus he gained over to him by enfeoffing, the nephew of the one with Amalfi, and that of the other with Sora.[4] Two men, who were invaluable to him, were entrusted with the conduct of home affairs, viz., Antonello Petrucci, and Francis Coppola. The former was his most intimate counsellor, to whom he was wont to refer every one. This man was often obliged to come out to him when on the chase, and then return in dust and dirt to the council in the city; sometimes he had hardly crossed his threshold, when fresh messengers would summon him back, although it was night. In return for his services, two of his sons were made counts and another an archbishop. Petrucci himself, though originally quite poor, was at last enabled to build churches and castles.

With the other, Francis Coppola, a merchant, the King entered into partnership. By allowing no one to buy, unless

[1] Pontanus, de bello Neapolitano, Haganoæ, fol. v. 4, S. 2.
[2] Pontanus, ibid. Dd. 4. Gg. 2.
[3] According to a document in Angelo di Costanzo, Istoria di Napoli, xix. 440, 467.   [4] Costanzo, 466.

Francis had already done so, and by permitting no trading ship to come into port, unless it had previously sold its cargo, as well as by treating the oil and wine market almost as a monopoly, he increased his gains to an extraordinary extent. Francis had in a short time a county, and an arsenal for his own ships.[1] By their advice and his own perseverance, the King became completely master of the country. The barons were obliged to maintain his stables. To his falconer he gave an abbey, and to the son of a Jew, in return for a sum of money, a bishopric.[2] The land was quite subject to him. He waged the wars of Italy. His power was steadily on the increase.

Brought up in the atmosphere of Ferrante's covert shrewdness, his son Alfonso developed into a totally different character, and one quite peculiar to the Italian princes of those times. They considered cruelty and licentiousness lawful things. To appear always in pomp—to hunt with hawks and falcons, which bore their arms in velvet and gold aloft into the air; at home to be seen in gorgeous apartments, surrounded by savants, musicians, and artists of all kinds; in public among the people to wear an imperious mien, and to be decorated with jewels; to be witty and eloquent; to command a goodly troop of soldiery, to perceive danger and to avert it: this appeared to them to be glorious and worth living for. There was no trace in them of the good qualities of human nature. They were unrighteous, and of true princely dignity they knew nothing; justice they considered bondage.[3]

This ideal, which instead of the strength and power that it intends, seizes only their shadow and their semblance, Alfonso followed; and whilst the others must be called generous, he was nothing less than niggardly.[4] He showed that he considered Petrucci's and Coppola's wealth to belong to the royal house. Petrucci only shrugged his shoulders when he heard of it, and tried to

---

[1] Caracciolus, de varietate fortunæ in Muratori, Scriptores R. I. xxiv. p. 69.
[2] Comines, vi. ch. xi. Porzio, Congiura, 116.
[3] Corio, p. 839. Castiglione Cortegiano, p. 388, and in other places.
[4] Laurentii Medicei Epistola apud Fabronium, ii. 269.

pacify the King by making him New Year's presents.[1] But Coppola was differently minded.[2] He leagued himself with the most powerful of the barons, Sanseverino of Salerno, who also felt himself in danger. Alfonso had been heard to say that Sanseverino looked almost like Balzo of Tarento. They met together by night in solitary places, devised plans for their protection, and gained over others also.[3] For all the barons began to fear Alfonso, as he threatened all who had not been zealous enough in assisting him in his military expeditions.

They leagued themselves with Pope Innocent VIII., who would rather have been possessor of Naples than only its feudal lord, and for the second time arrayed themselves in open war against the House of Aragon. Three Sanseverinos, two princes and a count, three Balzos, two counts and a prince, were the conspirators.[4] Many others, among them Caracciolo of Melfi, gradually joined them. They promised one another, with solemn vows, the Sacrament in their hands, to hold out together. But they were weak and undecided. After the first unfavourable issue they showed themselves inclined to come to terms;[5] when fortune favoured them, they again took up arms.[6] Their achievements were insignificant. When Alfonso had defeated the Pope and had laid siege to the city of Aquila, which adhered to the baronial party and was their chief hope, and was at the same time advancing in the kingdom, they forgot their vows, promised one after the other what was demanded of them, and surrendered.[7]

The Aragons had now asserted their superiority in a still more decisive manner than heretofore, and with their own forces. They next, father and son, resolved to wreak vengeance on their enemies.

Coppola and Petrucci had only taken a very doubtful, and at all events a very insignificant, part in the war; but they were the first victims of the peace. Ferrante pro-

[1] Caracciolus, p. 28.   [2] Porzio, Congiura, p. 28.
[3] Porzio, Congiura, pp. 39-49.
[4] Lodovico de Raimi, Annales Neapolitani, in Muratori, 23, 231.
[5] Macchiavelli, Istorie Fiorentine, viii. 343. Pontanus, bellum Neapol. II. h.
[6] Porzio. 80, 90.   [7] Porzio, 186.

mised to marry one of his nieces to one of Coppola's sons, and to celebrate the marriage in the new castle. Coppola and Petrucci rode up thither, each on a perfumed mule, and in all gala pomp; but as soon as they arrived both they and their sons were seized. They were all put to death.[1] The rest of the barons would have had time to escape on two barks,[2] and the Princess of Bisignan advised this course; but one was hindered in this way and another in that, and so remaining they were all taken on a single day,[3]—three Sanseverinos, three Balzos, and a Caracciolo. The people saw their food taken to them every day into the prison; but when the hangman was seen with the chain of the Prince of Bisignan, it was seen to have been all deception. In the church of St. Leonard, the patron saint of the captive, the Duke persuaded his father to commit the murder, and this executioner, or a slave, a Moor, did the deed.[4] Ferrante would scarcely listen to the expostulations of the Papal Nuntius on this matter. "Did not Pope Sixtus do with his rebels what he pleased? I shall also do the same with mine." This was the whole of his answer. Having delivered himself of it, he ordered the horns to be wound, and rode to the chase.[5] But what he had devised for his security threatened to become his ruin. Many had fled to Rome, and now sent messages to Spain and to France to implore help. In France, Prince Antonello of Salerno, who had escaped from his clutches, aroused his real enemy. Those who still remained in the country only waited for the day when they could again take up arms against him. His first care was to provide that they never should find an opportunity of doing so. Such was the position of the Aragons in Naples. Lodovico, the Moor of Milan, also owed to them his present position.

After the eldest son of Francis Sforza, Galeazzo Maria, Duke of Milan and Lord of Genoa, had been murdered, his widow, the Duchess Buona, took quiet possession of his

[1] Caracciolus, l. Raemi, 239.
[2] Literæ Lutotii de Nasis in Fabionii Vita Laur. Med. ii. 352.
[3] Passero, Giornale Napolitano, p. 50.
[4] Angelo di Costanzo, 479.
[5] Infessura, Diarium Romanum, p. 1980.

lands and cities in the name of her son, John Galeazzo, who was still a minor. This was very displeasing to Lodovico, Galeazzo's brother, who, when sitting in the Corte dell' Arengha with the Municipal Council, had to take his orders from the Castle and the Council of State, and none the less so to the third brother, Ascanio.[1] But as soon as they agitated against it they were driven out. But a war which Ferrante began at that time with Florence, with which city Buona was allied, as well as Ferrante's assistance, enabled these two fugitives to show themselves on the frontier, and to stir up valley after valley in revolt, until they came to Dertona;[2] whereupon, in a single day, forty-seven castles belonging to the discontents went over to them. The Borromei, Pusterli, Marliani, and all Ghibellines, rose in their favour. The disaffection spread even to Buona's Court. Whilst this confusion was at its height, Lodovico returned,[3] and took upon himself the conduct of affairs. But the attitude which he now adopted was quite unexpected. Although supported by the Ghibellines and in good understanding with the Guelphs, he would neither be dependent upon the one nor the other, nor consent to see the heads of these families, his rivals, in power. The Ghibellines, owing to whom the power of the Visconti had been established in all the cities, which Corio emphatically styles "ducal," he deprived of their weapons and of their head, his brother Ascanio;[4] he did not even spare those who had supported him in his flight; nay, he surrounded himself with Biragi, Terzagi, and Trivulzi, who had retained their Guelphish proclivities through centuries, and to their party he granted his favour and his castles.[5] Yet this was not done exclusively enough to gain to his side the whole party: its most distinguished head, John Jacob Trivulzio, was forced to seek safety in flight. With the House of Aragon he entered into the closest dynastic alliance. Of this house came the wife of his nephew, in whose name he governed. Moreover, he attached the Pope Sixtus to his house by giving to

---

[1] Corio, Istoria di Milano, p. 840.
[2] Diarium Parmense in Muratori, 22, p. 319.
[3] Diarium Parmense, p. 351.   Corio, p. 850.   Macchiavelli, Istor. Fiorent. viii.
[4] Corio, p. 848.   Diarium Parmense, p. 354.   [5] Corio, 869.

his nephew, Girolamo, Catherine Sforza to wife. He procured the peace of Bagnulo for the republic of Venice, when all Italy was against her, by which event he increased her power and made her well disposed towards him. Upon this league he relied: for his power had sprung up externally. Under its protection he advanced step by step to the supreme power within. At first, Buona's favourite merely came into the Council of State in order to carry some point or other, and would say, "Her Serene Highness the Duchess will so and so." [1] On Lodovico's initiative the twelve-year-old Duke went one day into the castle, had the drawbridge pulled up, and the favourite made a prisoner. "I will rule myself," he said, "and my mother may look after her widowhood." [2]

After this, Lodovico shared the sovereign power for a time with Eustachio, the commander of the castle. After the Venetian war, the young Duke helped his uncle, into whose power he had entirely given himself,' to get rid of him also. Having thus acquired the sovereign power, Lodovico showed himself kind and affable towards everyone, and perhaps the use he made of his power caused the way in which it had been obtained to be forgotten. He provided for the building of hospitals, the digging of canals, the foundation of churches and monasteries, and the protection of the country from robberies and famine. In accordance with the taste of the time, he fostered art and science. He summoned Leonardo da Vinci to Milan to be the instructor of the young nobles,[4] and gave him a salary. He was the first to have music publicly taught.[5] Jason de Maino, in Alciat's opinion one of the five first jurists of the Middle Ages, lectured in Pavia upon law to 3,000 students. Lodovico also honoured the grammarians. Demetrius Chalkondylas, who saw his auditorium in Pisa grow empty owing to Politian's more brilliant lectures, repaired with his Florentine wife and his favourite

[1] Diarium Parmense in Muratori, p. 351.
[2] Ibid.
[3] Senarega, Annales Genuenses, p. 523. Comines, Corio.
[4] Vasari, Vita di Leonardo da Vinci, iii. 21.
[5] Jagemann, Geschichte der Künste und Wissenschaften in Italien, iii. 650.

pupil, Johann Reuchlin, the teacher of the teacher of Germany, to his Court.¹ It cannot be said that the Prince laid out badly the 650,000 ducats which the country gave him. Bellizona's fêtes and entertainments, in which the people fancied to perceive the hand of the Prince himself, enlivened his Court, as did also Gaspar Visconti, who was considered equal to Petrarch.² His farm at Vigevene was a *chef d'œuvre* of rural economy. Here once had grown not even provender enough for the cattle, and no plant would flourish; only wild animals made their lairs in the low brushwood. Lodovico, who was first carried thither in the chase, cut dykes, and thus made meadows for the cattle, and then, by bringing manure upon it, produced tillage land that vied with any other.³ This done, he planted mulberry trees in long avenues, and lastly built spacious and cleanly stables with columns to hold 1,800 head of cattle and 14,000 sheep, and others for the stallions and mares.⁴ In this castle a son was born to him; here woods were preserved for the chase and hawking.⁵ The bounteousness of peace rested on the land. Every day saw new fashions and amusements, jousts and balls.⁶ It was of the utmost importance for him, so long as his rule was tolerated, to maintain the peace and the *status quo* in Italy, seeing that, were it disturbed, his ruin might easily ensue. But the present conditions depended, before all else, upon whether Lorenzo de Medici, the head of the Florentines, lived on the best of terms with the King of Naples and the ruler in Milan, or not.

Francis Sforza, principally owing to the assistance of Cosimo di Medici, had now become Lord of Milan, and, to the vexation of Venice, the Medici and Sforza had since then been the best of friends. When, after Galeazzo's death, the above-mentioned difference in the Sforza family arose, Lorenzo made cause with Buona; but the Milanese brothers and Ferrante attacked him, and succeeded so well.

---

¹ Jovius, Vitæ Vivorum, D.D., p. 37. Reuchlini Præfat. ad Gv. Hebr.
² Bouterwek, Italien, Literatur, i. 339. Roscoe, Life of Leo X., 113.
³ Carpesanus, Commentarii suorum temporum, ix. 1363.
⁴ Desrey on Monstrelet, 239.
⁵ Comines, Mémoires, p. 507. ⁶ Corio, last book. Beginning.

that he made his resolve, went forth, came to Naples, and entered into friendship with them.¹ Since then, the King was his nearest ally, and Lodovico his second; in conjunction with both he fostered a very dangerous feud against Ferrara, and eventually aided the King in the second Neapolitan war, which we have noticed. After it was over, Ferrante said, "I saved him, and he has now done the same for me." ²

Pope Innocent VIII., who had espoused the cause of the barons and had been defeated, was at first highly dissatisfied with this arrangement. He even protested in his secret garden at the palace, saying, "he did not recognize Ferrante as king, even though he called him such."³ He exclaimed, "I will put him under ban. If the Italians will not then assist me, I will cross the mountains, like the Popes did in the days of old, and appeal to those dwelling on the other side, and I know I shall stop their feuds and that they will help me."⁴ Lorenzo undertook to pacify him, in which he was successful, by giving his daughter to the Pope's son, Francheschetto Cibo, to wife.⁵ Hereupon a thorough change supervened. His old friends, Julian della Rovera and the Colonna, fell into disfavour with Innocent, who inclined to the Orsini, Lorenzo's relations and his old enemies. At last the Neapolitan complications were settled, and the King confessed that in everything he perceived Lorenzo's faithfulness and goodness.⁶ We see how it is that Lorenzo, owing to his position, became the mediator of Italy; upon it was founded the subsequent greatness of his house, for, owing to the co-operation of the three, his son John was made abbot of Miramondo in the province of Milan, of Cassino in the kingdom, and a cardinal of the church.⁷

And thus they all lived in peace together; all of them, except the Pope, in usurped lordships, each menaced by his subjects, and only careful that they did not anywhere find

¹ Macchiavelli, viii. Diarium Parmense, p. 335.
² Fabronii Vita Laurentii Medicis, ii. p. 369.
³ Literæ Petri Victorii, ap. Fabronium, ii. p. 344.
⁴ Literæ Philippi Pandolphini, *ibid.*, p. 353.
⁵ *Ibid.*, p. 313. Letters and documents.
⁶ *Ibid.*, p. 351.
⁷ *Ibid.*, p. 374, and in Roscoe, Leo X., the letters in Appendix, from p. 486 on.

assistance in any neighbour: each supporting the other. They are neither nations nor races; neither cities nor kingdoms; they are the first States of the world, and their origin is as follows.

The appellation of "State" was originally given to the friends most nearly devoted to a single family; and we find Foliugno dei Medici complaining that their "State" had decreased, only numbering fifty men instead of a hundred, and these ill provided with children.[1] The most illustrious members of the State, who came to Lorenzo with the deputies of the city, in order, as he says, to entrust to his care the public duties, were not from the country—for this is called "Dominio" and has not the slightest influence—but they were the friends, the old State, without which Lorenzo declared it difficult to live in Florence.[2] Now, as the party united with these "nearest friends," and the party was master of the city, and the city of the land, the name of the original unit became applied to the whole. Nowhere did real liberty exist. Whence, then, springs the lively impulse to perpetuate the "beautiful," through which this people at this time became the envy of and the model for all later peoples;—whence came the semblance, yes, the effect of liberty? It is the prime result of the antagonism of parties, ever covertly or openly existing, of the vigilance of all human forces engaged in conflict, of universal jealousy, which applies itself to art, energy, science, and antiquity, and of the reverence in which the savants are therefore held. Since the era of the migration of nations, Italy now for the first time stood independent, and displayed the greatest diversity in ideal unity. These States, though based upon violence and faction, entertained notwithstanding the most universal relations. Venice was built upon commerce, Florence upon industrial art and manufactures, the kingdom of Naples upon the great European balance of power, which had now found a moment of rest, the duchy of Milan upon the trade of war as it was followed by the Condottieri, and

---

[1] Foligno dei Medici, Notizia in Fabroni, ii. p. 7.
[2] Lorenzo dei Medici, Ricordi, *ibid.*, p. 42. A further proof is contained in Varchi, storia Fiorentina, ii. p. 8 : andavano cercando che lo stato si ristringesse e a minore numero si riducesse.

the State of the Church upon the idea of the supreme hierarchy. The nation was at the zenith of its culture. Would it not have been possible for it to have progressed and developed further in the same way, and so have exercised in later times more influence than it had to accept of others?

But this retired and peculiar world was convulsed by a great and violent movement. The sea is calm, and reflects the sky; then comes a storm: when it is past and gone, the sea is the same as before. If a movement and a storm comes into the hearts of men, there will also return a day of calm : but meanwhile the world has altered.

In the year 1480 Ferrante had two grand-daughters at his Court, who, it might be, often quarrelled when playing at his feet: Isabella, ten years of age, the child of his son Alfonso, and Beatrice, aged seven years, his daughter Leonora's child by her marriage with Ercole d'Este.[1] At the beginning of his career Lodovico betrothed the elder of these two to his nephew, John Galeazzo, who would one day be duke, and himself to the younger. Some time passed, and Isabella was taken to Milan: but while there was forced to see how the uncle governed her husband like a boy, and neither allowed him nor herself the least power; she endured it all the same. But the time too came for Beatrice to go as a bride to Milan,[2] and as Lodovico was actually prince, Beatrice and not Isabella was honoured as princess. Here, then, we see the younger girl with every wish in the pleasures of youth gratified, full of hopes, sometimes sitting as mistress at the games and tournaments in Milan, and anon at Genoa—whither she had come secretly to enjoy herself—so soon as discovered, the recipient of princely honours amid the gorgeous pomp of the merchants;[3] anon driving to her father at Ferrara with her ladies attendant, with many coaches and mules, the streets covered with carpets and green boughs, whilst the populace shouted her husband's name.[4] The elder, meanwhile, who was the lawful duchess, had the pain of being fettered to

[1] Diarium Parmense, p. 311. Diarium Ferrarense, p. 254.
[2] Diarium Ferrarense, p. 279.
[3] Folieta, Historia Genuensis, lib. xi.
[4] Diarium Ferrarense, p. 283.

a man, who was a mere nobody, and who even repeated to his uncle what she confided to him, and she had little prospect either for her own future or that of her children; for Lodovico now declared, that the sovereignty belonged to him, who was born whilst his father was reigning duke, rather than to the son of one who was born before,[1] and entered into negotiations to procure his investiture. A heart perceiving danger threatening its whole house and enduring in silence, were nothing less than divine. Isabella acted like a mortal in not tolerating this treatment; at first she complained in Milan, then threatened,[2] and finally appealed for assistance to her father in Naples.[3] She wrote, "Whilst his newly-born infant is designed to be Count of Pavia, we and ours are ever held in contempt, and are even in peril of our lives; and I am like a widow, a helpless woman. We have courage and understanding, and the people are favourable and pitying. Hast thou, then, the heart of a father, and love and generosity, and art touched by tears. Save us."

"We ought to help them," said Alfonso, "even if they were strangers to us." He consulted with his old father, and with his grown-up son. He then called upon Lodovico to crown his noble actions by the most noble of all, and to retire from the government in favour of his nephew. He received no answer. But in this silence lay the breach of friendship and peace between them; nay, the peace of Italy itself.[4] Alfonso's friends said Lodovico must be content to be "Podesta" in Milan; they wagered that he would not exist one month longer.[5] But he, on his side, thought that he possessed the means of securing his rule, and at the same time of endangering the existence of his enemy.

Now, Lorenzo dei Medici and Innocent VIII. at this time died in quick succession, and Alfonso as well as Lodovico had to cast about to gain the favour of their successors. Lorenzo's son, Piero, was heart and soul devoted to the Aragons, from whom, in the great hall at a splendid

---

[1] Comines and Georgius Florus, p. 3.
[2] Marcus de la Cruce to Trivulzio in Rosmini, ii. 192.
[3] Literæ Isabellæ. Given word for word in Corio, p. 884.
[4] All in Corio.   [5] Cruce to Trivulzio, 191.

festival, he had received his wife, Alfonsina Orsina.¹ But the successor of Pope Innocent was of entirely opposite feelings.

Amidst the universal corruption, it was a universal calamity, and discreditable to the whole human race, that, in the retired cells of the Conclave assembled to elect a Pope, amid high and holy ceremonies, and among men who had no further wants, and no one to provide for, it was not the weal of Christendom, so sorely in need, that determined the election, nor that of a nation—no, nor even genuine affections and emotions. The highest dignity in the Church was regarded as the inheritance of all cardinals; given, because alas! it was indivisible, to the one who promised the others most. Brother Albus of Venice, ninety-five years of age, who could scarcely talk any longer, and always nodded his head, still took 5,000 ducats.² He received them from Roderick Borgia (Borja) of Xativa in Valencia, and the others took like presents. The revenues he received from three cathedrals and several monasteries, whose head he was; the income derived from the vice-chancellorship that he held, as well as numerous alliances with foreign princes, furnished him with the means of making these bribes.³ Ascanio Sforza and Julian della Rovera still resisted him; but the former gave up his opposition when Borgia sent him four mules laden with silver into his house, and promised him the vice-chancellorship. The latter would not receive anything, kept complaining that the Italians were excluded, only at last to give in himself.⁴ Calamity was expected to result from the election. Sinibald de Sinibaldis died of grief occasioned by it. It is said that a tear was seen in the eye of the old Ferrante, whose rule, established by so many misdeeds, was threatened with utter ruin by this election.⁵

¹ Oricellarius in Fabroni, ii. 316. ² Infessura, Diarium, p. 2007.
³ Jacob Volaterranus, Rom. Diarium, p. 130.
⁴ Infessura, p. 3008, and Corio.
⁵ Infessura, 3009. Zurita, i. 15. In the Codice Aragonese of Trinchera this tradition is referred to Guicciardini, and denied, without mention being made of the reliable authors. The account which follows, however, records the hostile relations between the new Pope and the King of Naples, which immediately showed themselves. "Sappiate," it runs in a letter of the King, of 7 June, 1493, addressed to

The great Popes of early days provided, after their lights, for the Church; the later ones had nephews to provide for; and in these days even sons—Borgia, who called himself Alexander IV., had three of them, Juan and Joffred of the secular, and Cesar of the clerical profession, as well as one married daughter, Lucrezia.[1] Men said, "This man, who when Cardinal, made his son Duke of Gandia, what will he do now he is Pope?" The Sforza gained him over to them by giving John Sforza, Lord of Pesaro, to his daughter for a husband; he dissolved the marriage with her former husband, whom he satisfied with money. In the presence of one hundred and fifty Roman ladies, whom these clerics in frivolous play pelted with sweetmeats served up in more than a hundred silver dishes, the new betrothal was celebrated.[2] Hereupon the Pope nominated three Cardinals in the interest of the Sforza.[3] After that, he endeavoured to separate King Wladislaw of Hungary from Ferrante's daughter, in order that he might wed a Sforza; and, as Lodovico was allied with all his relations at Ferrara, Mantua, Forli, Pesaro, and Bologna, and had even gained over Venice,[4] and despatched his envoys and his letter to Charles VIII., Alexander entered into a league with him. Their plan was to put an army into the field under a joint commander. The Pope approved Lodovico's proposals that he should invest Charles,[5] and thereupon invited him to come.[6]

Antonio d'Alessandro (Cod. ii. 2, 43), "che 'l pontifice succedendo in pontificato, con la majore pace in tutta Italia : et con lo majore reposo che mai altro pontifice : stando tutti li potentati in summa amicitia : ipso pontifice non guardando al ben publico, ma sequendo el suo naturale." (Cf. Gregorovius, Geschichte der Stadt Rom., vol. vii. p. 329.) The accounts given in the Codice are of great moment for the epoch 1493-1494 ; yet they go so deeply into the details of the intricate and vacillating policy of those times, that their contents can on no account be inserted in this place; the general view here given will not be affected by this.

[1] Vannozza de Cattanei was the mother of Cesar, Juan, Joffred, and Lucrezia. Her monument stands in Santa Maria del popolo. Petro Luis, Duke of Gandia, was born of another alliance. Cf. Reumont, Gesch. von Rom. iii. 2, p. 838.
[2] Infessura, 2010, 2011.
[3] Senarega, Annales Genuens. in Muratori, 24, p. 534.
[4] Alegretto, Alegretti, Diarj sanesi, p. 827.
[5] Zurita, i. 26. [6] Infessura, Diarium, p. 1016.

That the adherents of the Aragon dynasty did not despair in the face of such dangers, was owing to their reliance upon the tried shrewdness of their old king, Ferrante. But he now appeared to have lost all the elasticity of life. He cared neither for the chase nor for games, and would even scarcely take food. No one could please him in rendering the small services of everyday life.[1] He was bowed down by the weight of years and the dread of this third war, by far the most dangerous of all, as the King of France was taking part in it; and he was moreover harassed by his barons. It was said that an ancient work had been found in Tarento, addressed to the King alone and his most intimate adherents. The people believed that therein was prophesied the destruction of Ferrante's race and dynasty.[2] Yet he did not abandon the cause as lost. He thought of paying tribute to Charles as his vassal, but his envoys returned with the presents he had sent. He next thought of securing Alfonso by a Spanish marriage, but King Ferdinand evaded it. His sole safety he now saw in going to Milan, and taking Isabella back home with him. But grief and fear, as well as the recollection of what he had done, broke his heart. At great festivals he was heard to give vent to frequent and deep sighs; in the midst of a conversation he would utter meaningless words, which, however, had reference to his danger.[3] In this state he died, two days after his return to the city, on the 25th January, 1494.

When Alfonso mounted at once his black steed, and, riding through the streets with a bold air, received the ovations of the people, there were still some who hoped. But the tradition goes that many were obliged to join in the acclamations under the point of drawn swords; and meanwhile the old Queen sat with her daughter Johanna in a dark room. They lamented: "Wisdom is dead, and light is extinguished. In what plight has he left us behind, and to whom? All power is gone: the realm is helpless and lost!" Alfonso came to them, and said: "I shall uphold the kingdom as well as did my father." But

[1] Caracciolus, de varietate fortunæ, p. 72.
[2] Giacomo, Cronica di Napoli, p. 173.
[3] Senarega, Annales Genuenses, p. 538, and Caracciolus, de varietate fortunæ.

they were afraid of his cruelty, and only implored him to spare the people.[1]

Alfonso's first care was to gain over the Pope Alexander, in which endeavour he was in so far supported by the King of Spain, as that he married Enrique Enriquez, his uncle's daughter, to Juan Borgia.[2] Alfonso promised the latter an estate of 12,000, the younger son Joffred one of 10,000 ducats, in addition to his daughter Sancia; so that the Borgia were thus received into relationship with the genuine as well as with the spurious House of Aragon. For the sake of these great advantages, Alexander forgot his former engagements, did not heed the protestations of the Consistorium, and sided with Alfonso,[3] an alliance that first caused alarm to the Cardinal Julian. On a former occasion, he had once invited the Pope to Magliano. The Pope came; but on hearing a chance shot fired, he feared it was a signal meant for him, and returned without tasting food.[4] Since then Julian had banded himself with the discontents in Ostia.

Now, when the Orsini were also reconciled with the Pope, he sailed with two "caravellas" through the pirate ships of Villamarino across to France, came into his legation at Avignon, and leagued himself with Charles.[5] Immediately hereupon, the Colonna, under their own standards, as well as those of Rovere and France, occupied Ostia, closed the Tiber, cared not that their houses were destroyed, and awaited the coming of the King.[6]

Alfonso was crowned on the 8th May. His coronation apparel was valued at more than a million and a half of ducats; yet, amidst all the pomp and splendour, he looked sad and brooding.[7] On this very day he heard certain tidings of the approaching French expedition. His silver shield could not gladden his heart, for he needed an iron one. Yet he did not think of awaiting the attack, as

[1] Zurita and Passero. Giornale, p. 57.
[2] Zurita, i. 29, 34.
[3] Diarium Burcardi in Eccardus, 2036, 2040.
[4] Infessura, 2010.
[5] Senarega, Annales, p. 539. Zurita, 34. Infessura, 2016.
[6] Burcardus, p. 2048.
[7] Passero, 61. Caracciolus de varietate fortunæ, 43. Diurnale di Giacomo Gallo, 7.

his father had advised. "Shall I hide," he said, "like a stag in the wood?" After he had got in the presents made him at his coronation, a whole year's income from landowners, and his tithes; and after the foals from his studs had been trained for military service, and his ships equipped with the latest inventions in bombs, he had an interview with Alexander at Vicovaro. In accord with the latter, he resolved to attack Lodovico on two sides [1]—with his fleet in Genoa, and by land in his own country of Milan. In view of the operations against Genoa, two exiles, Cardinal Fregoso and Obietto Fiesco, offered their services. They had been expelled in order that the city might obey Lodovico, and they now placed their hopes in the King of France.[2] He hoped to effect an entrance into Milan through the instrumentality of the Papal vassals, who were pledged to obey their suzerain; the upper hand he hoped to gain through the Guelphs, whose head, Trivulzio, marched with him; whilst the complete victory should be his through the devotion of the people to their own prince, John Galeazzo. In August, 1494, thirty-eight squadrons of horse started from the Abruzzi mountains; they were to take their way through the Romagna, in order to set free the young Duke of Milan.[3] Infantry they had none; but they had sergeants with them to recruit them. The land army was led by Ferrantino, the son of Alfonso; whilst the fleet, which put to sea at the same time, was commanded by Federigo, Alfonso's brother. Thus did the war in Italy break out.

Lodovico did not await the coming of his enemies without French help; he was to be aided against the landing troops, which the Neapolitan fleet had on board, by Duke Louis of Orleans, who had come to Genoa with a few companies of Swiss.

At last the beacon-fires flashed from cape to cape; the enemy was approaching. The Aragons then effected a landing on the Riviera, and occupied Rapallo [4] with their

---

[1] Benedicti Diarium. Corio, 919. Oricellarius, de bello Italico, p. 10.
[2] Senarega, Annales, 520, Folieta, 263.
[3] Emilia Pia to Gibert Pio, in Rosmini, 202.
[4] Georgius Florus, de bello Italico 7. St. Gelais, Louis XII., p. 82.

troops. But what availed these troops, which were neither picked nor disciplined—to-day recruited, and to-morrow disorganized—troops whose highest aim it was to scurry about and shout the name of their lord [1] who had hired them; what availed they against the Swiss battle array? They could not hold their position; Aubigny and one of the Sanseverin from the borders of Ferrara offered resistance to the troops advancing by land. Ferrantino, at all events, was warded off.

3. *Charles VIII. in Italy.*

Whilst the Italian League, as now constituted, was attacking Genoa and Milan by land and sea, King Charles was ordering processions to be held, and prayers offered up in all churches, in celebration of his victory over the Saracens.[2] After the old custom of French kings, he had the corpses of St. Denis and his companions brought up into the church from the vaults.[3] On the 29th of August, 1494, he attended mass at Grenoble, took leave of the Queen, and started for Italy. He had arranged who, in his absence, should govern the kingdom, and who rule each duchy. He had borrowed 100,000 ducats from the house of Sauli in Genoa;[4] the chamberlains had arranged his journey, and so, with high expectations, he proceeded from Briançon across Mont Genèvre, down the valley of Cesanne, and through the valleys of the Waldenses to Turin; mules brought up the baggage in the rear. At the gates of Turin they were received by Blanca, the lady of Savoy, seated on her palfrey, and by the young Duke, still a child, but who had been taught to express himself in graceful language;[5] for close relationship and frequent appeals for their decision in disputes touching wardships, had procured for the French kings the reputation of real suzerains in Piedmont. To the music of clarions and trumpets, the cavalcade passed through the streets, where Charlemagne's wondrous

[1] Nardi, Vita di Tebalducci.
[2] Baudequin MS. in Foncemagne, Memoiren der Acad. 17, p. 572.
[3] Desrey on Mostrelet, p. 228.
[4] Desrey, 214, 215.   [5] Georgius Florus, 6.

exploits were represented in devices.[1] The Princess gave her ornaments in pledge for a small loan. Philip de Bresse, the uncle of the Duke, joined the expedition; with a light heart they marched upon Asti, on the borders of Milan.[2]

Here Lodovico met the King. " In Italy," said he, "we have three great powers. One you have on your side, Milan; another sits quiet, Venice. How should Naples single-handed oppose him, whose forefathers have conquered us all together? Only follow me, and I will make you greater than Charlemagne was. We will drive these Turks out of Constantinople ere we finish."[3]

Before ever they had come up with the enemy, Lodovico took complete possession of Milan. John Galeazzo was sick unto death; but Lodovico had received the investiture with the dukedom from the King of Rome,[4] who had a few months previously wedded his niece. Now if Galeazzo were to die whilst the French army was in the country, who should then stand in his way? In Pavia Charles saw the sick man, whose mother had been the sister of his own, and who apologized even then for not having come to meet him, for he was too ill; but he offered him himself and his children.[5] A Pavian physician, who accompanied the King, assured Rucellai that it was evident he had been poisoned.[6] However, Charles bade him be of good heart, took his chain from his neck and hung it on him. He had scarcely reached Piacenza, when he heard of the young man's death.[7] Sympathy with the innocent victim was universal, as was the horror felt of him who was considered to be the murderer. Whilst the King invited the citizens to the funeral and gave presents to the poor, Lodovico hurried to Milan, assembled the Council of

[1] Philiberti Pignoni Chronicon Augustæ Taurinorum, p. 41.
[2] Comines and Desry, 2, 6. On the 1st September Charles arrived at Briançon, on the 5th at Turin, and on the 9th at Asti.
[3] Comines, p. 444.
[4] Documents in Corio, 900, 912, 935.
[5] Georgius Florus de expeditione Caroli, p. 9 (note in 3rd edition). Marino Sanuto, La Spedizione di Carolo ottavo in Italia, pubblicata per cura di Rinaldo Fulin. p. 671. Charles started from Asti on the 7th of October, and arrived in Pavia on the 14th.
[6] Oricellarius, de bello Italico, p. 33.
[7] Desry, 218. On October 18 Charles arrived at Piacenza; and on the 21st John Galeazzo died.

State, and proposed the son of the deceased as his successor.[1] "We need a man, and not a child," the Treasurer Marliano replied. All the members were of one opinion, that Lodovico must be their duke; they handed him the sceptre, a garment of gold stuff was brought and put on him; he then rode, accompanied by the notables of the city, to St. Ambrosio, and was there proclaimed duke by popular acclamation.[2] If Isabella had felt that her letter had caused her father a most perilous war, and her husband his death, what must her feelings have been now, when she heard that Lodovico was duke, and her children were without hope and robbed! The first she had endured, but this crushed her to the earth.[3]

The King stood on the borders of the Florentine and Roman territory. In Piacenza two Medicis came to him, Piero's cousins of the younger branch, yet more generous, more affable, more endeared to the people, and not less rich than him, but exiles, because, when at play with Piero, they had quarrelled with him and evinced French sentiments.[4] They told the King he need only advance into Tuscany, for he had friends in Florence. Among the old adherents of the Medici, there were many who were discontented with Piero. His father had once written to him, "Though thou art my son, thou art all the same no more than a citizen of Florence, like myself."[5] But the son of an Orsina, whose brother was Cardinal, whose father had been the mediator of Italy, and who felt himself even superior to the latter in point of physical strength, handsomeness, and graceful deportment, and, it might be, his superior in classical education—for he expounded Virgil to his brother, and could improvise cleverly[6]— might easily forget this warning. Like many others did, he forgot, over external show, what was really deserving of praise. He had no liking for agriculture and commerce, as his father had, but only taste for hunting, hawking,

[1] Florus Navagero in Muratori, 23, 201.
[2] Corio, p. 936; Lodovico to Aubigny in Rosmini, Trivulzio, ii. p. 206.
[3] Petrus Martyr; Epistol. xi. 193.
[4] Corio and Comines.
[5] Literæ Laurentii in Fabroni, Vita, p. 264.
[6] Literæ Petri in Fabr., Vita Laur., p. 298.

and Tuscan games with hand and foot, brilliant cavalcades by day, and nightly carouses.¹ He had a portrait taken of himself in a coat of mail.² In civic business, on the other hand, he approved what his counsellor, Bibbiena, proposed. It was not until Charles had crossed the high mountains and had arrived at Pontremoli, that Piero perceived how little the Florentines were inclined to support him against the King. "I never dreamt I should come into these straits," he wrote; "never have I mistrusted such great friends of this city, but I am forsaken by all, and have neither money, credit, nor repute, so as to be able to sustain the war."³ This he wrote when already on the road to Pisa to meet Charles, to deliver himself unconditionally into his hands.⁴ Only with the King's help was it possible for him to maintain himself in the city.⁵ The course he pursued was not so ill-advised as has been asserted,⁶ that of granting the King all

¹ Nardi, Istorie Fiorentine, p. 9.
² Jovii Elogia virorum illustrium, p. 187.
³ His letter to Bibbiena in Fabroni, Leo X., p. 262.
⁴ Second letter in same work. On 23rd October Charles left Piacenza, and arrived on the 29th at Pontremoli. On the 26th Piero started from Florence.
⁵ Georgius Florus, p. 9. Nerli Commentarj, p. 61.
⁶ In modern writings there has been attributed to Piero, una stoltezza veramente incredibile (Villari, storia di Girolamo Savonarola). We must not forthwith presuppose such a quality in a Florentine, a Medicean. All was antagonism of parties, more or less false calculation, and agitation of the moment. Extremely worthy of note are letters of the time of the crisis given in the collection of Desjardins, Négociations diplomatiques de la France avec la Toscane. We can perceive that Piero was at variance with his State in Florence, in consequence of his alliance with Alfonso, and his general attitude. For the Florentines were at heart well inclined towards France; they perceived the danger that threatened them from France with all the greater ill-humour, as it was not the policy of the Commonwealth, but merely a personal one of the head of their republic, that implicated them in it. Florence itself could not be defended against the superior forces of the French that threatened it from the sea side. Coerced by his opponents within, and menaced from without, Piero resolved to seek in person the favour of the King of France. He did this not without anxiety on his own account, and before setting out implored his fellow citizens to provide for his family, in case any disaster befell him. But as he went to the French camp in the double capacity of head of the Republic, and its envoy, his opponents in the city bestirred themselves; they appointed an embassage, which should either in conjunction with Piero, or without him, enter into negotiations with Charles VIII. They were also, resent

he wished, the fortresses of Sarzana, Sarzanella, Pietrasanta, Pisa, and Livorno, which command the mountain-road and the coast from the Magra to the mouth of the Arno.[1] He meant by this means to estrange him from his friends, and to gain him for himself. But he was far from being sure of this when he learnt that his action was condemned at home. He hurried back to Florence. In order to assert the sovereign power, he massed his troops under Pagolo Orsino, and proceeded—it was on the 9th of November, 1494, a Sunday evening—with an armed retinue to the palace. The assembled Signori were not in accord. One of them, of the name of Lorini, ushered in Piero, and refused to give up the key to the bell, with which the others intended to call together the people. But the latter had the upper hand. A Nerli and a Gualterotti, both sprung of families formerly Medicean to the core, stepped towards Piero, as he entered, exclaiming, " Alone and unarmed, otherwise he does not enter here." Others opened the bell-tower.[2] With Piero had returned one Francis Valori, hitherto envoy to King Charles, and convinced that he would not support Piero Medici.[3] This

to meet the French demands. Meanwhile, it had not cost Piero much difficulty to open negotiations with the French. He was really of opinion that he was doing his old ally, Alfonso, the best service, by throwing himself entirely into the arms of France. He did not hesitate to deliver into their hands the fortresses which the French coveted, until their business with Naples was settled. He at once issued orders to Pisa and Florence to receive the King of France in a manner worthy of his dignity and the old connection with him. The new envoys had not received any orders that were exactly contradictory; they only laid stress upon the authority of the Republic as such. Every minute the opposition to Piero in the city itself waxed stronger. He considered it wiser to return to Florence, in order to keep master of the city. But he was not quite assured of the protection of France; in the French camp it was, on the other hand, perfectly well known that he and not the Signoria, was the real enemy of France. One of the civic envoys, Valori, came back from the King, convinced that he would leave the internal affairs of the Republic to its own management. Thus it came bout that Piero, whilst thinking to gain possession of the palace, met with opposition, and the population rose up against him. The moment of the greatest importance; it was really decisive for the later times is Tuscany.
of Comines, 449. ² Nerli, i. i. Nardi, p. 13.
The alleged bulletins of Charles VIII.'s army (Pilorgerie, Campagne bulletins de la grande armée d'Italie commandée par Charles VIII.),

man mounted his horse, summoned the people to liberty, and increased their confidence.

Hieronymus Savonarola had for the last four years preached to the same people: "A king will come across the hills, a great king, sent of God to punish the evil, and to regenerate the Church."[1] This king seemed now to have come. As Piero went across the square, he saw stones flying about him, and the people at the sound of the bell running together towards the palace, and disarming his myrmidons. He saw these weapons of slavery, the few that had escaped his control, brandished for the emancipation from his own yoke.[2] Giovanni, his brother, shouted in the street, "Palle!" (Their watchword was Bullets.) They endeavoured to rouse their partisans in the suburb of St. Gallo; but no one stirred, and Pagolo's troops were afraid. Thus the Medici, Lorenzo's sons, left Florence without saving anything; their treasures, their jewels, those cups of sardonyx, the most precious antiquities, the 3,000 medallions, the manuscripts and books, which it was their pride to show strangers,[3] the gardens, in which the Torrigiani and Michel Angelos were brought up, all were left to the people to pillage. They yielded up the power which their fathers had possessed for sixty years and fled, for they durst not turn their steps to Charles, but they crossed the Apennines to Bologna.

The advent of him, in whom the prophets foretold a Saviour, and whom people loved to address as "Holy Crown," set also Pisa free on the same Sunday. How that came about is not without uncertainty. One historian relates much about Simon Orlando, who exercised great influence upon both people and prince.[4] On the way back from mass, or on the way thither, it is recorded how the people of Pisa, young and old, prostrated themselves before the King, complained to him of the great oppression

are worthy of note, in so far as they explain the political negotiations that accompanied the expedition of the King, and his intentions: they are, however, of little value for the internal Italian movements.

[1] From Savonarola's discourses in Fabroni, Vita Leonis X.

[2] Nardi, Nerli, Guicciardini.

[3] Comines, p. 451, 455. Vasari, Vita di Torrigiano, v. d. P. iii. p. 136.

[4] Jovius, Historiæ sui temporis, fol. 19.

which they had suffered for the last eighty-seven years at the hands of the Florentines,[1] and said that they wished to be free and under his rule. Hereupon the monarch, who had a tender heart and hated all unfairness, at once threw an inquiring glance at one of his counsellors, who accompanied him, his master of petitions, Jean Rabot, and when the latter had judged that they were right, and when all his knights showed their sympathy, he nodded to them and promised to maintain them in good freedom. Hereupon the people, shouting "Franza!" "Libertà!" and "Joy!" threw the Florentine lion into the Arno, and expelled the Florentine commander.[2] They add, that two strangers had a share in this; a Milanese, because of certain pretensions of the Sforza, called Galeazzo Sanseverino, and a Sienese for the sake of the Tuscan liberty, named Bartholomew Sozzini, a teacher of law at Pisa, and who had for a long time been a prisoner in Florence.[3]

So much for the story told by the Florentines and French. Since the day of its enslavement there have never been any Year-books in Pisa.[4] Charles intended to wrest this city from Piero; but as yet he could not know how the latter stood with the Florentines.

Those against whom he now advanced were partly his enemies, for their head had waged war against him, and partly his friends, in that they had expelled this their head. Upon the hills before Signa, with the unprotected plain of the city before him, negotiations were opened. Since Lucca, that was in nowise under an obligation to him,[4] had received him with offerings in its best palace, he now demanded the same of Florence, viz., perfect confidence and unconditional surrender to his good-will.[5] The Florentines appeared ready to accede to his terms, and brought him (on the 17th of November) the keys of the gates. Youths in French garments bore a Baldachin over his head and conducted him, all in arms, just as he was, past the mystery of the Annunciation to their cathedral,

---

[1] Desry, p. 219. Nardi, 12.   [2] Comines, 452. Ferronus, p. 10.
[3] Alegretto Alegretti, p. 836.
[4] Sismondi, note to p. 1406.
[5] Chronicon Venetum in Murat., 24, p. 8.
[6] Negotiations in Ovicellarius, de bello Italico.

and to the houses of the Medici.[1] But the subsequent negotiations did not proceed so smoothly. Can it be true, as is said, that Piero Capponi seriously challenged the French inside the city to fight a battle that his party had not dared to accept outside? Certain it is, at any rate, that the citizens and the French did not agree well together,[2] that the King feared treachery, and the town pillage.[3] At last an understanding was arrived at. The principal point of dispute concerned the House of Medici, which the King wished to have restored. However, he only so far attained his point, that the most rigorous edicts that had been launched against the Medici, their lives, and their house, were withdrawn. All else was left for the future. Pisa, Livorno, and the fortresses ceded by Piero were to remain in French hands until the conclusion of the expedition against Naples. The French reserved to themselves a great influence,[4] in respect of both policy and arms. After this had been ratified, the bells were rung, and "feux de joie" were kindled in the streets and squares. The king caused messages of peace, favourable to the renewal of liberty, to be affixed to the walls; and then prepared to continue his expedition to Rome and Naples.[5] Savonarola came and warned him to lose no time; God had sent him, of this he was assured, but he conjured him not to allow the insolence of his soldiery to bring to nought the accomplishment of his object.[6] Charles VIII. issued a

[1] Desry, 219. Nardi, 15.
[2] Macchiavelli, Decennale. Oricellarius.
[3] Macchiavelli, Clizia Commedia. Alto i. Sc. i.
[4] A very vivid picture of the mistrust existing between the French and the Florentines may be found in the Diario Fiorentino dal 1450 al 1516, by Luca Landucci, edited in the year 1883 by Jodoco del Badia. Therein we read under date of the 24th October (p. 85) : Che ognuno attese a riempiere le case di pane e d'arme e di scessi e afforzarsi in casa quanto era possibile, con propositi e animi ognuno volere morire lo l'arme in mano e ammazzare ognuno, se bisognassi, al modo del Vespro Siciliano. (Note to 3rd Edition.)
[5] Petrus Parentius, Daybook in Fabroni, Leo 263 (note to 2nd ed.). Désjardins, Négociations, i. p. 601. The text of the treaty has been published by Gino Capponi in the Archivio Storico Italiano, Sér. i. vol. i. pp. 362-375.
[6] Petri Criniti Carmen, cum Carolus ad urbem tenderet, in Roscoe, Life of Leo, i. Appendix, 510.   [6] Nardi.

kind of manifesto, to the effect that he had left his wife, his Dauphin and only son, and his realm; that he was not come to injure anyone, but to take Naples, that had been assured both to his forefathers and to himself by twenty-four investitures of Roman Popes and holy councils, and whose harbours and seaboard afforded him the best base of operations for attacking the Infidels. He demanded a free passage, otherwise he would proceed by force.

Florence having been metamorphosed by his advent, he next advanced against his second foe.[1] Pope Alexander was thrown more into perplexity than into fear. He said to Rudolph of Anhalt, who was at that time in Rome: "This King will demand the name of emperor, as he does the sovereign power. But assure Maximilian that I would rather have a sword at my throat than agree to it."[2] Ferrantino was advancing on the one side towards Rome; he had been long since forsaken by the Florentines, and then by the princes Urbino and Pesaro,[3] and by Catharina Sforza also, now that he had showed himself incapable of resisting Aubigny. The people declared they did not desire war with the French;[4] they even showed themselves hostile to him and barred his way. Without divesting himself of his armour,[5] he took the Roman road through the Romagna. The Pope seriously believed that, with the assistance of the Neapolitans, he would be able to withstand the King of France advancing from Tuscany.[6] He did not listen to the assurances of the Sforza and their adherents. Charles VIII. entered Siena through guirlanded gates;[7] he there proclaimed his ban against those that had been expelled, and left some soldiers behind him. In Casciano he received the youth of Pisa, who brought him an offering of roes, hares, and all other fruits of the chase.[8] Thus did Charles VIII. arrive within the territory

[1] Charles left Florence on the 28th November.
[2] Burcardus, Diarium, p. 2050.
[3] Balir Guidobaldo, p. 135.
[4] Passero, Giornale, p. 63.   [5] Zurita, f. 52.
[6] Burcardus 2053, and Zurita, p. 50.
[7] Desry, 218 (note to 3rd ed.). Sanuto, Spedizione di Carolo, viii. p. 144.
[8] Alegretto Alegretti, 835-837.

of the Church.¹ The Cardinal Perrault persuaded the inhabitants of Montefiascone to receive the King peacefully; for so had been the old and real promise of the Pope. As early as the 10th December he was praying before the relics of St. Rosa in Viterbo;² and there even an Orsino, whose family was closely allied with Piero and Alfonso, surrendered to him all his castles and supplies. On all sides, even on the Tiber, the enemy appeared; Comines narrates that it was an undoubted fact, that a portion of the city wall had fallen.³ Ferrantino, on hearing of the King's superior force, quitted Rome. Then the Pope sent his master of the ceremonies, to escort the King into the city.⁴ On the 31st December, 1494, he made his entrance by torchlight through illuminated streets, received by the ovations of the people.⁵ It could not be Charles' intention to bring about a reformation of the Church by force, or to seize the imperial power; purposing, as he did, to attack the enemies of Christianity, he dared not stir up the whole of Christendom against himself.⁶ But if he had Cæsar, Alexander's son, as a hostage in his train, he was assured of the Pope. If he occupied Terracina and Civita Vecchia, the chief harbours from the French to the Neapolitan coast would be in his hand.

There was at this time in Alexander's keeping a certain Zjemi, the brother of Bajazeth, who had fled from the latter to the Christians, but yet had many adherents among the Turks; a man of resolute principles, who would only kiss the Pope's arm, and not his feet. Charles, by taking this man with him, considered himself as good as

¹ Burcardus, Diarium, 2051.
² Desry, fol. 220. On the 22nd December Charles started from Viterbo.
³ Comines, 462 (note of 3rd Ed.). That is also narrated by Sanuto, a.a. O., p. 163.
⁴ Burcardus on the 31st December.
⁵ Tremouille's Memoirs, 147, 148.
⁶ By a letter of the Archbishop of St. Malo to Queen Anne, we definitely learn that the deposition of the Pope Alexander, and a thorough ecclesiastical reform was talked of. "Si nostre roy eust voulu obtempérer à la plupart des Messeigneurs les Cardinaulx ilz eussent fait ung autre pappe en intention de refformer l'église ainsi qu'ilz disaient. Le roy désire bien la réformaçion, mais ne veult point entreprandre de sa depposicion. Vide Pilorgerie, l.l. p. 135. N.B. Note to new edition.

assured of success against the Turks.[1] Having obtained these advantages, which were moderate, though important, he said, standing on the steps of the papal throne, "Holy Father, I have come to make my obeisance, as my forefathers did."[2] He was present at the ceremony of the universal Indulgence, received the blessing, and quitted Rome on the 28th of January, 1495.[3]

Now only Alfonso was left to deal with. Whilst in Rome he had entered into negotiations with the King through the Pope. He had offered him large sums of money; a million ducats down and 100,000 ducats annually as a kind of tribute. The Venetian Republic and the King of Spain were to guarantee the payment. But, certain of his hereditary right, and filled with his plans against the Turks, Charles VIII. rejected all his overtures.[4] Even then Alfonso did not abandon all hope. Charles would not, he conceived, be able to advance upon Naples before the spring; meanwhile he would fortify his frontiers, and succour would arrive.[5] He expected such aid from the King of Spain, who, on a proposal being made him for his youngest daughter for Ferrantino, had shown himself inclined to accede to the request. He had offered, through Ram Escriva, 500 lancers, and even a large army under a grandee, under certain conditions. It was known of Bajazeth, against whom the French expedition was so publicly proclaimed, that he was fitting out a great number of galleys for sea in Constantinople, and had others on the stocks, and further that the Natolian army had received orders to cross the strait by the first of March, and the Greek fleet orders to get ready without delay.[6] His envoy accompanied Alfonso from the army to the capital.[7]

But this winter was just like spring; no rain fell, and even in Lombardy there was no snow; the French expedition met with not the slightest inconvenience.[8] Nowhere

---

[1] Infessura, 2060. Alexander to Maximilian in Datt, Wormser Acten, p. 852.
[2] Desry, 220.   [3] Burcardus, 2064.
[4] Letter of the Archbishop of St. Malo to Queen Anne in Pilorgerie, p. 138 (note to new edition).
[5] Zurita, f. 49, f. 50.
[6] Chronicon Venetum, p. 11.
[7] Passero, p. 63.   [8] Diarium Ferrarense, p. 290.

did it meet with resistance; Aquila surrendered as soon as the French showed themselves. The Neapolitans began to inquire of one another whence all this success came. Many said, "It is a secret of God;" others, "Their Latin and Greek made them cowards."[1]

Alfonso himself was at length startled at the universal despondency. And as, in addition, the people rose up in tumult—the reason whereof was not known—and it was only Ferrantino's presence that calmed them,[2] Alfonso perceived that he could not stand his ground, and remembered the prophecies which had been foretold of him. He hid himself for three whole days; the consciousness of his wickedness paralyzed his energies. But when the people again rose with the cry, "The King must be dead, for who has seen him alive?" and he saw that all was lost as regards himself, feeling that he was loathed and hated with just cause, but that his son, innocent, uncontaminated, young, and brave, the darling of the people, would assert himself, Alfonso renounced the realm.[3] They all wept when Jovian Pontan drew up the document.[4] Alfonso bade his son mount a horse and ride through the city in company with his uncle Federigo. Even then, the horror did not leave him; the spectres of his innocent victims visited him by night; upon his conscience lay the warning of his father, after whose death, people believed all was going to destruction: "crime entices thee as with an alluring face, before thou hast committed it; afterwards, when it is done and a calamity has happened, it still retains its features; but they are now a hideous picture; for hairs it has snakes; it is a veritable Medusa's head." "We will away from here," said Alfonso to his stepmother, and when she desired to wait a little longer, exclaimed, "I will throw myself from the window. Dost thou not hear how they all shout the name of the French?" He tarried no longer, but fled to Mazzara into a monastery of the Olivetans.[5]

---

[1] Romoncine, Tesoro politico, in Vecchione, p. 107.
[2] Passero, 64.
[3] Passero (note to new edition). Gallo, 8. Cronica di Napoli di Notar Giacomo, 185.
[4] Bembus, 32, 33.
[5] Comines, 462-467. Tranchedin to Lodovico in Rosmini, 207.

With the intention not to yield, Ferrantino meanwhile joined his army at the pass of St. Germano. With the same intent, Alfonso Davalos held in front of him the rock of St. John, which was considered unsurmountable.[1] If they could only hold out for a while on the frontier, the people might be gained over, they thought, and succour arrive. But they could not hold their ground. One day, after the midday meal, Charles arrived from Bauco before St. John and ordered it to be stormed. He did not require to repeat his order, for one and all were determined to gain honour in his eyes.[2] On renewing their onslaught for the third time—for they met with staunch opposition—they gained the rock, and spared no one; they showed great cruelty. But Charles was at Garigliano.[3] The rapidity and fury of this conquest inspired terror into Ferrantino's friends and roused the courage of his enemies.

The citizens of St. Germano were no more for resistance. At Teano one night Messere Renaudo came to Ferrantino: "Sire," he cried, "away hence, else you are delivered over to the enemy by your own camp."[4] No hope remained, save in the citizens of Capua and Neapolis. On the 16th of February, Ferrantino felt himself sure of the Capuans; he thereupon hurried to the Neapolitans to gain these also over; he called a gathering of them in St. Chiara. "Ye Sirs, my fathers and brethren," he said, "do ye know me? Among you I grew up and was reared. Now that all forsakes me, and I have no one I can trust, will ye also forsake me? Yet not now! Only not for fourteen days. If I have then received no help, do as ye list." He stood before them in tears; they were silent, for many loved him. "Our lord," said a nobleman, "we have neither provisions nor guns." Ferrantino replied, "There are the keys of the new castle, go and take what you need; there are a whole year's supplies for the whole of Naples there." He was still speaking, when a messenger came with the tidings that the enemy was attacking Capua; in despair he rushed away and took the road thither.[5] On his arrival at Aversa, he learnt that of his

---

[1] Passero, 65.   [2] Villeneufve, Mémoires, p. 4.
[3] Chronicon Venetum, p. 13. Desry.
[4] Passero. Martinellus to Ascanio in Rosmini, 208.
[5] Passero, 66 (note to new edition). Giacomo, 185.

three first captains, Trivulzio had gone over to Charles with his whole army, which had been kept so long in pay for him. This he did on the very first day that he had an opportunity of reciprocating this outlay with his service.[1] The other two had fled, and the citizens, if not on the 16th, at all events on the 17th, had sent envoys to Charles, who begged for mercy with folded hands.[2] All the same, it is said, he ventured up to the walls of Capua; but here he was met by the Germans, who had alone remained faithful to him, by Caspar's and Gottfried's companies; they had made a sortie against the enemy on the other side, but had been abandoned by the Italians. They had hardly been permitted to withdraw through the town in parties of ten men each.[3] It was now evident that all was lost. Perhaps Ferrantino when he turned round to go back to Naples, still hoped, for had not his grandfather here resisted all his enemies? But he had to see that the nobles, instead of equipping themselves for battle, were plundering the Jews, and that the populace, when he went into the stables to give horses to his servants, ran after him and stole them. Now all was over; he felt that the hatred cherished towards his father and grandfather was now turned against himself. Full of despair, he drew his sword and turned about with the words, "What have I done unto your children?" But a faithful servant led him away to his castle out of the throng, for he had otherwise been murdered.[4]

Whilst, then, Alfonso Davalos held the castle with 400 Germans, whilst the houses round about the arsenal and some ships were being burnt down,[5] and whilst the old Queen lamented, "O fate, no lance has been broken, and thou dost ruin this kingdom!" and all were on shipboard, she, her daughter and the young King, in order to escape to Ischia, Jacob Caracciolo, without asking leave, opened the gate to the French herald, and shouted "Franza!" Hereupon, twenty deputies of the Neapolitans advanced to meet

[1] Florus, as against which Rebucco in Rosmini, Trivulzio, i. 227, is improbable.
[2] Desry.
[3] Jovius, Historiæ sui temporis, fol. 30.
[4] Passero. Johann. Juvenis, de fortuna Tarentinorum, p. 127.
[5] Chronicon Venetum, p. 13. Navagero, p. 1202.

Charles, with the words, "Holy Crown, thou hast been awaited these hundred years in Naples. Now thou art come. Enter as our King and Master!"[1] and Charles, whose success had been most brilliant, and who now saw this kingdom like the French duchies, united to his crown, entered as the rightful heir. Yet in Capua he fancied himself wonderfully reminded of his expedition against the Turks; Zjemi still lived. It was said that the prestige of the French had prevented the Bassa of Avlona from crossing, and had scared away the Turks from many islands, and even from Negropont they were flying to Constantinople. When Grimani with Venetians passed by Lepanto, they thought it was the French, and retired from the castle and the shore. The peninsula and the mainland gathered fresh hope.[2]

[1] Diarium Ferrarense, p. 294.
[2] Corio, 939. Bembus, 346. Benedictus, p. 1583. Chronicon Venetum, p. 8.

CHAPTER II.

SPAIN AND LIGA IN WAR WITH CHARLES VIII.

1495—1496.

1. *United Spain.*

AT this time Spain was first heard and spoken of; this country had a short time previously become consolidated into a united and powerful kingdom out of two disunited and feeble principalities, Castile and Aragon. With respect to Castile, the autograph of Alonso de Palenzia records that there existed a law of Henry of Trastamar to the effect that, "without permission of the King of France, no Englishman should go to Castile, nor a Castilian to England." Such a disgraceful compact was actually kept by these weak monarchs.[1] John I. relied in battle even more upon the French than upon his Castilians; John II. appeared to many to be almost bewitched by his favourite Alvar de Luna;[2] the Portuguese, Pacheco and Giron, after overthrowing Alvar, lorded it over Henry IV. Henry, though a huntsman, and an enemy of baths and wine, but deprived of noble indignation and manly strength by early profligacy,[3] had scarcely turned away from them—not to be his own master, but to take another favourite—when they revolted, and with them all the nobles. They declared his daughter Joana to be illegitimate, and favoured his brother's succession, and, when he died, that of his sister Isabella; but she did not desire to be called queen, and was content that the succession should be assured to her issue.[4]

[1] Ferrera's Spanish History from this Manuscript, vii. B. p. 47.
[2] Rodericus Santius, Historia Hispanica, iv. c. 31.
[3] Hernando Pulgar, Claros Varones, p. 4.
[4] Antonius Nebrissensis, Rerum a Fernando et Elisabe gestarum Decades, p. 801.

Near relatives of this family ruled in Aragon, yet with no better fortune, in spite of their having inherited from Ferdinand I. a crown adjudged him by the three counties of which Aragon consisted, great estates in Castile, and valid claims to Naples. These claims Alfonso took over from his son, and succeeded in establishing them; yet he afterwards gave Naples to his illegitimate son, and separated it from Aragon. The estates in Castile devolved upon Henry; but at Olmedo, where he fought against John II., and was defeated, they were lost to the house, and came into the hands of those Portuguese favourites. Even the crown was in danger, when John of Aragon, to whom it had passed, was attacked by his eldest son, and by all the Catalans.

Let us now represent to ourselves how the union and the consolidation of these kingdoms was brought about. The same men who had seized the Aragon estates had procured for Isabella the succession in Castile. Now, when John's enemies were dead and he triumphant, and they now began to feel alarmed, Isabella betrothed herself with the man whom they dreaded most, with Ferdinand, the youngest son of John, and his heir. Seated on a mule, in disguise, Ferdinand came to Valladolid to celebrate the nuptials;[1] then they did not hesitate to swear allegiance to Joana, and to offer her hand and realm to the King of Portugal.[2] This was the origin of the war, a war that was waged on all points between Fuenterrabia and Gibraltar at the same time: a war in which John Ulloa strove against Roderich Ulloa,[3] his brother, Peter Zuñiga against his father,[4] and the Count of Salinas against his sister,[5] and the cities that sided with Aragon, and their castles, that favoured Portugal, also strove together. But at last Ferdinand and Isabella were victorious at Toro, and succeeded in ridding the country of the enemy. They founded the monastery of St. Francis in Toledo, and proceeded in two directions to pacify the country—the Queen to the Andalusian cities, and the King to the castles on the Duero. Against the castles—for, as a fact, the country had been

---

[1] Ferdinand himself in Zurita.   [2] Antonius Nebriss, p. 802.
[3] Antonius Nebriss, p. 821.   [4] Idem, 835.
[5] Idem, 895.

pillaged, and all robbers had sheltered themselves in them —he was assisted by the cities and their Hermandad, who, in order to punish robberies and murders in the streets, squares, and houses, maintained 2,000 horsemen and a proportionate strength of infantry.[1] They lent their assistance, as though their sole aim was the general peace, yet their object was also a political one in the interest of Ferdinand. He wrested the castles from his enemies. Isabella, meanwhile, presided at tribunals of justice at Seville every Friday, surrounded by bishops and lawyers, and with clerks before her. But here, where the Duke Medina Sidonia and John de Cordova were of her party, and the Marques of Cadiz and Alonso d'Aghilar against her, and where the enmity of the old Christians, the new converts, the Jews, and the neighbouring Moors, divided streets and families,[2] her rigour was ineffectual. She resolved to pardon all offences, save and except heresy. This latter, with which the judgment hall of the Hermandad was as incompetent to deal as the Dominican inquisition, which had been long since abolished, was reserved for another tribunal.

In September, 1478, she quitted Seville; on the 1st of November, Sixtus IV., who at the same time revoked the dispensation granted to the King of Portugal to marry Joana,[3] gave the Kings (under which title Ferdinand and Isabella were now known) the right to appoint inquisitors against heretics, apostates, and their patrons.[4] Unexceptionable accounts testify[5] to the fact, that it was the representations of Thomas Torquemadas, a prior of the Holy Cross, who declared that "those who had been converted, went by night into the synagogue, kept the sabbath and the Jewish Easter, and celebrated, barefooted, the day of Remembrance," that primarily caused the institution of this tribunal; a lamentable fatality, if true what Pulgar states,[6] that the Torquemadas were also originally Jews; and that it was a quarrel between the converted and the unconverted Jews that brought the Inquisition upon the people of Castile and Aragon. But if

[1] Antonius, 851.
[2] Antonius, 861.
[3] Ferrera's Hist. of Spain. Vol. xi. sec. 235.
[4] Llorente, Histoire de l'Inquisition. Vol. i. p. 145.
[5] Marineus Siculus, p. 481.
[6] Claros Varones, p. 24.

we remember that the influence of the Jews over the grandees, due to their farming their revenues, their affluence, and their relationship to them, conflicted secretly and at all points with the King's interests,[1] that the first order of the Inquisitors threatened the Marques of Cadiz, an opponent of the monarch's, in case he sheltered the fugitive Jews, and that it was a Jewish book against the Government that brought matters to a crisis,[2] we have a consecutive account before our eyes. The Inquisition harmonized with the Hermandad in form—for they each had originally two judges and a fiscal—as also mainly in scope; viz., the completion of this war and the consolidation of the royal power, under the cover of a far wider plan; yet the ecclesiastical power of the one was far more arbitrary than the civil power of the other. After some hesitation, Isabella had the Quemadero erected on the plain before Seville, between the four prophets;[3] the monastery of the Dominicans in the city was soon too small to hold the accused,[4] and 5,000 houses in Andalusia were empty.[5] But they began to obey. So soon as Pacheco consented to resign a great part of his estates, and the King of Portugal to renounce his claims, and when everybody surrendered, the civil war came to a close, and the royal power was at the same time re-established. Yet these institutions still continued under the pretence of general policy, and others were added to them. When the grand masters of two of the Spanish orders of knighthood had died, and the third was inclined to retire, Ferdinand undertook to manage all three. In truth a goodly power; for the order of St. Iago alone could put 1,000 heavy cavalry into the field; and a table of the fifteenth century ranks its grand masters among the princes and independent heads of Europe.[6] Further, since the Pope had given way in the matter of

---

[1] Caracciolus, Epistola de Inquisitione, in Muratori, Ser. 22, 97 (note to new ed.). Cf. as to the condition of the Jews, Reyes Catolicos in Prescott, " Hist. of the reign of Ferdinand and Isabella the Catholic," i. p. 243.
[2] Llorente, pp. 148, 149.   [3] Llorente, p. 152 and fol.
[4] Ferrera, xi. sec. 320.   [5] Marineus Siculus, p. 483.
[6] In Sanuto's Venetian history in Muratori, xxii. 963.

some disputes touching the episcopal chairs of Saragossa, Cuenca, and Tarragona, the rule was established that no one could be raised to the rank of bishop upon whom the King had not previously declared his willingness to confer this dignity.[1]

Let us now observe: the Hermandad was the reflex of a former independent coalition of the citizens against the nobles, and it now committed the civic power into the hands of the King. The Grandmasterships, through the Encomiendas, bound the knights who had received of them, as well as all noble families, out of gratefulness or expectation of future favours, to the King. The latter, by his Inquisition and the election of bishops became almost the head of the clergy. We perceive that it was not so much that Ferdinand and Isabella extended the royal power handed down to them from their ancestors, as that they gave it a new basis; they placed themselves at the head of the estates who might have resisted them, and who resisted their forefathers, and, concentrating their powers in their own persons, became their real chiefs. In all this the Church, by supplying them with the Inquisition and Mayorazgen, and by gradually making over to them for ever the Tercias of the ecclesiastical tithes, rendered them the greatest service, and they had no more dangerous foes than the enemies and apostates of the Church of Rome. The traditional liberties still continued; even in Castile the noble might surrender his fief back into the King's hand,[2] and retract his allegiance, whilst the citizen might shut his house against the royal officer;[3] but obedience to duty became established. The rigorous Isabella, she who rode in person after the son of the Almirante, Fadrique, who had broken her safe-conduct and fled, that Isabella who had the Alcadian, who had killed a royal servant, hanged on the very spot where he had committed the deed, and who ordered the hand of the other, the Great Alcaldian Villenas, to be cut off for allowing it,[4] soon

---

[1] Mariana, de rebus Hispaniæ, xxiv. c. 16.
[2] Mariana, xiii. p. 599.
[3] Hallam from Marino, Ensayo critico, in The State of Europe during the Middle Ages, i. p. 762.
[4] Ferrera, viii. p. 92.

brought it about that travellers from Spain told it as being one of the wonders of that land, that there no wrong was done, not even by the authorities themselves, but that speedy retribution followed.[1] There sat Isabella (before her her escutcheon quartered with a castle, a staff, a lion, and an eagle), amongst the images of the saints in her chapel; Cardinals, Archbishops, Bishops, and Orators, on the one side, and the Connetable, Almirante, Dukes, Marques, and Counts, on the other, the priests in full canonicals before her, all awaiting her sign.[2] Her diplomacy aimed at absolute power over an orthodox kingdom.

Now that the internal disorders had ceased, and the constitution was in process of development, the kings turned their eyes unceasingly towards the outer world, the Christian world, too, but principally the infidel. According to the example of their forefathers, Ferdinand the great and the holy, the four Alfonsos, the Emperador, Ramon the noble, and the eleventh, who ventured not to wage war with the Moors until they had first been victorious in a civil one, but who engaged in the former as soon as they had succeeded in the latter. Thus did they, under the standard of the Cross, each division under a crucifix, as the song goes, invade the plain of Granada.[3] They swore not to leave it until they had taken the city; they centred the attention and the obedience of the whole nation upon this point, and at last conquered it. But as the different kingdoms had always been in the habit of dividing beforehand what they intended to conquer, and were hardly less jealous of what they coveted than of what they had already taken, so at the present time did they claim the African kingdoms of Oran and Tlemsan for the crown of Aragon, and for Sicily, Tunis, and the eastern slope of the Atlas. These claims were also confirmed by the Pope, and they hoped to push on in an easterly direction to Egypt, and to come as far as Jerusalem. In the West, Castile claimed all that had formerly been Mauritania and Tingitana. This led to a war with Portugal. At last they agreed together, that, with the exception of Melita and Caçaça, Portugal should

[1] Senarega, Annales Genuenses, in Muratori, xxiv. p. 534.
[2] Marineus Siculus, p. 506.
[3] Guerras Civiles de Granada, by Perez de Vita, tom. iii. p. 145.

be at liberty to conquer the whole of Fez. But this was of minor importance. Those maritime expeditions, in which the Portuguese, planting their standard ever further and further afield, had learnt of an eastern and Christian monarch, the King of Abyssinia,[1] and by which they hoped —for already someone had been in Goa and had discovered the Cape—to find this potentate, and by his help, proceeding along the coast,[2] to arrive at India, and the land of the spices, were endangered; for Pope Alexander had promised the conquest of the whole of Africa to the united crowns. But, finally, the old treaties remained valid; the right of navigating to Guinea and the coast downwards was assigned to the Portuguese,[3] and they needed not allow another to sail the same way. But Providence willed that something unexpected should result from these differences; and what actually happened far surpassed human calculations. In Lisbon there often sat together two brothers from Genoa, Bartholomew Colon, who drew maps for the use of sailors,[4] and Christopher, the elder, who had navigated with varying fortune the inner sea, and the outer from the Canaries to Iceland.[5] These two discussed together what was well known, and became convinced that the safest plan to discover that land of precious stones, pearls, and spices,[6] that Sypango of which Marco Polo had written,[7] a land into which Christianity could be introduced, would be, not by voyaging along the coast of Africa, but by sailing ever westward, and thus circumnavigating the globe. But no King, no Duke, and no Signorie, would believe the brothers. At length the two Kings, in their joy over the victory of Granada, being at Santafé three months later, took the advice of the above-named Alonso Quintanilla, he who first invented the new Hermandad,[8] and hazarded

[1] Barros, Asia, iii. c. 2, 3, 4.
[2] Sommario Pietro Martir's in Ramusio, 3, 1.
[3] Mariana, xxiv. c. 10.
[4] Antonius Gallus, Commentariolus de navigatione Colombi, p. 300.
[5] Jagemann, Geschichte der ital. Literatur, iii. iii.
[6] Petrus Martyr, decas Oceanea, i. f. 1.
[7] Barros, Asia, iii. c. 9.
[8] Oviedo, Sommario, in Ramusio, iii. f. 80, compared with Antonius Nebrissensis, p. 847.

this venture. They put three Caravellas (small ships) at the disposal of the elder Colon, and had them manned for the most part by sailors from the vicinity of Palos.[1] Tradition goes, that these coast seamen, after spending week by week between heaven and water, only gazing upon seaweed, and seeing no land, threatened to murder their captain. The captain the while, working by day with the lead, and by night keeping his eye intent upon the fixed stars, and even in his dreams full of visions of success, remained firm of purpose, and managed to curb all opposition; until at last looming clouds inspired hopes, and in the night a sailor shouted, "light and land;" when day broke, hills, high trees, and green land were discovered; he shed tears, and falling on his knees, said the "Te Deum Laudamus." They erected on the coast an enormous cross, heard the notes of the first nightingale, saw the timid good people,[2] and returned to tell their king of the country they had taken possession of in his name.[3]

God's gift and the discovery this excellent man had made primarily led to the continuation of the Castilian-Portuguese differences. The wind drove the returning party to Lisbon. As soon as the King of Portugal saw that the natives, who had been brought back, looked like the Indians, as they had been described to him, and heard from Colon, that he had there been told of a land called Sybang,[4] he began to be afraid that his scheme had been anticipated. He requested the Kings to sail, not southwards but, northwards, according to the old compact.[5] They believed him to be right, and that they had come to the point where east and west touched; they little knew the size of the world; they bargained long together, and

[1] Oviedo, p. 81, and Dillon's Journey to Spain, ii. 102.
[2] All taken from the "Sommarios" of Pietro and Oviedo, p. 16, p. 810, and from the Decas, i. 1 (note to new edition). It is evident that in this short mention of the great event neither its worldwide importance could be enlarged upon, nor its course critically examined; it appears only to be treated in its local origin with reference to the undertakings which at that time proceeded from the Iberian peninsula.
[3] Christophori Columbi Epistola in Hisp. Illustr. ii. 1282.
[4] Barros, Asia, iii. 9.
[5] Zurita, Historia del Rey Hernando, i. f. 30, 31.

finally offered a prize to him, who, starting 370 leagues from the Canary Islands, should discover Portugal towards the east, and Castile towards the west.[1] This was quite a different matter from their Fez and their Tingitana; but they still went on in the old fashion.

Such were the operations of the united kingdoms against the Infidels, and, if the conquest of Granada was celebrated in all Christian lands with feasting and games, how much more did not the report of a new earth and a new mankind ring throughout Europe! These kingdoms now turned their eyes again towards the interior of Christendom. The grandees had delivered up those crown estates to which they could show no legal title, and which were, at the lowest estimate, computed to be worth nearly thirty million maravedi. Cadiz and the Isla had been recovered from the Ponce, and Roussillon had been given up. The time had come, in which the idea of a united Spain for the first time asserted itself. The Pope initiated the title "Serene Kings of Spain," seeing that European, Bætic, and a portion of Lusitanian Spain had become united in the sense in which the title "Catholic King" is said to have been originally framed.[2] In the same way as the regenerated unity of the French realm impelled Charles VIII., so did the unity of Spain, asserting itself now for the first time, induce Ferdinand and Isabella to look towards Naples. The rights of the one clashed with those of the other.

2. *Alliance between Spain and Italy.*

The two Sicilies had from time immemorial been the source of strife between the Spanish and French houses, a strife which began with the death of the last Hohenstaufen, and had not as yet been fought out. It was on the point of being taken up on both sides by third houses. At first it had been carried on between the Barcelonian House of Aragon, the heirs of Conradin, and the Anjous, who had

[1] Zurita, f. 36.
[2] Marineus Siculus, p. 164. Francis Tarapha, de Regibus Hispaniæ. Hispan. Illustr. i. p. 567.

been called in by the Pope, that is, between the Provençals and the Catalans, who are in reality one race, of the same origin, and speaking the same language. The former took Naples, the latter Sicily, and ever since they had been in feud with each other.

Secondly, this long-standing dispute devolved upon Alfonso I. of the House of Castile, and the younger branch of the Anjous. Alfonso with the Catalans was victorious, and gained possession of Naples. Although before the people he took his stand upon the new right of a certain adoption, although it had been revoked, yet he confessed after the victory that his greatest joy was, that he had regained the possession of his ancestors.[1] From this dates the war of Ferrante with John of Anjou.

Thirdly, when the rights of the Anjous had at length passed to the crown of Paris, the united kingdoms, in opposition, felt themselves pledged to protect the interests of Catalan. Ferdinand had ofttimes been urged by the barons to make war on Ferrante, but had always answered, "He is my brother-in-law."[2] But now if Charles was victorious, he would lose one prospect, viz., his rights, and saw even Sicily threatened. The Kings of Spain were bound by the treaty of Roussillon, but had never approved the enterprises of Charles VIII.

While Charles was making his preparations, they proposed to him an expedition against Africa with their rights to support him; when he was already in the Alps, they equipped a fleet in Viscaya; when he turned against Tuscany, they endeavoured to rouse Lodovico's ambition by offering him an alliance with their house and a royal title. Charles arrived at Florence; they then despatched Lorenzo Figueroan to Venice, in order, it may be, without any declaration, to arrange an alliance.[3] But when the French King was in arms at Rome, and had already occupied the cities of the Church, they laid hold of a clause in their treaty, "*reserving the rights of the Church*," a clause which Charles agreed to, as long as Alexander was Sforzian and belonged to his party. Ferdinand was the first

---

[1] Marineus Siculus, de Vita Alfonsi, v.
[2] Zurita, "Casado con su hermana."
[3] Zurita, f. 38, 41, 46, 47.

to make it important by helping to win over the Pope. Whenever the Catholic Kings bestowed any care upon Christendom, it was agreeably to their own interests. Relying on this clause, their envoys,[1] one for Aragon and one for Castile, betook themselves to the States of the Church, met Charles near Rome, and, on his refusal to accede to their demand that he should restore the cities and uphold the treaty, tore up the document embodying it. It cannot be exactly called faithlessness, but a faithful observance of treaties it certainly was not. Ferdinand and Isabella then took under their protection Alexander, whose son had long since fled from the French King, and Ferrantino, who had betrothed himself with their niece Joana, and had fled with her from Naples, and promised them certain Neapolitan castles as security for their war expenses. They were now in a position to form a new league against Charles.

Now after Charles had left Lodovico the Moor, differences arose between them on account of some transactions in Tuscany, Rome, and Naples. Serezana and Serezanella, which had been objects of contention between the Genoese and Florentines until Charles's arrival, Lodovico had vainly hoped to obtain from the latter for his city. He found fault with the peace concluded with Alexander, because he found himself not sufficiently benefited by it.[2] He was vexed on seeing his rebels, the Milanese Trivulzio, and the Genoese Fregoso and Fiesco taken into Charles's service at Naples, and in consequence refused to allow French ships to anchor at Genoa.[3] Meanwhile a danger threatened him nearer home. Duke Louis d'Orleans, upon whom there had devolved, through a legitimate daughter of the House of Visconti, better claims to Milan[4] than those were which the Sforzas deduced from an illegitimate offspring, was at Asti, as though only waiting for a favourable opportunity to assert his rights. His servants openly declared that he would soon be Duke of Milan; and as

[1] Argensola, Annales, p. 50. Florus, p. 15.
[2] Lodovico to Ascanio in Rosmini, ii. 208.
[3] Lodovico to Charles in Rosm., 213.
[4] Extrait d'un discours, touchant le droit sur le Duché de Milan, by Tillet. Comines, Preuves, ii. 321.

he was collecting troops, and had at least no resistance to fear from Charles, Lodovico began to tremble for his own power.[1] He addressed himself first of all to Maximilian, who had only a short time previously solemnly conferred upon him the investiture,[2] and who, among all princes, was almost his nearest relative. Maximilian, too, had received Alexander's message, and might well be anxious for the imperial dignity. His envoys throughout Italy also complained when they saw lilies where the eagle should be, for the suzerainty belonged to the German King.[3] Yet most of all was he moved by this, and was ever repeating it to the princes of the land: Charles was threatening Genoa, and Louis Milan, so that it was imperative to take immediate steps against them. But the need of the Venetians was more urgent than Maximilian's, and quite as sore as Lodovico's. They feared for their own existence, now that Aubigny had penetrated as far as Forli. They raised money when Charles was in Florence; directly he reached Rome, without meeting with resistance, they gathered a force of several thousand light Albanian cavalry, their Stradiotti;[4] and now that he had Naples, and the castles had fallen into his hands, and they had heard of Louis' plans, they were seized with the utmost fear. One morning they were sitting together, as was their wont, sixty or seventy in number, in the Doge's chamber, when the French ambassador entered. They sat, with their eyes fixed on the ground, and their heads resting on their hands. No one broke silence, no one looked at him. The Doge then spoke: "Your master has the castles of Naples, will he remain our friend?" The envoy assured them that such would be the case.[5] What troubled them was not exactly the destruction of the unity of Italy alone, but their own danger. For we must remember that Louis d'Orleans' pretensions to Milan might also be extended to a great part of the Venetian possessions, which once had been in the power of John

[1] Instructio Casati in Rosmini.
[2] Sanseverin to Lodovico in Rosmini.
[3] Allegretto Allegretti, Diarj di Siena, p. 838.
[4] Chronicon Venetum in Muratori, xxiv. p. 8, 9, *seq.*
[5] Comines.

Galeazzo Visconti, his ancestor, and which were later conquered by the Republic. If the one were taken, there was certainly reason to fear for the other.

We see that Maximilian, Lodovico, and Venice were natural allies. It was to Ferdinand's advantage to join this league, not by himself, but with his allies Ferrantino and the Pope. But could Lodovico trust Alexander, who had only shortly before this broken faith with him? Suarez insisted; it was not his power, but his name that was wanted.[1] Should they, moreover, receive into the league Ferrantino, who no longer possessed anything or could afford any assistance? Yet, all the same, his ambassadors went to Worms and appeared before the German King, praying to be included in the alliance.[2] At length, on the 29th March, 1495, after frequent negotiations had been carried in secret, even by night, an understanding was arrived at. Suarez exclaimed, "Charles made the wound, and we have found its cure."[3] The Venetians now invited the French ambassador again. "We have concluded an alliance," said the Doge, "against the Turks for the peace of Italy and the security of our possessions." A hundred nobili were there, holding their heads high, bold and joyous, for they knew that an army of more than 50,000 men would take the field against Charles.[4]

The ambassador departed, as is said, surprised and perplexed. On the stairs Spinello, the Neapolitan envoy, met him with a beaming face and in a fine new dress. Coming down, he begged the secretary who accompanied him to repeat to him what the Doge had said.[5] It is Comines of whom that is related; he himself will not confess to it; he asserts that he knew all. In the afternoon the envoys of the allies, to the number of fifty, were conveyed in pleasure barks, decorated with the arms and ensigns of their respective masters, to the strains of music and song, through the Grand Canal, between the marble halls on

---

[1] Zurita, f. 61. [2] Datt, de pace publica, p. 523.
[3] Peter Justinianus, Historica Veneta, from Hieron. Donatus, Apologia, p. 148.
[4] Comines, Mémoires, i. p. 490.
[5] Bembus, Historiæ Venetæ, p. 34-36.

either side. They passed under the windows of Comines, and the Milanese envoy, at all events, pretended not to know him. In the evening, torches, cannon, and illuminations proclaimed the new league.[1] Ten days later, Venice had 21,000 men in the field; on Palm Sunday the league was proclaimed in the countries of the respective allies. Comines and Louis d'Orleans wrote six times within six days to France that fresh troops were needed. King Charles was informed of the danger that was approaching.

3. *Retreat of Charles VIII.*

It is both the life and the fortune of the Germano-Latin nations that they never become united. These negotiations and these preparations, with which the real struggle of the Spaniards and French began, were the beginning of a thorough and wearisome grouping of factions that completely altered the face and form of Europe. In the first instance, when Charles's expedition threatened danger to the Turks, they were advantageous to the latter.

Zjemi was now dead. There have been preserved to us an instruction sent by Alexander to his Turkish ambassador, and letters of Bajazeth to the Pope, of perfectly horrible contents: "The Pope might be pleased to raise Zjemi from the troubles of this world into another, where he might enjoy greater repose; in return for which he, Sultan Bajazeth Chan, would pay him 300,000 ducats."[2] And it is well that we have reason to doubt the genuineness of the letter. However, Zjemi died suddenly; and whilst the Christian writers speak of poison, the Turkish annals[3] contain this passage: "Mustapha Bey killed Zjemi with the help of the Pope." Little blame is due to Charles for not having actually embarked on the expedition he had intended to make, and on which he had already despatched the Bishop of Durazzo and the Despots

---

[1] Comines. Carraciolus, Vita Spinelli, Cariati Comitis, p. 43.
[2] Burcardi Diarium, p. 2056.
[3] Leonclavii Annales Turcici, p. 154. Daru, Histoire de Venise, iii. 164, from Saadud-Din-Mehemed-Hassan.

of Morea.¹ He would gladly have concluded a treaty with Ferrantino. Federigo, too, before the Liga was formed, came once more, found the King sitting under an olive tree near the new castle, and begged an estate for Ferrantino, and the title of King; but Charles cautiously answered, "Not here, but in France;" and thereupon they separated.² He contented himself with bringing nobles, citizens, and people of Naples into peace and harmony. All the barons came to pay allegiance to him, and received back their estates, which they had lost through the Aragons. With the exception of a few, who still held out, all cities sent their syndics with the keys, and received favours,³ Tarento, for instance, permission to select its syndic from among the middle class of citizens, the Onorats,⁴ and the Neapolitans a like permission to elect an Eletto, with a council of twelve from their midst.⁵ He remitted the propertied classes 200,000 ducats of their annual dues, and to those who had nothing he promised 12,000 ducats as an annual present. He fed the poorest on Maunday Thursday.⁶ How could he fail to feel contented and happy when he visited the wonders of the land—the grotto of Posilippo, which he was told was the artificial work of Virgil, the wondrous springs, the chasms in the earth, full of hot wind⁷—and gazed on the fatness of the land in spring?

[1] Oricellarius, p. 66.
[2] Desry, 223. Passero, 70. (Note to new edition.) Giacomo, 188. The negotiations can be followed in a letter of the King, dated 28 March, 1495, to Bourbon, which contains this passage : " Frédéric (Federigo) me supplia et requist, que je voulasse bien laisser à son nepven (Ferrantin) le tiltre du royaume et quelque pension pour vivre telle qu'il me plairoit adviser." The king replied, before his departure his right and title to the kingdom had been investigated in France and solemnly recognized, and then further, " Je n'estois point deliberé de riens laisser ni quitta de mon héritage et dudit tiltre—que s'il s'en vouloit venir en France, je luy donneroye pour son état xxx mille livres de rente et xxx mille livres de pension chacun an, et des gend'armes, avecques ce que je le Maryerois en quelque lieu de mon royaume de manière qu'il auroit cause de se contenter " (Pilorgerie, Campagne et Bulletins, p. 212).
[3] Passero, 7.
[4] Joh. Juvenis, de fortuna Tarentinorum, p. 127.
[5] (Note to new edition.) Giacomo, 204. Gallo, 67. Cf. Reumont, die Caraffa von Maddaloni, i. p. 124.
[6] Lettre à la Duchesse de Bourbon in Godefroy, 739.
[7] Desry, 224.

And when he sat at the tournament, and saw how French and Italians tilted in the ring together, and how the Princess of Melfi rode as straight as a knight on her horse, the red and white feathers waving from her hat, her hair floating in dainty tresses about her frill and the knightly tunic of green-gold embroidery;[1] these amusements made his heart glad. With satisfaction he noted in his letters the restoration of good order and justice in the land hitherto so oppressed, and the homage paid him on all sides in consequence. They evince the feeling that he had happily accomplished a great undertaking. In the midst of these pleasures, the news of the Liga and its preparations reached him. The restoration of Roussillon and Artois had been in vain. How would his powerful foes in his rear at Milan, Venice, and Rome have permitted a Turkish campaign? In order not to be cut off from France, he must of necessity return thither. Once more he entered the city, with a crown on his head and an orb in his hand, to make and to receive the vow.[2] The citizens lifted up their sons of five, ten, and twelve years of age to him, in order that he should dub them knights.[3] He appointed Bourbon Montpensier viceroy, lord, and commander of the kingdom, took one half of his troops with him, and returned on the road by which he had come.[4] He hurried, in order not to be overtaken by the heat.

The Pope fled before him from Rome to a stronghold;[5] those who are well-informed assert, that Charles would otherwise have taken further steps against him.[6] In Siena he heard the complaints of the reformers against the Nove—that is, the factions of the city,—and took the part of the complainers, who called him their king and lord. He left a garrison behind him there.[7] On the first day of his arrival at Pisa, the children greeted him, all dressed in white silk, embroidered with lilies; and, on the next day, the men—they desired to be his subjects; on the third, the ladies and

---

[1] Lettre, ibid. [2] (Note to new edition.) Giacomo, 190.
[3] André de la Vigne, Histoire du voyage de Naples, in Godefroy, p. 200.
[4] Idem, and Desry, p. 2246.
[5] Navagero, Historia Veneta, p. 1204.
[6] Oricellarius, de bello Italico, p. 68. [7] Allegretto Allegretti.

citizens' wives, but these barefooted and in mourning, praying: "he might see fit to take them under his protection."¹ These good people had scarcely a piece of fine cloth left in their shops that they did not give to the commanders of the army.² Particularly they gained over the Swiss, who appeared before the King at the play with axes at their necks, and begged him to guarantee the freedom of the city. Charles so far agreed as to say that he would act so that everyone should be contented.³ And there he stood again at the foot of the Apennines, where, from the Magra across to the Taro, a pass that the Longobards deemed right to fortify with castles and strongholds⁴ separates Tuscany from Lombardy. In Naples the Liga had been ridiculed in a comedy;⁵ and as yet Charles had seen no enemy, nor feared any. But Savonarola had told him that the God who had brought him in would surely lead him out; but, because he had not ameliorated the condition of his Church, he would be scourged.

The Liga had already actually occupied Naples, that he had only just quitted, as well as the territory of Milan that lay before him. There there appeared under Gonzal d'Aghilar Ferdinand's Viscayans, Galicians, and horsemen. Gaeta revolted, and Ferrantino pushed forward into Calabria. This first attack was repulsed by the French, who took Gaeta, not even sparing those who clutched the crucifix for their protection,⁶ and drove Ferrantino back. Only one Neapolitan, of the name of John Altavilla, comported himself bravely. Seeing the King fall with his horse, he dismounted, gave him up his own, and with a soldier's death gained the eternal glory of fidelity.⁷ All the rest fled. But now Otranto, of its own accord, raised the Aragon cry of "Fierro;"⁸ and in Naples, when two persons met in the street, they asked, "Brother, when comes the Sponsor?" meaning Ferrantino. The decisive issue was expected in a

¹ André de la Vigne, 204, 205, 206.   ² Nardi, p. 24.
³ Comines, 501.
⁴ Paulus Diaconus, v. 27, vi. 58.
⁵ Burcardus, Diarium Roman., p. 2067.
⁶ Passero, 74.
⁷ Jovii historia sui temporis, 48.
⁸ Galateus, de situ Japygiæ, p. 14.

short time. On the 4th of July the beacons of Capri announced that he was really coming.[1] Lombardy was in great commotion on both sides. The Duke of Orleans, immediately on the outbreak of hostilities, took the field forthwith with his lancers, Gascons, and Swiss, which were sent to the King's assistance.[2] He was invited to go to Milan and Pavia, for the new taxes that Lodovico had imposed had excited the populace. Following the two Opizi, he had been received in Novara, and proclaimed Duke. Immediately on the receipt of this news, Lodovico betook himself to the Venetian envoy, to entreat his good services with the Republic; he pressed a valuable emerald into his hand.[3] He himself collected all his energies to rid himself of the enemy. Venice bestirred itself in real earnest. In spite of its strong army in the field, it issued orders throughout the province that one man of every family should equip himself for active service.[4] The allies at once invested Novara, and intercepted Charles's retreat. It was improbable that he would advance by way of Bologna; yet all the same they prepared to meet him there. He must either take the road from Parma or from Genoa. Early in June, a strong force was in position in the Parmese mountains; and Lodovico wrote to Genoa, "We are ready; get ready also." On receipt of this message, Conradin Stanga made every preparation for resistance.[5] If Charles took the road by the Riviera, Louis of Orleans would be isolated; but, on the other hand, did he take his old road across the mountains, he would be obliged to forego all hopes of conquering Genoa, his fief, that Lodovico had now forfeited. He chose the more difficult of the two; he chose to march across the mountains,[6] whilst Fregoso, Julian, and Philip de Bresse made an attack upon Genoa. On his road he was continually reminded that he had Swiss with him. This soldiery had

---

[1] Passero, 72, 76.
[2] St. Gelais, Extraict d'une histoire in Godefroy, p. 180 (note to new edition). His feelings are shown by a letter of 23rd April, given by Cherrier, Histoire du Charles VIII., vol. ii. p. 491 : "Je pense faire ung tel service au roi, que en long temps en ira parlé."
[3] Corio, 941, and Jovius, 38.
[4] Chronicon Venetum, p. 23.   [5] Chronicon Venetum, p. 23.
[6] Chronicon Venetum, p. 21. Comines.

always caused him much trouble. At the very outset, on the expedition to Naples, their sacking of Rapallo roused almost the whole of Genoa to arms against them. In Siena their bad discipline again made itself felt. In Rome it was within an ace that an open battle took place between them and the Spaniards; and in Naples, on one occasion, the shops had to be closed in consequence of their tumultuous behaviour.[1] And now, on the retreat, they fell upon the city of Pontremoli with pillage and murder, in spite of the assurances of the commanders to the contrary, because they thought that they had something still to avenge from their previous march through.[2] Their exuberance of health and physical strength incited them to take disproportionate vengeance for every little insult. The same exuberance of health and vigour, however, rendered them amenable to every good impression. In the same way as they had formerly offered to forego the pay for which they had undertaken to serve, on condition that Charles would promise to guarantee the liberty of Pisa, so now did they soon repent that they had destroyed supplies that were urgently needed, and represented to the King that if he would forgive them they would harness themselves to [3] the cannon that he was at a loss how to transport across the mountains. A brave knight of the King's retinue, of the name of De la Tremouille, undertook to lead them. He once, while still a boy, and Louis XI. was fighting with the barons, in childish earnestness took the side of the King, and in his early youth rode away from his parents to serve King Charles. He now threw off his upper garments; and when the Swiss, in gangs of one hundred to two hundred men, attached themselves to a cannon, and, pulling all together, dragged it forward a distance, then to be relieved by a fresh relay, he would himself lend a hand, and address them with words of encouragement. He had trumpets and clarions sounded until they were over the summit, and down at the bottom of the steep hill, where men and horses rested. He then appeared, black from the intense heat of the sun, before

[1] Florus, Allegretti, Burcardus, and l'assero.
[2] Comines. Spazzarini, Framenti Storici, in Rosmini, ii. 217.
[3] Comines, 508.

the King, who said, "You have done like Hannibal did; I will so reward you that also others shall gladly serve me."[1]

With difficulty they made their way from the source of the Magra, that flows to the one sea, to hard by the springs of the Taro, that flows to the other. At length the last summit was gained. There they saw before them Lombardy, covered with ripe waving corn and fruit and grapes, dight with smiling villages, and intersected with streams. But in the foreground, not far from the foot of the range, they descried countless tents, and the standards of Venice and Milan—an army of nearly 40,000 men. But unmolested they pursued their way down, and on the 5th July the King took his repast at Fornovo.[2]

He was resolved not to make terms, but to accept battle. On both sides of the Taro the valley of Vergerra broadens out down towards the Po, surrounded by hills. On the right bank, the Lombards had taken up their position. What can have been the reason that they did not occupy both banks, and so directly face the enemy? They mainly wished to protect the Milanese territory and Parma, which was always in a state of sedition, against attack; Lodovico himself was strongly opposed to a battle.[3] They were drawn up in nine divisions and 140 squadrons; for their wont in battle, as in more serious tournaments, was as follows: the greater number remained in camp and looked on, whilst the divisions one after another successively attacked, fought, and relieved each other.[4] Although under arms, they allowed Charles's army to occupy the left bank of the shallow river. Forthwith the 3000 Swiss kissed the earth, placed themselves with Engilbert's Germans and the King's gigantic marksmen in the vanguard, and advanced against the enemy. The rearguard and the "Bataille," with the great standard surrounding the King, consisted of the hommes d'armes.[5] The latter made

---

[1] Jean Bouchet, Histoire de Mons. de la Tremouille, in the Mémoires, xiv. p. 150.   [2] Desry, 225.
[3] Benedictus, Diarium, p. 1589. Balt. Visconti to Lodovico in Rosmini, ii. 218. Carpesanus, Commentarii, 1213.
[4] Excurs in Porzio, Congiura dei Baroni di Napoli.
[5] Comines, 521. Desry, 226.

the sign of the cross on their foreheads and thirsted for the fray. The King sat on his one-eyed black charger, Savoye, a splendid beast. The colours of France and Brittany waved in the plume of his helmet; the crosses of Jerusalem adorned his tabard; to-day his forehead, his eyes, and his whole visage flashed war. He spoke: "What say ye, sirs? Will ye live and die with me? Be not afraid, though they are ten times our numbers. God has led us hither, and he will lead us home."[1] Whilst he was creating new knights, some shots were fired, and three divisions of the enemy, in a storm of rain, dashed across the river; the Milanese against the vanguard. When the Milanese saw the lowered spears of the Germans and Swiss, they hesitated to attack. The Venetians under Gonzaga, mounted upon great horses in full cuirass, even better harnessed than the French, were in splendid array. The Stradiotti, who were destined to fall upon the flank of the royal army,[2] shouted "Marco Victoria."[3] An actual collision took place only between the regular cavalry of the Venetians and that of the French. When the first advanced to the charge, the French sentinels cried, "The enemy is there!" Someone said to the King, "Forward, Sire!" He drew the centre and the rearguard together, faced about, came close to the enemy, and met his first onslaught.[4] The charge was directed against his right wing, and was dangerous so long as lances were being used, for those of the Italians were longer. As soon as swords were resorted to, the left wing of the King's army, the twenty shields under the standard of Aymar de Prie, the noblemen of his house, and some valiant Germans,[5] fell upon Gonzaga's flank, which tapered off to a thin end, and afforded no broad front, as was their habit. When at length the Milanese, who had lost courage, were broken and hurried down the banks with drawn swords, Gonzaga himself turned towards the river.[6] A real melée took

[1] André de la Vigne, p. 209.
[2] Comines, whence Guicciardini. Oricellarius, p. 70.
[3] Navagero, Storia Venet., p. 1206.
[4] Symphorian Champier, Trophæum Gallicum in Godefroy, 306. Graville to Bonchage in Rosmini, 218.
[5] Mémoires of de la Tremouille, p. 153. [6] Benedictus, p. 1597.

place, in which even the French baggage boys surrounded the cuirassiers, four or five round each, and with their mattocks drove holes through their armour. But an Italian squadron charged once again, and penetrated as far as the King.[1] But he warded off the onslaught with his right hand and by the aid of his horse. The royal army was beyond doubt in advantage; yet it was no decisive one. Pitiglian, who escaped from French captivity, and rode back into the Italian camp, kept shouting, "You have conquered," until they halted; and, as the French saw many lances held aloft, they did not venture to follow up their victory.[2] The Taro flowed with blood. Trivulzio had a bottle of water fetched therefrom for his little son, who was thirsty, as though it were red wine.[3] The boy said, "How salty is this wine!" "My son," answered the father, "there is no other in this country."

The French had repulsed an attack that was never very seriously meant. They had not gained any real victory, but they were enabled to continue their march. The battle took place on the 6th July; on the 7th, before daybreak, whilst mass was being sung and the watch-fires were still burning, the King arose, without sound of trumpet or war-cry, and took a way, along which all the fortresses were occupied and shut their gates against him, so that his knights often came with a handful of hay—for they had not more wherewith to feed their horses—and the army marched from early morn until late at night, ofttimes so thirsty, that wherever there was a pond or a pool they jumped in up to their middle.[4] Along the whole line of march

---

[1] According to an account of Gilbert Pointet, the intention of the allies was to take the King prisoner (Pilorgerie, Campagne et bulletins, p. 356) :—" Nous rompre et prendre ledit seigneur aussi fièrement que vindrent lesdits ennemis, aussi fièrement furent-ils recueilliz, tellement que quasi tous furent tuéz." But he distinguishes from this the charge upon the King, who had only three warriors about him :—"Il avait son espée traicté combattant contre les ennemys." (Note to new edition.)

[2] Bembus, p. 44. Jovius, 43. Corio, 949. Nicole Gilles, Chroniques de France, f. 117.

[3] Rebucco in Rosmini, i. 268.

[4] Comines, 537. Vimercatus to Lodovico in Rosmini, ii. 221. Gilles.

they left fresh graves behind them. In the same days two other battles were fought.

On the 6th July, Julian advanced towards the French into the plain of St. Spirito, to attack Genoa. The Spinola and Adorni made a sortie,[1] which was repulsed; but on the 7th the Genoese assaulted Rapallo, which was in the occupation of the French, and made a simultaneous attack upon their ships in the bay—both with good success, so that Julian lost courage, and took the road[2] upon which the King had proceeded. The most important event of all took place at Naples. On the 6th July, Ferrantino appeared with sixty-nine sail in the Gulf of Naples; but he showed himself neither resolute nor quick. But, on the morning of the 7th, as he was sailing past Naples from Torre, as if bound for Puzzuolo, he suddenly heard from within seditious cries, stopped, and approached. He saw the flag of Aragon flying upon the bell-tower of Carmelo; and then heard the loud pealing of bells. Then a bark shot up to him, whence came shouts of "Lord King, the city is yours."[3] A certain Merculian, so Jovius narrates,[4] the previous day crept stealthily in from the fleet and assembled the friends. When they were about to lay hands on him, the tumult burst forth—someone having produced an Aragon flag from under his coat; hereupon general shouting, waving of flags, and ringing of bells. Some ran to Maddalenna, where the King had alighted, fell at his feet, and brought him a horse. He rode to the gates between Alonso Pescara and his private secretary Chariteo,[5] who was making Provençal poems the while. The whole populace came out of their houses. They caught hold of his sword, and did not heed being wounded so long as they could kiss his hand or his coat; and ever and anon they shouted "Fierro" so loudly, that he turned to Chariteo and quoted from Juvenal, "It is iron, that they love."[6] So they came into the city, whence the French were flying

---

[1] Senarega, 553.
[2] Folieta, p. 270. Senarega, 554.
[3] Passero, 75.
[4] Historia sui temporis, f. 49, 50.
[5] Edictum Friderici in Vecchioni to Passero, p. 106.
[6] Passero, 77. Juvenalis, vi. 112.

and were being robbed or slain.¹ Gaetanians were seen with a Frenchman's heart between their teeth. Jean Rabot, who lived in luxury and opulence, scarcely saved the most indispensable clothing of his household.² But the people kissed the King's feet, the ladies wiped the sweat from his brow, and maidens threw garlands in his way; all cried, "Long live our true sovereign." At the same time the Venetians fell upon Monopoli and took it, and Federigo captured the city, court, and castle of Trani, and threw its captain, who defended himself with only eight others, into the hold of his galley. In the whole kingdom the Aragon party was astir and doing.³ After these events, having at last arrived at Asti across the dyke of Tortona, Charles could no longer dream of conquering—he must confine himself to rescuing the Duke of Orleans, who had meantime been shut in Novara, and was in great distress.

By permission of Maximilian, Friedrich Cappeler of Pfirt and Georg von Wolkenstein had brought 10,000 Germans, probably Tyrolese and Suabians, across the Alps;⁴ and these, after having been reviewed by Lodovico and his wife, lay with the Venetians in one camp, living in tents full of abundance (there being before the door of almost each one a spring of water), well paid and contented.⁵ In order to procure suitable troops for the French, wherewith to oppose this force, the Bailiff of Dijon repaired to Switzerland. On the 24th of August he was seen on large ships, with music, drums, and joyous cries, sailing up the lake towards Lucerne from the Cantons, where he had been well received.⁶ In Lucerne he feasted daily with his friends, was lavish with his money, and was regarded as a prince. The latest decrees prohibiting foreign expeditions were not heeded. Where the magistracy insisted on their observance, the young men climbed over the walls. Where it was permitted, the flags floated on the gates and were put up on the conduits. Even old men, who had seen the

---

[1] Villeneufve, Mémoires, p. 13.
[2] Lettre in Godefroy, p. 717.   [3] Villeneufve, p. 873.
[4] Acta of Worms in Datt, 873.
[5] Benedictus, Diarium.
[6] Ludwig von Diesbach's letter to Lucerne in Glutzblotzheim, Schweizer Geschichte, p. 516.

Duke Charles at Nancy, went also. And so they marched, troop by troop, from Martinach, across the mountains, and down to Ivrea. On the 7th of September, the first detachment, all grand, martial fellows, appeared before the King in Moncagliere.[1] And none too early; for Duke Louis in Novara, who, although suffering from intermittent fever, was yet obliged to visit the guard every day, and his brave companions-in-arms, ill from bread made of hand-ground coarse meal from unripe corn,[2] signalled their great distress by three times lowering and raising their torches each night on the highest towers. Even this flour was exhausted, and in the streets there were dead and dying to be seen.[3] Charles now despatched some Swiss to Provence, to cross thence to Naples; but the greater part of them he kept in his camp at Vercelli. Their numbers increased daily, and made the enemy fear for the result of a battle, and therefore more inclined to make terms.[4] An arrangement between Charles VIII. and Lodovico had been already mooted. The first opportunity for the opening of overtures was made by the death of the Marquise of Montferrat, when Charles, on the occasion of settling her inheritance, sent a message to Gonzaga, expressing his sympathy. This led to the envoys of both parties incidentally talking of peace. At first, heralds went over, and concluded a truce, by virtue of which the Duke of Orleans was permitted to leave Novara, and received food for his troops. Hereupon negotiations were opened as to the peace itself. There sat in Lodovico's chamber, himself, his wife, and the envoys of the League, on one side of the table, and on the other the French; at the end were two secretaries for the two parties and the two languages, and the negotiations were carried on between them. Frequently, when one, two, or three Frenchmen all began talking at once, Lodovico interrupted them with "Ho, ho! one at a time;" and thereupon himself carried on the conversation. He brought it about, that at the expiration of fourteen days, on the 9th of October, all parties

---

[1] Tschudi Supplementum MS. In Fuchs, Mayländische Feldzüge, i. p. 212. Stettler, Schweizer Chronik, 325.
[2] Benedicti Diarium, 1603. Notizie di Novara in Rosmini, 222.
[3] Benedictus, 1619.
[4] André de la Vigne, 226.

were agreed.¹ He promised to support the French from Genoa, as it was a fief of Charles, against Naples, as soon as his country belonged entirely to him again. Upon these conditions peace was concluded. Early on the morning of the 10th, the Venetians burnt their camp, and marched away.² How could it, as Bembo says was the case, have been so disagreeable to them, when the danger that they had dreaded was removed, and the expense that they so unwillingly bore was at an end ? The treaty moreover was concluded under their very eyes. The Duke of Orleans, a part of the French nobility—the numbers of his adherents are reckoned at about 800 lances—and the Swiss, who had joined the expedition in order to enrich themselves, submitted but unwillingly to the arrangement. But Charles VIII. kept saying, "I have sworn to it, and I will keep it." His intention was to pacify Upper Italy, in order to save Naples for himself.³ He now came to Lyons, paid his vow in St. Denis, and found France just as he had left it; yet the movement that he had begun in Italy was still stirring.⁴ Scarcely ever has a military expedition been undertaken, that, after such a brilliant beginning, resulted in fewer immediate consequences, and which was yet indirectly of the greatest influence upon the world. Charles's expedition may be regarded as the last enterprise undertaken in the chivalrous spirit of the Crusades. This spirit now disappeared. But from this expedition sprang that great rivalry between the Spanish and French monarchies that from this time forth filled the world, whilst Italy was at the same time broken up.

The ideal unity of the peninsula we have traced above has never been re-established. Italy became the battlefield of neighbouring nations, and the sovereignty over it the prize for which they continuously strove. Also in the Germans the Roman expeditions, which appeared to have been almost forgotten, revived.

[1] Comines, 553-557.
[2] André de la Vigne, 227.   Benedictus, 1622-1624.
[3] Comines, 553-557.   [4] Desrey, 227-228.

4. *War in Naples*, 1495-1496.

In Naples the war still continued. Its object was the possession of the city. This was gained by the favour of the populace, who drove the enemy into his castles, and who, each placing as much as he could give into a collection box, paid 500 men for their King, and who even marched against the Swiss at Sarno, and repulsed them. It succeeded further, because the enemy in his castles despaired of all help. After the peace of Novara, two Genoese ships arrived, and the French hoped that Lodovico had sent them to their assistance.[1] But Lodovico had never intended any such thing. When the Venetians called out to the Genoese sailors, "Qui vive?" the latter replied, "St. George and Fierro! Fierro!" Hereupon in the city, trumpets, flying flags, and congratulations on the part of the Sopracomiti; in the castles, sheer despair.[2] The castles surrendered. Capua, Nola, and the greater part of the west coast, followed their example; and following the Colonna, who had gone over, Aquila and a part of the Abruzzi did the same.

Gonzal had also advanced from Reggio. The whole southern tableland of Calabria, and Sila, which was conquered by the ambushes, stratagems, and surprises his soldiers had learnt in the Alpujarras, in a northerly direction as far as the foot of the mountain range, where a steep road, in winter quite impracticable, hewn in the solid rock, leads from Rotigliano to the Cosentian villages—all this, together with the places lying on both sides, he had taken either by force or faction. Here he stopped.[3] It was now December. In spite of their sudden change of feeling, it is not quite correct to complain of the inconstancy of this people. Whenever a party which has received its affections with its birth, and which has seen itself the victim of sudden oppression, becomes roused at the first opportunity, this must be called obstinacy rather

---

[1] Passero, 78-90.   [2] Villeneufve, 43-45.
[3] Zurita, f. 72, compared with Séjours d'un officier en Calabre, 1821. Geographically better than Bartels.

than inconstancy. We will suppose two almost equal parties, united not only by disposition, but also by property; for the one has often lost its goods to the other, or wrested them from it in return. In their case, a successful campaign and battle won, or favourable tidings, may help up the one, whilst a chance accident, and the crime of an individual, may oppress and dishearten the other; so that, in order not to subject itself, but to await another opportunity, it hastes to secure itself on this occasion as far as possible by making terms. No one will accuse the English of natural cowardice, but in those days they acted in the same manner, and for the same identical reasons. Where relationships are sundered by disunion, by an enmity which only aims at the recognition of a privilege, or a superiority of the one and not the complete destruction of the other, in proportion as hatred is weakened, is martial ardour diminished. Often, when they had already taken the field in order to fight, the Aragons thought of the losses of their Anjou relatives, would not engage and were considered cowardly.[1] Under such circumstances, the war could not be brought to a close in a moment.

From the west he turned eastwards across the hills. Here there stretches away the well-watered plain of Apulia, arid notwithstanding, on which, at all events in those days, not a single tree grew, and where fennel stalks served as fuel. Upon this plain there was no village, but at harvest time the respective owners of the soil came from their towns and castles with waggons and oxen, remained all night in the open, and only returned when they had finished their work. At times, there grazed upon the royal meads of Tavoliera, sixty miles in extent, a strange herd of cattle.[2] For towards the winter there came down from the Abruzzian mountains, passing by Serra Capreola, several hundred thousand sheep, goats, and beeves, who remained there until the early spring, when they returned to the fresh herbage of their hills. In those days they were the King's best source of revenue in Foggia, as they once were of the Roman Republic, bringing in 100,000 ducats. In order to collect this revenue, there hurried

---

[1] Zurita, f. 86, 96.   [2] Leander Alberti, Descriptio Italiæ.

across it in February, 1496—Ferrantino to Foggia and Montpensier to St. Severo. In the little guerilla warfare which they began there a marvellous deed is recorded. About 700 Germans under Ferrantino, who had taken the road from Troja to Foggia, were suddenly surrounded and attacked by several thousand French. At once forming a ring, they beat off the enemy with their muskets; and then, for they wished to proceed on their way, they opened their ranks, and 200 of them dashed ahead to clear the road. But their captain, Hederlin, had fallen; they bound his corpse on a horse, took it in their midst, and pushed forward. They would then have remained unharmed, had they not had to cross a river. In so doing they divided their forces, which made it easy for the enemy to attack them. Over the whole field of Marsaria, and along the road, lay corpses, just as life and blood had left them. They all died. Italians and Spaniards have sung their praises once or twice since then; but never a German.[1] This deed is remarkable not for its success, but for the prowess displayed. Yet Ferrantino immediately after had the advantage again. He had pledged five places in Apulia, the best situated in the country, to the Signorie of Venice for their war expenses, and pledging was almost tantamount to selling. The Stradiotti, who in return for this transaction joined him, even took the cattle away from the French, which were being driven for them to St. Severo.[2] Here, there, and everywhere, always attacking and never awaiting the enemy's attack, they made the King master of the plain, so that both Lodovico in the west and Venice in the east aided Ferrantino to victory; yet the Republic afforded by far the greatest assistance. In the south, Gonzal, as early as February, had mounted up to the Cosentian villages on the hills, had subjected Cosenza, except its castle, and all the fortresses of the Crato valley, whether they would or no, as well as the whole mountain chain as far as the second passes, where it slopes down from Castrovillare to Campo Temesse, and had instituted everywhere Aragon judges.[3]

[1] Jovius, 71. Passero, p. 97. Zurita, 73.
[2] Bembus, 57. Also Guicciardini, ii. 149.
[3] Zurita, 84, 96.

The Colonna had possession of the Abruzzi in the north, the western and eastern slope of the hills were Aragon;[1] and so the French were obliged to pass through their midst into the province of Molise, although they were disunited, without money, and ignorant of hill-warfare. Ferrantino immediately went in search of them there. At Morcone they both again faced each other; at Frangete only a ditch parted them. A collision appeared to be inevitable. In Naples, processions were held for two days, because the King would have to fight at Benevento. In Calabria, too, he was not quite safe. In Laino were gathered the barons that had fled before Gonzal, and who now cherished the plan of joining Aubigny, who was still at Tropea, in order with united forces to relieve Cosenza. Before they could make up their minds,[2] Gonzal sallied forth at night, seized the passes, occupied the bridge between the city and castle of Laino, possessed himself of both, and took fourteen barons and many knights prisoners.[3] Whilst he was coming up from the south, Ferrantino drove the enemy before him from the north, by way of Ariano and Jesualdo, from place to place, until he caught him up in Atella.[4] Here he occupied the hills, covered with woods and vineyards, which surround the valley on three sides. He only left the road from Venosa open. This road Gonzal blocked.[5] When now the French made an attempt to break through, Ferrantino was the first to break his lance upon them; and when his knights said to him, "Sir, how dare you expose yourself so much?" he replied, "It is my affair also." In this way he fired the zeal of his troops, and soon drove the enemy back.[6] The latter hoped against hope in their King, but he was too far away, and they were perishing from hunger. They accordingly begged for a thirty days' truce; if at the expiration of it they were then unable to take the field, they pledged themselves to leave the kingdom and surrender their strongholds. The days passed; succour did not arrive, and at length they were all

---

[1] Tarfia, Historiæ Cupersanenses, in Grævius. Ital. Thes., ix. p. 48.
[2] Passero, 100.
[3] Jovius, Vita Consalvi Magni, p. 220.
[4] Baldi Gundubaldo, p. 156.   [5] Zurita, 91-95.
[6] Passero, 101. Unrest, Oesterreichische Chronik, p. 798.

—for Aubigny had also surrendered—conducted to the coast. Here, heat, hunger, and dire diseases left only 1,500 men out of 6,000, and these took ship in such an exhausted condition that they had almost to be lifted on shore, if they were ever to breathe the air of the land again.[1] Others came into captivity, sat behind wooden and iron gratings in dark cells, where they saw no living creature, except perhaps the Moor who brought them their food.[2] At last they were set free. These fugitives might be seen, with the iron chains of their captivity still about their necks, betaking themselves to holy places and to the court of the King. They were contented to see his face once more; they took his presents, and wished him long life.[3]

After this great victory over the French, on the 5th October, 1496, Ferrantino returned with his young wife to Naples.[4] The people, whom he had allowed to choose a fuller as their Eletto, who was permitted to carry the Mappa[5] on Corpus Christi day, which had been a privilege of the nobles—and who, if he lived, might hope for many other favours at his hand—loved him from the bottom of their hearts. Many of them imitated him, how he raised and bowed his head,[6] and they believed they had a hero in him. And now he came back to them; but he was sick to death. The people spent the whole night before the saints on their knees. Early in the morning, they carried a wonder-working image of Mary through the streets, and brought it to him; in the evening there followed in grand procession, clerics and laymen, men and women, and even the nobles, behind the head and blood of St. Januarius, which their Archbishop carried before them through the streets, until they were come to the gate of the palace. Here the old Queen knelt down, and the people cried, "Misericordia." He spoke to them, and said, "Finish your prayers; God will do as seemeth him best," and then died. "O our master," they said, "wherefore hast

---

[1] Schodeler in Fuchs, iii. Anshelm.
[2] Villeneufve, Mém., p. 74.
[3] Villeneufve, Mém., p. 87.
[4] Passero, 105, 107. (Note to new edition.) Giacomo, 205.
[5] Passero, 101, 102. Giacomo, 209.
[6] Cortegiano, from Castiglione, vol. i.

thou left us so soon? Thy prowess, thy prowess in battle, equalled by no hero of old, where is it now? By thy death it is gone." Another said, "How shall I now live, O my master, I that have borne so many hardships to earn thy favour?" Some reminded that he had often been in danger of poison; but he had escaped such a death, and now he had passed away gently at the goal of his victories.[1] Federigo, his uncle, succeeded to the throne in his stead.

And now it almost appeared as though Charles's expedition, which certainly never vanquished the Turks or took Jerusalem, was not even productive of any lasting effects upon Italy—Lodovico and Federigo were even reconciled. Yet it was not so in reality. The Florentine Popolares, the Orsini, who now opposed the Pope instead of the Colonna, as well as the unconquered cities in the kingdom, Tarentum, Bitonto, Sora, Roca Guilielma, formed a strong party, and every day Charles, their suzerain, thought of returning to them again. These were confronted by the Liga. The Italian members of it would have been quite contented with a victory over their enemies in Italy. The foreign members desired more. Ferdinand was thinking of his claims to Naples, and made inquiries of the Pope in respect thereof.[2] Maximilian hoped, with the assistance of this Liga, to strike a blow at France itself.

[1] Passero, 107-110.
[2] Zurita, i. 101-103, whence Mariana, 26, 14.

CHAPTER III.

1. *Maximilian of Austria and the Empire.*

IN reality Maximilian wished first of all to aid the Liga to conquer in Italy, and then to place himself at its head, and attack France.

He was lord of Austria and the Netherlands. It might have been about 600 years previously that, between the Alps and the Bohemian frontier, the mark Austria was first founded round and about the castles of Krems and Melk.[1] Since then, beginning first in the valley towards Bavaria and Hungary, and coming to the House of Habsburg, it had extended across the whole of the northern slope of the Alps until where the Slavish, Italian, and German tongues part, and over to Alsace; thus becoming an archduchy from a mark. On all sides the Archdukes had claims; on the German side to Switzerland, on the Italian to the Venetian possessions, and on the Slavish to Bohemia and Hungary.

To such a pitch of greatness had Maximilian by his marriage with Maria of Burgundy brought the heritage received from Charles the Bold. True to the Netherlander's greeting, in the inscription over their gates, "Thou art our Duke, fight our battle for us," war was from the first his handicraft. He adopted Charles the Bold's hostile attitude towards France; he saved the greatest part of his inheritance from the schemes of Louis XI. Day and night it was his whole thought, to conquer it entirely.

But after Maria of Burgundy's premature death, revolution followed revolution, and his father Frederick being too old to protect himself, it came about that in the year 1488 he was ousted from Austria by the Hungarians,

---

[1] Kurz, Beiträge zur Geschichte von Oesterreich, iii. 226 (note to new edition). Cf. Büdinger, Oesterreich. Geschichte, i. p. 167.

whilst his son was kept a prisoner in Bruges by the citizens, and they had even to fear the estrangement of the Tyrol. Yet they did not lose courage. At this very time the father denoted with the vowels A. E. I. O. U. ("Alles Erdreich ist Oesterreich unterthan"—all the earth is subject to Austria), the extent of his hopes. In the same year, the son negotiated for a Spanish alliance. Their real strength lay in the imperial dignity of Frederick, and in the royal dignity of Maximilian, which they had from the German Empire. As soon as it began to bestir itself, Maximilian was set at liberty; as soon as it supported him in the persons of only a few princes of the Empire, he became lord in his Netherlands. The standard of the Kennemer, with its device of bread and cheese, floated before Leyden for the last time, and the last Hök, Philip of Ravenstein, surrendered Sluys to him.[1] It was the same help that secured him the Tyrol, and which enabled him to reconquer Austria.[2]

Since then, his plans were directed against Hungary and Burgundy. In Hungary, he could gain nothing except securing the succession to his house.[3] But never, frequently as he concluded peace, did he give up his intentions upon Burgundy. He might have hoped to compass them if Anna of Brittany had only been his wife. On the day that he learned that she was not to become so, he threw himself in a fit of bitter disappointment into the saddle, and appeared again and again on the race ground.[4] But on this occasion the German Empire took no account of his indignation. But now that he had allied himself with a Sforza, and had joined the Liga, now that his father was dead, and the Empire was pledged to follow him across the mountains, and now, too, that the Italian complications were threatening Charles, he took fresh hope, and in this hope he summoned a Diet at Worms.

Maximilian was a prince of whom, although many por-

[1] Pontus Heuterus, Rerum Austriac. Hermanni bellum Gelricum, 530.
[2] Speech of Berthold of Mayence of the year 1492 in Müller's Reichstagstheatrum.
[3] Document in Sambucus, Appendix ad Bonfinium.
[4] Ehrenspiegel, p. 1368.

traits have been drawn, yet there is scarcely one that resembles another, so easily and so entirely did he suit himself to circumstances, so little was he controlled by one occupation or one inclination,—a prince of whose character his contemporaries have left behind them detailed descriptions, yet not a single satisfactory history. His soul is full of motion, of joy in things, and of plans. There is scarcely anything that he is not capable of doing. In his mines he is a good screener, in his armoury the best plater, capable of instructing others in new inventions. With musket in hand, he defeats his best marksman, George Purkhard; with heavy cannon, which he has shown how to cast, and has placed on wheels, he comes as a rule nearest the mark.[1] He commands seven captains in their seven several tongues; he himself chooses and mixes his food and medicines.[2] In the open country, he feels himself happiest. He rides by copses listening for the nightingale,—it may be to the forests of Brabant, to hunt the boar,—to the Tyrol mountains, where he has forbidden the hunting of the chamois because firearms have left so few remaining.[3] Here he leaves his horse behind, and in pursuit of them climbs the steep rocks where, if he makes a false step, he may fall four hundred to five hundred fathoms, and where sometimes, when the climbing iron has given way, a bush or projecting stone alone has saved him from destruction, and where, on one occasion, in the Hallthal, he heard the avalanche thunder at his back.[4] The common people tell stories of how he was once let down by strong ropes from the heights into the valley beneath, and on another occasion, when this was impracticable, and a crucifix was already raised towards him from the valley as though to receive his dying prayer, an angel rescued him from the Martinswand.[5] On his return from such an expedition, his fowler brings him all manner of singing

[1] Weiskunig, 83, 90, 99.
[2] Grünbeck, Historia Friedrichs und Maximilians, p. 84. Cuspinianus, Maximiliani in Vitæ Imperatorum, p. 613.
[3] Weiskunig, 91.
[4] Grünbeck, Ehrenspiegel, 1381.
[5] Pontus Heuterus, 343, and the legends.

birds into his chamber, who drown his very voice in their melody. Or, again, he goes to one of his servants' weddings, or listens confidentially to the prayers of his subjects, or it may be relates a story to his counsellors and secretaries. Sometimes he dictates a piece from his enigmatical and almost unfathomable works,[1] a note for his diary, as, for instance, how priest Lasla is to compile the Chronicles,[2] or one of his very exact instructions as, for instance, how it were possible with a makeshift musket to shoot across into the kitchen[3] at Beutelstein, or perhaps a letter. Such is his character. But this has little to do with history. What really distinguishes his public life is that presentiment of the future greatness of his dynasty which he has inherited of his father, and the restless striving to attain all that devolved upon him from the House of Burgundy. All his policy and all his schemes were concentrated, not upon his Empire, for the real needs of which he evinced little real care, and not immediately upon the welfare of his hereditary lands, but upon the realization of that sole idea. Of it all his letters and speeches are full. Yet each individual plan he keeps extremely secret. There are projects that he communicates to none of his counsellors.[4] At such times he places the foreign embassies in positions where they learn nothing, and from which they cannot escape. Then he sends his cook only an hour in advance of himself, when he intends to take a journey.[5] Whenever he fancies his plans are discerned, the veins in his neck swell, and he becomes wroth.[6] It will sometimes happen that the matter upon which he is bent, after he has undertaken it, presents difficulties for which he is not prepared,[7] but, as he has always other schemes, which lead to the same end, he soon forgets his failures. Thus, in such matters, he behaves like a huntsman, who is bent upon climbing a very steep

---

[1] Grünbeck, 90. Henric. Pantaleon, de Viris illustribus, p. 1. Roo, Annales rerum ab Austriacis principibus gestarum, 316.
[2] A passage therefrom in Hormayr's Oesterr. Plutarch, v. 159.
[3] Instruction in Göblers Chronika der Kriegshandel, f. 1.
[4] Macchiavelli, Principe, c. 23, p. 60, out of the mouth of Pre Luca.
[5] Macchiavelli, Legazione alla corte di Massimiliano, p. 193.
[6] Hubertus Thomas Leodius, Vita Friderici Palatini, lib. iii. No. 7.
[7] Histoire de Bayard, 179.

hill, first by this path and then by that, and if he fails, attempts another and yet another way without losing patience; for it is now quite early in the day, and he gradually mounts higher and higher, his sole care being to hide himself from the wild animal he pursues.

In March, 1495, Maximilian came to the Diet at Worms. He showed himself in his full chivalrous bearing, when he himself entered the lists with a Frenchman, who had come to challenge all the Germans, and conquered him. He appeared in the full glory of his regal dignity, when he sat in public between the archbishops and his chancellors. On such occasions, the Count Palatine sat on his right and held his orb, on his left stood the Duke of Saxony and held his sword; before him, facing him, stood the envoy of Brandenburg with the sceptre, and behind him, instead of Bohemia, the hereditary cupbearer of Limburg, with the crown; and grouped round him were the rest of the forty princes, sixty-seven counts and lords, as many as had come, and the ambassadors of the cities, and others, all in their order.[1] Then a prince would come before him, lower his colours before the royal throne, and receive enfeoffment. One could not perceive that this mode of enfeoffment involved any compulsion upon the King, or that the insignia of royal power resided in the hands of the princes.

At this Reichstag the King gained two momentous prospects. In Wurtemberg there had sprung of two lines two counts of quite opposite characters. The elder was kind-hearted, tender, always resolute, and dared "sleep in the lap of any one of his subjects."[2] The younger, volatile, unsteady, violent, and always repentant of what he had done.[3] Both were named Eberhard, but the elder, by special favour of the Imperial Court, also governed the land of the younger. In return for this, he furnished 400 horse for the Hungarian war, and despatched aid against Flanders. With the elder, Maximilian now entered

[1] Bernh. Herzog, Elsasser Chronik, ii. f. 150, in Datt, de pace publica, 613. Linturius, Appendix ad Rotewinkii Fascicul. tempor. in Pistorius, Scriptt. Germ. ii. 594.
[2] Pfister, Eberhard in Bart, p. 60.
[3] Ulrich's lamentations in Sattler, iv., and in Spittler's Geschichte von Württemberg, 46.

H

into a compact. Wurtemberg was to be raised to a dukedom—an elevation which excluded the female line from the succession—and, in the event of the stock failing, was to be a "widow's portion" of the realm to the use of the Imperial Chamber.[1] Now, as the sole hopes of this family centred in a weakling of a boy, this arrangement held out to Maximilian and his successors the prospect of acquiring a splendid country. Yet this was the smaller of his two successes. The greater was the espousal of his children, Philip and Margaret, with the two children of Ferdinand the Catholic, Juana and Juan, which was here settled.[2] This opened to his house still greater expectations,—it brought him at once into the most intimate alliance with the Kings of Spain.

These matters might possibly, however, have been arranged elsewhere. What Maximilian really wanted in the Reichstag at Worms was the assistance of the Empire against the French, with its world-renowned and much-envied soldiery.

For at that time in all the wars of Europe, German auxiliaries were decisive. The troops upon which Wasiljewitsch depended when he led his Muscovites against the Poles,[3] and those who subjected Sweden to the Union,[4] were German, as were also those which died in England for the cause of the Yorks on the place[5] where they had awaited the battle. Those who made the possession of Brittany by the crown of France uncertain, as well as those who conquered it, were also Germans;[6] the defenders as well as the conquerors of Naples; the subduers of Hungary, as long as it suited them, as also those who saved it in going home with their booty,[7] all were Germans. But these were the quarrelsome, wandering portion of the nation, those hirelings against whom the peace proclamations were directed. In Germany there still lived peasants, like the Ditmarses, who awaited a victorious

[1] Pfister, 271, 297.
[2] Zurita, f. 79. Petrus Martyr, Epp. 96.
[3] Letter in Raynaldus, Annal. Eccles. xx. 141.
[4] Kranz, Vandalia, xiv. 27.
[5] Polydorus Virgilius, Historia Anglica, 26, 729.
[6] Müller, Schweizer Geschichte, v. 318.
[7] Maximilian's proclamation in Datt, 496.

army, under a king of three realms, behind their walls, and defeated it, and who hanged the Danebrog in a village church. In the cities there dwelt behind their impregnable walls and their cannon, citizens versed in the use of arms, who practised their good arts and games until irritated by an enemy, when they met him, as the Strasburgers did Charles the Bold before Nancy.[1] Less secure were perhaps princes and lords, yet these had castles to protect them against the first attack, and feudal tenants and faithful subjects ever about them. If Maximilian had united the whole of this power in his hand, neither Europe nor Asia would have been able to withstand him. But God disposed that it should rather be employed in the cause of freedom than for oppression. What an Empire was that which in spite of its vast strength allowed its Emperor to be expelled from his heritage, and did not for a long time take steps to bring him back again?

If we examine the constitution of the Empire, not as we should picture it to ourselves in Henry III.'s time, but as it had at length become—the legal independence of the several estates, the emptiness of the imperial dignity, the electiveness of a head, that afterwards exercised certain rights over the electors,—we are led to inquire not so much into the causes of its disintegration, for this concerns us little, as into the way in which it was held together.

What welded it together, and preserved it, would (leaving tradition and the Pope out of the question) appear, before all else, to have been the rights of individuals, the unions of neighbours, and the social regulations which universally obtained. Such were those rights and privileges that not only protected the citizen, his guild, and his quarter of the town against his neighbours and more powerful men than himself, but which also endowed him with an inner independence; those rights and privileges that secured his rightful possessions to the greatest, and his existence to the least; a legacy left by each generation to the succeeding, unalterable either by emperor or empire who had confirmed them, but which were without them

---

[1] Königshofer, Strassburger Chronik, 379.

a mere nothing. Next, the unions of neighbours. These were not only leagues of cities and peasantries, expanded from ancient fraternities—for who can tell the origin of the Hansa, or the earliest treaty between Uri and Schwyz?—into large associations, or of knights, who strengthened a really insignificant power by confederations of neighbours, but also of the princes, who were bound together by joint inheritances, mutual expectancies, and the ties of blood, which in some cases were very close. This ramification, dependent upon a supreme power and confirmed by it, bound neighbour to neighbour; and, whilst securing to each his privilege and his liberty, blended together all countries of Germany in legal bonds of union. But it is only in the social regulations that the unity was really perceivable. Only as long as the Empire was an actual reality, could the supreme power of the Electors, each with his own special rights, be maintained; only so long could dukes and princes, bishops and abbots hold their neighbours in due respect, and through court offices or hereditary services, through fiefs and the dignity of their independent position, give their vassals a peculiar position to the whole. Only so long could the cities enjoying immediateness under the Empire, carefully divided into free and imperial cities, be not merely protected, but also assured of a participation in the government of the whole. Under this sanctified and traditional system of suzerainty and vassalage all were happy and contented, and bore a love to it such as is cherished towards a native town or a father's house.

For some time past, the House of Austria had enjoyed the foremost position. It also had a union, and, moreover, a great faction on its side. The union was the Suabian League. Old Suabia was divided into three leagues—the league of the peasantry (the origin of Switzerland); the league of the knights in the Black Forest, on the Kocher, the Neckar, and the Danube; and the league of the cities.

The peasantry were from the first hostile to Austria. The Emperor Frederick brought it to pass that the cities and knights, that had from time out of mind lived in feud, bound themselves together with several princes, and formed, under his protection, the league of the land of Suabia. But the party was scattered throughout the whole Empire.

In almost every German house was a division into an elder and a younger line; and, as though fated, it happened that one, generally the younger, clave to the Emperor. Of the Bavarian House, it was at last that of Munich; of the Palatinate, that of Veldenz; of the Wurtemberg House, the Urach line; of the Saxon, the Dresden; of the Hessian, the Marburg; and of the Guelph, the Brunswick. Most friendly to the Imperial House were the Houses of Brandenburg and Baden, which were for a long time undivided; the most hostile to him, since Frederick the Victorious, the Palatinate. He who takes in hand all historical documents, especially the electoral rolls of the ecclesiastical princes, and narrowly scrutinizes these dry historical details, will be able to discover, from Frederick II.'s time, a new history, unlike Häberlin's, founded upon persons and living actions.

But it is not that upon which the Emperor's hallowed position in the nation reposed. This was based before all else upon his dignity, the sublimest in Christendom, the keystone of that social order, and upon the custody of traditional rights—a custody, so to speak, of times past for times to come, which lay in his hand, and which was bound up with the distribution of new rights through the medium of privileges and fiefs. His position was based, moreover, upon the universal judicial office he filled, as well as upon the great influence he exercised upon public matters by his motions, proposals, and party in the "Reichstag." "His name is great," says a papal deputy; "in a land of factions he can do much. Everyone looks to him; and without him nothing can be done."[1] In this respect there were, however, great deficiencies. Freedoms were often bestowed out of mere personal considerations, and to the prejudice of others; judicial business was frequently kept in arrear, if the parties did not come to court with sufficient money; domestic matters were often made affairs of general policy, and real needs neglected. The princes complained that the Em-

[1] Campanus ad Cardinalem Papiensem in Freherus, ii. 148.

-peror did not consult them, but his counsellors. Much arbitrariness, the taking as much as one can get, on the one side, and uncomplaisancy and unwillingness, doing as little as need be, on the other, were observable in his régime.

Maximilian had first intended to remain fourteen days at Worms; and, before Charles had returned from Naples, with the help of the vassals of the realm, to undertake an expedition against him. Yet his proposal did not express this intention. It was as follows: "Whereas the Turk twice each year assailed Christendom; and whereas the King of France threatened to bring the prerogatives of the Empire and the Church into his power, a speedy and, more than this—for they had equipped themselves for a long campaign,—a continuous aid for ten to twelve years was needed." [1]

But here lay the chief difficulty, to induce a constitution only framed for peace, or at most fitted to carry on a short war, to undertake a protracted campaign at a distance. To this end either the dormant military power of the vassals, princes, knights, citizens, and peasants could be utilized, or else the lansquenets, who were always ready to serve for pay. But the feudal system had fallen into decay, owing no less to the Emperor, who left the individual unaided, than to the individuals who did not, on their part, support him. It still lived on only in respect of "Mine and Thine," and not with any view to war; it existed more in claims and in parchments than in actual fact. It was impossible to unite the first in military obedience for any length of time, so as to undertake a real campaign. Maximilian's intention, therefore, was to raise money through his claims upon them, and with this money to form an army of lansquenets. This was the tenour of his proposal.

This proposal was received by the estates at Worms in full assembly at the city hall. Hereupon they withdrew—the Electors into one chamber, the princes into a second, and the emissaries of the cities into a third, and began to examine article after article. The printed

[1] Reichstags acta von Worms, 13.

records do not quite disclose the relations of the princes to the electors; but of the cities thus much we know, that their commission was, to agree to what the gracious lords resolved, and only to protect the interests of each individual city. They would not, even when asked, make known their opinion until the princes had declared theirs. They often learnt from the Elector of Mayence what had been proposed to them, and what they had determined upon. In case they had any scruples they sent, perchance after their meal, to him direct. The King when confronted by the full assembly appeared at a great disadvantage. In case he desired a rapid decision, he was even obliged to go out whilst they were deliberating, and await outside the result.

These estates, then, that have in their hereditary independence as little in common with the representative estates of a military monarchy, as the Empire of those days with a political state, answered the King, that, before all else, order in the Empire must be secured. When, in 1486, Frederick pressed them for assistance against the Hungarians, they cast in his teeth complaints as to his judicial conduct; and when, in 1492, he proposed a French campaign, they replied, following the example of Berthold von Mainz : "It was an evil innovation, the reckoning of assistance in money. Many were excused the contribution; many paid only half; many, again, too late; those that paid it were ruined; and, finally, it was spent for different objects than it had been granted for." All the same, they did not declare themselves against pecuniary assistance, but they wished to counteract those two evils by the aid of the tribunals, and by assisting in the appropriation of the moneys voted.

At the present moment, both parties, they and the King, pursued their own ends. On three occasions, Maximilian was particularly pressing. The first occasion was in April, when the preparations of the Duke of Orleans threatened Milan, and Charles's retreat menaced the Pope and Genoa, and he could still hope to find him in the field, far away from his country. But the princes took upon themselves to propose to him a Council of State, with him as president, but which should contain sixteen members, composed of the Electors, the four archbishoprics, the four countries and the cities, and which should, in reality, exercise all internal power. In this first dispute Maximilian gained the day. Berthold von Mainz said, "They did not wish to mortgage the King's person for this assistance they voted him; they would acquiesce in his wishes and trust him." Acting upon this sentiment, they promised him that, although he rejected their Council of State, they would, within six weeks, raise 100,000 guilders from the estates; 50,000 he should raise himself, and both sums should be covered by a general tax levied on the country; only he should not leave the land before peace, right, and a tolerable state of order was established. This was the first time.[1]

The peace was not established, the money was not paid, and the six weeks had long passed by.

On the second occasion, when Charles was in the Florentine country, and messengers announced that Milan was in danger, he declared as follows: "For two days, from eight o'clock in the morning until eight at night, he had busied himself with the peace project; in two days he hoped to have settled it; in the meanwhile they should be good enough to vote him the money." Many were opposed to this, especially the cities. But he prevailed upon some princes to grant him the money; and Berthold induced the representatives of the cities to write, at all events, to their respective homes. He was successful on this occasion also. It was in July.[2]

After this, at the beginning of August, when Novara was being besieged, and a victory of the Swiss was apprehended, in case the lansquenets, who had been sent thither, were not regularly paid, he made fresh demands. But on this occasion he could prevail upon nobody. On the afternoon of the 4th of August he adopted the plans provisionally, and on the 7th definitively, and received on the 9th a fresh vote of 150,000 guilders.[3]

What can it then have been that the King was unwilling

---

[1] Acta, § 25. Müller's Reichstagsstaat, p. 11. Besserer's letter to Esslinger in Datt, de pace publica, 521.

[2] Acta § 47, § 55, § 56.

[3] Acta §§ 69-74, in Datt, de pace publica, pp. 873-883. Cf. Ullmann, Kaiser Maximilian, i. p. 374.

to face? Certainly not the public peace, that had been so often proclaimed, but the Supreme Court of Judicature, a Court constituted with the advice and consent of the Diet, and which, moreover, as was plainly evidenced by later references to the events of this day, was composed in the way in which it was intended to compose the Council of State, so that hereby a great part of his absolute judicial power was taken from him. Yet in the matter nearest his heart still greater difficulties presented themselves. It was resolved to raise an universal "*pfennig*" *tax*—no small contribution, as it would amount to the thousandth part of the property of the public, and in many districts, taxes and assessments were at this time unknown.[1] The object would have been to bring every individual in all Germany immediately under the central imperial government, and always to keep a good sum in reserve for public matters.

This "pfennig" was for the King, but it was not proposed to leave it to his absolute control. Seven imperial treasurers should be told off to raise it, and an annual diet appointed to keep watch over its application. On the evening before the "Feast of the Purification" in each year, King, princes, and all estates should assemble, and remain a whole month together to deal with the public peace and law. This assembly could not do aught but diminish the King's independence and his whole prestige. What availed him the money, when another could determine how it should be employed? But on this occasion it could not be avoided. With but few knights, without any reception, Maximilian arrived in Frankfort. On the great Braunfels there, he delivered the simple red judge's staff with its black handle to the first justiciary, Eitel Frederick von Zollern, and then, in disgust that his chief object had been defeated, betook himself to the Tyrol. Charles was home again; in Milan peace prevailed, and all his plans had been bridled.[2]

---

[1] Kanzow, Pomerania, ii. xiv. 414.
[2] § 57, 7, Datt, de pace publica, 606, 717. Vogt, Rheinische Geschichten, iii. xiv. 365. MS. of Latom in Lersner's Chronik von Frankfurt a/M., 128.

2. *Maximilian's First Expedition to Italy.*

In the Tyrol, Maximilian was visited by the ambassadors of Italy; they represented to him that "the King of France was every day threatening to return. The Popolares at Florence, his keenest partisans, had been bold enough to attack Pisa. Against the former, as also against these latter, they prayed him to come and wage war, and not, when they had so great need of him, to be again thwarted by a Reichstag." Maximilian turned his attention entirely to Italian affairs, and inclined to the hope that he would be able, even without material assistance from Germany, to carry one of his plans.

The condition of things in Pisa and Florence was now as follows. When King Charles took Pisa under his protection, he forgot that it had ever been Ghibelline, had declared against the Anjous and against his rights, and that its last action had been to hoist the Burgundian colours.[1] Later, he came to terms with Florence, and only insisted upon an amnesty for Pisa. Relying upon this, the Florentines commenced the war. The castles upon the heights of Eva and Elsa, originally belonging to Pisa, and not far from the coast, were soon taken. Livorno surrendered to them, and Charles gave orders to his captain in the castle of Pisa to surrender this also.[2] But the captain acted contrary to expectations. Whether or not it was compassion, bribe, or, as is said, a lady of Pisa, who pleased him but too well, he disregarded his sovereign's commands. When the Florentines, upon his invitation, rushed through suburbs, fortifications, and across the Arno, in order to take the city and to receive the castle from him, he fired amongst them and hurled them back. He was the first to make the people of Pisa perfectly free, by surrendering to them their castle.[3]

But what sort of liberty is that, which from the first outset hesitates to protect itself? It was enough for the people

---

[1] Sismondi, Histoire des Républic Ital., viii. 152.
[2] Nardi, Istorie della città, 26. Guicciardini, ii. 121. Jovius, Historiæ sui temporis, 56. [3] Comines, viii. 567.

of Pisa not to be subjected to their old enemies. And he who protected them against their foes was also acceptable to them as their lord and master.

When, then, on the occasion of the renewed attacks made upon it by Florence, Lodovico and the Venetians took the part of Pisa, they may, perhaps, have intended to injure the French party; certain it is that Lodovico reflected, that the city formerly belonged to the Visconti, and that it was favourably situated for both Genoa and Milan; and certain it is that the latter considered what an excellent acquisition Pisa would be to the Apulian cities which were already theirs, and to Tarento, which had just raised the cry of "St. Marco," and how it would enable them to plant their standards on the Tyrrhenian sea. At first, as though no one knew the others' thoughts, they held together; but every day Lodovico became more jealous. He retired. His general, on being invited to advance, once answered that he must first take his breakfast. But matters did not come much further in this way.[1] It was a very brilliant idea of his to help to pass on this war to the German King, his nearest relative, who was an enemy of the Popolares, and no friend of Venice.

When, in May, 1496, Trivulzio came across the hills, fortified Asti, and spread the report that close behind him were coming the Duke of Orleans, and after him the King, with 2,000 hommes d'armes, and 10,000 Gascons and Swiss; this induced the Venetians—for Charles threatened to avenge their attack upon Fornovo—to agree to Lodovico's proposal.[2]

Accordingly, in July, 1496, Lodovico set out with his court and journeyed to Valtellino, and thence by way of Bormio across the Umbrail to Münster, there to await Maximilian. The next morning, before daybreak, the Emperor arrived attired in a black hunting costume, at his side the golden bugle-horn, and accompanied by 200 huntsmen with the long poles, with which they clamber from rock to rock, and by many nobles all decorated with the Burgundian Cross of St. Andrew. After the meeting was over, he might

[1] Chronicon Venetum, 36. Bembus, Historia Veneta, 66. Bursellis, Chronicon Bononiense, 914.
[2] Ebel, Anleitung, die Schweiz zu hereisen, iv. 510.

have been seen following the chase on the highest peaks of the Umbrail Joch—merely to gaze up at which made the spectator dizzy—his feet shod with climbing irons, where the cleft rocks ran sheer down into the abyss beneath. Meanwhile, the Duchess sat in a small hut, and chamois were driven down from the ravines and round the jagged rocks, and the sport went on before her eyes. In this way they amused themselves. The most important event, however, was, that Maximilian entertained the proposals of the Italian envoys: "they should pay him 40,000 ducats every three months, and he would then come and wage their war for them."[1] But first he must return to Germany.

In his ill-humour he had dropped all the resolutions of the Diet. At all events, he ought, by his presence in the first assembly, to have inaugurated the new constitution; but when the Day of Purification had arrived, he said that in Worms he had been treated as no city treated its mayor, and thereupon remained away. A few plenipotentiaries came, but in a short time everyone went home. In the meanwhile, the "Pfennig" had been raised; abbots and ecclesiastics paid it, and the cities also paid it into the hand of their parsons. But as the assembly, which should determine how the contribution should be expended, had broken up, how was it likely that any should show great eagerness, especially as all were unaccustomed to these proceedings, and annoyed at their property being investigated? Maximilian, accordingly, at Whitsuntide, 1496, wrote: "Each one should appear at Lindau with his soldiers all ready equipped, and with the money that had been raised by tax to pay them." Immediately afterwards, just as if nothing had been pre-arranged and pre-determined, he demanded that, "eight days after St. John's Day, the summer solstice, the strength of the nation should accompany him across the mountains, for King Charles was already on the march;"[2] and in August he wrote that he was full of great hopes for the success of his Roman campaign; the country

---

[1] Ghilinus, de adventu Maximiliani in Italiam, ap. Freherum, iii. 82. Navagero, Stor. Venet., 1207.

[2] Letter of the Esslinger in Datt, de pace publica, p. 550. Maximilian's proclamation, *ibid.* 544, 546. Trithemius, Chronicon Hirsangiense ad annum 1496.

should support him at once with loans and the "pfennig" tax.¹

But how was the campaign to be begun, without the fiat of the Empire? That it did not come to this in no way disheartened him. The princes of his party afforded him some assistance, namely, those princes that at that time were living at his Court at Innsbruck. The deputies of a few Swiss cities accompanied him. Yet his real army was to be provided by Italy. In Linz he took counsel with his son Philip. Philip, who now ruled the Netherlands, came merrily, sometimes taking part in the "bird-shooting" of respectable burghers, and sometimes joining in the patrician dances. At the manor-house at Augsburg, where they made a pile of maypoles and garlands forty-five feet high for the St. John's Day bonfire, the fairest damsel with a wax taper in her hand kindled it with him in the dance, whilst the trumpets, cornets, and kettledrums all brayed to the fire and the dance.² In Linz his father disclosed to him his bold plans. He hoped to keep the French back from Italy and Livorno ; Florence would then league itself with him; nay more, aid him to cross over in René's interest from Tuscany into Provence. This done, Philip should invade France from the Netherlands and Ferdinand from Roussillon. In Lyons, they might all three meet, and then Burgundy would be won.³ With these hopes, in August, he took the 200 horse that he had equipped, and induced Albrecht of Saxony to follow him with some infantry; and in the hamlet of Meda, beyond Valtellina and Morbegno, between houses and gardens, he met the envoy of the Pope and Lodovico. In Vigevano they took counsel together.⁴ A few days.

¹ A letter of Maximilian of the 29th August from Carimate (read instead of Calmia) in Datt, p. 552 *seq.*
² Pontus Heuterus, Rerum Aust. i. 15, p. 230. Gassers, Augsb. Chronik, 257. Cursius, Ann. Suevici. ³ Zurita, i. 98.
⁴ Maximilian proceeded from Augsburg, where he had resided for two months, about the middle of June, 1496, to Innsbruck, by way of Landsberg. Here he remained from the 27th of June to the 5th of July (Reports of the Venetian envoy, Francesco Foscarin, in the Achivio storico Italiano, t. vii. p. 734, 749). Thence he journeyed by Imst (10th July), Pfunds (13), and Nauders to Mals, where he arrived on July 17. On the 20th the meeting with Lodovico took place at Münster. Maximilian escorted Lodovico on the same day as far as Mals. From

later, the Venetian envoys arrived. The first danger, the arrival of the French, was past. In France, Louis d'Orleans, when his baggage was already on the road and he was about to start between evening and morning, suddenly changed his mind, and Charles did not wish to compel him. It would have been all the easier to have attacked Asti, but the Venetians would not give it up to the man who had refused them Pisa. An immediate attack upon Florence was concerted. In a short time Maximilian stood before the towers of Livorno, in order to first wrest this city from it—full of schemes for the future.[1]

The Florentines at that time owned sway over 800 walled towns, consisting partly of such as were closed in the evening and opened in the morning—the half at least with a market—as well as over 12,000 open hamlets. One hundred and thirty towns brought them every St. John's Day a taper or a piece of cloth, and owned the city as their protectress.[2] Such was the power they exercised over Pistoja and Volterra by party influence, by their commerce and money over Arezzo, which they had purchased from Courcy

Mals, which he left on the 26th July, he returned to Imst, where he arrived on the 2nd August (not on the 28th July, as Ullmann, Kaiser Maximilian, i. p. 447, states; or in Foscari's report in the Arch. stor. Ital., vii. p. 790, "Jeri Giunsi in questo loco dove si trova l'Arciduca Filippo e nel quale S. M. arrivo il di precedente;" by jeri, seeing that the letter was dated 4th August, the 3rd is meant, and accordingly by "il di precedente" the 2nd August is denoted—in the "Itinerarium Maximilians," by Stälin, Forschungen, i. p. 355, Imst does not occur), and had an interview with his son Philip. On the 4th August Maximilian again left Imst, and proceeded by Landeck, Prutz, Pfunds, and Nauders to Mals, which he reached on the 13th. Thence he set out on the 15th, and betook himself by Bormio, Tirano, Sondrio, and Carimate, to Meda, where he met on the 31st August the envoy and Lodovico. On the 1st September Maximilian went back to Vigevano (Vigevene), where he arrived on the 2nd, and Lodovico and the papal legate on the 3rd of September (Sanuto in Arch. stor., vii. p. 946). (Note to 3rd edition.) On the 13th September (Foscari's Report in Arch. stor. Ital., vii. 865, Sanuto Diarii, i. p. 304; cf. Rawdon, Brown, Ragguagli sulla vita e sulla opere di Marin Sanuto, pp. 35, 40).
[1] Senarega, Annales Genuenses, 560. Burcardus, Diarium, 2075. Ghilinus, 88. Comines, 576. On the 23rd of September Maximilian started from Vigevano, and proceeded by way of Tortæa (Foscari, a. a. O. p. 886) to Genoa, which he reached on the 27th. Here he embarked on the 8th October.
[2] Benedetto Dei, in Varchi, Istorie Fiorentine, 262.

d'Enguerrand,[1] over Cortona, that had surrendered to King Ladislaw and had been bargained by him to them, over Pisa, that had on one occasion been betrayed and sold to them by Gabriel Visconti, and on another by the head of the exiles, then the head of the city—for the city had resisted and had called back its exiles into it—and, finally, over Livorno, which Thomas Fregoso had made over to them for 100,000 ducats.[2]

Now we must remember that not all the 10,000 fathers of families at that time in Florence belonged to the ruling classes, for the most of them were burghers without the rights of citizens. The benefit of the city, as it was called, was shared in by only 576 houses of the greater, and by 220 of the lesser, trades, but never by more than 2,000 citizens. They had also private property; and the 800 palaces and the 32,000 estates in the vicinity of the city were for the most part in their hands. It was these 2,000 against whom Maximilian waged war.[3]

In spite of their great affluence and power, they had not as yet forsaken their original employment, trade, nor abated their innate severity of life. They had 270 woollen factories which imported wool from France, Catalonia, and the best that England could produce, and exported cloth to South Italy, to Constantinople, and by way of Brusa to the whole of the East. They had eighty-three manufactories for silk, brocade, and damask, for which their own ships fetched the silk from the East, and which found their chief markets in Lyons, Barcelona, Seville, London, and Antwerp.[4] The East sent them silk, and the Western world wool; they manufactured both, and exported their silkstuffs to the West and their woollens to the East, and thus ministered to the wants of the world. Hence it came that their first "Signori" were cloth and silk merchants, and the third a banker.[5] Their thirty-three banks, for instance, having agencies in all parts,

---

[1] Sismondi, Histoire des Républ. Ital., vi. 407, vii. 287.
[2] Belius, Historia Patriæ in Grævius, v. 27, 42, 90.
[3] Varchi, Digressione intorno il governo di Firenze in the Istorie, ii. 65. Istorie, 208.
[4] Benedetto Dei in Fabroni, Vità Laurentii Medici, ii. 337.
[5] Neumann, Introd. to Aretinus, Staatsverf. von Florenz, 39.

did perhaps the best business of all, they founded the fortune of the Medici.¹

The first business of such a Florentine was to go to early Mass. This done, in summer clothed in black Lucco, frilled round the neck, and a black silken cap with a long point, and in winter in black mantle and cowl,² he walked through the streets to his business in the market or in the palace. At midday, after dinner, he saw his children and related to them a new or an old story.³ He then arranged his papers, or went to the Loggias that the patricians had at their houses. They always addressed each other as "thou;" and only a knight, a doctor, or an uncle was called "you" and "sir." Almost everyone bore the nickname that had been given him by his playfellows in his youth. The beautiful language that the whole of Italy learnt from them was formed in their society. At Ave Maria they were all at home. In winter, they stood with wife and child for a while around the fire; and whilst the lower orders, and those that lived by the sweat of their brow, made good cheer in the inns, they themselves partook of a frugal meal at home at three o'clock at night. Many stayed up half the night with their silks and before their "Caviglia."⁴

Among these rich, influential, educated, and solemn people, a Dominican monk of Ferrara, one Hieronymus Savonarola, had succeeded in making himself universally esteemed. He was, it is true, strict with himself and others, a solitary walker, a monk by inclination, and a man who also knew how to control his rough voice. He admonished his monasterial brethren to give up all their property. He spared no one, not one of his fellow-citizens, the Brescians or the Florentines, nor his liege lords, the Pope and Lorenzo di Medici, and all this could not help securing him a certain influence. But what made him really powerful were, before all else, his doctrines and his prophetic gifts.

Now his doctrines are really worth examining:—" Like a piece of iron between two magnets, so does the human

---

[1] Roscoe, Lorenzo's Life, from his Ricordi, 120. Benedetto Dei.
[2] Varchi, Storie, p. 265.
[3] Macchiavelli's comedy, Clitia, act ii. sc. iv. p. 141.
[4] Varchi, 261, 267.

soul waver between divine and earthly things, and between belief and feeling. Its purity consists solely in withdrawing itself from the love of things earthly, and in voluntary flight to God. Sacrament and prayer lead to him; his nature it is that draws it heavenwards to participate in its goodness.[1] But the *soul* has a domestic enemy, an adversary in the form of a friend, the flesh, that rebels against it, and oppresses it to sin. With its help the devil lays snares for it, like the vulture after the heart of its prey. Since the world began he has deceived and devoured it a thousand thousand times, yea, a number without end and count, and is not yet satiated, but still lurks and waits like a hungry wolf. The world accordingly is divided between two banners, of Christ and the devil, a black and a white one.

"Now the sinner is like a dead man, reft of life. His face is dark, he durst not open his eyes. God hates him. A man may pour bad wine from his golden vessel and keep the vessel; but God breaks both, sin and the vessel of sin. And no one begs for mercy of God, as in Florence no one dares to entreat for an exile.[2]

"The faithful, on the other hand, when he bows his knee, when he follows the commands of Love, when he disregards all things earthly, and only aims at being merged into God, feels God and is illuminated by him. In this way, a simple man and a maiden of low estate come further than Plato and Pythagoras came. But he who is by nature inclined, and who is quite free of earthly care, by constant habit, and watchful carefulness attains in his old age the greatest bliss, he sees God. Such a man communes with angels and saints; and the devil has no power over him, but he over the devil.[3]

"When the wicked man's day is done, where is then his pomp? His journeying and his riding? His hurrying and scurrying, and his golden ornaments? Down, down, where

---

[1] Savonarola de simplicitate Christiana, 80, 18, 78. Edition of 1615. Triumphus Crucis, i. c. 12.

[2] Seven consoling sermons by Hieronymus Savonarola in Latin.

[3] De Simplicitate, 13, 41, de divisione omnium scientarum, edition of 1594, p. 793. Dialogus, solatium itineris mei, ed. of 1633, p. 165, 228. Expositio orationis dominicæ, edition of 1615, p. 190.

his body is food for worms. But the soul is free, begins to think of itself and to lament: O woe! who hath soiled my vesture, which by baptism was made whiter than snow, and made it now more filthy than pitch? Satan then comes to it and says: 'My playmate, stand up, I have done it. For thou hast followed my advice and worked faithfully with me. Come, follow me into my kingdom. There is hunger without meat, thirst without drink, there is an unquenchable, dull, violent, smoking fire, and by the side of it, cold without measure and remedy. Come with me. The devils are coming to meet thee with their song of lamentation.'[1]

"But on the other side, the joy of the elect cannot be described in language. It will be splendid and clear, like the sheen of the sun, quick like the ray of light that in one moment gleams from east to west. Being with God he will know all things, present, past, and future; he will wish for nothing that he cannot obtain; there will be a life and existence in constant admiration, in sweet delight, in ecstatic love, in the ceaseless singing of praises, in bliss and triumph, without ending for evermore."[2]

When Savonarola enunciated this doctrine, with an eloquence that often appeared like a jubilant cry and shout of triumph,[3] and especially when he corroborated it out of the Holy Writ, the Florentines, as he himself has said, stood and gazed at him like marble pillars, with their faces turned to his.[4] It was all the more impressive, this doctrine, because it distinguished good and evil, like in their city Gibellines and Guelphs, Bianchi and Neri, had often been contrasted. Besides, they considered him a prophet. He had foretold the advent and the victory of Charles, and had prophesied in unmistakable language the expulsion of the Medici.[5] The majority believed him perfectly. He was master of their minds, and in the new order of things in Florence he attained the greatest influence.

It was Piero's nearest relatives and friends that had

---

[1] Sixth Sermon. Solatium itineris mei, lib. vi. de vita futura, p. 250.
[2] Seventh Sermon. Solatium, 254-263.
[3] For instance, Sermo in vigilia nativitatis Christi.
[4] Triumphus Crucis, p. 100.
[5] Fabronius, vita Laurentii Medici, ii. 291.

summoned his enemy to Tuscany, that had expelled him from the Signorie, and overthrown him. Not as though they were minded to share their government with the populace—when would this ever occur to the ruling party in any city?—but, because Piero intended to be prince, they hated him. They hoped under Lorenzino and the junior line of this house to attain to greater influence. With this idea, immediately after Piero's flight, they summoned a parliament. They called it a parliament, when they collected the people together on the square by the sound of a bell, placed armed youths at all the entrances, who thrust back everyone that was displeasing to them, and then, finally, allowed the collected throng to vote by acclamation. Such a parliament, on this occasion, by loud consentient voices, entrusted the conduct of public affairs to a Balia of twenty men,—that is, the supreme government.[1]

Savonarola, whose theory based the right of government purely upon agreement,[2] opposed them, and preached his principle that all true citizens ought to participate in the sovereign power. He even convinced some of the leading men. Antonio Soderini publicly professed his views; others visited him at night. Owing to this, differences and regular dissensions gradually arose, which were followed at last by a peaceable and complete dissolution of the Balia.[3]

The new order of things was framed in accordance with Savonarola's principles. All those who enjoyed the benefit of the city, that is all whose fathers and grandfathers had, since the political government of the Medici, been adopted into the three dignities of Signori, Gonfalonieri, and "good men," that is chosen, were declared eligible, and entered into the government under the name of the great Consiglio. Such an arrangement is far from being an exposition of the rights of man; for Savonarola conceived of social distinctions and grades to have been original and given by God:[4] to many it will appear to have been no-

---

[1] Nerli, Istorie Fiorentine, 58, 63. Cf. Sismondi, Histoire des Républiques Ital. xii. 233. [2] Savonarola, del Governo.
[3] Nardi, Le Storie della città, 23. Corio, Istor. di Mil. 966.
[4] Savonarola, de simplicitate vitæ Christianæ, 65, 70, 85, 90.

thing more nor less than an enlarged aristocracy. Only inside the Consiglio no privilege should be tolerated. It received a thoroughly democratic constitution. Just as in Venice there were Doge, Consiglieri, and Pregadi above the Great Council, so here also the Gonfalonieri had the administration of justice, and the eight Signori and the Council of Eighty the essential attributes of government. In Venice the greater part of the dignities were conferred for life, but, in this case, for two months and not by a regular election. Only after certain names in respective quarters of the city had been proposed by chance, by lot, did voting take place upon them. The elections were rather committees and commissions, than official elections in our sense of the term. "A city is well governed," says Savonarola, "when the magistracy have short notice given them of the day when their stewardship shall be inquired into. What otherwise is the meaning of free election? for everyone will only be obedient to the best."[1] For this assembly a hall was at once built. It was the largest in Italy, and yet was finished in a marvellously short time. It was approached by broad steps. The middle was occupied by long and cross benches for the burghers, on each side upon a raised dais three yards high and broad were seats for the Eighty. At the east end, the Gonfalonieri and Signori had their places, and here two doors led into the chambers set apart for secret deliberation, and for the registry of taxes; at the west end there stood a tribune and an altar, with a picture of Fra Bartholomew, at which mass was held. The hall had also an ecclesiastical appearance, and Savonarola said: "the angels have assisted in the work."[2]

This constitution was in full operation when Maximilian was investing Livorno. There was no demand now for brocade or cloth; the Stradiotti laid waste the country estates; there was no importation either by sea or land, for Siena also was hostile, but that made little impression upon the citizens. They came in such numbers to hear Savonarola's sermons, that, in spite of its great size,

[1] Nerli, 44, 66. Varchi, Digressione intorno il governo, 67; Savonarola, del Governo.
[2] Vasari, Vita di Simone Cronaca, iii. 253.

galleries had to be built at the entrance of the Church of Maria del Fiore opposite the pulpit, as in a theatre. The fasts were most strictly observed. The games that the monk condemned were abandoned; and, in view of the approaching war, they awaited the arrival of the fleet that Charles was fitting out in Marseilles. But soon they had to learn that this fleet had been wrecked in a storm. Weiskunig narrates that Maximilian saw the French fleet arriving; and hereupon, as soon as he had weighed anchor and spread his sails, there came first a cloud, and from it wind, and then more clouds, and thereout there arose such a storm, that the enemy's ships were driven with him into the harbour, and part in battle and part in storm were wrecked and lost. Where was now their hope and the promise of God's immediate help that the Dominican brother had made them? Yet they retained sufficient courage, even at this critical moment, to receive within their walls a host of fugitives, who had been beggared by the war. They could not do aught else but carry the image of the Virgin through the streets, followed by all men and women, clerics and children, with psalm-singing, prayers and lamentations. They had just arrived with their tabernacle at St. Mary's Gate, when they perceived a messenger on a mare careering across the Trinity Bridge, and waving an olive-branch from afar. They stopped and listened; some ships fitted out by their merchants, which had long struggled with the same storm, had at last, owing to the wind having unexpectedly shifted, been driven right past Maximilian into the harbour, and so to Livorno. The news was true. They seized the horse's reins; everyone wanted to hear it for himself from the mouth of the messenger. The historians do not record it, but we may imagine how fervently they thanked God, the God of their prayers, for these tidings.[1]

What saved them, thwarted Maximilian's plans. And now the Florentines would not entertain the idea more of being separated from Charles VIII., of whose return Savonarola had always reminded them. Livorno was held for them by Swiss legions. Moreover, the south-west wind

[1] Nardi, 29-32. Weiskunig, 201, and in other passages. Ghilinus, 90.

levelled their enemy's tents on land, and scattered his ships on the sea. Maximilian, meanwhile, saw the months, within which the money was promised him, draw to a close; the Marchesci and Sforza party were already at variance as to which should hold the harbour when they took it; and he heard of letters from Venice itself, written with the object of inciting the army against him. Overcome by the feeling of the impossibility of being able to achieve anything under such circumstances, he said, "No! against the will of God and men, he would not wage this war." He turned towards Pisa, arrived at Vico, appeared as if he intended to do something, but did nothing, and, though invited to the chase, hurried away to Pavia and home to Germany.[1]

Since then the Florentines cherished no doubt of Savonarola's prophetic mission. At Christmas, 1496, 1,300 children under eighteen years—for only with their eighteenth year were they wont to adopt the "Lucco," and to rank as young men—partook of the Sacrament with the priest. On the ensuing fasts the children of every quarter went to the houses and begged for the "Anathem," that is "things damnable." Their distribution into companies, their processions, and songs at vespers under conductors were familiar.[1] The men gave them cards, dice, and dice-boards, the women false hair, paint, and perfumed waters. Many produced their Morgante, Boccaccio, and indelicate pictures; some sacrificed their harps, remembering perhaps for what purposes they had used them. Bartholomew Baccio took the naked figures—for they should not be where young maidens congregated—from his workshop and offered them. On the market-place was raised a scaffold in the form of a pyramid with many steps mounting up to it, and upon this all these things were piled. On the day of the Carnival,

---

[1] Jovius, Historiæ sui temporis, 83. Navagero, Storia Venez., 1207. Zurita, 108, and Coccinius, de bellis Italicis, 277. Macchiavelli, Legazione a Pisa. The French ships put into the harbour of Livorno on the 29th Oct. (Foscari in the Arch. Stor. ital. vii. p. 938. Sanuto, Diarii, i. p. 373); about the middle of November Maximilian raised the siege. On the 16th Nov. he was in Vicopisano, on the 2nd Dec. in Pavia, on the 26th in Mals; at the commencement of the year 1497 he returned thence to Innsbruck.

[2] Varchi, 259, 265.

the whole people came together, and the Signori were seated. Then came the children from the mass all dressed in white, with olive-branches round their heads and red crosses in their hands, and sang Italian hymns of praise. Four advanced to the Signori, received from them burning torches and lighted the pyramid, which blazed up amid the blare of trumpets. The while alms were collected for the indigent poor.[1]

The severe religious tendency of this city forms a material link in the struggle between the Liga and the French party. By declaring against the Pope, who regarded himself as the head of the Liga, it gave the quarrel a new phase.

In Ferrara, Savonarola's native place, we remark a similar condition of things. Frequent fasting was observed, blasphemy was punished, and swearing was prohibited. "Massari" were sent through the streets to report on everything. There is no doubt what was the object of all this. The inhabitants of Ferrara, who had but little sympathy with the Liga, because it united both their natural enemies, Venice and the Pope—being, as they were, of French sympathies, even to wearing French dresses and shoes—endeavoured to counteract the Pope's influence by still deeper piety.[2] In spite of the great perils surrounding them, they made processions every third day. In the King of France, Charles VIII., we remark a kindred tendency. He asked his doctors whether or not the Pope was not bound to hold a Concilium every ten years, and whether, in case he neglected to do so, the princes were not entitled to hold it; and further, in case all the others neglected this duty, whether the King of France alone could not hold it. He made known his intention of restoring the order of Benedict to its original form, and of permitting no bishop to absent himself from his church.[3] Savonarola was the head of all enemies of the Liga and the Pope. He condemned the wealth and the pomp of the clergy, for thereby the barrier was broken which separated Church and world. By this means the

---

[1] Nardi. Vasari, Vita del Fra Bartolommeo, t. iii.
[2] Diarium Ferrarense, 320, 323, 386.
[3] Questions in Garnier, xx. 519. Brantome, 39. Comines, 592.

children of the world had entered into God's vineyard. But God's Word still endured, and by no means were they bound to trust a prelate as much as it. Nay, no one should sit on an ecclesiastical chair except so long as his works were not prejudicial to the operation of the doctrine. Acting in accordance with these principles, he invited Charles orally, and the German and the Spanish King in writing, to undertake the reformation of the Church. But it could not but be that he roused this hierarchical antipathy against himself. A man named Mariano de Ghinazzano, who had once preached at his side in Florence to the admiration of the classical scholars, hurried to Rome to the Pope, and there began one of his sermons with, " Cut this monster off from the Church, holy Father!"[1]

Whilst Pope Alexander at that very time gave dispensation from oaths, in order that his enemies might die in prison,[2] he resolved at the same time to use his ecclesiastical weapons against Savonarola and his adherents, as being heretics. But before this, he had another battle to fight out with the partisans of the Liga in his own land, the Orsini.

The Orsini were no despicable foes. They had defeated his son, the Duke of Gandia, to whom he had committed the staff of the Church to war against them. He was obliged to call Gonzal to his aid. Gonzal had first taken Taranto, that had in vain flouted the colours of the Marchesci—for the Liga would not allow Venice to take its side[3]—and had subjected Sora to Federigo. He now vanquished a pirate, who had taken Ostia and threatened to starve out Rome, and compelled the Orsini to make peace. Willamarino's ships at that time flew the Neapolitan, Papal, and Spanish flags all at once. They were now victorious everywhere. Even Cardinal Julian entered into a compact.[4]

---

[1] Meditationes in Psalmos, Lugduni, 1633, p. 128. Von Gewalt und Ausehn, B. 7. Letters in Mansi, Nardi.

[2] Zurita, i. 97.

[3] Johannes Juvenis, de fortuna Tarentinorum, vii. 3. Navagero, Stor. Ven. 1209.

[4] Jovius, Vita Gonsalvi, 220. Arnold von Harve, Reise im Conversationsblatt of 1823, No. 2. Burcardus, 2080.

After this, when the Pope had now leisure to turn his attention to Savonarola, it happened that a factious rising in Florence aided him, and he it. The leading Florentines could not forget the power they had enjoyed under the Medici in former days, and their sons would not submit to the rigorous discipline of the monk. Probably under the impression that Piero would now have learnt to know them better, they allied themselves with his professed adherents, the Bigi (they called themselves the Arrabiati), in order to effect his recall. They were not successful. Benivieni, whom the Signori in their alarm sent to Savonarola, often related how he found the brother reading in a book; he looked up and said: "O ye of little faith, God is with you! Mark ye, Piero will come as far as the gates and will then turn back." Nardi adds: "And so it really happened. One of them that had been seized by the Medici, having escaped, came before daybreak to the gate in order to close it, whereupon Piero having found it closed and all quiet, returned." But how fierce and violent must this faction in the city have been, to bring such an excellent and pious man, as the monk was, from his path.[1] To him especially is due the law that where anyone is accused of a political crime, he shall not be judged by Signori, or a Commission as a court of last instance, but shall be allowed to appeal to the Consiglio. This law mitigated the Italian usage, that every victor should, as of right and under certain legal formulas, be able to decide the question of life and death in the case of his adversaries. But in August, 1497, when it was believed to have been discovered who had taken Piero's part, Savonarola allowed his good law to be infringed, and the accused were denied the right of appeal. His opponents became, in consequence, only more violent and mysterious.[2]

The Pope now sided with them. The Tuscan Dominicans, whom Savonarola had separated from the Lombards, the Pope ordered again to unite, interdicted him from preach-

[1] Nerli, 71. Nardi, 36. Jovius, Vita Leonis, 19. Cf. also Matthiæ Döringii Continuatio Chronici Engethastani in Mencken, Scriptores Rerum Saxonicarum, ii. 53.
[2] Macchiavelli, Discorsi, sopra la prima deca di Livio, c. 44.

ing, summoned him to Rome, and appointed the Lombardian Vicar of the Dominican order as his judge. But Savonarola continued preaching, took daily more brothers into his convents, and refused to recognize his judge, saying "he could not come to Rome on account of his enemies." It availed him nothing that in Florence signatures were collected attesting the fact that his doctrine was sound and productive of good fruit. In spite of all he was placed under ban.[1] Since then, his life depended upon the fact, that his party never allowed its enemies to become strong, for, by the then existing law, he could be at once put to death. The Pope only required the secular arm.

In Florence, however, towards the close of the year 1497, open dissensions burst out. Some of the clergy condemned the processions of others, some the Communion that others celebrated, and some again, as in an heretical city, desired not to perform divine service any longer. The Franciscans, the old opponents of the Dominicans, joined the party of the Arrabiati and the Pope. Sometimes the brother found his pulpit soiled. On one occasion some young men lifted a heavy money-box during his sermon, let it fall and fled. He was escorted to church by armed men, and whilst he was preaching one stood by him with a halberd. But sometimes, when some of the Arrabiati joined the Signori, and the others were timid, he remained in his convent.[2]

Yet he did not lose courage. The moral of his teaching was that a pious and learned man must not give way to a wicked and ignorant Pope.[3] He comforted himself in his convent with his successes. "Every day a greater number, out of yearning for a more perfect life, forsake parents, friends, and goods, and betake themselves where each must do or not do as his superior wills; where no one has anything except what he absolutely needs, and where he can for a time be deprived by his superior even of that. But here everyone becomes daily calmer, and

---

[1] Alexander Papa priori, etc. Responsio fratris Hieronymi in Burcardus, and in Gordon, Vie d'Alexandre, Appendix ii. 488. Epistolæ Petri Martyris xi. 191.
[2] Nardi and Nerli.   [3] Von Gewalt und Obrigkeit. G. 3.

confesses that Christ is his only joy. Only he who prays without ceasing attains to a holiness, from whose rays his face beams with rapture."[1] He found himself in the midst of the struggle between "Popolares" and "Arrabiati," the Liga and its enemies, the true and the Roman Church, between heaven and hell. He openly interpreted those two flags, the black and the white, in this sense. He felt certain of victory. At Christmas he published his book on the "Triumph of the Cross." Therein he represented Christ upon a triumphal car, above his head the gleaming ball of the Trinity, in his left hand the Cross, in his right the Old and the New Testaments; further below, the Virgin Mary; before the car, patriarchs, prophets, apostles, and preachers; on either side the martyrs and the doctors with opened books; behind him, all the converts; at a further distance the innumerable crowd of enemies, emperors, powerful rulers, philosophers, and heretics, all vanquished, their idols destroyed, and their books burnt.[2]

But the longer it lasted, the more furious waxed the conflict. At Shrovetide, 1498, his children desired to repeat the celebration of the previous year; but the torches were torn out of their hands. At first, the children, and then even the men, stoned each other. A significant instance of the extent of the feud was afforded by the action of the painters, Baccio and Albertinelli. They had always worked together, and had had all things in common. They now left their workshop. The former went into a convent, the other became innkeeper.[3] How was it possible that these differences could be settled but by force? When, at last, a Franciscan monk presumed to declare that he would prove in the fire that certain doctrines of the Dominicans were erroneous, it appeared also to the latter that they had found another and the true decision—the ordeal. The Franciscans argued thus. If Savonarola would allow their monk to perish in the fire, he was no saint; and upon this they built. The others, who were half mad, who indulged sometimes in the

[1] Triumphus Crucis, 121, 195, 114.
[2] Triumphus Crucis, p. 11. Macchiavelli Lettere, tom. vi. ed. 1783, p. 6.
[3] Vasari, Vita del Mariotto Albertinelli in the Vite, iii.

market places in round dances to the accompaniment of an ecclesiastical ballad, and who had chosen for their war cry "Viva Cristo," hoped to conquer by the truth of their faith. During the sermon, hundreds cried, "Look! look! I will go for thy doctrine, O Lord, into the fire." Accordingly two piles of oak logs and brushwood, well saturated with pitch and oil, were built up side by side, 40 feet in length, leaving a very narrow passage between them, and on the 7th of April the Signori, on this occasion only Arrabiati, sat awaiting the trial.[1]

The Franciscans came quietly, the Dominicans with burning torches, red crosses, and loud hymn, preceded by Savonarola. The monks approached the pyre, the Dominican seized the host. At this moment the crisis arrived. The Franciscans would not permit him to have the host, as this was a trial of the whole Christian faith, but he would not be prevented. Hereupon ensued a quarrel, confusion, a rain of missiles, and a general stampede. Some rushed into the convent, others resorted to arms. It now came to scenes of violence, and the Arrabiati were not for allowing the favour of the Signorie and the propitious moment to pass by without taking advantage of it. They attacked the Popolares in the streets and in their convent; and, although they did not take the convent by storm, they remained masters of the situation. Savonarola did not take part in it. At first he exhorted his followers from the pulpit, afterwards he prostrated himself in the choir of the church and prayed. When all was quiet, he went out, and delivered himself up to his enemies.[2]

This occurrence undoubtedly made the Liga victorious in Italy: the Arrabiati were as devoted to it as the Popolares were to the French. On the 7th of April the Arrabiati asserted their supremacy in Florence; on the 8th, Charles died, and the Liga was victorious even in France. Charles was at last busied with the internal affairs of his

---

[1] Nardi and Nerli, Declaratio fratris Hieronymi, in Burcardus, 6. Eccardus 2090.

[2] Nardi and Nerli. Burcardi Diarium 2087, 2094. Excerpta ex Monacho Pirnensi, probably a pamphlet, mentioned by Trithemius in Mencken ii. 1518.

realm. Of his Great Council he formed an ordinary Court of Judicature, consisting of seventeen members, something similar to the later "Reichshofrath" of the Germans; in all Commanderies he had a general book of customs compiled; he intended to live upon his demesnes, and twice every week he sat to hear the complaints of the poor. Having made all these arrangements, and equipped with better alliances, he was again about to attempt to assert his right to Naples. Savonarola, too, had always referred to his return. But on the 8th of that month, whilst on his way to a gallery to look at a game of ball, he suddenly fell down, and, though a moment before in perfect health, was in a few minutes a corpse.[1]

Many are of opinion that this event first determined Savonarola's fate. Many accusations had been brought up against him; and as often as the scourge was inflicted, he confessed all that was wanted. But as soon as he came to himself again, he denied everything, saying that "on the rack he would certainly confess to it again." Meanwhile his soul searched its own heart. His pride was broken; if he ever had thought himself holy, this feeling was now passed. It often seemed to him as if Despair, with a strong army with lances and swords, with the standard of Justice before it, and surrounded by instruments of torture, appeared in the town, called him from afar, and, coming nearer, whispered into his ear all his sins; and then again Hope, shining with the light of heaven, would comfort him. He spoke to himself thus: "Thou hast loved the Lord many years, and hast wrought out of love to him; then didst thou exalt thy heart; then didst thou follow thine own thoughts, and live in the vanity of thy mind; then did the Lord take his hand from thee, and thou art like a sinner plunged into the depths of the sea." He had only just arrived at this holy self-enlightenment, when he was doomed to die; his body was consigned to the fire.[2]

[1] Garnier from the Lettres patentes, 515, and a letter of Charles there cited. Comines, 591. St. Gelais, 120. Bayard, 56. Brantome, 44.
[2] Meditatio in Psalmum; "In te Domine speravi," i. "Quam morte præceptus absolvere non potuit," 84, 97. (Note to 2nd Edition.) The history of Savonarola has since then commanded the greatest attention in all civilized countries, and has been the subject of various treatises. The account that I have recorded here as the result of former studies, I

With his death the essence of his doctrine and his influence in no wise died out. Simon Cronaca, a good master, honoured him whilst he was alive, and spoke of him now that he was dead. Even at the expiration of thirty years, the accomplishment of his most famous prophecies was expected to take place. But at that time, as we have said, the Arrabiati attained the first offices. They did not now consider the recall of Piero necessary for their safety. They were so devoted to the Liga, that all its members, except the Venetians, considered it better to restore Pisa to them.[1]

3. *Extension and Ascendency of the Liga.*

Thus the object of the Liga was attained, and Italy subjected to its views. But the extension and the ascendency of the Liga is fraught with other consequences for the whole of Europe, and later times. The alliance of the Houses of Hapsburg and Aragon is one result of the conditions which obtained during these years. Ferdinand knew how to draw the princes of the outer sea into the sphere of his alliances, and among them first Don Manuel of Portugal. He had protected him whilst he was still Duke, and had made military preparations in his favour when he inherited the throne after John's death.[2] But Don Jorgan, John's natural son, of whom all were afraid, was led by Jacob Almeida before the King to kiss hands,[3] and war was dispensed with. Ferdinand promised his daughter Isabella to this Manuel. Isabella, who considered a second marriage a bad thing, demanded that Manuel should at all events expel from Portugal the Jews and all those whom the Inquisition had condemned. She would not consent to be his wife until he had pro-

could not alter by the light of them, although on the occasion of a lengthened visit to Florence I have not neglected to make researches. I still hope to be able to publish in a later volume the results of my labours at that time, that have especial regard to the history of Florence in the first epoch of the Medici.
  [1] Vasari, Vita di Simone, detto il Cronaca. Zurita i. 143.
  [2] Zurita, 78.
  [3] Hieronymi Osorii re rebus Manuelis libri, xii., lib. i. 3, a.

mised her this.[1] After that day, peace and union subsisted between Portugal and Spain for a century and a half.

At the same period, in August, 1497, and ever since the alliance with Bretagne, Ferdinand negotiated with Henry VII. of England. If Spain and France quarrel, England must take part in it. In June, 1496, Henry joined the Liga;[2] he received hat and sword from the Pope, and received the envoys of all the allies.[3] His counsellors asserted that this was tantamount to bringing the war to England; but this monarch, who never cared about taking the field, except it might be against a rebel, well knew what he was about, and that he was working at the iron wall, with which, as he said, he intended to gird his realm.[4] But, at present, great dangers threatened him from without: in Flanders, from Margaret of York, widow of Charles the Bold, who, if she did not actually incite his first rebel, Lambert Simmel, who declared himself to be Edward Warwick, she, at all events, aided by 2,000 Germans, whom she found means to send to his assistance, raised him to certain importance.[5] It was not doubted, that the second rebel, Perkin Osbek, who called himself Richard Plantagenet, was also really her creature.[6] His most reliable support the latter found in the Scots, where King and nation united in their eagerness to cross the Tweed. James IV. allied Perkin with his house, brought him across the borders, ravaged the country, and was alternately in his palace and on the frontier;[7] whilst the people, whenever a truce was made, broke it on their own responsibility. The proposed marriage of Catherine of Spain with Arthur, Prince of Wales, could not fail to affect both sides, both Flanders and Scotland. Ferdinand was thus enabled to render the King of England secure on either side. At first, through the Austrian alliance, the

---

[1] Zurita, f. 124. Osorius i. p. 14.
[2] Burcardus, 2067 (note to 2nd edition). Cf. Brown Calendar of State Papers, i. 247.
[3] Chronicon Venetum, p. 41.
[4] Baco, Historia Henrici Septimi, p. 300.
[5] Polydorus Virgilius, Historia Anglica, lib. 26, p. 730.
[6] Baco, p. 194.
[7] Buchananus, Rerum Scoticarum, lib. xiii. 460, 465.

treaty of general intercourse between England and Flanders was renewed, "rebels were to be extradited, including Margaret's territory."[1] The English merchants came in triumph to Antwerp, and Maximilian, though hesitatingly, promised to ignore the so-called York.[2] In Scotland, Peter Ayala was plying his negotiations with sly circumspection, in order to draw the King into the great political league. He understood how to persuade Perkin—and this appears to have escaped the notice of the English historians[3]—that the Kings of England and Scotland were already agreed, and that there was therefore nothing left to him but to flee; and when Perkin, on the ship of a Spaniard of St. Sebastian, had joined the rebels of Cornwallis, he persuaded King James not to undertake the invasion of England just at that moment,[4] upon which Perkin fell into Henry's power. King James then married Margaret, daughter of Henry VII.,[5] whence resulted a long peace between the Scots and the English, and finally the union of both kingdoms. The close relationship in which James stood to John of Denmark, who possessed Norway and claimed Sweden, cemented the peace which Danes and English had, after a long war, recently concluded.

The chief members of this League were Ferdinand, Henry, and Maximilian, the old allies of Bretagne, yet now united, not merely by their advantage, but by the blood of their children.

All that now remained was that, if not Henry, at all events Ferdinand and Maximilian should, as they had agreed, invade France. But this scheme was confronted by the consideration that hereby Ferdinand had some-

[1] Baco, p. 268. Treaty in Rymer. Wagenaar, Allgem. Gesch. ii. 269.
[2] Zurita, pp. 88, 99.
[3] Hume and Rapin, besides Baco and Polydorus Virgilius, the source of all.
[4] Zurita, p. 134.
[5] Buchanan 488 (note to new edition). From the information given by Bergenroth, "Calendar of State Papers," i. p. 97, it is plain that the chief impetus to this alliance was given by the Catholic kings, who only regretted that they had not two daughters to dispose of, so as to be able to marry one to the King of England and the other to the King of the Scots, and therefore counselled that a marriage should be arranged between the latter and the daughter of the former.

thing to lose, whilst Maximilian would gain. Between Aragon and France there lay certain frontiers, where ravaging was so regular, that whenever anyone went on a pilgrimage, or took to him a wife, he had to submit to a good rifling at the hands of both parties. Thus in this war also, Enrique Enriquez crossed the frontier, and pillaged for three days and three nights on the other side; thereupon well-armed Gascons, Swiss and French, appeared, and the French succeeded in surprising the Castle of Saulses; and hereupon, out of apprehension for Roussillon, Ferdinand concluded a truce.[1] Maximilian was discontented with these doings. Not only the death of Charles, but a new phase of German politics, aroused him to fresh hopes.

After his return from Italy, his prestige in the Empire was at first at a low ebb. The Elector of the Palatinate was on good terms with Charles, sent knights into his pay, entreated a good reception for his merchants, and delegates of both sides held meetings.[2]

The setting aside of the Decrees of Worms made the Elector of Mayence extremely discontented. He openly complained of Maximilian: "From above to below there was little trace of earnestness; contrary to their resolutions Milan and Savoy had been regranted; he was ill pleased to find that ordinances were made and sealed, and yet not adhered to; in this way the Empire could not possibly maintain its position."[3] Maximilian also perceived that he could not undertake anything, until he had gained over both Electors and the Chancellor of Mayence, Doctor Stürzler. He never put in an appearance at any meeting of the Diet. However, in consequence of the death of the elder Eberhard of Wurtemberg, he effected a change. For the former, whilst appointing for his cousin and heir a council of twelve men, four from each estate, without whom he could do nothing, but who without him could

---

[1] Hubert Thomas Leodius, Vita Frederici Palatini, ii. No. 45. Comines, 581. Zurita, 79, 114.

[2] Epistolæ Galliæ Regis Caroli et Philippi Archipalatini, in Ludewig; Reliquiæ Manuscriptorum, vi. 96.

[3] Müller, Reichstagstheatrum, ii. 144. Also in Hegewisch. Leben Maximilians, i. 144, and in Menzel.

discharge the daily business of the State, and perform even the most important functions, if he did not accept their invitation to appear,[1] had entrusted to this Government his principles, and his devotion to the Emperor. But was it likely that the younger Eberhard would follow his cousin after his death, seeing that he never cared to follow him in his lifetime? Immediately after his arrival, he dismissed the old Councillors, took a prisoner, a Doctor Holzinger, out of gaol, and made him Chancellor. Thereupon Hug von Werdenberg refused to be Chamberlain longer; the twelve complained that Eberhard intended to surrender the estates to the Count Palatine; but the estates were not minded to agree to that. They took his servant prisoner, and seized his cities. He escaped with silver and jewels to Ulm. The Estates, the new Chamberlain, the Councillors, the Chancery, the officials and the courtiers turned against him, and renounced their allegiance.[2] Maximilian, alarmed for the estrangement of the country, hurried thither, and heard both sides. But for what purpose? It seems that he had previously decided upon his verdict, " that both land and Councillors had acted aright; the young Ulrich should be Duke under the guardianship of the twelve, and later should receive Sabina, the King's niece, to wife; but that the country should not, as was formerly determined, pass to the Empire, but fall to Austria."[3]

Eberhard renounced his duchy, repented of his action, fled to the Count Palatine, assigned to him his silver plate and all right and title to his land, repented of that also, and was imprisoned in Lindenfels until his death. But Wurtemberg was devoted to the King.[4]

In the new prestige that the treaty with Wurtemberg had gained for him, Maximilian appeared in June, 1498,[5] in the Reichstag at Freiburg, which had eight months previously commenced. On this occasion he received from the

[1] Esslinger, treaty of Eisenbach; Geschichte Ulrichs von Württemberg.
[2] Ufkündigung der Pflicht, in Sattler, i., Suppl. No. 12. Document A., p. 157. Naucleri Chronographia, at end.
[3] Sattler's Geschichten, p. 32. Mandat Lünig, ii. 722.
[4] Sattler, 33. Eisenbach.
[5] Neidhart's letter to the Reichstag, in Datt, p. 594.

estates 70,000 guilders, without reckoning what had been received by the "pfennig" tax in his hereditary lands.[1] It appeared now possible for him to acquire Burgundy, if not Bretagne. With this hope he let his army advance to the frontiers of Burgundy. The bold lansquenets boasted that if the victory was this time theirs, France and Switzerland also would be in their power.[2]

[1] Datt, p. 904.
[2] Hugi, Vogt zu Domeck, in Glutzblotzheim.

CHAPTER IV.

THE FALL OF THE HOUSE OF SFORZA AND ARAGON.

1. *Louis XII. and Venice against Milan.*

THE situation was now as follows. The attacks of the French upon Naples and Milan had leagued the King of Spain and the Pope with Ferrantino, and Venice and Maximilian with Lodovico. Ferrantino had mainly been saved by Ferdinand, whilst Lodovico owed his safety principally to Venice. In the midst of the dissensions that Charles's advent had produced in Mid-Italy, a Spanish general from the one side and Maximilian himself from the other had taken the field against the French party. This party had been completely defeated. Round and about France itself there had become formed, in the interest of the League, an alliance of all potentates.

Relying upon this, Maximilian, in the summer of 1498, undertook a three-fold attack upon France. He sent one corps against Langres,[1] a second against Chalons,[2] and a third, under the command of his Marshal of the free county, Guillaume de Vergy, against Dijon and Burgundy.[3] Three thousand Swiss were in his pay. He expected the help of the Liga, and considered himself assured of success. But the first corps was weakened and lamed in its movements by the heat, which suffocated the horsemen in armour, and also by a want of provisions, which was increased by the soldiers, who, impatient to see fire, preferred to burn down the rich villages to plundering them. The second was driven back by the rains. The third saw the enemy approach and retire, but concluded a treaty.[4] This

---

[1] Life of Götz von Berlichingen, p. 7.
[2] Zurita, f. 152.
[3] Fugger's MS. in Kurzbeck's notes to Weiskunig.
[4] Weiskunig, 260.

campaign was crowned with so little success, that it has been overlooked by all later historians.

These failures were due to the fact that the Liga at this precise moment had ceased to exist. Ferrantino was now dead, and his successor was hated by the King of Spain. Venice was in feud and almost in open war with Lodovico on account of Pisa. But the new King of France succeeded in gaining for himself those who had defended Milan, as also him who had defended Naples. He drew the Pope to his side, and repulsed the attacks of Maximilian. He made matters look at the moment as though there never had been a Liga. It is our acquaintance, the Duke of Orleans, now King Louis XII.

He was standing, the story goes, at his window, without knowing that Charles was dead or even ill, when the royal bodyguard drew up before him, and shouted "Vivats" to their new Lord and King.[1] On this he spoke, as well as he knew how, in terms of laudation of Charles VIII., sprinkled his body with holy water,[2] and received the fealty of the Grandees.

Louis was a perfectly developed man, more in the apogee than in the perigee of life, and already a little afflicted with the gout.[3] That wildness of his early youth, when his chamberlains dared not chastise him unless disguised —for fear he should revenge himself—that impetuousness of later days, disclosed at revelries, tournaments, and in domestic wars, were passed and gone.[4] Still he was more vigorous than any other prince, and chivalrous to boot. The first thing he conceived he ought to guard was his honour. Whoever attacked him, or accused him of the smallest breach of faith, would be contradicted with the sword. After that, his lands and his rights were nearest to his heart. "I will endure everything," said he, "save where my honour and my lands are concerned."[5] He had not such bold plans as had Charles, and had not Maximilian's love of conquest. Only his rights he was resolved to assert,

[1] Corio, Storia di Milano, 967.
[2] Extrait d'une histoire in Godefroy, 198.
[3] Maximilian to Esslingen, in Datt, 564.
[4] Extrait de l'histoire de Louis, 337.
[5] Zurita. Macchiavelli, Legazione, v. 355.

and therefore did not select a "Plus Ultra," but a porcupine for a symbol. It was he who was the author of that grand saying, "The King does not avenge what has been done to the Duke." He preferred to sell his demesnes for the purpose of carrying on his wars, to exhausting his poor subjects with taxes.¹ The same feeling made him forbearing and kind towards others. But increasing years made him more saving every day. His first action was to defray the expense of his predecessor's interment at Blois out of the savings of his own private exchequer.²

The internal government he committed from the first into the hands of the Archbishop of Rouen, George d'Amboise. When at the Court of Louis XI., George had taken the side of the present King, even in opposition to his own brother. For his sake he had suffered imprisonment, for endeavouring to advantage him at the expense of Charles VIII. They were only three years apart in respect of age, and devoted one to the other with perfect confidence; and, especially since Dunois' decease, George was entirely in the confidence of his master.³

The first duty of the King and his Archbishop was to provide that the internal peace was perfectly assured. Charles's sister, Anna of Bourbon, demanded, at all events, a compensation for the increment her grandfather, her father, and brother, had acquired for the Crown. She was content when her daughter Susanna was guaranteed an almost relinquished right of succession in all the possessions of her house.⁴ The Prince of Orange regained his sovereignty. As many of them as had been afraid of Louis, because they had offended him whilst Duke,—perhaps in his feud with the Queen Regent,—were comforted, when he showed a mark of favour to the brave Tremouille, who had formerly taken him prisoner, and marked the names of the others with the red cross of pardon.⁵ Only he would not brook any limitation of the

---

¹ Monstrelet, 249.
² Histoire de Charles in Godefroy, 169.
³ Le Gendre: Vie d'Amboise, 12, 27, 39.
⁴ Zurita. Garnièr, Hist. de France, tom. xxi.
⁵ Vie et gestes de la Tremouille, 158.

rights of the Crown. A new tribunal decided against René's claims to Provence. The weightiest question that he had to determine concerned Bretagne, which by Charles's marriage with Anna had become attached to the Crown, but which, owing to his death, had now become separated from it again. Louis XII. did not scruple to divorce his wife Johanna,[1] in order to re-marry with his predecessor's heiress, Anna. Johanna was certainly not beautiful, neither had she borne him children. She now betook herself to Bourges, where she entered with some sisters into the order of the Annunciation, was most charitable to the poor, and was reverenced as a saint[2] by the people, who always remained attached to her.

Anna made it a condition that Bretagne should neither pay taxes, nor have officials appointed in it, nor be called upon to make war, without her special permission. Louis blended on his coins the arms of Bretagne and France.[3]

Upon other coins, as soon as he had entered Paris, he styled himself King of Naples and Milan.[4] He was certain of his rights to these countries, he had fought for both; and he now wished to enforce them. It was a great advantage to him that the Liga collapsed, nay, that one-half even took his side. After Enrique Enriquez had been killed in a revolution at Perpignan, and Roussillon was threatened by the French, and was not minded to defend itself, Ferdinand concluded a treaty with Louis, securing his own interests and the possessions of the House of Burgundy; yet it did not include Federigo.[5] The Pope hoped to obtain from Louis so many advantages for his house, that he was quite ready to pronounce the divorce from Johanna. The Venetians sent him sixty falcons from Candia and two hundred valuable furs, as a coronation present.[6]

The successive enterprises of Louis with the Venetians, with the Pope, and with Ferdinand, are distinguished more by unity of event than by unity of action. Never

[1] Decret in Nicole Gilles, Chroniques de France, 118.
[2] Hottingeri Historia Ecclesiastica.
[3] Coins in Daniel, Hist. de France, iv. 596.
[4] Coin in Daniel, 597.
[5] Zurita, 140.
[6] Petrus Justinianus, Historiæ Venetæ, 359.

more than one of his allies was engaged at a time; they appear as so many distinct and different enterprises.

The first was the expedition against Milan. It was supported by the feud between Venice and Lodovico.

After Savonarola's death, when the Florentines again attacked Pisa, Lodovico took the side of the assailants, for it belonged to them; Venice sided with the attacked, for a man ought to keep his word of honour. Hereupon, the Venetians won over Pitigliano, and Lodovico the Marchese of Mantua. The former threatened a French alliance, the latter replied that such would be to their own damage. In the Council of the Pregadi conflicting opinions were expressed; some old fathers could not conceal their apprehensions; others were for combating Lodovico unaided. Others again, those who detested him to the bottom of their hearts:—for if ever they had a secret plan would he not at once adopt public measures to thwart it, and a neighbour, served by their traitors, was the most intolerable of all:—this third party proposed an alliance with France.[1] How could Lodovico believe that they, who had waged a great war against a man, because they would not have him for a neighbour when Duke, would call him in, after he had become King? He never apprehended this. He continued his hostile operations against Pisa, without paying any attention to the Venetians, who supplied it with both money and men.

In this quarrel he really retained the upper hand. Paolo Vitelli was entrusted by him with the command of the Florentines, and, with his assistance, he succeeded, between June and October, 1498, in taking castle after castle round about Pisa, as well as Vico and Librafatta, and in reducing the city to extremities. Against him the Venetians tried first of all their own resources. They knew that they were deceived by the lords in the Romagna, and yet they enlisted them. Thus they were enabled to place a large body of cavalry in the field, though not without the heaviest expense; 16,600 horse in all. They then, now by Bologna and now by Perugia

---

[1] Chronicon Venetum, 53-57.

and now again by Siena, attempted to threaten Florence itself which lay on the other side of the Apennines. On one occasion Alvian succeeded in crossing over, and stood against Paolo Vitelli.[1] But though their men hurried by day and night to his succour through the Ferrarian land, no less did the Sanseverins, Lodovico's cavalry, spur their horses, and ride day and night to come to Vitelli's aid at Forli, Imola, and Faenza. At last great detachments, as many as 300 men at once, deserted from the Venetian camp, which was shut up in the hills, " for they had neither straw, nor money, nor bread." Others dashed after them to take from them the recruiting-money, until the whole army became disbanded; so that this undertaking resulted in failure for Venice.[2] In their indignation at this ill-fortune, " for which Lodovico was alone to blame," they resolved on a campaign against him himself. They left Ercole of Ferrare, who was not even their particular friend, to settle the Pisa affair. Meanwhile, they made a proposal to King Louis: they offered to assist him with 6,000 horse in an expedition against Milan, on condition that he would guarantee them a portion of the territory of Cremona and Ghiara d'Adda. The King no sooner saw the conditions than he acceded. On the 10th of February the agreement was arrived at. He that had attacked Lodovico, and the city that had mainly defended him, were now both leagued together against him.[3] Lodovico was not dismayed. He considered himself the most sagacious man in Italy. On one occasion, when the papal master of the ceremonies wished to explain to him how to address a cardinal, he answered, " Have you ever seen a Duke of Milan who has done what I have done? I shall know also how to act on this occasion."[4] In Milan there might often be seen a painting of a rose branch, with the motto, "With time," or a painter's brush, with the motto, "With merit and time."[5] The mulberry tree, " that only shoots forth its leaves when

[1] Nardi, Istorie Fiorent. Nardi, Vita di Tebalducci, 57, 63. Bembus, Histor. Venet. 87.
[2] Diarium Ferrarense, 355, 357.
[3] Chronicon Venetum, 67-72. Bembus, 93.
[4] Burcardi Diarium, viii. 63.
[5] Leunclavius, Pandectæ Historiæ Turcicæ, 193.

spring is at hand, and then quicker than all other trees," he may perhaps have regarded as the emblem of his cleverness.[1] He said, "In one hand he had peace, and in the other war; but even in war a quill pen could do more than the sword."[2]

Time was the only thing his shrewdness took into calculation, in other respects it employed the boldest schemes and the most dangerous means. Alfonso of Calabria assisted him against Venice, and Venice against Alfonso. His country was on one occasion defended for him by the Duke of Orleans, notwithstanding he desired it for himself, and on another by Maximilian, to whom it belonged of right. His cavalry had emblazoned on their standard a Moor with his right hand holding back an eagle's wing, and with the left strangling a dragon. Lodovico was a gambler, who staked the whole of his existence upon a throw of the dice; for he knew the dice belonged to him. He only accepted advice from the stars. He never concluded a truce, even for three days, without consulting his astrologer.[3]

I cannot say what his astrologer may have told him on this occasion; but, as things were, he needed not to be much alarmed. His brother Ascanio—a man ever full of schemes and secrets, and untiring[4]—was with him, and kept the Gibellines, as he did the Guelphs, on his side; under these circumstances, he was justified in feeling assured of his country. Should he then fear an attack on the part of Venice? In the Turks he could arouse an enemy to that city, who would keep it sufficiently employed. Or should the lances of the French strike terror into his breast? He had other and stronger fortresses to throw in their way. More dangerous it would be if Louis enlisted Swiss; for no Italian infantry could cope with these. But Lodovico also was firmly allied with Schwyz and Unterwalden, and with Berne and Lucerne;[5] and in case these could not prevent an enlistment being

---

[1] Jovius, Elogia Virorum bellica virtute illustrium, 196.
[2] Chronicon Venetum, 53.
[3] Benedicti Diarium, 1611, 1623.
[4] Arluni, de bello Veneto, i. 22.
[5] Tschudi MS. in Fuchs, Mailändische Feldzüge, i. 234.

made by the French, they could, at all events, easily provide him with an equal number of their men, whom he could lead against the King. In this way he was on an equal footing with his enemies. Through his alliance with Maximilian, and through the lansquenets who, in consequence, were at his disposal, he was even superior to them. Besides, it did not so much depend upon the collective strength of the States, as upon how much money each could employ. Lodovico was thus of good heart. Three years previously he had had coins struck, one of which had a device of a snake, his emblem, guarding a lily, and another that of a snake bending down the cup of a lily, a sign of his power over France:[1] at this time he had a picture in his hall of an Italy full of cocks, hens, and chickens—intended to represent Gauls and French—and in the midst of them a Moor sweeping them out with a broom.[2]

2. *Swiss and Suabians implicated in the War.*

Maximilian was as much interested in this struggle as Lodovico.

Valentina, Louis' grandmother, had a hundred years previously helped to kindle the deadly enmity between Burgundy and Orleans. An Orleans was now reigning in France, and possessed even Burgundy; and the head of the House of Burgundy was King of the Germans, and demanded Burgundy back. The Sforza, whom the former attacked for his grandmother's sake, the latter was bound to defend for the sake of his wife. The Duke of Guelders, who was related to Louis, Maximilian plotted to destroy for being a rebel to him; so that they were enemies on three accounts.

Although Maximilian's son, Philip, had been obliged to promise never to attempt to take Burgundy by force of arms, and moreover to serve King Louis against every

---

[1] In Rosmini, Trivulzio, i. 255 (engraving of).
[2] Nardi, Istorie, viii. 63.

soul without any exception,[1] yet he was never inclined for peace: "peace was like corn that had been harvested while yet unripe; by peace he would never conquer his land." In vain René and Frederick the Wise endeavoured to mediate.[2] Forthwith in the country of the Duke of Guelders, who had received French aid, the war was continued which had been already waged at Livorno, and on the Saône.

It is evident how closely Lodovico and Maximilian were allied. Lodovico desired no treaty with France, if the German King had none, for he cared not to sever himself from him.[3] Maximilian repeated: "the Duke would be able to defend himself without foreign aid; but, in case he could not do so, he would in person come to his assistance with the whole strength of the Holy Empire, and protect Milan as well as the Tyrol."[4]

As, owing to this alliance, the balance of power was in Lodovico's favour, it was important for the French King to try to occupy the German King in another way. He could cause him trouble in Germany, and there are letters extant, wherein he reminds the Count Palatine of the century-long alliance of their dynasties, and promises one of his sons a pension at his Court, and to another high ecclesiastical dignities.[5] But how, if he found ways and means of attaching the Swiss to himself, so as to be enabled to avail himself of their infantry; to ally them so closely with himself that Lodovico would receive no assistance from them, and at the same time to involve them in war with Maximilian, so that he would have to fear for himself, and would not dare to come to the assistance of another?

Without any action on his part, the desired opportunity arose. The incident that in the year 1498, George Gossenbrod von Augsburg, Royal Councillor of Tyrol, journeyed with his wife to the watering-place of Pfäffers,[6] and there

---

[1] Jean Amis, Procès Verbal, in Garnier, xxi. 108.
[2] Zurita, f. 121. Spalatin, Life of Frederic the Wise, 78.
[3] Lodovico to Brascha in Rosmini, ii. 256.
[4] Somentius to Lodovico in Rosmini, 258.
[5] Instruction of Mathieu Pelleyt in Ludewig, Reliquiæ, vi. 117.
[6] Stettler, Chronik des Uechtlandes, p. 329.

met an enemy, Count Jörg von Sargans,[1] and that the latter tried to take him prisoner, was ordained to determine the course of public affairs, and bring this great struggle to a head.

Count Jörg had once schemed to bring the Tyrol to the crown of Bavaria, and on that account had been outlawed by the King.[2] Unconcerned thereat, he lived with only one cook in the castle of Ortenstein by selling his estates, and slept in the tower, where his bed may still be seen; for he was on terms of friendship with the monks of Chur, and made common cause with them. The Abbot in Pfäffers, to whom Gossenbrod thanked his preservation and who was also a friend of Maximilian—the latter confided to him his schemes and successes—was forced by Jörg to leave his monastery. Now between Chur and the Tyrol there had existed, since time out of mind, differences, which had lately been revived. These differences affected the Engadin as far as Pontalt, where their frontiers touched the jurisdiction of the Minster in the Münsterthal, to which both laid claim, as also the hereditary office of cup-bearer, which Maximilian declined to receive, as former Counts had done, as a fief from Chur.[3] Gossenbrod availed himself of this feud to take revenge. He mocked the monks of Chur and encouraged the Tyrolese, until the latter, who had been posted by him in strong detachments on the border,[4] invaded and took the Münsterthal; the others at once sallied out and recovered it. Upon this, both appealed to their allies; the monks summoned to their aid the "Upper League" and the ten tribunals, with which they formed the "Grey League," and the people of Uri, with six other Swiss towns, with whom they had allied themselves since 1497, and "until the end of all things";[5] and these all called in all the others who were members of the federation.

The Tyrol called to its assistance the princes, lords, and cities of the Suabian Confederation.[6] In a trice the whole frontier bristled with arms; on the one side the Swiss, and

[1] Müller's Schweizer Geschichte, v. p. 322.
[2] Müller, p. 190.   [3] Münster, Cosmographie, p. 763.
[4] Pirkheimer, de bello Helvetico, p. 13.
[5] Simleri Respublica Helvetiorum, p. 36.
[6] Gasser, Augsburger Chronik, p. 258.

on the other the lansquenets; each waited to see what the other would do.

This was not a plot of the King of France, yet the event relieved him of perplexity. It was, as yet, doubtful whether there would be war or not, for Maximilian could not be anxious for it, and, moreover, on the 5th February, 1499, the decree [1] of Lucerne declared that terms had been arrived at, and that it was doubtful whether the places that favoured Milan would join the others. It came to pass quite spontaneously. In German countries it frequently happens that between neighbouring hides and marks, but most especially on the border, there arises an enmity engendered of boasting, scoffing, and claims; a hatred such as exists between two brothers who have quarrelled, and which is the more intense in proportion as its cause is less recent. The least occasion arouses it. So here, when the Swiss, thinking peace was assured, retired from their frontier and passed through Gutenberg, the German lansquenets crept on all fours over the walls and lowed at one another like cows. Where the Rhine separated the two peoples, the Germans dressed up a cow, danced with it and cried that they had the bride, and the others should send them the bridegroom. In Bendre they christened a calf "Amman Reding;" [2] and amused themselves at Constance, Dieffenhofen, and elsewhere with variations of the same joke. Enraged thereat, some Zurichers and Zugers crossed the Rhine on the 6th of February, routed the enemy, and ran across hedge and ditch away to the Lake of Constance, where they again defeated the lansquenets, whose leaders had become desponding and wished to return, with such onslaught, that they drove some of them into the ditches, where they were drowned, others into the morasses, where they died of cold, others fled before them to Ulm and Augsburg, where they told their tale of terror.[3]

This event made war a certainty and united the Swiss. Schwyz and Unterwalden-in-the-forest, Lucerne and Berne had already joined the Liga; and Glarus wanted to

[1] Abschied in Glutzblotzheim, p. 77.
[2] Stettler, 331. Edlibach and Tschudi in Glutzblotzheim.
[3] Pirkheimer, de bello Helvetico, p. 14. Tschudi.

be the fifth canton to do so.[1] They had joined it in Maximilian's interest, who, owing to this, had Swiss envoys with him on his Livorno expedition, and Swiss soldiers in his expedition against Burgundy. The same cantons were allies of Lodovico. But now this League, if not expressly opposed to Lodovico, was certainly in arms against Maximilian, by whose counsellors the feud had been caused, and whose lansquenets had made it burst forth. The confederation held better together than did the Liga; all the cantons united for war. Louis saw it, and being himself on good terms with Venice and the Pope, and as in the interior of Germany, the Houses of the Palatinate and Bavaria-Landshut, both opposed to the Austrians, were most closely allied, he offered the Swiss his alliance.[2] Although Lodovico let it be known that he "had never supported the Suabians, and he desired to be mediator between them and the Swiss,"[3] for he too saw the danger, and although there were many among the Swiss who were opposed to a war with Austria, yet the contrary opinion was the prevailing one: "for what had the House of Austria ever done for them, save abuse in words and war in deed; but that was the way to bring its plans to nought." On the 21st March, 1499, they all concluded a treaty in these terms:[4] "The King promises to assist them in their wars with men and money, and to give in peace, besides, to every canton 2,000 Rhenish guilders annually, in return for which they concede to him free enlistment, and to no one else in opposition to him;"[5] and appended their ten seals to the document. They then emblazoned the Crucifixion on their standards and guarded their frontiers.[6]

High among the mountains, where spring the sources of the Inn and the Etsch, along the Rhine valley lying between the Senniwald of Appenzell and the red wall of the Vorarlberg, on both shores of the Lake of Constance, down

[1] Stettler, 325-328.   [2] Tschudi in Fuchs, p. 239.
[3] From Lodovico's letter, p. 240.
[4] Stettler, 337. Glbl., p. 93.
[5] Anshelm Berner Chronik, ii. p. 360 (note to new edition).
[6] Unrest, Oesterreichische Chronik in Hahn, collectio monumentorum, tom. i. p. 803.

to where the Rhine has finished his course and leaps downwards to the plain, they stood; "Grey Leaguers" against Tyrolese, Appenzeller, and St. Gallers against the King's lansquenets and countrymen, the nine cantons in Thurgau against Constance, and the cities of the Suabian League, with Zurich and Solothurn, against the nobles of Sundgau and Hegau. Between them flowed the Rhine and adorned both its banks with the gorgeous mantle of spring. But among them many a Suabian might have been heard to boast, how he would fire and burn in the enemy's country, that St. Peter would not for the very smoke be able to find the gate of heaven; and, should he die, his comrades were conjured to crush his bones to make powder wherewith to exterminate the foe.[1] The Swiss, on their side, swore by the saints that they would take no prisoners, but slay all their enemies, as their fathers had done before them.[2] The former only wished to vent their hatred, the latter to protect their freedom that was threatened; and thus they waged their war.

At the same time, the confederates on one occasion crossed the Rhine to attack the Wallgauers, whilst the Leaguers crossed the bridge of Constance against the Schwaderloch. Hereupon the "Landsturm" was called out; on the Suabian side, by the firing of shots, and on the Swiss side by smoke, and the people ran to their places of rendezvous. Thurgauans, Bischofzellers, and St. Gallers assembled at the Schwaderloch to the assistance of the whole League, and sallied forth to find the lansquenets. These were already on their way home, their waggons full of corn,[3] and their muskets and field-pieces hung with pans, kettles, and all manner of pillage. But their enemies, by taking shorter roads through the woods, caught them up and engaged them in bloody encounters, and only when the leader of the infantry, Burkard von Randeck, who was considered the bitterest foe of the Swiss, had fallen, and the leader of the horse, Wolf von Fürstenberg, had taken flight after a

---

[1] Stettler, p. 331 (note to new edition), Anshelm, ii. p. 302.
[2] Proclamation of 11th March and a Military Ordinance in Glutzblotzheim, p. 86.
[3] Tschudi in Gltzbl., p. 103.

chivalrous struggle, the lansquenets left both their muskets and booty behind, and fled towards the city-bridge, and to the ships in the lake.[1] This was the battle of Schwaderloch.

Meanwhile Allgauer, Etschländer, and Suabians collected at Frastenz. The miners came out of their pits, arrayed themselves in steel, vaunted themselves greatly, and came to the battle. They did not dare to follow up their enemy, but entrenched themselves behind ramparts, and so awaited his onslaught. Above them, on the top of the Lanzengast were posted 300 rifles, and at its foot the miners.[2] The Swiss advanced against them in two divisions; a compact body against the rampart in the valley, whilst sharpshooters to the number of 2,000 scaled the Lanzengast. Heini Wolleb rode at head of the first detachment of the 2,000; he then dismounted, ordered them to kneel, and said the Lord's prayer: he cried, "in God's name follow me." He led them through the ravines, where each one had to draw up his fellow by his lance,[3] first into the fire of the rifles, and then into close quarters with them, until they were routed; this done, they attacked the miners, and drove their first and second line behind their entrenchments; and here, already victorious, he met with the main body.[4] With united forces, they scaled the great barricade, and saw the enemy drawn up in three bodies, in act of preparing his guns for action. For one moment they threw themselves flat on the ground, until the shots had passed over their heads: they then wanted to rise up. "Not yet, confederates!" cried Heini, "wait for another salvo, and then at them." They all knelt down except himself. He, a tall, powerful man, stood up in the midst of all to maintain discipline; careful for all, but fearless for himself. The bullets flew again, but all missed save one, and this laid him low. "Lay me by and attack them," he cried.[5] Within two hours the Suabians had been driven from their camp. The corpses with their red crosses floated down to Feldkirch. The Wallgauer

[1] Pirkheimer, p. 15.
[2] Stettler, p. 341.
[3] Tschudi in Gltzbl., p. 99.
[4] Hauptman und Fähndrich an Luzern, Glutzblotzheim, p. 522.
[5] Stettler, 342.

came even upon the battle-field to the victors with the sacrament, priests, women, and children, and begged for mercy.[1] The Suabians took comfort and said, " Where is now your Wolleb ? " The Swiss replied, " He is playing dice with Randeck."

The Swiss were everywhere in advantage. From Thiengen the lansquenets retired before them in their shirts, a white staff and a piece of bread in their hands.[2] The lady of Blumeneck carried her husband away from the castle as the dearest treasure that she was allowed to take. On the Malsian heath the three bands of the Tyrolese fled before the "Grey Leaguers" when the horn of Uri echoed from afar.[3] The King's troops, on the other hand, climbed the topmost hills commanding the Engadine, and pursued the enemy down the side. But when they had reached the valley, they found the bridges, across which they had to go, on fire, villages, in which they intended to pass the night, in flames, and stores that they wanted to eat, all destroyed. They, the plunderers, had to pluck grass to satisfy the cravings of hunger, and were half mad from want ; the fresh waters of these mountains were their sole comfort.[4]

Such was the character of this war : on neither side was the motive love of conquest. No! it was merely defence and revenge. They entrench themselves, sally forth, pillage, plunder, burn, and return home again. The neighbouring cities might easily, at that time, have joined the League of the Confederates (but these were as cruel as their enemies), and throughout the whole of Suabia, on every Wednesday and Saturday, after the sermon, they prayed for the League, the widows and orphans, and the general peace.[5] Conquest was not the intention of the Swiss either; their war served no one save the King of France.

And so it came about that Maximilian became involved in a desperate struggle. Lodovico had to forego all assistance from him, and found himself, as he was

---

[1] Münster, Cosmographie, p. 631.
[2] Stettler, 343. Tschudi and Anshelm in Gltzbl.
[3] Stettler, 345.
[4] Pirkheimer, 19-21.
[5] Crusii Annales Suevorum, i. 513.

his ally, even deprived of Swiss aid. Danger threatened him, if the French succeeded at the same time in leading Swiss against Milan. To effect an arrangement with the Swiss, Lodovico sent Galeazzo Visconti with thirty horses across Wallis to Berne. Schwyz, at all events, declared for him, but all to no purpose: he could not bring about any arrangement.[1] There was only one way of escape, viz., if Maximilian were to engage the Swiss in such a conflict, that they would forget to lend their aid to others.

In July, 1499, Maximilian came upon the scene. The daily invitations addressed to him by his people had at last induced him to leave those enemies in Guelders he was for ever pursuing, and never catching. In an open letter to the estates of the realm he enumerated the crimes the Confederates had committed against the Empire and Austria; and he succeeded in raising a considerable number to assist him. In a short time, a strong army of the Empire and the League was assembled at Constance. The soldiers of Guelders and Burgundy were at Dorneck under the command of Count Fürstenberg, He felt sure of success.[2] If the Swiss ever really offered him, as is related, that they would serve the Empire, and wage his wars against the Turks, it must have been on this occasion.[3]

He threw them into great alarm and trepidation, yet did not succeed in preventing them from joining the French. Yet when Louis XII. made them a proposal in these terms, " He was taking the field, in order to take his hereditary land of Milan; how if his allies showed themselves on the hills with only three thousand men?", the Cantons refused him this request; but a few thousand individuals were induced by his pay—for their Fatherland had nothing to give them—to forget their country, and, in spite of all, to join the King's *hommes d'armes*, who were collecting at Asti.[4]

The issue to be fought out by both sides lay alone in

[1] Fuchs, 242. Weiskunig, 271.
[2] Weiskunig, 261. A letter in the Swiss Museum and in Glutzblotzheim, 113.
[3] Unrest, Oesterreich, Chronik in Hahn, Collect. Monument., i. 803.
[4] Tschudi MS. in Fuchs. Proclamation of 22 June.

arms and open war. If only Maximilian was victorious over the Swiss, Lodovico could join the Suabian League, and this might come to protect Milan.[1]

On the 13th July, 1499, with his artillery, and accompanied by knights in coats of mail and waving plumes, Maximilian advanced over the bridge of Constance against the Schwaderloch. Scarcely recognizable in his old green tunic and his great hat, he rode about and gave his commands. The Eagle of the Empire waved in the hand of the Schenk of Limburg. The astrologers prophesied success. He waited for the enemies to come down from the mountains; but they did not come. He therefore resolved to hunt them out in their native hills; and many of his followers expected, as he himself did, to strike a grand blow. But his nobles remembered Sempach and Charles the Bold. Should they spill their noble blood upon peasants?[2] The captains of his Wurtembergers declared that, "they were tired out with marching, and must wait for the strength of the whole Confederation to come up." They would not follow him. The King threw away his glove, and rode off; they returned hastily to the city.[3]

After this, Count Fürstenberg, at all events, resolved to make a raid from Dorneck. One day a provost of the Cathedral at Bâle had a banquet prepared in the Cathedral tower, in order, with his friends, to look out upon Dorneck in flames. The same day, Nicholas Conrad, bailiff of Solothurn, sat at table at Liechstall, when he learnt that the castle was threatened. He did not wait for the other Federals to come up, but with his own followers mounted the heights above the enemy's camp. The horsemen were scattered about the villages; the lansquenets were drinking and dancing, or else shouting and quarrelling, their captains made themselves comfortable in long clothing. Upon this camp the bailiff fell, and the Bernese and Zurichers followed him. At first it looked as if they must succeed without more ado.[4] But when the disciplined

---

[1] Lodovico to Stanga in Rosmini, ii. 261.
[2] Götz von Berlichingen Leben, 19. Münster, Cosmographie, 632.
[3] Coccinus, de bellis Italicis, ap. Freherum, ii. 278. Tschudi.
[4] Dornecker, Song and Letter of the Bernese Captains in the Appendix to Glutzblotzheim, 524, 526. Stettler, 352.

lansquenets had drawn themselves up in line, and were supported by their cavalry, it was doubtful, and some Swiss fled into the woods near the Scharfenflue. All at once horns and shouts and the sound of feet. Both sides looked up to see who was coming, and which party's lot was to be victory and life, and whose defeat and death. There appeared a flag, folded like a banner; it was the flag of Lucerne. The brave fellows, the Lucerners and Zugers, had been informed of the battle that was raging and had seen the fugitives in the wood; they forthwith hung up their knapsacks on a great pear tree,[1] came, and fell upon the enemy. The Federals, thereupon, took courage, and the lansquenets lost heart. Count Heinrich fell, and four thousand men with him. Maximilian's hopes were over. At first he shut himself up in his castle at Lindau, and would not admit any of the princes; but soon he composed himself. In the evening he opened his door, and dined in public; he then gazed from his window at the stars, and spoke of their nature.[2] He was inclined for peace; accepted Galeazzo's mediation, and consulted with him at Schaffhausen. But before any terms were arrived at—nay, even before any regular meetings had taken place, even whilst fighting was going on in Hegau, and Laufenberg was being threatened,—the French threw themselves upon Lodovico.

Lodovico saw his fate approaching. Against him was arrayed, on the one side, the same Trivulzio whom only three years previously he had publicly denounced with the words that "a halter awaited him as soon as caught;" the same Trivulzio, against whom he had roused warrior upon warrior to prove to him his treachery and cowardice; that Trivulzio, of whom he had at last had a picture exhibited in all his cities, representing him as hanging by the legs,[3] had now 1,500 lances and 15,000 men on foot under his command. On the other side, the Venetians were arming against him. He had hoped for assistance from the Swiss, but they were leagued with his enemies. He had hoped in the Germans, but they were engaged in war with the

---

[1] Inscription by Gerber, *vide* Glutzblotzheim, p. 134.
[2] Pirkheimer, p. 24.
[3] Documents in Rosmini, ii. 224, 244; i. 276, 299.

Swiss. He had hoped even a little in the Arrabiati at Florence; but they were engaged on a campaign against Pisa. Finally, he had relied upon Bajazeth; but how could Bajazeth help him? for Venice was fitting out two armies, one against the Turks, and one against him.[1] At this critical moment, all his foreign alliances, that had made him what he was, failed. The pen availed him nothing; the sword could alone decide. He still relied upon his castles, and those favourites in them, whom he had from the first honoured more than his party; he still hoped in his two armies on his two frontiers, who were not to engage the enemy in open battle, but to come to the assistance of the menaced castles; he hoped, finally, in the fidelity of his Milanese, whose beneficent lord he had ever been.

But even this calculation proved false. For castle after castle surrendered as soon as Trivulzio showed himself. Those favourites of Lodovico were Guelphs, and their head, Trivulzio, was more to them than he was. The garrison of Valenza had just prepared itself to give the enemy battle outside the walls, and awaited his attack, when the commander, Donato, let him in through the castle, and they saw themselves taken in the rear. At one stroke, Dertona, Voghera, and the whole country across the Po was lost. It is said that Trivulzio had brought with him 300,000 escus for the commanders; that Donato received 5,000; and that there was no custos, and no official in any castle in the Milanese land, that had not been bribed.[2]

Everything now depended upon the saving of Alessandria, and into it Galeazzo Sanseverino threw himself with one of the two armies. Lodovico meant to exert all his strength to keep it. He summoned Francis Sanseverino, who was in command of the other army, to come to the aid of his brother.[3] But many energetic warnings were addressed to him, and this commander's name was mentioned to him among fifteen others suspected of treason. "Whom shall I trust if not Francis?" he exclaimed. He had loaded

---

[1] Chronicon Venetum, 96.
[2] Corio, 969. Jusmondus to Lodovico in Rosmini, ii. 271. Antonius Ex Marchionibus in Rosm.
[3] Nardi, iii. 62. Senarega, 568. St. Gelais, 147.

him with favours, and had treated him as a son. Yet, when Francis had arrived at the Tessin he refused to cross and come to his brother's assistance. Lodovico persuaded himself of his inability to do so without risking a battle, and this must, under all circumstances, be avoided; but everybody else said, Francis' treachery is patent.[1]

In this strait, Galeazzo thought also on self-preservation. He saw his walls crumbling under the enemy's fire and his foes making ready to storm his citadel. He would not surrender, and neither would he defend himself to the last push. He arranged with Constantin de Montferrat, one of the leaders of the enemy, for permission to march off privily: and, accordingly, on the 28th August, 1499, between the third and fourth hour of the night, Galeazzo and his *hommes d'armes* took to flight. They took different roads; some the direction of the Po, in order to gain the main road, others the road to Montferrat, to reach Milan by way of Genoa. They were four hours gone, when the *reveille* sounded in the French camp, and the pursuit of the fugitives began. Galeazzo, two Sforza, the Count of Melzo, and Luzio Malvezzo escaped across the Po.[2] But in Montferrat, Constantin could not keep his plighted word; the *hommes d'armes* were deprived of their horses and weapons.

The city had fallen; the country was defenceless; and Galeazzo's army was annihilated. "Haste," wrote Lodovico to Visconti: "Quick, haste to his Imperial Majesty; announce to him this calamity. Kneel before him and implore him not to allow us to perish, but to come at once to our aid with as great an army as he can muster. In this citadel we will shut ourselves up and wait until His Majesty comes to deliver us."[3] That was Lodovico's first resolve, and he still relied upon the Milanese, whom he considered faithful to him, and whom he had already organized into companies. But their feelings towards him proved unreliable; they were willing to remain faithful to their lord, but it should, if possible, be to their advantage, and certainly not to their harm. To risk life for him, life that

---

[1] Lodovico to Somentius. Corio, 971.
[2] Lodovico, Commissione ad Ambrogio et Martino, Corio, 979.
[3] Lodovico's Letter in Rosmini, i. 322.

was to them the greatest of all goods, never entered into their calculations.¹ When the Venetians were come across the Oglio and would entertain no new proposals, Guelphs and French sympathizers showed themselves even in the capital. On the 30th August, the Treasurer, Landriano, was attacked on his way to the palace by an insolent fellow, who had twelve horsemen in his pay, and was thrown wounded under his horse. This occurrence showed Lodovico plainly that he could not count upon the Milanese, and could not trust himself and his family to them.² On the following day he lifted up his sons, Maximilian, aged nine, and Francis, seven years, kissed them, gave them into his brother's keeping, and sent them with his treasure to Germany. This done, on the 1st September he chose four men; these again co-optated eight others from the first families, all Ghibellines. He granted each of them an estate, and committed the government into their hands.³ He too intended to cross the mountains. After having committed his castle and his jewels⁴ to the keeping of Bernardino da Corte, whom he had brought up and raised from the dust, and had received the kiss of fealty from him, all was arranged, and he said to his companions, "God be with you." He then went forth alone to the Church of the Madonna delle Grazie. His wife, Beatrice, the companion of his prosperity, with whom his luck had died, lay here entombed. Here Leonardo da Vinci had painted them both, him with the elder child on his lap,⁵ and her with the younger. The beams of the setting sun slanted through the windows. He stood at the foot of her grave. The brothers of the convent escorted him out of the church. He looked once more around. What a close texture of coloured threads, and how unchangeably interwoven, happiness and fortune, guilt and calamity, is this mortal life! He burst into a flood of tears. Thrice he turned round, and then stood long lapsed in thought and motionless, with his head bowed to the earth.⁶ In the

[1] Chronicon Venetum, p. 93.
[2] Corio, 973.   [3] Corio, 973.
[4] Burcardus, Diarium Rom., 2103. Commissione, 980.
[5] Vasari, Vita di Leonardo da Vinci, in vol. iii.
[6] Histoire MS. de la Conquête de Milan in Daru, Histoire de Venise, iii. 221.

castle yard, meanwhile, the bustle of horses and men, who were to escort him on his way, was heard. The next morning, at break of day, they all took the road to Como. Of all other cities the people of Como were the most Gibelline and ducal in their sympathies. Once again did they welcome in their Prince, and give him quarters in the episcopal palace. The following morning they came together at his command in the garden by the lake. He stood amongst them on a rising knoll and addressed them.[1] "Citizens, my most faithful subjects! My fortune stood high, but now it has changed. I have spared neither energy, nor friends, nor strength. Yet all in vain; no one can resist treachery. I will now give way a little to fate, and will not struggle against God, will not destroy so many peoples, and still save my own. I go to my nephew, the serene King of the Romans; I go to him, and hope, with his assistance, in a short time to return as conqueror. Follow, then, my advice. When the French come, do not oppose them, but obey them. But preserve your allegiance to me, so that when I come I may not be received as an enemy, but as your true and best lord and master. If I can do you any favour, tell it me, for I am still among you." Codito, a citizen, answered him in these words. "With thy departure, O Prince, we pass from day to night. If thou wilt still do us a favour, relieve us of toll for ten years, so that we may each day praise thy generosity, and deliver the citadel into our keeping." He did not hesitate to grant the first request, but at the second he showed some hesitation. They shouted loud: "Go not away from us, Prince! we will have no other prince but thee. But if thou wilt go, give into our hands the castle, wherein is our safety and our destruction." Whilst he was granting this petition, a cry was raised that the enemy was already in the Borgo. He instantly embarked, and sailed up the lake to Valtellina. Having arrived at the baths of Bormio, at the foot of the Umbrail, on the frontier of his land, he rested once more, and then crossed over into Germany.[2]

[1] Corio, 976. Paulus Jovius, Elogia.
[2] Corio, 977. Senarega, 567.
[3] Chronicon Venetum, 102, 108, 122. Bembus, 98.

Venice had avenged and, at the same time, compensated itself for the loss of Pisa: for Cremona surrendered, and in the cathedral there an altar was raised to St. Marco. Louis XII. had acquired the inheritance of Valentine. Bernardino da Corte in the castle quieted his scruples, on the King making him rich presents and a yearly allowance, and assigning to him the treasures and the artillery of the fugitives.[1] He kindled no torch and waved no flag, as he had promised his lord to do, to announce good or bad tidings. Unattacked by the enemy, he surrendered to them the impregnable fortress, the sole refuge of his benefactors. By this treachery he drew down upon himself the contempt of the one side and the curses of the other. But he could not endure it long; he went forth and hanged himself.[2] The King now came into his new country. Attired in a white mantle and turban, he rode through the white draped streets of the city: and some were heard to call him the Great King, their deliverer.[3] In order to win the most influential classes over to him, he allowed the nobles to hunt the big game, gave the professors greater incomes, and made the appointments of officials permanent. He then caused it to be publicly announced in the open squares and streets of Milan, that tolls upon wine, wheat, corn, millet and nuts, should from thenceforth be no more levied in the town and suburbs, or within the ecclesiastical district of Milan, whilst other burdens should be removed in the whole dukedom. He lowered the taxes, moreover, to 622,000 livres;[4] he thought thus to satisfy everybody. Genoa, too, recognized his suzerainty. After Corradin Stanga had been recalled, and the Adorni showed themselves more and more violent, many became averse to Lodovico. Now that he had fled away, the Adorni were also obliged to abandon their castles, and to fly. When the King arrived, the city sent twenty-four men to him, who arranged a capitulation, and thereupon received the oath of the new governor, Philip of Ravenstein, to it. He

---

[1] Burcardus, 2103. Ferronus, p. 48.
[2] Tschudi in Glutzblotzheim, 188.
[3] Chronicon Venetum, 119, 120. Burcardus, 2107.
[4] Ferronus, iii. 49. Forma Cridæ in Rosmini, ii. 278. Gilles, Chroniques de France, f. 120.

now ruled as far as Lesbos, as far as where the Genoese had formerly swayed.[1] The less powerful princes joined him. The Marchese of Mantua entered into his service,[2] and Ercole of Ferrara, whose falcons and leopards he had had brought to him at Milan, put himself under his protection and claimed his friendship.[3] The Popolares at Florence approached him by sending an embassy. When it came to war, the young Arrabiati chose them a leader, whom they called "Duke," and the Popolares another, whom they called "King," and they both gave performances in the market-place, displaying their respective tendencies.[4] The party of the Popolares, owing to Lodovico's fall, gained the upper hand, and came to renew their old relations to France. Venice is Leonardo's lion, whose breast opens and is full of lilies.[5] As the Pope also was dependent upon the assistance which the French rendered him against the Sforza of Romagna, and as the Anjous in Naples longed for the arrival of the King, he, hitherto only Lord of Asti, had suddenly become by far the most powerful potentate in Italy. Having happily accomplished all these things, he returned to France.

The quarrel at Milan had not, however, as yet been finally disposed of.

Lodovico, far from giving up his cause for lost, thought of Ferrantino; how he once had fled away and had returned to his own, chiefly owing to the people of Naples and the favour of the Milanese. As late as November, the King heard in Milan the cry of "Duke and Moor!" and, in December, a coin was seen bearing the device of a Moor and a Turk, with the motto: "In winter we will fiddle; in summer we will dance."[6] Here also public opinion was manifested in play; when the boys, representing the two parties of the King and the Duke respectively, played together, the Duke's adherents were always the conquerors, and brought the leader of the royalists, who played King,

---

[1] Senarega, 563-570. Folieta, 272.
[2] Chronicon Venetum, 122.
[3] Diarium Ferrarense, 370.
[4] Filippo Nerli, Commentarij, p. 80.
[5] Vasari, Vita di Leonardo da Vinci., tom. iii. p. 25.
[6] Diarium Ferrarense, p. 375, 377.

back to the city dishonoured, tied to the tail of an ass.¹ Lodovico considered himself sure of Milan. In Switzerland, Galeazzo Visconti negotiated, to his advantage,² a peace with the neighbouring Germans. Lodovico himself was obliged to pay the fine levied upon Wallgau and Bregenzerwald, and undertake to pay the 20,000 ducats, without which Constance would not cede the provincial Court of Justice in the Thurgau to the Seven Cantons, which demanded it. It was only after this was arranged, that the other differences were on the 22nd of September submitted to arbitrators at Bâle; where a thanksgiving service was held in the cathedral and the peace ratified.³

On the conclusion of peace, the Swiss Cantons again evinced their old tendencies and dissensions. Lodovico had also here a faction favourable to his cause, and, as he could again avail himself of the lansquenets, he determined to dare a second struggle.

In the green Alpine valleys, on either side of the St. Gotthard, dwelt the Ursers and Levantines; the latter consisting of eight Italian communes, originally connected with the cathedral and the leading houses of Milan, and the former, a German settlement, ruled by the people of Uri. The valleys were perpetually in feud, usually about the pasturage, and each called its patron to its aid. But, sometimes, when the people of Uri drove their oxen through Levantina to the market of Varese, they themselves were insulted, and became thus the more enraged. On such an occasion, in 1402, Levantina was forced to acknowledge the protection of Uri. That was no sufficient advantage for the people of Uri. The pass of Bellenz is so narrow that the town, with its three gates, could entirely close it. They also acquired Bellenz, partly by force and partly by purchase. Since then they had, on this account, fought many a battle with Milan. There was a time when they had given up both. Francis Sforza had restored Levantina to them (and "in gratitude for this they had to bring every August four falcons and a new crossbow to Milan"), but not Bellenz.⁴ They conceived that they had

---

¹ Chronicon Venetum, p. 137.   ² Pirkheimer, p. 27.
³ Document in Fuchs, p. 269.
⁴ Simler, Respublica Helvetica, p. 43. The rest Müller and Ebel.

an established right to this place also, and followed the Duke of Orleans to Novara: they were always on his side, because he had promised it them. But now that the Duke no longer thought himself bound by his promise, which was made under other circumstances, Lodovico, who had changed sides with them, was inclined to promise them something.[1] Like the oxen of Uri, the horses of the Valais had also their market in Milan; thence the "Grey Leaguers" procured certain tuns of corn and wine. They could not live without the Dukedom, and enjoyed old privileges from the Sforza. Lodovico knew how to turn all these conditions to his account.

First of all, as it appears, he availed himself of the state of affairs in Uri. For at the self-same time, in October, 1499, he promised Bellenz and Val Bregna to the people of Uri,[2] and Galeazzo collected some troops for an incursion into Vatellina.[3] But on this occasion—for the Bailiff was also at this moment enlisting troops, and the cantons called back their sons who had gone away; and the King promised the people of Uri various possessions—the troops were disbanded as soon as collected.[4] But one advantage accrued to Lodovico therefrom. The Bailiff dismissed many in the midst of winter without pay, and some were frozen to death on the tops of the mountains. By these doings he made himself and the King enemies enough. These enemies, the universal dissatisfaction, and the relations subsisting between the Grey Leaguers and the Valais, Galeazzo availed himself of to make a second attempt. The Valais declared that the King was an intolerable neighbour;[5] 2,000 Grey Leaguers enrolled themselves at Chur under his standard. All whom the Bailiff had wronged or rejected he welcomed to it. In January, 1500, he was enabled to venture over the mountains between the Engadine and Valtellina.[6] His advent was victory. At the first cry, Chiavenna opened its gates; the Gibellines of

---

[1] Lodovico's Capitulation in Müller, v. [2] Fuchs, 274.
[3] Stettler, 361.
[4] Tschudi in Glutzblotzheim and the proclamation of Lucerne of the 7th January, 1501, in Glutzblotzheim, p. 532.
[5] Hans Krebs in Fuchs, 171.
[6] Benedictus Corius, Historia Novocomensis, 58.

Lugano and Locarno rose; the people of Bellinzona reconquered their castle for the Duke. The French fled from Como, in dread of Ascanio's arrival. John Orelli marched into Pavia, and, as there was a lack of corn, provisioned it with chestnuts.[1] All depended upon whether the Duke's party in Milan would be able to hold that city.

In Milan, the Gibelline families, the Landrians, Marlians, Visconti, Cribelli, and especially some ecclesiastics amongst them, would never obey Trivulzio. On one occasion, even, they made common cause with the French prefect against him.[2] Between the Gibellines and Guelphs there existed an open feud. Sometimes no one dared to speak of terms. Sometimes the leaders had a conference and concluded a formal peace. Trivulzio, who behaved himself as these party leaders were wont to do when they were victorious, ever kept alive the arrogance of the rest. When then, on the 1st February, 1500, the tidings arrived that the Sforza were there, both rushed at once to arms. Trivulzio, with his Guelphs, was the first to occupy the square between the cathedral and the palace. The Gibellines showed courage, and surrounded him and his men. The two parties kept up a contest of words. As long as Trivulzio was honey-tongued, saying that: "he desired no better luck than to share Milan's fate; he was willing to die for his country, but that they must be faithful, and that then they would obtain great liberties," his opponents only replied with mockery; "was he not the same person, who had always sought his own advantage in his country's calamities? Was he not the old fox that had ever deceived them? He was only now making them promises that he would never be able to keep." But when he began to command them to lay down their arms, threatening that the King would destroy the city, they also became violent. "If Guelphs could carry arms, Gibellines could do the same; instead of giving orders, he would now have to receive them; but why was he still allowed to live? If his life was the ruin, his death would be the saving, of his

---

[1] Bened. Jovius, Historia Novcom., 60. Zurita, i. 176. Life of Aloysius Orelli, 40.

[2] Arluni, de bello Veneto, i. 7. Andrea da Prato, Cronaca, in Rosmini, i. 337.

country." One Gibelline or other was for ever shouting these words; each hour that the Sforza drew nearer, their courage waxed stronger. The next morning, Trivulzio retired to the park and the castle. In the city nothing was heard but "Duke and Moor, and death to the Guelphs." All the shops were closed, and the streets barricaded; Trivulzio saw that the city was lost, provided for the castle and fled to the Tessin.[1]

These tidings, with the invitations from his party, reached Lodovico in Innsbruck. He was not yet ready, he had not lansquenets enough, and Maximilian did not approve of his starting at that moment;[2] but Lodovico could not be restrained. He took Claude de Vaudrei's Burgundian horse, lansquenets as many as he had, and crossed the Alps.[3] They came from the villages and towns to meet him, saying, "All hail, Lodovico our prince!" The people of Como brought him in triumph into their church. All the nobles in a body met him before the gates of Milan. As a sign of his mercy, he carried a green ensign, upon it embroidered a Moor, dressed in gold, touching the shoulders of four barons kneeling before him. Thus did he enter the city.[4] After this, the people of Cremona only waited for an occasion to revolt from Venice, and in Genoa the rulers did not dare to commit the watch to any Italian, for the city was full of the report that, "John Adorno had written and was on the march with succour from Naples."[5] In Ferrara itself three hundred boys followed the drum of a Servite monk; they thundered at the door of the Venetian Visdomino, and shouted "Moor!"[6] The whole country would at one stroke have come into Lodovico's hand, had not the unfaithful surrendered their castles; these must be retaken, were he to assert his supremacy. He raised his army, in spite of their small pay, to 12,000 men and 2,500 horses; his brother Thomas followed him with the guns that he had just had cast in Germany. He

[1] Epistola Hieronymi Moroni ad Varadeum in Rosmini, ii. 280. Chronicon Venetum. 137.
[2] Maximilian's letter of complaint of the year 1507, in Fuchs, ii. 91.
[3] Benedictus Jovius, 61.
[4] Ibid., and Ferronus, iii. 51.
[5] Senarega, 571.
[6] Diarium Terrarense.

said to the people, "I will be your prince and will be your brother; but you must help me with money." Now, although many thought that they had made sacrifices enough for him, and others did not believe that they could rely upon his good fortune, most of them perceived that his need was their need, and assisted him. Hereupon Ascanio besieged the castle at Milan, and he that at Novara.

Trivulzio, in the face of this movement, had retired upon roads which the peasants endeavoured to render impassable by trees and stones, in return for which he left their villages desolate in his track, and proceeded despondently—for his own party upbraided him—past Pavia to Mortara and Vercelli. Thither the King despatched La Tremouille to take the supreme command; thither also came a few Swiss, who had been in the pay of Cesar Borgia.[1] But to withstand an army as great as that which Lodovico had with him, fresh recruiting must be resorted to. For this the Florentines and Venetians gave money, and the Archbishop of Sens and the Bailiff started at once for Switzerland to effect this.

The Swiss of those days were bold in the face of steel, but weak in the presence of money. They were united as soon as they had an enemy before them; but before that disunited, as also in negotiations. As they have no great general interests to consult, they blindly follow each special and momentary advantage. If those who joined Lodovico's colours remained faithful to his cause, whilst others were allowed to give their oath of allegiance to the Bailiff representing the opposite side, the murder of relatives by relatives, and a domestic war, terminating with the break-up of the federation, might ensue. It was, perhaps, owing to these apprehensions that they did not agree to the first offer of the Bailiff on the 21st February: "The King," they said, "should first of all pay up all arrears and confirm the terms;" and so, grumbling to himself: "it will be a matter of crowns, and so I suppose I shall have to open the purse," he left the assembly, and went through place after place.[2] On the 11th March they again assem-

---

[1] Moronus ad Varadeum, 285. Chronic. Venet., 143. Ferron.
[2] Anshelm and Tschudi in Glutzblotzheim, p. 171.

bled. Maximilian represented to them that: "in their terms with the French King, the Empire was excepted from those countries against which they were to lend assistance; but Milan was now a crown land, and Lodovico a subject, a vassal, of the Empire." That was at that time no unfounded assertion, as Lodovico had completely allied himself to the Romo-German King; but now that they had received their money, they would not listen to any counter reasons.[1] The Zurichers chose a captain and "Venner" for their companies; the Freiburgers sent their counsellors with them. Although the enlistment was at once prohibited in Berne,[2] the people, in spite of the prohibition, followed the drum. They marched, some up the Soane and across the Bernhardin and the three Cantons over the St. Gothard, and came to Vercelli. They did not know what they were doing. Many a one had a brother, a brother-in-law, or a father opposed to him in Novara.

Either the oath would have to be broken, or the federation was at an end.

Lodovico still called his camp the most happy;[3] he still hoped to draw all those who had crossed over the hills to his standard. He thought to make use of the people of Uri, and sent a message to the Swiss to this effect: "Bellenz, Mendris, Lugano, Locarno, and Val Maggia he would cede to them, give them 40,000 ducats at once, and pay a yearly sum of 24,000, if they would only rid him of the King."[4] Thereupon, the common people of Berne, in both city and land, having, as they probably had, relations on both sides, implored their counsellor, their Bailiff, to see that peace was made. This counsellor proposed[5] to the federals to dissuade both princes and both lords from using the sword, else great damage and great strife was unavoidable; and in this direction the German envoys likewise exerted their influence. As a matter of fact, a resolution was arrived at on the 31st March, such as Lodovico desired: "On the 8th of April two deputies from each canton should meet in the inn at

[1] From Tschudi in Fuchs, p. 287.
[2] Berne to Maximilian, p. 299.
[3] Lodovico's signature in Fuchs, p. 304.
[4] Stettler, 364.   [5] Letter of Berne, 298 and 302.

Uri, and thence haste, in God's name, to bring the two princes to an understanding."[1]

But before the decree was made, the French sallied out. Lodovico was bold enough to oppose himself outside the walls to a threefold stronger army than his, and to draw up Swiss to face Swiss. But both stopped; they refused to fight each other.[2] He retired to Novara, his enemies after him. He awaited, it appears to me, the decree, from which he hoped everything, and that succour, which on the 9th of April had arrived at Como.[3] At length the decree arrived; but it was not so unequivocal that the French could not make use of it. People were not in Lucerne quite at one in the matter; the ducal party had gained something, but not everything, and the essence of the decree was quite contradictory in terms: "The soldiers should be warned by both sides to return home, or, at all events, to go over to one side.[4] It is evident that this determined the matter. The French could rely upon faithful men; Lodovico had to deal with captains who defrauded him of 500 guilders in a single levy.[5] These latter went over into the enemy's camp, and let the enemy into theirs. The two became almost one. It was soon resolved to interpret the resolution in favour of the French. The cry was raised, "It is all over with the Duke."[6] The French then came so close to him that they might almost have taken him prisoner in a room.[7] When he complained of the conduct of his captains, they answered: "When did they ever promise to fight against federals: if he only wanted counsel, he should apply to his wise counsellors; but if he looked to them for advice, theirs was that he should mount a good horse, and ride off to Bellenz or Eschenthal."[8] In this state of perplexity, he entered into negotiations with the leaders of the French,

---

[1] Resolution in Fuchs, p. 292; in Glutzblotzheim, p. 174.
[2] Kergicht Meyers in Gl., 175.
[3] Benedictus Jovius, Hist. Novocom., p. 61.
[4] Resolution in Glutzbl.
[5] Resolution in Gl., p. 532.
[6] Anselm in Fuchs, 309.
[7] Tapfer vogts Vergicht in Fuchs, 321.
[8] Pfisters and Zehwegers Vergicht in Fuchs, Glutzb., and in Aloysius Orelli's life, p. 54.

and Ligny was for allowing him to escape; but the others opposed this, and Trivulzio said : " He is as good as ours."[1] The enemy without, treachery within ; for his Italians also became weary and drew back. There was only one way of escape, namely, that which Æmilius Paulus advised to Perseus, and of which Cato gave an example to the great Romans—the last expedient in the struggle with fate, before one succumbs. But Lodovico was not the man to perceive it or seize it.

On Friday morning, the 10th April, 1500, Lodovico Maria Sforza, called the Moor, sat in his room at Novara, read, and appeared to pray. Galeazzo Sanseverino entered and said: " he had only looked for two hundred Swiss to give him an armed escort, but had not found a single one." Then came certain Swiss captains and said: "they were obliged to go. Would he venture to escape in their midst, he should disguise himself and come." He hardly heard them, but went on reading.[2] They came again to him. " All is ready," they said. They found him still hesitating. So throwing a Swiss blouse over his scarlet skirts,[3] they sat him, partly by force and partly with his will, upon a horse, put a halberd in his hand, concealed him in their thickest company, and rode out of the gate. The French stood on both sides with lowered spears, and with guns ready pointed, so as to find him and not allow him to escape.[4] Some of them fell upon the lansquenets, and upon the Burgundians, and took Jacob von Ems prisoner.[5] Others rode up to the Swiss : " they had him, and for dear life they should surrender him. Did they not point him out, they were undone."[6] The cavalcade stopped. The Duke, now a Minorite, and now a Swiss trooper with a halberd, once taken, but again let go, as he was not recognized, was here, there, and everywhere, and few knew him. At last the Bailiff rode up and offered 500 ducats to him who would point him

[1] Morone to Varadeus.
[2] The same, Vergicht in Fuchs, 331.
[3] Anton, p. 110.
[4] Zimmermann's Vergicht, 323.
[5] Bebelii Epitome laudum Suevorum, p. 141.
[6] Brüchli Scherers, Tapfervogts Vergicht.

out.[1] Thereupon a man of Uri, by name Turmann, who was standing behind him—a man of whom nothing evil had ever been known before—was allured by the proffered lucre, and lifting up his hand, said in a low tone, "There!"[2] No one resisted. The Bailiff seized and recognized the Duke, and struck him with the flat of his sword across the shoulders. Trivulzio stept up to him and said, "Sforza, you have your reward."[3]

At the first report, the Milanese rushed terrified from their houses to the palace. Ascanio went out to them and said, "The Moor is a prisoner." He said nothing more. He had forgotten his eloquence. He thought only of his own escape.[4] Francis Sforza had had five sons, all excellently endowed by nature and well brought up by their wise mother; but the first was murdered by conspirators; the second fled away from his sister-in-law and was drowned; the third died in exile. The fourth was Lodovico, and Ascanio, too, the fifth, did not escape the fate of the others. He fell into the captivity of Venice. No city was able to defend itself. They came out everywhere to meet the victors with olive branches.[5] But the victors treated them as great criminals. The Vogheresi also waited for Ligny, their lord, but he rode by them, as though he did not see them. They began to entreat him, but he would not hear until Louis d'Ars interceded for them. They brought him

[1] Paulus Jovius, Epitome Historiarum, p. 87.
[2] Scherer's Vergicht, 322.
[3] Anton, p. 110. Ferronus, 52. Monstrelet, 230. In the "Anzeiger für Schweizerische Geschichte" for 1884, No. 80, p. 279, is published a letter of Geoffrey Carles (of the 15th April, 1500), who belonged to the French, who, at the revolt of Milan, in January, 1500, had retired into the citadel, and in which is also stated that Lodovico had endeavoured to escape among the Swiss, to whom he made great promises. The French let the Swiss file by man by man. They recognized Lodovico also by the fact that he could not speak German (Cognitus pour ce qu'il ne sceut respondre Alemand). The treachery of Turmann is not mentioned. Everything is attributed to the work of the French commander. So, also, in Trivulzio's letter to the Signorie (in Sanuto, Diarii iii., p. 226). But we must, after all, take our stand upon what the Swiss accounts tell us. (Note to 3rd edition.)
[4] Arluni, de bello Veneto, i. 2.
[5] Chronicon Venetum, 151.

silver plate, and he gave it at once to Bayard.¹ The latter said: "God forbid that the gifts of such wicked people should come into my hand," and distributed it among others. "He will become the most perfect man, I say," said Ligny. In this way they took possession of the country. In Milan the heads of the leading Gibellines were impaled at the palace gates, the rest were spared.² But the two Sforza were sent to France. Bourges and Loches lie not far apart on the left bank of the Loire, Bourges with its round high tower, commanding the country for miles round;³ thither came Ascanio; Loches with its towers and bastions built on a steep rock, and surrounded by such deep moats that the English declared it to be impregnable.⁴ Here Lodovico was interned. Here he often spoke with his servant from Pontremoli of his sins and his fate.⁵ "That is the star of Francis Sforza," said the astrologers in Italy; "it means fortune for one man, but disaster for his descendants."⁶

As Maximilian was engaged in this war, he was also affected by this disaster. On that same momentous 10th of April on which Lodovico was taken prisoner, he opened a Diet at Augsburg. His prestige in his Empire did not alone depend upon internal development, it depended almost still more upon his war and peace, and upon his extraneous successes. Now that, since the diet of Freiburg, the four military enterprises in which he had been engaged had failed, viz., in Burgundy, in Guelders, in Switzerland, and Milan, he was forced to acquiesce in a Government, such as had already been proposed at Worms. It consisted of twenty members, an elector, a spiritual and a temporal prince, a count, a prelate, and fifteen deputies, These twenty had the right of summoning the princes in small numbers or collectively, of deciding upon war, of recruiting infantry and horse for the "pfennig" impost, that they were to administer, even of

---

¹ Bayard, p. 84.
² Chronicon Venetum, 162. Seyssel, Louanges du bon Roi, p. 48. Supplement to Monstrelet.
³ André du Chesne, Antiquités, p. 482.
⁴ Ibid., p. 520.
⁵ Paul Jovius, Elogia, p. 200.   ⁶ Arluni, de bello Veneto, i. 24.

resolving upon the conquest, which might perhaps succeed, and finally, of making peace again.¹ What then remained of the royal dignity? "They would have liked to depose us," said Maximilian, "but a certain person required time and leisure." On the 2nd of July, 1500, this Government was resolved upon. As early as the 21st, Louis XII. went to meet an embassy sent by it; he had to expect more assistance from it than resistance to his plans. He had gained a complete victory over Maximilian.²

3. *Pope Alexander VI. and his Son against the Vassals of the Church.*

Had it really been so with Francis Sforza's star, as was said, its pernicious effect would have extended to the whole of the Sforzian-Aragon dynasty. It turned out to his ruin that the Pope had entered into a league with Louis XII. But, in order to make clear to ourselves how the Pope was situated, it is necessary to begin with a general sketch.

Laws and customs, representing the unity of society in each individual member, do not merely exist for the purpose of protecting others against you, or you against others, but also for the purpose of protecting you against yourself. Moderation and self-restriction, the neglect of which entails self-destruction, and which inclination and arrogance will notwithstanding never tolerate, become by means of them a habit, and lead him, who submits to them, unharmed and peacefully through all the days of his life. Yet, as the human race ever needs new laws, some one must be raised up to originate and guard them, and over such a one their restrictive force cannot have power.

A great danger this, and yet one which high and low ever vie with each other in arrogating to themselves, and which the Germano-Christian nations, while yet united, reposed in a single individual, a greyhead chosen by grey-

---

¹ Gasser, Augsburger Chronik, 258. Regiments-ordnung in Müller's Reichstags-staat, 25-48.
² Maximilian. Kurzer Begriff Seiner Reichs-verwaltung, p. 120. Monstrelet.

heads; a man who, with the exception of his name, had given up all connection with the world, and whom they believed God's Spirit did not allow to go astray. But inclinations are exceedingly deep-rooted and obstinate, even in old men; and who is there that could be dead to the world and yet rule it? It was fortunate that the Popes were not entirely without fear, neither when they fought with the Emperors, nor when the Gibelline party was at its height, nor when they were at Avignon in the power of the French kings. After this, they were held in check by the schism, the fear of a fresh schism, or by the proximity of the Turks.

It was only when they had become accustomed to this constant fear, and when, in the whole of the Western world, there was none who could withstand the coalition even of the few that the Pope could always command, that he became quite fearless. Two things tended to make this a particular misfortune; corrupt election, and the prevailing infidelity. Would a strong man, whose mind in the course of a long life had become impure by sensuality, greed, and all the vices of the world, on having attained this position, be more likely to employ it to a good or an evil end? A fear of Him, of whose being he knew nothing for certain, could not restrain him. Alexander every Maundy-Thursday imitated the Author of the faith by washing the feet of twelve poor men; but the feet had first to stand in a golden basin full of perfumed herbs, and a Cardinal had first to pour water over them out of a golden vessel, and not until then did he touch them.[1] Reliable diaries accuse him of a sensuality that found its gratification even in that of others, of a cruelty that employed murderers[2] by day and night, and of a villainy so elaborated, as by means of promises to induce a man, good in other respects, to confess to something that he had not committed, and then to punish him as if he had been guilty of it.[3] A man who had once spoken ill of his son, he punished by cutting off his hand and the tip of the tongue, and caus-

[1] Anton Harve, Reise 3.
[2] Raphael Voleterranus, Vitæ Paparum, p. 167. Burcardus, Valerianus de infelicitate literatorum, p. 272.
[3] Burcardus, 2085.

ing the latter to be exhibited stuck on the tip of the little finger.¹

Through his son Don Juan, to whom Federigo had promised a principality in return for his enfeoffment, this Alexander had become closely connected with both Federigo and all the Sforza and Aragons. But, in consequence of Juan's sudden death—his body was found in the Tiber ²— this connection began to be severed. Juan, as the German chronicles relate, was Alexander's joy, and his soul was wrapped up in him. He now sat from Thursday to Sunday shut up in his chamber, without eating and sleeping, and always in tears, and thought of abdicating; for his wickedness was the cause of his son's death.³ On Sunday he came forth, went on foot to St. Peter's, ordered five cardinals to re-arrange his Court, and bade his children leave it.⁴ But his children controlled him. All his passions were in still greater intensity found in his son Cesar: sensuality, thirst for power, bloody revenge, also the power of concentrating all his mental forces upon a single object, and his open-handed and apparently generous and princely bearing.⁵ Cesar was an active, well-grown man, skilled at throwing, riding, and at slaying the bull when running with a single blow; his dark-red face was full of pimples, that readily festered, and gave to his eye keenness and brilliancy and a snake-like movement, which he only restrained a little in the presence of women.⁶ After his brother's death, which was attributed to him himself, his tastes were all for arms and princely honours. Instead of removing from the Court, he proposed to his father to relieve him from the office and dignity of Cardinal, and to endow him with a principality.⁷ The Church is built up upon the inextinguishable character of the priestly state, and it was quite without precedent that the highest rank in it should be given up. Yet this objection did not

---

¹ Burcardus, 2137.
² Burcardus, Diarium, 2082. Zurita, f. 125. Mariana, xxxi. p. 169. Guicciardini, iii. 182.
³ Matthias Döring, Continuatio chron. Engelbusi, Ap. Menken, iii.
⁴ Nardi, ii. 42. Burcardus.
⁵ Petrus Martyr, Epistolæ xv. 143.
⁶ Jovius, Elogia virorum bellica virtute clarorum, 201-203.
⁷ Burcardus, also in Gordon's Appendix, 57.

trouble the Pope much, and, as a matter of fact, he proposed to Federigo that he should give his eldest daughter and Don Juan's possessions to Cesar.[1] Now Joffred Borgia and Lucretia Borgia, the latter of whom had been torn away from the side of John Sforza of Pesaro and married to Alonso of Bisceglia, were already allied to the Aragon house by marriage. But Federigo knew Cesar. A quiet, moral, noble gentleman as he was, and a father who loved his daughter so tenderly, could not sanction this. The Sforza plied him with entreaties upon entreaties, representing to him that the Pope would otherwise take other steps for the destruction of Italy. But his reply was that: " nothing in the world should induce him; rather would he die a poor nobleman, and endure all the ills of the world, than do this. They should not mention it again." From that time Alexander began to enter into serious negotiations with France. After Louis XII. had promised Valentinois to Cesar, the latter came into the Consistory of Cardinals: "in spite of always having been addicted to the world, he had ever been raised to spiritual dignities and benefices. His propensities would not be curbed. He now gave back his benefices, and begged to be relieved of his office."[2] How could he be refused what had long since been determined and settled? In short, in Oct., 1498, he made his public entrance as Prince into Chinon, where Louis was holding his Court. Sixty-six laden mules preceded him; he himself rode in, covered from his hat, in which gleamed ten rubies, down to his boots, with precious stones. His horse was shod with silver shoes; and behind him there came twenty-four mules caparisoned in red velvet.[3] The Pope was at one time heard to say that, "he would give a fourth part of his papacy if only Cesar would not return;" and at another—for he believed himself offended—" If only Cesar were there, he would act differently;"[4] and hence we can perceive how completely he was in Cesar's power. In France, Cesar received Valentinois, the bishop of which styled himself Count, as a Dukedom, and in May, 1499, Charlotte, Alain d'Alibret's daughter, to wife.[5] Through this mar-

[1] Bercardus, 2098. [2] Burcardus, 2096.
[3] Brantome, Capitains étrangers, from an original.
[4] Zurita, 159, 160. [5] Fleuranges, p. 12. Ferronus, p. 48.

riage he became related to the King of Navarre and France. He next schemed to attain a larger lordship. If Louis attacked the Sforza in Milan, he, on his part, would ruin the Romagnan vassals, and all the vassals of the Church.

In September, 1490, Lodovico fled for the first time. In November, the Pope declared the nephews of the former to have forfeited Imola and Forli.[1] Cesar did not recollect that their father, Girolamo Riario, after having risen to power, lived like he did, and what his end was. With French and Swiss assistance, Cesar made war upon Catharine, Lodovico's sister and Girolamo's widow. The lady had no support. Florence and Milan had formerly been allies. The former favoured her, because her Court was full of Florentines;[2] besides, her third husband, Giovanni di Pier Francesco dei Medici, had come from Florence, and her son at times enjoyed the emoluments of office there.[3] The latter city was so devoted to her that, for a time, Giovanni da Casale, Lodovico's agent, had the whole government in his hands, and was present at her most secret audiences.[4] Aided by both, she had in the previous year resisted the Venetians, and in this had supported both, especially Lodovico, with troops.[5] But now Lodovico was an exile, and her enemy was lord of Milan. Now, too, in Florence, instead of the notables, who were her friends, and the friends of her late husband, Giovanni Medici, and of her child, the Popolares were supreme; and although she went thither saying, "the holy evening of the Florentines was her festival also," they still considered it dangerous to resist the French and Cesar. In consequence of this state of things, Imola, both city and citadel, was soon lost, and the nobles welcomed the enemy into the city of Forli.[6] The citadel of Forli, that had been so strongly fortified by Pino Ordelaffi as to appear impregnable, still held out. Catherine, who, since her husband's death, had withstood all her enemies, herself commanded it, went about on the walls, and was not

[1] Burcardus, 2107.
[2] Macchiavelli, Legazione alla Contessa Caterina Sforza, lett. iv. p. 16.
[3] Commissione a Macchiavelli, p. 1.
[4] Macchiavelli, Legatione, lett. ii. 7.
[5] *Ibid.*, p. 17.   [6] Nardi, ii. 61.

daunted.¹ In order to compass her rescue, a musician took a poisoned letter to Rome, and desired an audience of the Pope. His chamberlain was a native of Forli, and with this chamberlain's help he thought he would be able to succeed. Yet he betrayed him. "Didst thou think to escape, in the event of succeeding?" "At all events," was the answer, "I should have saved my Princess; she reared me up, and I would suffer a thousand deaths for her."² Cesar had promised 10,000 ducats to whomsoever would bring her to him alive; but amongst such faithful adherents he could not hope to find a traitor. She took no notice of the Pope's promise to grant her an annual allowance; she met Cesar's attacks with energy. At last the wall was pierced by 400 shot, and was scaled. She defended herself to the last; but at last she was taken, and brought before Cesar. The French captain demanded the 10,000 ducats; Cesar then spoke of 2,000. "Wilt thou break thy word?" answered the former, and was on the point of killing her.³ After this she enjoyed many long years and much honour in Florence. Lodovico's return delayed this undertaking, for, on account of it, French and Swiss had to turn towards Milan.

After a while a messenger brought the tidings of Lodovico's captivity. The Pope gave him 100 ducats. The Romans shouted "Orso and Franzia" in the streets.⁴ Cesar, who had since received the mantle, hat, and staff of "Gonfaloniere" of the Church, advanced against John Sforza at Pesaro.⁵ John relied upon his people, upon Venice, and Urbino. In his hall, the nobles and citizens at his request had promised him allegiance and assistance; immediately afterwards he discovered a conspiracy. He hurried to Venice, that had always protected him; but on this occasion he remembered how he had received Turkish ambassadors. The Duke of Urbino gave him poor encouragement, saying he ought to keep himself for a better opportunity.⁶ When Cesar approached, he fled, and abandoned to him both city and country. Pandolf Malatesta would not await him at Rimini. Be-

---

[1] Chronicon Venetum, p. 128.
[2] Burcardus ii. 61.
[3] Chronicon Venetum, 135.
[4] Burcardus, 2116.
[5] Burcardus, 2114.
[6] Baldi Guidubaldo, 215.

fore that year, Venice had sent a Proveditor to protect him, so that Cesar had to return, whilst he hurried to the feet of the Signorie,[1] to express his gratitude. But now Venice had declared for the Pope, who had granted to her ecclesiastical revenues wherewith to fight the Turks; his people hated him, and so he also fled. Hereupon, now that everything appeared to succeed, in November, 1500, Cesar advanced against Faenza.

The Faentines were distinguished among all the Romagnans for their harmony and their industrial cleverness; their linen was the whitest; their potteries had acquired a reputation; and they had, moreover, been renowned for their loyalty, ever since they had defended Bolgheri against Frederick II.'s superior force, and had saved them from harm.[2] At the time of which we speak, there lived two youths, descendants of their old princes, the Manfreddi, of whom the elder, Astorre, aged fifteen years, was an angel in cleverness and beauty. Their sole ally was the winter; but they made such good use of it that Cesar retired on the tenth day. In April, 1501, he came again. They killed 1,000 of his men to sixty citizens on their side; 1,400 they blew up in a bastion.[3] The Pope sometimes, out of ill-humour, did not go to chapel. But Cesar was not weakened by his losses, as the charitable offerings of piety were at his disposal; but they were ruined by their success. At last, utterly exhausted by three successive attacks, they surrendered, after Cesar had guaranteed them safety, and liberty to their princes.[4] Since that time Cesar was called Duke of Romagna, and up to this point Louis suffered his undertakings. But when he threatened Bologna, John Bentivoglio, under French protection, resisted him, and escaped with a few fines.[5] When after this he made an irruption into the Florentine land, as though intending to restore the Medici, the King and his own father warned him to depart; and he was obliged to content himself with money and a "Condotta."[6] When

---

[1] Chronicon Venetum, 241.
[2] Leander Alberti, Descriptio Italiæ.
[3] Zurita, i. 209.   [4] Diarium Ferrarense, 393, 395.
[5] Nardi, 70.
[6] Nardi. Nerli, v. 86. Macchiavelli, Discorsi, i. 38.

he made a descent upon Appiano of Piombino, the King would not have been displeased had Genoa previously acquired the fine fresh-water harbour by purchase. But Cesar was too quick; and having Elba and Pianosa, its Prince was obliged to relinquish to him Piombino, and take refuge in the Scrivia Valley, on the estate of a Spinola.[1] Even Alfonso of Ferrara was not strong enough to resist him, and was obliged to make terms, by marriage with this family.

Cesar is like a wolf in the fold, that has made friends with the shepherd. His soldiers wore a sword belt from the right shoulder to the left thigh, representing a scaly snake, picked out in gold and colours, darting downwards with its seven heads.[2] But what symbol could express the damnation of a man who, during these struggles, came once to Rome, caused the St. Peter street to be closed, and six human beings brought out, and hunted with arrows, whilst he stood by and shot them until they died like hunted game;[3] who promised Astorre his liberty, and then outraged this innocent boy, this noble blood, in an unnatural manner; and, still fearing him, at last caused him to be thrown with his brother into the Tiber,[4] a stone attached to his neck.

God's judgment was over Italy. Destruction was abroad, and stalked from one palace to the other. Only the real Aragons, Federigo and his house, still survived; but destruction was in their wake. At the first attack upon the Sforza, Alfonso da Bisceglia, Alexander's Aragon son-in-law, fled from Rome. If he had only not returned! But now, when crossing the square of St. Peter in broad daylight,[5] he was attacked by murderous bands, and, thrice wounded, was carried off to his house; but, as he did not succumb at once to his wounds, Cesar employed his executioner, Michelotto, to despatch him in bed.[6] Beatrice,

---

[1] Senarega Annales. [2] Baldi Guidubaldo, p. 216.
[3] Burcardus, 2121. [4] Nardi, iv. 71. Burcardus, 2138.
[5] Burcardus, 2123.
[6] Passero, 123 (note to 2nd edit.). Cf. Römische Päpste, vol. xxxvii. p. 33, and Paolo Capello's account in the appendix to 3rd vol., No. 3. Peculiar are the ten Neapolitan accounts, from the reports which reached the Court of King Federigo, for instance, in Giacomo, who describes very exactly the wounds inflicted, p. 235 : " Una alabardata alla spalla, una ferita dereto la testa et una stocchata in li fianchi."

daughter of Ferrante the elder, and wife of King Wladislaw, was far away in Hungary. After losing a better husband, she had brought the crown to this one. But Wladislaw was long since tired of her. Alexander, who had always hitherto been prevented by some consideration or other, now pronounced his divorce from her. Anna of Candale, of the royal house of France, took her place.[1] In Federigo himself, the life of this dynasty was threatened. When Milan was for the first time conquered, the French volunteers boasted, "they were now in the midst of a hundred years' war without a day's peace;[2] they had still to war against the Turks, and to cross the Alps, but first of all to Naples." Federigo had sometimes attempted to negotiate, but he only found himself dallied with. In April, 1501, the preparations were no longer a secret; and, in May, Louis communicated his intention to the German council of the realm, which had concluded a truce with him until the 1st of July, and had tied Maximilian's hands.[3] In June, the army advanced into the Florentine country; and in Rome arbours were made for the men, and cribs for the horses, whilst a residence was prepared for the King.[4] Many thought then how closely Ferdinand was related to Federigo, and how the former, even in breach of his treaty, had come to the aid of Ferrantino, and saved him, and how Gonzal was in Messina ready for action. A long war—possibly a reversal of the whole of the French successes—might be expected. Federigo had asked Gonzal if he could depend upon him, and he answered: "my master is your friend."

Yet it was not so. Ferrantino would scarcely have been so energetically supported had he not been married with Joana, Ferdinand's niece. For the old kinship, from the time of the first Alfonso, was hateful to him, as it had ousted his line from Naples. Federigo, also, had looked for a new alliance and had begged for Ferdinand's youngest daughter, or his niece Joana, for his son;[5] but he refused the first proposal and for the second demanded an exorbitant dowry.

[1] Burcardus, 2116.   Zurita, 180.   Petrus M., epist. xi. 190.
[2] Burcardus.
[3] Altobosto's statement in Müller's Reichstags staat.
[4] Burcardus.   [5] Passero, p. 120.   Zurita.

He now began to think of his own claims. He had formerly negotiated with Charles VIII. upon the matter of compensation for his pretensions to Naples, in case Charles should invade it, to take the form either of Calabria, which should be detached from the kingdom, or of a partition of the whole of Italy between the French King, the German, and himself the Spanish King.[1] Charles was dead. Next, in the early commencement of Louis XII.'s reign he concluded a treaty with him, without, however, including Federigo.[2]

When then this King was making ready for his campaign, Mosen Gralla, Ferdinand's ambassador, visited the Cardinal of Amboise, and said to him, as though only expressing his own ideas: "how if you were to come to some arrangement with us respecting Naples, as you did with Venice regarding Milan;" Amboise had always feared the Spanish pretensions, and so replied, "We two shall have to keep up the friendship between our kingdoms."[3] But Gralla had long since received his instructions from his master. On the 22nd September, 1500, a real treaty was arrived at, in these terms; "The territory of Naples to be divided into two halves; one half, comprising the Abruzzi and Lavoro with the title of kingdom, to belong to Louis, the other, consisting of Apulia and Calabria, as a dukedom, to Ferdinand. A further arrangement especially respecting the Dogana to be come to after the conquest."[4] This treaty was still unknown when the French entered the Florentine territory. But on St. Peter's day, 1501, both envoys submitted it to the Pope, who at once enfeoffed both princes.[5] This was the first tidings that Federigo received of what was proceeding against him. Thereupon Gonzal sent him a message to the effect that: "he renounced his fief in Naples, for that he was obliged to renounce[6] the oath he had taken in respect of it." Glad of heart was the Pope when he saw the French army, 2,000 horse and 12,000 infantry strong, with 42 guns, file past in the garden of the Castel St. Angelo on its way to the Neapolitan frontier.[7]

[1] Zurita, 132-138. Comines, end.
[2] Zurita, f. 140.
[3] Zurita, f. 168.
[4] Zurita, f. 192.
[5] Guicciardini, iv. 266.
[6] Zurita, f. 212.
[7] Burcardus, 2131.

When Federigo looked about him, he found nothing upon which he could rely. The east coast was in the hand of Venice, and the strongholds, by virtue of old treaties, in those of Spain. Should he trust in his barons, who would not even all be present at his coronation,[1] who outlawed in their respective territories all who adhered to him, and whom he could only possibly have subjected with Gonzal's assistance.[2] The Colonna alone were faithful, but these alone were of no account, entrusting, as they did, their estates in the State of the Church to the cardinals. Their stewards were compelled to swear allegiance to the Pope, and an assembly of Roman citizens resolved to destroy their Marino.[3] Federigo's sole hope lay in the cities, and he had their walls repaired and hand-mills provided, whilst the peasants were driven in and located in barns.[4]

There is no spectacle more depressing than a country which allows itself to be subjected without drawing the sword. Gonzal was master of fifteen towns, without transporting a single horse thither. After Capua had held out for a moment, thanks to German mercenaries, the Count of Polenta rode out, as though he wished to see how things stood with the enemy, and, whilst doing so, surrendered a gate.[5] The city fell. Now Federigo lost all hope of being able to resist. The two great kings were his enemies, and on the march against him; the Pope was leagued with them, and his vassals were in revolt. He now only thought of how he should be able to save himself and his family, and avoid his country being given up to the ravages of war. Before the gate of the Arsenal in Naples, the King assembled his citizens and nobles and addressed them: "since fate was driving him away, he released them from their oath."[6] He himself came to the following arrangement with the French: "if within six months he could not appear at the head of an army, he should retire to France upon estates which should be assigned him, and thither should bring also his treasures, his acquaintances and friends."[7] Hereupon he betook himself to Ischia. Thither came also Beatrice of Hungary, and Isabella of

---

[1] Zurita, f. 126. [2] Zurita, 130, 132.
[3] Burcardus, 2129. [4] Caracciolus, Vita Spinelli, p. 47.
[5] Arluni, i. 17. Zurita, 215. [6] Passero, p. 125. [7] Zurita, 218.

Milan, his whole family and the few that still remained faithful to him. He never again was able to show himself with an army in the field, and so remained in France. How different were his expectations and how different all anticipations thirty years previously, when, in the flower of youth and hoping for the hand of the daughter of Charles the Bold, he passed through Rome![1] He was neither king nor heir to the throne, but the cardinals strove together as to which should be the first to welcome him. In him the whole of the dynasty of the Aragons was extinguished, as well as that of the Sforza; both of which a short time previously had flourished before all others in Italy. If we inquire what they achieved, the answer is that it was owing to them that, almost for the first time in their history, the Italians remained for a while free from the influence of foreign nations. If Francis Sforza had not become Lord of Lombardy, the French would have been it: had Alfonso not given Naples to a spurious son, a Spanish viceroy had been already established there. It was due to this assertion of their independence, that the Italians, untrammelled by foreign influence, and in progressive movement and rivalry within, were enabled within a somewhat limited sphere to develop their intellectual energies to a degree that the Germanic-Latin nations have ever regarded as the highest perfection of culture they ever attained. They acknowledge the fact that every new science and art traces its birth to this era. These two families had to separate, chiefly on account of two women; the one called in the French, the other the Spaniards: after they had weakened each other, union availed them nothing. The two invoked friends joined hands, and destroyed both. They both sprang up together, flourished together, perished together.

After this event, it was possible to journey under the French flag from the Pyrenees to Naples. The Spaniards advanced further at the foot of Italy. In order not to be completely ruined by this powerful enemy, Maximilian was obliged at Trent to promise the King of France the fief of Milan.[2] Three independent and pre-eminently active

[1] Jacob Volaterranus, Diarium Romanum, xxii. 95.
[2] Dumont, iv. 1, 16.

members of Christendom were now annihilated, and only three large States still existed in Italy. That was the result of Charles VIII.'s movements. But we have deeply to regret it. We always regret it, whenever a peculiar existence, one of God's own creations, perishes. But one consideration may tend to calm our feelings.

Do we but remember that Otranto was once in the hand of the Turks, and that a certain Boccalin, on another occasion, ceded to them Osimo, that sometimes the kings and at others the barons of Naples summoned them to their aid; do we, moreover, reflect that their agents were well received at Pesaro in the Papal State, and that, on Lodovico Sforza's invitation, they made an incursion into Frioli; do we remember how unanimous and powerful they always were or soon became, and how disunited and weak the Italians showed themselves, we cannot deny that Rome might just as readily have fallen into their hands as Constantinople, and that the same fate which befell the Hungarians might easily have overwhelmed all Italy, and primarily Naples, to which the Turks already raised pretensions. But now more powerful neighbours occupied the frontiers, and offered them resistance.

The Turks themselves, and almost the whole Mohammedan world were involved in this war.

Abuayazid, whom we know as Bajazeth, induced by the messages of Lodovico the Moor, considered that Louis XII. after conquering Italy would probably realize the other plans of his ancestors, that it was an insult to him that Venice forced the Turkish ships to salute theirs, and that now that he had remained five years quietly in Stambul, the day had at last arrived when he could take Inebecht, that is Lepanto.[1] Entertaining this idea, he gave Andrea Zancani, who entreated peace of him, only an Italian letter of compact, which he did not consider binding, and not a Turkish.[2] Whilst Andrea went joyfully on his way home, thinking that "the Othman of the Othmanis, the Grand Turk, had assured him of all

---

[1] Leunclavii, Annales Turcorum, p. 35. Ejusdem Pandectæ Historiæ Turcicæ, p. 192.

[2] Bembus, Histor. Venetum, 91a, 92a.

good will," the latter equipped 270 ships for sea in the Hellespont, collected 250,000 horses in Adrianople, and despatched them in June, 1499, to pillage Zara.[1] But in August they set out, he by land, and his fleet by sea, both bound for Lepanto. Antonio Grimani awaited the fleet at Sapienza. Antonio, from being a prosperous merchant, in whose hands earth appeared to turn into gold, had become supreme commander of the Venetian forces, and they believed they had in him an Alexander or a Cæsar.[2] He had kept back in harbour a ship of pilgrims about to sail for Jerusalem for this holiest deed, namely, to do battle against the Infidel; he had already issued his orders to the effect that: "he would, with God's assistance, attack the enemy," but when the Turks sailed out from Portolungo, and the Christians from Sapienza, both sides showed themselves but little inclined for the combat, and, after manœuvring about, turned back. At length both sides became more resolute. The largest Turkish ship put out for action. Two other Christian ships had just made ready to engage her, when there came from Corfu that valiant hero Andrea Loredano and joined the fleet. The crew shouted their acclamations, and after having asked the general whither he wished him to go, embarked on one of the ships. They put out and 'grappled the Turk. All three caught fire. Whilst the Turks hastened to rescue their men in boats, the Christians stood thunderstruck. Loredano made no attempt to escape, he said: "under this flag I was born, and under this flag will I die," and threw himself into the flames. The rest jumped into the water, and were taken prisoners. Thus was this battle lost.[3] Grimani retreated; the Turks came before Lepanto both by land and sea, and took it.[4] Two thousand others pillaged in Frioli, so that in Treviso, and even in Mestre, the inhabitants dared not to open their gates. Zancani who was sent against them dared not venture out of Gradisca.[5]

Zancani was banished; Grimani was exiled also. In

[1] Chronicon Venetum, 74.
[2] Chronicon Venetum, 125, 126. Jovius, Elogia, p. 300.
[3] Chronicon Venetum, 86, 96, 109. Petrus Justinianus, p. 354.
[4] Annales Turcici.   [5] Bembus, 105, 106.

the following year, Melchior Trevisano, Grimani's most bitter enemy, went against the Turks, but neither was he able to capture Cephalogna, nor relieve Modon, but Abuayazid took Coron, Modon,[1] and Navarino. We must remark that at the same time the Moors of Granada rose against the kings of Spain. Ximenes, Archbishop of Toledo, had softened the hearts of some Alfaquins by gifts of silk dresses and red hats, and a Zegri by imprisonment and presents, and then baptized them, as well as a large number of others from Albayzin. But when he had burnt upon a pile nearly five thousand of their books, all beautifully wrought in gold and silver and artistically decorated, the people revolted, killed his servants, and scarcely spared him. The King came sorrowfully to the Queen: "their monk had undone all their conquest."[2] Three days later, the Moors living in the city recollected themselves;[3] in order to escape punishment they allowed pictures to be hung in their mosques and submitted to baptism. But the Moors of the mountains, who dwelt upon the impracticable peaks of the Alpujarras and of the red, white, and snow-bound Sierra, could not be pacified.

Two brothers, D'Aghilar by name, took the field against Moors and Turks. The elder, Alfonso, against the Moors, and he was slain. Since a great number would by no means become Christians, they retired to Africa, and every day their foists went backwards and forwards to transport them thither.[4] In order to hold the remainder in check, soldiers were left there. The younger brother, Gonzal, the great captain, went to the assistance of the Venetians, and his advent brought them good fortune. Abuayazid, who was lamed by gout, had returned to his palace to study the Averroes, and Trivisano had just returned from his pursuit, full of pride that within sight of Europe and Asia he had succeeded in hanging some of his enemies on the gallows.[5] Gonzal combined forces with him in order to capture the castle of Cephalogna; he sent in word to the Turkish commander Gisdar: "that it was the victors of Granada who were attacking him." The Turk answered, "Has not each of

[1] Petrus Martyr, xiii. 217.
[2] Gomez, Vita Ximenis, 958-961.
[3] Zurita, 172.
[4] Zurita, 202, 203.
[5] Zurita, 195.

us seven bows and seven thousand arrows? besides, the day of our death is from the first written on our brow,"[1] and in the sense in which he spoke, he defended himself with his accustomed weapons. The Viscayans withstood all his arrows, scaled his castle, and killed him. This done, Gonzal turned towards Sicily and Naples. But afterwards Portuguese ships and even papal troops came and took part in the Turkish war. The French troops stormed Mitylene eighteen times. The Christians did not succeed further than to surprise Santa Maura, and even this they were obliged to restore as the price of the peace. What Venice had lost remained lost; it had but little advantage from Cremona, and Lodovico comforted himself in his prison with the reflection that, at all events, one ally had not broken faith with him.

[1] Jovius, Vita Gonsalvi.

BOOK II.

INTRODUCTION.

THE position of the Latin and Teutonic nations at this time may be briefly summarized as follows:—.
Italy had been visited by a great disaster; it was not political unity, which the country had really never possessed, that was imperilled, but that internal accord and that independence in dealing with foreign countries, which stood in its stead. These were lost and gone, and this result had been effected, not so much by Charles VIII.'s expedition, and its immediate consequences, as by the feud between Venice and Milan, and the Pope and Naples. The papal authority, which lorded it over Naples, was mainly instrumental to this end.

Alexander VI. cannot aptly be compared with the Popes of the thirteenth century, who, when hard pressed by the enmity of the Hohenstaufens, appealed to the French for aid to rid themselves of them; in his case, the marriage of his infamous son, an alliance supported by the one and opposed by the other side, was the motive for delivering Naples at once into the hands of the French and Spaniards. The after-consequences of this step swayed the destinies of Italy in the ensuing centuries.

Of all princes of those days, Louis XII. was the most powerful. Of all the ordinances by which he guaranteed the French an appropriate constitution, and gained for himself in their esteem a place between St. Louis and Henry IV., the following is, perchance, the most characteristic: "A judicial post should never be venal: in the event of his commanding such a thing, the Chancellor should not seal it; and, in the event of his having sealed it, neither Bailiff nor Seneschal should obey." Such was the ordinance which by the King's unbiassed will placed law above arbitrariness.¹ In this way he kept his people well inclined towards him. Not merely his own subjects in Italy flocked to his Court, but the deputies of the several independent States in almost still greater numbers. Every day there arrived mounted couriers bearing letters, instructions, and money; everyone was desirous of currying favour with a member of the King's Council. No prince or city in Italy felt themselves secure without being first assured of French protection. Florence was itself powerful, yet was not in a better position than the rest.² In addition to politics, the daily occupations of Louis were hunting and hawking. With the month of May, the huntsmen made their appearance at the Court all dressed in green, and with horns and hounds. In September, when the stag-hunt was over, the falconers appeared in their cocked hats, and took the place of the others.³ Louis followed them both, through field and through wood.

His principal allies were Alexander VI., the kings of Denmark and Scotland, and certain German princes.

Alexander had assigned the legation at the Court of France, the most important office the Pope had to bestow, to the Cardinal Georges d'Amboise for life; and this was considered such an extraordinary act of favour, that the University of Paris opposed it. The neighbours and vassals who enjoyed Louis' protection, were taken likewise by the Pope under his. The Duke of Urbino allowed exiles and refugees free asylum and social intercourse at his Court; Alexander had guaranteed him his nephew's succession. John Bentivoglio relied upon his new treaty with Cesar, founded ironworks in the mountains near to Bologna, and cut canals in the plain; believing it was for his children.

The Baglioni, Vitelli, and Orsini, were in Cesar's pay. Pandolfo Petrucci was the head of the Nove, and being, through the three privy councillors, chief of the whole municipality of Siena, became also, in the persons of these his friends, allied with the Pope. Ercole of Ferrara pro-

---

¹ Ordonnance of 1499. Article 40 in Röderen, Mémoire pour servir à l'histoire de Louis XII. Paris, 1822, p. 255.

² Macchiavelli, Legazione alla corte di Francia, iii. 64, 66, 80.

³ Fleuranges, Mémoires, 19.

ceeded to build palaces, to ride behind processions, and to live carelessly in theatrical pleasures; his son was married in the Lent of 1502 to Lucrezia Borgia. Alexander remained the devoted friend of the King.[1]

James IV. of Scotland, who, since his marriage with the daughter of Henry VII., had forgotten his English wars, was building in Falkirk, celebrating tournaments at Stirling, and receiving constant visits from French knights.[2] Both expeditions of the King of Denmark were unsuccessful; that against the Ditmarshes, whom he, in league with France, had attacked against Maximilian's wish, at the time of the Milanese War,[3] failed, by reason of the enemy's bravery; that against Sweden was completely foiled by Sten Sture, and in 1502 he was forced to rest. Several German princes maintained an open understanding with France; since the treaty of Trent, they paused in their opposition to Maximilian.

This combination was confronted by another, a genuine family union, formed by the house of the Catholic Kings', and cemented not only by league, but by blood-relationship. In the year 1497, all the children of Ferdinand the Catholic were together, with the exception of Juana. Juan, with his consort, Margaret, was destined for the Spanish throne; Isabella for the Portuguese, Catharine for the English, and Maria for some other throne, which was at present the object of negotiation. At the Court all was still; all who desired to gain favour, went about with downcast eyes and modest paces; the royal pair had prescribed the strictest ceremonial, extending even to the interchange of kisses on hand and mouth, between the ladies of the Court.[4] But here changes were taking place, which were of great import for the State then existent, and of the greatest for posterity.

Just as all had begun to hope that the unity of Spain under a native sovereign had, in the person of Juan's son,

---

[1] Castiglione, Cortegiano. Baldi, Vita di Guidubaldo, vi. 223. Bursellis, Chronicon Bononiense, 912. Allegretti, Ephemerides Seneuses, in Muratori, 23, p. 763. Diarium Ferrarense, 325, 358, 276.

[2] Buchananus, Rerum Scoticarum, lib. xiii. p. 468, ed. Francf. 1624.

[3] Geppardi, Hist. of Denmark and Norway, ii. 41. Note 2.

[4] Zurita, i. 118. Petrus Martyr, p. 99. Marineus Siculus, 567.

been now for ever established, Juan died. He had been the hope of the realm. A prince by birth, and a gracious and good prince, is a great blessing. But now black flags floated over the walls of the city, and for forty days all business ceased. All the inhabitants were dressed in black. If a grandee rode out, it was only his horses' eyes that were undraped. The child, too, of which Margaret was delivered after Juan's decease, died as soon as born.[1]

Hereupon Isabella, who had since become Queen of Portugal, returned with her husband, and after receiving at Toledo the allegiance of the Castilians, as successor to the throne, she came to Saragossa, in order to obtain it likewise from the refractory Aragons. The whole peninsula would in course of time have thus become united; but whilst at Saragossa Isabella also died, and her son Miguel shortly after her.[2]

Thus the succession devolved upon Juana, the consort of the Archduke Philip, and passed to the house of Hapsburg with all the greater certainty, since on St. Matthew's day, 1500, she gave birth at Ghent to a son, Charles. "The lot fell upon Matthew," said the old Queen of Castile, and rightly, for round the life of this child was centred the greatest combination our nations have for centuries known. In the year 1502, Philip and Juana were in Spain; now received by the Commanders of Orders, so gorgeously attired that even their stirrups were of gold, and anon welcomed by that Biscayan nobility, who begged for a bounty in order to be able to celebrate high festival. And then the succession was assured them; in Toledo by the prelates, grandees, and procurators of the cities of Castile; in Saragossa, by the bishops, by the thirty-two Ricoshombros, and the deputies of the Cavalleros and Infanzones; in Aragon by the Jurada of the city.[3]

Meanwhile, Catharine had gone to wed herself with Arthur, Prince of Wales; Maria to marry with Manuel of Portugal, and Margaret, Juan's widow, with the Duke of Savoy.[4]

All these houses formed a natural union. The French

---

[1] Comines. Petrus Martyr, p. 100, 106.
[2] Osorius, de rebus gestis Emanuelis, i. 19. Zurita, 139.
[3] Hubert Thomas Leodius, Vita Friderici Palatini, lib. ii. Zurita, 227. [4] Treaty in Dumont, iv. 1, 15.

League and the family of the Spanish Kings, confronted each other face to face. Philip, at once vassal of France and heir to the throne of Spain, made a compact with Louis to the effect that their children, Charles and Claudia, who were both as yet in the cradle, should one day marry, and thus became the mediator between both parties. This induced Maximilian to abandon completely the interests of the Sforza, and, in October, 1501, to promise the King of France to invest him with the fief of Milan. Philip journeyed through France on his way to Spain, sat among the peers in the justice hall, came before the King, and readily comported himself as a vassal. Juana, on her part, gave Claudia a large diamond, in testimony of the new alliance. Philip also prepared to return through France.[1]

At this time our nations ruled over hardly a single foreigner, and were subjected to none. We find even the Grand Master of Prussia now refusing allegiance to the King of Poland, and this action of his found the support of many German princes. Iwan Wasiljewitsch's attack upon Livonia in the year 1501 was repulsed by the general, Walter von Plettenberg, in two great battles; peace for fifty years being thus secured. At this juncture a general campaign against the Turks, who were now engaged in war with Venice, would have been a feasible undertaking. Immediately after the treaty with Maximilian, and when Christendom was enjoying universal peace, Louis proclaimed this crusade.[2] For this, both France and Italy, and upper and lower Germany, but especially the latter, had been prepared by a marvellous apparition of certain coloured crosses, which were said to have suddenly made their appearance everywhere, upon linen and wool, and upon dresses and all manner of cloths. Maximilian, in anticipation of this war, founded a special order of knighthood.[3] But, as yet, Italian affairs, as well as those of the usurping powers, were not so firmly established as not to engender a fresh quarrel, a quarrel destined to become even yet more wide-spreading than the former.

---

[1] Pontus Heuterus, Rerum Austriac. libri. From the MS. of Lailaing, Philip's fellow traveller, p. 259.   [2] Appendix to Monstrelet, 247.

[3] Joh. Francisci Pici Mirandulini Staurostichon. Carmen ad Maximilianum. Apud Freherum Rer. Germ. tom. ii.

CHAPTER I.

1. *The War in Naples and Romagna.*

IN Naples a fresh war broke out between the Spaniards and the French. The immediate cause was the treaty of partition, which they had concluded together. In this partition, Lavoro and the Abruzzi were guaranteed to the French, and Apulia and Calabria to the Spaniards, whilst four smaller provinces, the two Principati, Basilicata and Capitanata had not been expressly divided. Now, seeing that, according to the fundamental institutions of these countries, institutions inaugurated by the Emperor Friedrich II., the Principati shared their court of justice with Lavoro, whilst the other two had one in common with Apulia,[1] a little good-will—especially now that the Dogana question had been settled between them—would have sufficed to settle this dispute also, had not there been other motives for quarrelling, notably, the internal factiousness of the country. The Colonna, whose possessions lay in the French share, placed themselves under the protection of Spain, whilst several towns in Apulia raised the French banner. The Angiovines summoned the French to Calabria, whilst the Aragons called Gonzal to the Abruzzi. The self-same factions were already engaged in fighting for Manfredonia and Alramura.[2] It turned out, that, live in whatever division they might, the one party would only obey the French and the other only the Spaniards, whilst these powers were always ready to help them to gain the ascendency. The attitude of their respective armies was decisive for the issue. When, on one

---

[1] Lebret, History of Italy, iii. 166. From Matthaeus Afflictus.
[2] Zurita, 231, 219. Jovius, Vita Gonsalvi, 230.

occasion, the Spaniards had made an incursion as far as the springs of Troja, and a skirmish was the result, Ive d'Allegre sent a message to Mendoza, inquiring, " Whether this meant an open breach, and was intended to rouse them from their tranquillity; if so, he was ready to give satisfaction." Mendoza replied, " We came to Italy, I and my army, not for peace, but for war. We would gladly engage, even without orders." And this was the feeling of the most. At this time the two commanders, Gonzal and Nemours, who had advanced close to each other, the first to Atella, and the latter to Melfi, often met at the high altar of a chapel dedicated to St. Antony, situate on the ridge of the Apennine chain which lay between them. But, in spite of all their orders to the contrary, the struggle broke out quite spontaneously.[1]

On the 12th July, 1502, when the Spaniards forcibly entered Tripalda—alleging it was a widow's portion, belonging to Juana, the sister of their King—and when Aubigny set forth from Naples to recover it—holding it belonged to the French share—open war could no longer be avoided.[2]

Gonzal, who had under his orders but few of his 5,000 men—for he had brought so many with him—was at once obliged to fall back. In his Apulia lay one of the four castles, which were considered the strongest in the whole of Italy,[3] viz., Barletta, and thither he proceeded. The French pursued him. They forced Pedro Navarra to retire from Canossa, though with honours.[4] In August they took Quadrata and Bisceglia; and by September they had all the Sanseverins of Bisignan, Bitonto, Melito, Capocho and Acquaviva di Conversano for them. Of the whole of Apulia they left the Spaniards nothing but Bari, Barletta, and some surrounding places. These districts also were attacked by the French, and first and foremost Barletta, " for the honour of their chivalry;"[5] for Bari was being defended by a woman, Isabella, the widow of John Galeazzo.

[1] Zurita, 238, 240.
[2] Passero, Giornale Napolitano, 129.
[3] Leander Alberti, Descriptio Italiæ, p. 369.
[4] Petrus Martyr, 15, 140.
[5] Jovius, Vita Gonsalvi, 235. Zurita.

"We are still six miles away," wrote Nemours on the 19th November, "and keep the enemy shut in; the King shall see that we defend his rights staunchly, and that everything is going from good to better."[1] In December, Aubigny advanced to Calabria. He fell upon the Spaniards, —they being here also much too weak—at the very moment they were in the act of retreating across the Aspromonte and through the passes upon Retromarina. They managed, however, to make good their escape; but the whole of Calabria, with the exception of a few castles on the sea-board, was lost to them. They held their ground in Gerace and in the Motta.

The rest of the Spanish possessions (like the plank of a ship fought for by drowning men) was the object of a chivalrous war, waged with good weapons. Here were the heroes whom Ariosto had seen when he began to sing of his Rüdigers and Rinaldos. In Calabria we meet with that Imbercourt to whom, whenever there was a battle to fight, the heat of an Italian noontide seemed like the cool of morning, and with that Aubigny who, in order to ransom him, although he had been preferred before him, sacrificed even his silver plate.[2] Before Barletta were the discreet La Palice, to whom the enemy first gave the title of "Marshal," and Montoison, who, though bowed down by weight of years, was still, when on horseback, the falcon of the fray; there, too, was Fontrailles, called the "Fearless," as well as many others of those who, if there was a battle to fight, and they happened to be on shipboard, contending with contrary winds, would land, and march one hundred leagues in three days.[3] Of their number was also that Bayard who, from the very hour when his mother came down from the tower to give him her small purse at parting, and to commend to him four virtues—the fear of God, truth, an obliging and a generous disposition—had never neglected a single day to practise them. He always prayed, before leaving his chamber, and no one ever heard him praise himself. Once when he had captured 15,000

---

[1] Lettera del duca di Nemorsa a Ciamonte in Macchiavelli, Legazione al duca Valentino, 222.

[2] Brantome and Garnier, from Anton's MS., 362.

[3] Brantome, 115, 116. Anton, Histoire de Louys XII., p. 159.

ducats, and another, though he had no claim, demanded them of him, he first of all established his legal right; this done, as soon as the money had been paid down, and his adversary remarked, "I should be happy for all the rest of my life if I only had the half of it," he replied, "Then I will give you just half;" and thereupon gave him the one half and his followers the other. "O, my lord, my friend," cried the other, upon his knees, "no Alexander was ever so generous."[1] Bayard's life is as clear as crystal, his heart ready in every danger, and his soul mild and gentle. The Spaniards resemble the French; but the resemblance is that between the Moorish and Christian knights of Ariosto. Among them was the small, thin Pedro Navarra, who had raised himself from a common soldier to the dignity of Count; no rock was so hard that he could not mine it; his mouth tightly closed, his nose pointed and severe; a thick and pointed beard fell from his chin.[2] There, too, was Pedro de Paz, who, when mounted, could scarcely be seen above the head of his horse; a squinting, withered, and deformed dwarf, yet the boldest heart in the world. He, accompanied only by his Moor, each with a torch, he himself with a naked sword in hand, ventured into the ill-famed grottoes of the Gaurus, in order to dig out hidden treasure; for he recked ghosts as little as he did the enemy in the battle.[3] Their leader was Gonzal Fernandez Aghilar de Cordova, whose plumed crest had, in his first battle, been seen thick in the midst of the fray, now a real captain. He never interfered when Spaniards, who made disgraceful conditions, were slain by their fellows for degenerate conduct; but that an enemy retiring under treaty should be robbed of a gold chain, this he never tolerated, and even himself pursued the robber even into the sea. He said, "I would rather tame lions than these Asturians;" but yet he tamed them. His infantry consisted of those whom the Spanish soil

[1] Histoire du bon chevalier Bayard, commencement, 407, 113. Brantome. Pasquier, Recherches de la France, from the Histoire.
[2] Jovii Elogium Navarræ. Vita Alfonsi Estensis, 171. Fleuranges, Mémoires, 84.
[3] Histoire de Bayard, 114. Passero, Giornale, 151.

would no longer tolerate, on account of their crimes; but he made them all loyal to his King, ambitious, untiring in besieging and defending, and dauntless in the battle.[1] He was the first to combine in a single corps Spanish, Italian, and German soldiers, an organization that proved irresistible for a century and a half. At the head of men like Leyva, Pescara, Alva, Farnese, and many other famous leaders, who for one hundred and fifty years hardly ever quitted the field with that army whose nucleus he had first formed, he may fairly be considered as being the great captain of all.

These, now, and their comrades, fought, not merely for victory but, for the prize of strength, dexterity, and chivalrous bearing. Sometimes individuals would engage in a single-handed combat; they first knelt down and prayed to God, threw themselves flat upon the ground, and kissed it, and then appealed to the sword.[2] It might happen that the French would announce that on the morrow they would prove that their *hommes d'armes* were superior to the Spanish; whereupon the Spaniards would come in like numbers to the appointed place, in order, as they said, to fight for their King's, their country's, and their own honour.[3] Or both sides, the one coming from Rubo and the other from Barletta, charged each other on horses with iron masks about their heads, and plates on their breasts and shoulders, and struggled together until one side was exhausted and gave way. Or they would have recourse to stratagem in order to gain the advantage; the French, for instance, would fly, but only to the ambush which they had laid, whereupon the Spaniards on their part would retire also, but only behind their ambush, so that the French were again compelled to fall back, yet not unwillingly, for they had still a third ambush in reserve, and this was their last, enabling them to remain the victors.[4] In this chivalrous rivalry the Italians also joined. In Barletta, which Gonzal defended

---

[1] Jovii, Vita Gonsalvi, 206; further Castiglione, Cortegiano, iii. 287.
[2] Histoire de Bayard, 103.
[3] Zurita, 249.
[4] Ferronus, Rerum Gallicarum, lib. iii. p. 59.

against the besiegers with his Spaniards and Italians, a French prisoner once observed to a Spaniard, that the Italians were cowards by nature, and their allegiance but empty air. "Were ye not there, we should extinguish them as water extinguishes fire."[1] This roused the Italians to challenge the French to a duel of thirteen to thirteen on the plain lying between Andria and Barletta. This duel took place on the 13th February. The Italian historians and poets have graphically described it; how that both sides confronted each other like two high forests, between which flowed a small brook, and how that the French attacked the others in vain—for Ferramosca restrained the ardour of his Italians—and how that the latter at length made their onslaught, like a subterranean mine, that seethes internally until at length it bursts its bonds and sends rock and castle into the air,[2] and conquered, driving twelve before them, and taking them prisoners (the thirteenth was slain); whereupon they were received with the ringing of bells and salvos of artillery, and with the cry of Italia and Hispania.[3]

Thus was the war protracted from June, 1502, until February, 1503. The Spanish were at a disadvantage, but they held their ground. During precisely the same months, Alexander also warred in the Romagna in the self-same cause, yet in how different a manner and degree! He well knew that the King, if not requiring his help, needed at all events his sanction, and he knew how to gain both sanction and help.

Cesar renewed his campaign in the Romagna with insatiable greed, duplicity, and violence. In June, 1502, he planned an expedition against the Varani of Camerino, and borrowed for this purpose Guidubaldo of Urbino's artillery. Guidubaldo had, besides, made him a present of a few thousand men and a horse splendidly caparisoned. Cesar, in return, saluted him as the best brother he had in Italy, yet he did not long rejoice in this name, for this

---

[1] Passero, 133. Jovius, Vita Gonsalvi.
[2] Marie Hieronymi Vitæ, 13. Pugilum certamen, Milano, 1818, vs. 316 and 390.
[3] Jovius. Guicciardini. Sabellicus. Carpesanus, 1250. Brantome, 106, wrong.

expedition was primarily directed against him. On the 20th of June he was sitting at supper in the shady vale of Zoccolanti, when at sunset a messenger appeared and announced that "Cesar's cavalry was advancing upon his city Fossombrone."[1] He struck on the table and sprang up; he felt he was deceived. At that instant other messengers arrived with the news that: "the enemy had been seen in the vicinity of Marino and San Leo, and that Cesar himself was advancing upon Cagli." Guidubuldo saw that he was defenceless, and caught in a net. He assembled the citizens of Urbino and addressed them. "A year has 365 days, and a day twenty-four hours. Of these days one, and of these hours one will be auspicious for my return." Thereupon he took flight. On the mountain roads on which he sped, hired peasants shouted after him the murderers' war-cry of "Carne Ammazza." Soon he heard bells ringing, the firing of shots, and the crackling of fire all around, intended to rouse the whole country to find him. On one occasion he was only saved by a girl, who was coming from market and gave him some information; but yet he succeeded at last in eluding the enemy.[2] His country, his city, and his library, in which he frequently studied with his tutor Odasio, fell into Cesar's hands.

In July Cesar also took Camerino. Old Julius Varano, who has been compared to Priam, because he only saved one son in a foreign country, he allured with all his other sons by specious promises, and then caused them all to be strangled.[3] In August he allied himself afresh with Louis XII.; which done, in order both to make Bologna the capital of his duchy, as also to give his father the glory of having in his day conquered a city, that no former Pope had been able to conquer,[4] he turned against the Bentivogli.

For these ends he made use of the Baglioni of Perugia, the Vitelli in Città di Castello, of Oliverotto da Fermo,

[1] Baldi, Vita di Guidubaldo, duca d'Urbino VI., 234. Nardi, Istorie Fiorentine, iv. 78. Burcardus, 2138. Raphael Volaterranus, Vita Alexandri, 166.
[2] Lettera del duca Guidubaldo, in Leoni, Vita di Francesca Maria, p. 15-21, in documentary form in Baldi's excerpts.
[3] Baldi, Vita, 253.
[4] Macchiavelli, Legazione al duca Valentino, 200.

and of all the Orsini. All these were warriors by inclination and profession. Of the first named, it was said that they were born with the sword at their side; the second had been the first to introduce Swiss arms into Italy. They pursued each their own aims and ends, as, for instance, Oliverotto, who, by murdering seven leading citizens of Fermo, who were related to him and had brought him up, made himself master of the city. Thus acted the others also, who were desirous of restoring the Medici to Florence. Cesar indulged them in this.[1] But now that he had allied himself with the King, and had begun to oppose their enterprises and to attack the Bentivogli, whose case was almost like theirs, they were filled with apprehension that, "the ruin of all the lords in the State of the Church had been resolved on." They thereupon sent envoys and assembled. They entered into a close alliance with Petrucci and Bentivoglio, and at last in Magione decided to make war upon Cesar.[2]

They resolved the war, and the Urbinati commenced it. The signal for its outbreak was given on the 5th October by a carpenter, who let a beam, which he was instructed to convey to the castle of San Leo, fall upon the drawbridge there.[3] Thereupon, in an instant, armed men rushed across the bridge and took the castle. Thence the cry of "Feltre and Duke" spread through the whole duchy, and stirred it up in revolt. In the city the peasants, who had come to market, first seized the cannon, and then gained the castle. Guidubaldo returned, and even those who only saw him lying on a bed—for he was at that time suffering from his malady, the gout—went away satisfied. Camerino summoned the last of the Varani.[4]

But what could have been the reason that the allies of Magione, menaced as they were and warlike as they were, did not attack Cesar, who was all defenceless at Imola?

[1] Leander Alberti, Descriptio, 125. Macchiavelli, Principe, 8. Nardi, 81.
[2] Macchiavelli, descrizione del modo tenuto dal duca Valentino nell' Ammazzare Vitellozzo Vitelli, etc., 92. Nardi, 83.
[3] Cesar's own story in Macchiavelli, Legazione, p. 130.
[4] Baldi, Vita di Guidubaldo, vii. 7 f.

They did not wish to destroy him; they only were for showing him how indispensable they were to him. Cesar knew that full well. "They wished to secure themselves, and nothing further," said he. He sent and asked them why they had deserted him, urging that only the title belonged to him, and that theirs was the possession of all his conquests, both those of the past and those to come: "he sent them a blank sheet of paper with his signature, and only waited for their conditions." And now that Alexander had remarked to Cardinal Orsino that he would perhaps resign his papal chair in his favour, they believed that they had attained what they wished. The Cardinal smiled and said: "The Pope needs me, we are always good friends."[1] On the 25th October, Paolo Orsino went to Cesar about the matter of the treaty. Cesar now said: "They are ogling me; I will abide my time."[2]

In Imola he received not only the assurances of King Louis, the proposals of the Florentine Popolares, and money from his father, but in June he gathered round him 230 French lancers, 2,500 soldiers, half French and half German, 2,500 Italian soldiers, a Bolognian refugee with mounted riflemen, and some Albanians; all in his pay. Meanwhile, Paolo journeyed with the draft of the peace proposed from Imola to Perugia, and thence to Magione and the camps of his friends, and minded no trouble, convincing one after the other, and although Vitellozzo Vitelli remained a long time obdurate, he also was at last overpersuaded, and signed it.[3]

On the 2nd December the following treaty was agreed to: "Cesar to receive back Camerino and Urbino, but to give a pledge to the Bentivogli by arranging a matrimonial alliance between their respective houses, and to use the old weapons again."[4] Hereupon Cesar ordered the barons to take the field against the revolted districts and against Sinigaglia; he himself remained with his army at Imola. He only gave audience to very few, and only then to those from whom he expected to hear important news; he only

[1] Burcardi, Diarium, 2142.
[2] Macchiavelli, Legazione, 161.
[3] Macchiavelli. Legazione, 145, 156, 174, 183. Del modo Tenuto, 94.
[4] Zurita, 261.

admitted three or four servants to his presence, and never left a certain chamber before nightfall.¹ It was never possible to learn from him what his purposes were; but his confidantes said, "We have been wounded with daggers and we are now to be healed with words: Even children would laugh at such terms."²

The treaty with the Orsini restored forthwith to Cesar both Camerino and Urbino, but only under the condition that the people and Guidubaldo's private possessions should be protected. Sinigaglia was next prevailed upon by four heads of the Orsini, namely, Paolo, Vitellozzo, Oliverotto, and the Duke of Gravina, to promise to surrender its castle, but only to Cesar himself.

The time he had longed for had at length arrived. On the 31st December, 1502, he advanced with his army upon Sinigaglia. Vitellozzo was not for awaiting his coming: but as the others trusted Cesar, and Paolo coaxed him to remain, he did not care to break the league. Unarmed, and attired in his citizen's cap with its green lining, he mounted his mule and rode forth to meet him. Their troops were quartered in the outlying villages, with the exception of Oliverotto's companies; and these latter dispersed at Cesar's request, "for fear they might otherwise quarrel with his troops about their quarters." The four chiefs escorted him to the lodging prepared for his reception. He would not part from them, "as he had something to say to them." Full of apprehension—but they could no longer refuse—they entered his apartments with him. Now he had them in his clutches.³ His principles were: "He who does not avenge himself, deserves to be insulted." He said, it is right to deceive those who are experts in all treachery and treason.⁴ He had always conspired not merely against lands, but against the head of their sovereign lord as well. When the door was closed behind them, Michelott, the privy executor of all Cesar's murders, stepped forward with a few armed men. Each

---

[1] Macchiavelli, Legazione, 250 f.
[2] Macchiavelli, Legazione, Celt., 23, p. 215.
[3] Macchiavelli, del modo tenuto nell' Ammazzar, 95, 36. Nardi, 85. Guicciardini, Book v. 290.
[4] Macchiavelli, Legazione, 266, 268.

of them was addressed with, "Sir, your are a prisoner," and forthwith they were thrown into prison. Their troops were surprised and slain. Cesar, talkative and vivacious once more, rode through the streets.

The work begun by the son was continued by the father. He invited the Cardinal Orsino to him, as if to narrate to him the story of the fall of Sinigaglia; but on the Cardinal looking down into the courtyard from the room into which he had been shown, he saw his mule being unsaddled and led off into the papal stables. He and all his friends with him were captives also.[1]

And now for murder and conquest, and the final accomplishment of these schemes and undertakings. Oliverotto and Vitellozzo, bound back to back, the former accusing the latter—it was the anniversary of the death of the Seven of Fermo,—and the latter praying for the spiritual blessing of the same Pope who had condemned him to die, were, on the first night of their captivity, strangled with one rope; the other two suffered shortly after. The Cardinal's mistress, in male attire, brought the Pope a valuable pearl, his mother sent a sum of money, and the Cardinal promised a still more considerable sum. But all these endeavours could only attain a momentary alleviation of his lot. His life could not be saved. When he died, all the world was convinced that he had been poisoned by order of the Pope. Their houses in Rome were pulled down; and an Orsina of eighty years of age was compelled to seek shelter under a public archway. Almost all their castles, the cities of Perugia and Città di Castello, as well as many towns, fell into the hands of the Pope. Cesar compelled the Sienese to expel Petrucci.[2] Never in history had the State of the Church known a Pope so powerful as Alexander. Both factions of barons had been expelled, if not utterly annihilated; there was now not a lord in the land, save his son and his son's family—for the Bentivogli and the Esti had been received into it—Siena was conquered, Florence friendly, all successfully accomplished.

It was primarily the name and assistance of France

[1] Burcardus, 2148.
[2] Macchiavelli, in both passages. Burcardus, 2150. Carpesanus, Historiæ, p. 1248.

that achieved this result. When Cesar was in peril, Louis said: "Whoever helped Cæsar he would love the more the quicker he did it; he would give the Pope and his son the whole of the State of the Church."[1] As the Orsini were in negotiation with the Spaniards,[2] their destruction redounded likewise to Louis' advantage. It was expected that Cesar's troops would come to the aid of the French in Naples.

The Decision in Naples.

In February, 1503, Gonzal, now shut up in Barletta, appeared to be in a sorry plight. Neither the German nor yet the Spanish troops, for which he had written, made their appearance. The transport of supplies was impossible so long as the French galleys under Prejean held the sea; and yet troops and supplies were both urgently needed.[3]

A change for the better began when, before the very eyes of the Venetians, some Spanish sloops and galleys succeeded in becoming master of so much extent of coast, that Prejean hurriedly threw his guns overboard, set free his slaves, forsook his ships, and escaped by land. Six days later, Gonzal dared once more leave Barletta. Whilst Nemours was gone to subdue a revolted town, he himself succeeded, after storming for seven hours, in reducing Rubo, and taking many brave men prisoners, and among them Palice. His courage increased, but as yet he was much too weak to make an attack in full force. But lack of provisions impelled him to risk it, and he was preparing to try his luck in a sortie on the following ing day, when a Venetian ship laden with wheat, and immediately afterwards a Sicilian corn ship, put into harbour. Three others brought 7,000 tumbanos of corn with them.[4] He was thus enabled to wait for reinforcements. On the 8th March, the Spaniards arrived at Reggio[5] with

[1] From Louis' letters in Macchiavelli, Legaz., 156.
[2] Zurita, 261.
[3] Caracciolus, Vita Spinelli, in Muratori, xxii. p. 50.
[4] Zurita, 266, 267. Jovius, 245.   [5] Zurita, 256.

THE DECISION IN NAPLES.

3,000 Catalonian, Galician, and Asturian infantry, and 300 heavy and 400 light cavalry. On the 10th April, the 2,500 Germans—the contingent Maximilian had promised,[1] and Joan Manuel had paid—at length arrived in Manfredonia, under the command of Hans von Ravenstein. Now the Spaniards were equal, if not superior, to the French in numbers. They were in a position to carry on the war in earnest. Serious encounters had already taken place in Calabria. Near Terranuova, the Spaniards from Gerace and Reggio were collected under the joint command of Andrada Caravajal, Benavides, and Antonio Leyva. In the plain below, but across the river which intersects it, Aubigny showed himself, and sent his herald Ferracut up into the Spanish camp: "They should come down into the valley where he had once vanquished the bravest king." The Spaniards gave the herald a silver dish and a golden goblet, replying: "They would come." They then came down, and, the infantry covered by the cavalry, crossed the stream in the plain. At this moment Aubigny attacked Benavides.[2] In Ubeda and Baeza the lion of the Benavides and the black standard of the Caravajals had often met in conflict.[3] But now Caravajal forgot the old feud, and with his Ginetæ made an onslaught upon Aubigny's rear. The French were defeated. Aubigny, surrounded by his body guard of Scots, escaped to Gioia.

This took place on the 20th April. On the 27th of the same month Gonzal left Barletta with all his forces also to do battle.[4] The French, stationed at Canossa, saw him depart and likewise set out, but neither side very willingly. Gonzal had received provisions, but no money; he scarcely succeeded in quieting his Spaniards with promises of rich booty and with the small sum of six carlins[5] for nine months' pay. The French had received express orders from their king to finish the business forthwith, otherwise

---

[1] Vide also Viti Prioris Eberspergensis Chronica Bavarorum, in Œfele, ii. 739.
[2] Jovius, Vita Gonsalvi, 251. Zurita, 278.
[3] Molina, Nobleza del Andaluzia, Sevilla, 1518, fol. 217 and 222.
[4] Petrus Martyr, 16, 147.
[5] Zurita, f. 330.

he would summon them home again to their wives, and send other Hommes d'Armes in their stead.

Here stretched away the treeless plain of Apulia, and the month of April always scorches there. Of Gonzal it is told how his Germans in early morning licked the dewdrops from the high fennel stalks, and for very thirst fell down exhausted at noon; how he refreshed them with the last drain of Ofanto water the bottles contained; and how at last he let the most weary mount behind the horsemen. Nemours will have had to contend with no lesser difficulties on his march. Yet, after ten months of weary waiting, the satisfaction of at length finding themselves face to face with the enemy enabled them to endure their hardships, and, on the 28th April towards evening, both arrived in extreme exhaustion before Cerignola. The Spaniards, who were the first to arrive, threw up light entrenchments in a vineyard.[1] But as soon as the French came up, and both armies saw each other, they forgot exhaustion and thirst—the soul conceals within it secret wells of ever revigorating refreshment—and the armies prepared for battle. On either side, the infantry was in the centre, and the cavalry on the flanks. Nemours was by no means inclined to risk the attack; but was compelled to it by the pressure of Ive d'Allegre and the other captains. In order to show, as he said, who he was, he dashed at the trench behind which the Germans were posted. He came up to it, wheeled about, came up to it again and cried, "We must over this blunt wall." Whilst dashing at it in full career, a German gun laid him low,[2] and his comrades, who met with an equally hot reception, began to retire. Further to the left, the Swiss attacked, though somewhat later; but as soon as they perceived their commander, recognizable in his white plume, and at the same moment many others also, laid low by the Galician bullets and javelins, they likewise turned and fled. Allegre, who led the left wing and was furthest in the rear, dared not then attempt aught further. The Spaniards were left victors on the field, and passed the night in the French bivouac. Nothing further

---

[1] Jovius, Vita Gonsalvi, 254.
[2] Ferronus, Rerum Gallic., vol. iii. p. 66.

was now needed to give the Spaniards the upper hand in this kingdom, rent and torn as it was by factions. The understandings which Gonzal had maintained from the Abruzzian Mountains as far as Castel a Mar awoke to life and energy. On a single day he took thirty castles, and on the 13th May with the cry of "Spagna," "Spagna," the Count of Tramontano opened to him the gates of Naples. Inigo Davalos brought the keys of the castle of Ischia. Rocca Guilielma, that since Charles VIII.'s expedition had held for the French, fell in June. Meanwhile, Andrada took stronghold after stronghold in Calabria, and at length Aubigny himself surrendered to him. With the exception of Gaeta, whither the French army had fled, almost the whole kingdom was now in the hands of the Spaniards. At the end of July Navarra went to that stronghold, in order to try the same means as had opened to him the fortress of Naples.[1]

We shall now consider the great change which was brought about by the death of Alexander VI., which took place in August of this year. During the agitation for the election of his successor, French and Spaniards fought together. In Rome, even the troops were on one occasion arrayed against each other. This event, however, exercised no immediate influence upon the war in Naples. The decision there depended solely upon the superiority of arms.

In October, 1503, a fresh French army, under the Marquis Gonzaga, made its appearance on the Gariglian, in order to invade the lost provinces. The Spaniards were resolved to prevent their crossing the river. Accordingly, both armies marched backwards and forwards for a while, intently observing each other, until Gonzal threw a bridge across at Sessa, and, under cover of his guns, which mounted on barks swept the river, actually succeeded in gaining the opposite bank. As soon as he had crossed, a battle began, in which Gonzal fought on foot, and a Spanish ensign who had lost his right arm exclaimed: "Have I not still the left?" and again seized the standard. In this encounter the French held the bridge and

[1] Passero, Giornale, 138. Jovius, 258. Zurita, 291.

the head of the bridge, but they never advanced a step further.[1]

But the opposing armies were not kept apart so much by the river, although it actually separated their camps, as by the bog on either bank—for the season was very wet, and the country as far as Montdragon almost one great morass. Some of the Spaniards kept the outer lines of the trench they had dug; the rest were encamped under oaken huts.[2] The French endeavoured to find shelter in the neighbouring villages, at all events for their horses; the Swiss companies lay alternately in the camp and in the same villages. Both armies were in need of provisions, money, and clothes.[3] This depressing state of things resulted in the very reverse of the merry war before Barletta. Words of abuse were heard more than ring of arms. The Spaniards were abused for their stealing and hanging proclivities; the French were called drunkards; the Swiss were called cattle-vultures, and the Germans "Schmocher;" whilst the Italians were called "Bougres."[4]

The question was, which of the two would hold out the longer. Gonzaga hearing himself called "Bougre" by his own French, and all disaster attributed to him, would no longer tolerate this want of discipline, and so drew up an account of his operations, and after having it signed by his captains, left the army. Gonzal, on the other hand, who was beset by his bravest officers, stating that they could and would not endure this state of affairs any longer, replied: "Rather a step forward to encounter death, than one back to victory," and so held out."[5]

At length the enemy crossed over and attacked. On the 29th December, 1503, Gonzal made an onslaught upon the French bridge, and a simultaneous attack upon their camp with his main army, which, with Alvian's assistance, he had been enabled to bring across the river. This battle

---

[1] Jorii Gonsalvus, 263. Petrus Martyr, 261. Zurita, 313 f. Passero, 141.
[2] Macchiavelli, Legaz. a. c. d. R., 316, 342, 382.
[3] Caracciolus, Vita Spinelli, 52.
[4] Zurita.
[5] Ferronus, Rerum Gallic., vol. iii. pp. 70, 71.

decided the fate of the kingdom. Bayard fought like a hero, but all in vain; the French disorganization was too great, and the onslaught of the Spaniards overwhelming. Gonzal was victorious on both banks. In Gaeta, too, whither the French had fled, the Spanish standard was flying on the 3rd January, 1504. The French were obliged to retreat homewards; many by sea—the ships set sail as soon as they were filled, none waited for the other—the rest by land; the latter said to Gonzal: "Give us strong horses to bring us back again."[1]

Yet this favour was not to be theirs so readily. The superiority of the Spaniards was due to their greater proximity, owing to the possession of Sicily, between which and Naples subsisted an old natural alliance, as well as to the prudent and cautious treatment of the factions opposing one another in the south of Italy; for this was Gonzal's peculiar merit, that of controlling different factions and nations by the exercise of his ascendency, as might be seen in the manner in which he succeeded in uniting Colonni and Orsini in one and the same camp. He did not spare his enemy. The remainder of the Anjou army was vanquished in the Abruzzian mountains, and in Otranto by Morgan and Pedro de Paz; the Marquisates of Bitonto and Salerno were seized, and many barons dispossessed.[2] Gonzal rewarded his captains and those of the Orsini clan amongst them, with the estates of those thus expelled, and ruled the kingdom entirely in the spirit of the Aragon party.

At the same time, the French and Spanish forces were opposing each other, not only on the Neapolitan frontier, but also on the borders of Roussillon.[3] Here Ferdinand, in person, protected those garrisons, that wrote to him saying: "they were ready to die, only he should see that he did not lose many brave men," as well as the frontiers of his own empire. On showing himself on French soil with 20,000 infantry and 8,000 lances, he obtained in November a truce for Roussillon.[4]

[1] Sabellicus, Euneades, 12, 2. Bayard, Guicciardini, 330. Jovii Gonsalvus, 267. Zurita, 315-317.
[2] Treaty in Dumont, iv. 1, 52. Zurita, 321.
[3] Appendix to Monstrelet, 236. [4] Petrus Martyr, Epistolæ, 151, 2.

In the February following their reverse, this truce was also extended to Naples, where the French still entertained the greatest hopes.

A Change in the Papacy.

The former good understanding between the French and the Pope did not long endure. The French complained that he had appropriated the purchases of supplies made by their commissioners in the State of the Church,[1] and consequently, that their troops had been compelled to fight at an inconvenient season; that he had despatched troops to Aquila, but only for the purpose of seizing it for himself; and, finally, that he had taken good care that Cesar's army should not support the French.[2] If we inquire what it was that could have estranged him from the French alliance, to which he owed all his successes, we find the reason in the state of affairs in Tuscany. Cesar had twice threatened to attack Florence, and on each occasion Louis XII. had dissuaded him. Louis had granted all that he was capable of granting. His most faithful allies, the Popolares at Florence, could not possibly be sacrificed to the Borgia. But this very city of Florence, on the other hand, Ferdinand the Catholic was ready to leave to the Pope. He had long since proposed to the German King to make Cesar King of Tuscany.[3] Here we can perceive how great the prestige of this Pope was. The King of France was desirous of making his son lord of the Mark and of Romagna, whilst the King of Spain was even for making him King of Tuscany. For the struggle between the two princes it was of vital moment to which side the Pope would incline. Hitherto he had been regarded as a supporter of the French. But now, when a French envoy could be attacked and almost slain in the streets of Rome, now that envoys from Pisa, who had long since offered their city to Cesar, and enemies of the Florentines

---

[1] Garnier, 399. From Anton's MS. compared with Monstrelet and Gilles. Chroniques de France, 121.
[2] Carpesanus, 1254.   [3] Zurita.

had the *entrée* of the Court, and now that the Pope most energetically opposed the union of Florence and Siena, which Louis XII. exerted himself to compass by the restoration of Petrucci,[1] it was palpable that the Pope was abandoning the French cause, in order primarily to conquer Pisa, Siena, and Florence. When Francis Trocces, the favourite of the Pope and his privy chamberlain, attempted flight, and was seized and put to death the same night, this act was ascribed to the suspicion that Trocces communicated to the French the plot that was being hatched against them.[2] We have it from the most unimpeachable source, that in March, 1503, Alexander proposed to the Catholic King to enter into a league with Venice in order to expel the French from Italy.[3]

Thus the whole success of his campaign in Romagna would have been turned against Louis, and a league formed against him, like as against Charles VIII. In the same way as when in league with the French Alexander had conquered the State of the Church, would he now, deserting his former allies, have conquered Tuscany in league with the Spaniards. He would have become master of central Italy, and a powerful arbiter between the great powers.

Everything bearing on these undertakings had been well weighed and considered, save and except one thing, and this occurred. Alexander died, and Cesar at the same time fell dangerously ill.[4]

Alexander also had been ill for a few days previously to his decease, but little more was known in the palace about his state of health than that he was ill of a fever. But, after his death, which took place on the 17th August, the sight of his corpse, with the face black as coal, and the tongue so swollen that the mouth would not close, a sight more ghastly than had ever been observed in other dead bodies, gave rise to sinister reports.[5] It was said that the

---

[1] Cardinal Soderini in Macchiavelli, Legazione alla corte di Roma iv. Titzio in debret a. p. a, 544.
[2] Carpesanus, 1255. Biagio Buonaccorsi, Diar. Fiorent., 78.
[3] Zurita, f. 270.
[4] Macchiavelli, Principe, c. 7.
[5] Burcardus in Brequigny, Extraits et Notices, 66, 67.

Pope one evening went to a banquet in the vineyard belonging to the Cardinal Adrian of Corneto, at which he intended to poison several rich cardinals; being thirsty, he called for wine to drink and by mistake drank of the wine which Cesar had told his servant was the best, but which had been really poisoned for the purpose of murdering the guests. Cesar also partook of the wine, and both he and his father were carried off half dead. Cesar was sewn up in the reeking hide of a mule, and escaped death, but Alexander died.[1] The Cardinal of Corneto told the historian, Giovio, that the poison, which carried off the Pope was intended for him among others, and that he narrowly escaped.[2] Others added that Alexander had forgotten the sacred host that he was in the habit of carrying about with him for protection; others, again, that the compact he had sealed with the Devil had expired, and his Satanic majesty had come in the form of a courier to fetch him away.[3]

At all events, in the midst of his greatest expectations, his career was cut short.

It has been said, that the Pope had sometimes been warned, as though by God, in the midst of his crimes. For instance, by a flash of lightning that once struck the ground before him, just as he had persuaded the Archbishop of Cosenza to accuse himself guiltlessly,[4] —by a popular tumult, from which he barely escaped with his life into a church,[5] immediately after he had caused Alonso da Bisceglia to be put to death—and he likewise received the express warning of the astrologers that he would die for his son's sake.[6] There never was a Pope, who so completely postponed all ecclesiastical considerations to secular interests, and still less was there ever one, who strove to compass his ends by such terrible means. No acquisition of land has ever been stained with so much blood

---

[1] Guicciardini, iv. 314. Petrus Martyr, 269. Mariana, 222.

[2] Jovii Vita Gonsalvi, 260 (note to new ed.). I have given in my History of the Popes the results of certain later investigations. In my opinion they place the matter beyond all dispute. Cf. S. W., vol. 37, p. 35, and the Appendix in vol. 39.

[3] Tommaso Tommasi in Gordon, Vie d'Alexandre II., 298.

[4] Burcardus in Eccard, ii. 2085.

[5] Zurita, i. f. 186.   [6] *Ibid.*

and cruelty, as was his foundation of the papal territory by stamping out all its small potentates. But this appropriation was not after all intended for the papacy, a single despot was to unite it all in his hand, and this despot none other than the Pope's own son. What a check would not such a principality exercise upon future popes!

After Alexander's decease, Rome and Romagna became involved in the greatest confusion. In Rome, Cesar was master of the Monte d'Angelo; he had a large body of men under his command and, moreover, his father's treasure stored in two large chests, which he had removed from the palace.[1] But since he lay sick, the cardinals were not prevented from enlisting troops, the Orsini now too ventured again to make their appearance. It is related of Fabio Orsino that he slew one of Cesar's attendants and washed his mouth and hands in the blood. The citizens often closed the streets and shops because of the tumult of the fighting parties.[2]

In Romagna, the authorities, Cesar's adherents, fled, and the lords of the land returned. When Guidubaldo came back to Urbino, even the patrician ladies under captains followed the drum through the streets in the evening, to show that they also were ready to fight for him.[3] In Città di Castello a golden calf was carried through the streets as a device of the Vitelli. Sinigaglia, headed by the Rovere, flew to arms at the bidding of the Cardinal Julian. Giampaolo Baglione returned to Perugia under French protection. The others likewise returned from their several asylums.[4]

But how matters would develop depended entirely upon the election of the new pope.

The cardinals hastened to meet. Ascanio Sforza was once more released from his tower at Bourges, in order that he might give his vote for the French candidate. John Colonna came from Sicily, where he had been living upon an annual allowance from the Catholic King. He was

[1] Burcard in Brequigny, 67, 68. Victorellus ad liacconium, 1356.
[2] Sismondi, xii. 289, from Ulloa. Raphael Volaterranus, Vitæ Paparum, 167.
[3] Baldi, Vita di Guidubaldo, ix. 115.
[4] Baldi, viii. 108, ix. 116-122.

entirely Spanish in his leanings.¹ As soon as the French forces occupied Nepi, the Spanish advanced under Mendoza to Marino, both places being in close proximity to the city. Under the protection of the French party, both in the conclave and in the field, Georges d'Amboise publicly aspired to the highest dignity in Christendom. Gonzal was not less open in his counter-declaration: "If the Holy Ghost would choose another than Caravajal, the Spanish party would not oppose the choice."² But neither Amboise nor Caravajal were elected. Both parties were finally agreed in the choice of one Piccolhomini, of Siena; in him, sitting as Pius III., the Spaniards fancied they saw a friend, whilst the French saw only in him an enemy, as Pius II. Piccolhomini had been their foe.³ The Spaniards appeared to triumph. But Pius had scarcely taken possession of the Vatican, and had not even entered St. John Lateran, when he died, and the struggle between the rival parties began afresh. Baglione and Alvian once more entered Rome with their troops; the former with his French on the right bank of the Tiber, and the latter with his Spanish on the left. Immediately the cardinals met in conclave, both sides retired.⁴

Now at this time, Julian della Rovere, who had always proved the boldest in opposing three popes,⁵ a man whom even Alexander admitted was a man of his word, the same man, who had just directed the defence of the Castle of Sinigaglia, enjoyed the greatest esteem of all the cardinal body. He was a native of Savona, and might be considered a French subject. He had always favoured the party of the Colonna, and was not altogether unacceptable to the Spaniards. Now that Amboise despaired of becoming pope himself, and Ferdinand of placing a Spaniard in the chair, both parties were unanimous in favour of this Julian. He had always been well disposed towards the Venetians, and he now promised security for Cesar. And so it came to pass

---

¹ Zurita, 299. Arluni, de bello Veneto, i. 21.
² Zurita, 329.
³ Epistola Francisci Cardinalis Senensis in Ciacconius, 1356. Gilles, Chroniques de France, 121.
⁴ Macchiavelli, Legazione alla corte di Roma, 285.
⁵ Infessura, 1977. Jacobi Volat. Diarium.

that, within an hour after the close of the Conclave, he was sitting at a separate table as pope, signing the contract of his appointment by the cardinals, and placing on his finger the papal ring that had already been engraven with his monogram.[1] He styled himself, slightly changing his baptismal name, Julius II. In this choice the French believed they had gained a victory such as the Spaniards had vaunted in the case of Pius. At all events, Amboise, who, in addition to the French legation, received also that of Avignon, and whose nephew was the first cardinal, lived harmoniously together with him in the palace and assisted at his most privy councils.[2] The next difficulty to be encountered was the state of things in the Romagna, which became more and more complicated. On the part of Tuscany, there offered their services to Gonzal. Aretins and Pisanese, with Pandulf Petrucci and Julian Medici; on the part of Genoa, both French and Adorni; and on the part of Lombardy 600 nobles and Ascanio Sforza with them.

For, precisely at the time that Julius became pope, the Venetians invaded the Romagna. They occupied the country round about Imola, purchased Rimini from the Malatesta, and threatened Faenza.[3] But as this country owned Cesar as its suzerain, and since Julius, though promising to let him remain so, had not undertaken to defend him, this invasion, consequently, resolved itself into a war between the Venetians and Cesar.

Therefore, when the Pope upbraided them for their conduct, asking, "Whether he had done them so few services, that they had resolved to rob the Church during his pontificate," they replied : " it was a robber, and not the Church that they were attacking : and that they were ready to pay their contribution." Whereupon the Pope replied : that "though he wanted lords over his cities, he only wished for such as he could control," and held frequent counsel.[4] Although Cesar was not exactly an acceptable personage—

[1] Macchiavelli, Legazione alla corte di Roma, 287-293. Zurita, 330. Burcardus in Eccard, 2159, in Brequigny and in Rainaldus, Annales Ecclesiastici, vol. xx. p. 2.
[2] Macchiavelli, Legazione, 361, and in many passages.
[3] Bembus, Historiæ Venetæ, 145-147. Sansovino Orig. 79.
[4] Macchiavelli, Legazione a. c. d. R. 300, 305, 320.

for how could he possibly trust him?—the Venetians were even less desirable.

Since his father's death, Cesar appeared to have lost all confidence, boldness, and decision. He even vacillated in the papal election; to-day concluding a treaty with Amboise and on the morrow with the Colonna; to-day promising to join one army, and then on the morrow betaking himself to the other. But, as soon as the first intelligence of the Venetian operations reached him, he completely lost his senses. Men said of him: "The strokes of adverse fortune have stunned him, and he no longer knows what he wants."[1] Where we see men displaying energy as soon as disaster befalls them, we shall always find them at the bottom to be good and noble natures; those, on the contrary, who are not such only appear strong for so long as they are in good fortune and no longer.

In order to invalidate the excuse advanced by the Venetians, Cesar expressed his readiness to surrender for a time all his castles and towns to Pope Julius. But the latter, apprehensive lest it might be difficult for him to restore them again, refused the offer.[2] He considered it to be best for Cesar to proceed by sea to Spezzia, and thence to go by way of Ferrara, whilst the army advanced against Imola through the Tuscan and Perugian territory. Cesar was neither supported by Florence, nor yet by Baglione; but he made the venture. On the 19th November, 1503, he despatched his army through Tuscany, whilst he himself went to Ostia, to take ship. He still hoped that the star of his fortune would return; but all the world mocked at him: "Whither," said they, "will the wind waft him, where will he meet with his troops again?"[3] Everything depended upon his relations to the new Pope, and upon the latter's good-will towards him.[4]

[1] Soderini, in Macchiavelli, Legazione, 319.
[2] Macchiavelli, Legazione, 337.
[3] Macchiavelli, Legazione, 332. Burcardus, 2139.
[4] The divergent opinions that have been expressed about this event cause me to reproduce here, more in detail than I have done in the text, the account given by Zurita, who utilized the intelligence received by King Ferdinand. According to Zurita, the proposal to deliver over his castles to the Pope proceeded from Cesar himself. He wished to secure

CH. I.]   A CHANGE IN THE PAPACY.   211

He was but two days gone, when Julius received tidings, that Faenza was in the greatest danger of being taken by the Venetians, and that it was open to doubt whether Cesar would arrive quickly enough, and with sufficient forces, to be able to take energetic measures. These tidings deprived the Pope of sleep, and in the night of the 22nd November he resolved to risk it and to accept Cesar's strongholds for the time being. In the morning he summoned Cardinal Soderini to him; but he still kept

them from Venice, that would recoil in terror before the name of the Church. Soon after he repented of his offer, and was kept under restraint until he had performed his promise. He was taken to Ostia, with the express assurance that he should enjoy complete liberty as soon as the strongholds had been given up. He was under the care of the Cardinal de Santa Cruz. Two galleys were put at the latter's disposal, in order to release Cesar, as soon as he had kept his word. The Cardinal was invested with full powers to this end not only by the Pope, but also by the College of Cardinals, and it actually came so far that of the three castles in question, two were surrendered, and a money security given in the case of the third, so that the Cardinal set him at liberty. At this moment the war between the French and Spaniards that had been interrupted by a truce threatened to burst out afresh. Cesar, who was still well furnished with money and accustomed to pay his soldiers well, and who was fawned on as their lord and master by those insolent characters who are charmed by wild and cruel deeds, and being, as he was, thoroughly well acquainted with the internal relations of the various Italian factions, and accustomed to turn them to his own account, would have been welcome as an ally either to the French or Spaniards. Gonsalvo sent a message to the Cardinal of Santa Cruz to the effect that he would oblige the King of Spain if he would contrive that Cesar joined his side (seria gran beneficio de toda la Christiandad divitirle de otras empressas: y que no se diesse lugar que veniesse a Francia); which now comes to pass. Cesar came with a strong escort to Naples, but it was not his intention to remain long quietly here. His first idea was to prevent the surrender of Forli to the Pope, which had not yet taken place, to revive the war in the Romagna, and to retake Urbino and the other cities, which had been lost to him. He was desirous, for this purpose, of employing the Spanish and Italian infantry, with which Gonzal had gained his victories. Gonzal quickly perceived that Cesar was influencing his troops, and being moreover informed that he was in communication with Forli, began to be apprehensive lest he was plotting, not merely to renew the war in Italy, but to weaken him (Gonzal) so much that Naples would be forced to fall into French hands. Thereupon he resolved to make sure of this dangerous personage: the King approved his conduct. (Zurita, 324.) Mariana has borrowed his remarks from Zurita, and has not made them clearer, though he has lent them a classic colouring. (Note to 2nd Edit.)

his own counsel, for he wished not to do wrong, and did not confide to him his resolve. Towards evening he again sent for him, told him, and sent him after Cesar. But now the latter refused. On the 29th, he was brought to Rome by the papal guards; when there, he was sometimes to be found in Magliana, and sometimes in the treasurer's apartments, or in Amboise's lodging. He there heard how Baglione had surprised and annihilated his army; and so, at length, he consented to surrender the signs of power, to which the governors of his castles were pledged.[1] But they delayed and made fresh difficulties. It was not until April, 1504, that the castles were delivered to the Pope, and Cesar again enjoyed full liberty in Ostia.

Thus it came to pass that Julius II. interfered against Venice on the part of Cesena, Imola, and Forli, as now being their immediate lord, and defended these cities against attack. But, meanwhile, Faenza was lost. We shall next see what important events resulted from its fall.

In Ostia, Cesar had a fresh seizure of his old vacillation. His father had first of all been French in his sympathies, and then Spanish, and then again French, only to end with being Spanish once more. Lezcan, and the Marquis of Final, both set out at the same time to Cesar, the latter offering French aid, and the former a Spanish escort. What should he do? Louis was a relation, and always kept his promise. Ferdinand had the reputation of being faithless, and the Aragon escorts were well known, as was also the fact that, a short time previously, Federigo's son had been allured to avail himself of them, and had been made prisoner, and carried off to Spain. But was he still capable at that time of making a choice? It might be said that his fate was upon him. Lezcan was the first to come, and Cesar followed him. In the same way as Michelott stepped up to his prisoners, so did at last Runno de Ocampo address Cesar with the words: "Sir, you are a prisoner." Cesar drew a deep sigh, surrendered himself, and was in-

---

[1] Macchiavelli, **Legaz.**, 347-339, 355, 366, 373. Baldi, Guidubaldo, 147. Burcardus and Nardi.

terned in a castle in Spain. This firebrand, the Spaniards said, was safe in no other hands but in theirs.[1]

Later, Cesar escaped from the Castle and reached Navarre once more, but was slain, shortly after his flight, in a skirmish.

[1] Zurita, 328. Jovii Gonsalvus, 274. Mariana, 233. Guicciardini, vi. 339.

CHAPTER II.

VARIANCES BETWEEN THE HOUSES OF SPAIN AND AUSTRIA.

THESE Neapolitan affairs are intimately connected with a quarrel between Spain and Austria, which broke out even before their negotiations had been concluded.

When, for instance, Philip, in the early part of the year 1503, set out on his return journey to the Netherlands through France, the Spanish cause at Naples was in a sorry plight, and Philip believed himself commissioned to conclude a treaty with Louis. He had arrived at his Court in Lyons,[1] and, on the 5th of April, had just agreed upon a peace with the King, a peace, of course, most advantageous to him and to this effect: "That Naples should be governed in the name of Charles and Claudia, but with his co-operation, and should at a future day devolve upon them," when the prospects of the Spaniards at Naples improved. They now entertained hopes of victory, and Ferdinand ordered his Commander-in-Chief to disregard any orders he might receive from Philip.[2] In vain his heralds came and departed; instead of the peace, the battle of Cerignola took place. Philip had long been on bad terms with his father-in-law; the latter had refused him the appanage of a prince, had, in Roussillon, prohibited his attendants being provided with horses, and had given orders to have all the cannon at Salsas ready for action whenever he visited that fortress.[3] Both foresaw Isabella's death, and that they would then have to fight for the succession in Castile. This Neapolitan affair further fanned this misunderstanding. The quarrel with Ferdinand's envoys, who denied that Philip had been com-

[1] Hubert Thomas Leodius, de vita Friderici Palatini, p. 41.
[2] Zurita, 259, 260.   [3] Zurita, 258.

missioned to conclude a peace, at first deprived this young and noble prince—who was ill—of consciousness.[1] But he soon recovered. In his own name he now concluded an alliance with Louis, which was proclaimed in Lyons in August. It was aimed immediately at Ferdinand. Louis promised the Archduke 1,000 lances for the conquest of Castile, as he knew that he would need them.[2] Philip then induced his father, who was always in accord with his son, to join this alliance and to reiterate his promise touching the Milanese fiefs, which had not yet been bestowed; and to this step Maximilian was also induced by the state of affairs in Germany.

1. *Maximilian, through the influence of the French Alliance, Victor and Lord in Germany.*

It is worthy of remark how intimately connected German domestic affairs were with French war and peace.

The council of the realm, which had been constituted after Louis' victory over the Sforza and Maximilian, passed, as early as September, 1501, independent resolutions of its own. But owing to Maximilian having, on the 3rd of October following, entered with Louis into the league of Trent, not one of its resolutions was put into force; nay, from that hour it entirely fell to pieces.[3] For a whole six months neither "Kammergericht" nor "Hofgericht" was held throughout the Empire, the estates lost prestige, there was no prospect of a Diet, and public peace was not to be dreamt of. In spite of this, the Neapolitan war of Ferdinand and Maximilian against Louis was, as we have seen, allowed to break out in June, 1502, before any steps were taken. In July, the electors assembled at Gelnhausen, to inaugurate yearly meetings, to which they proposed to summon all classes, each bringing his neighbours, in case the King himself did not appoint any day and place of assembling.

The intention was the same as that with which certain

[1] Pontus Heuterus from Lalaing's MS. as it appears.
[2] Zurita, i. 289 ; ii. 9.
[3] Müller; Reichstagsstaat, i. c. 21, sec. 3; c. 23.

days in the year were set apart at Worms, and a committee of the realm appointed at Augsburg; namely, to deliberate upon such subjects as war with the Turks, the public peace, the high court of justice, and all internal matters. Such meetings were actually held.[1] To these the Electors referred everything that Maximilian demanded of them individually; and when he summoned any of their number before his Court they flatly contradicted him.[2] All the decreeing power now left to the King was the right of reversing appeals, and the bestowal of expectancies.[3] During the months in which the French were victorious in Italy, the disunion was most strongly marked. Maximilian loudly complained of Berthold von Mainz, stating that: " he was most vexed with him, because he had not followed his suggestions in the Reichstag at Worms; and had, moreover, always hindered him in his endeavours for the prosperity of the realm and Christendom."[4] In February, 1503, he would gladly have made common cause with the Swiss, who crossed the St. Gothard to defend Bellinzona, and would with them have entered Milan, in order to settle the Neapolitan question, had it not been that the situation at home tied his hands. To enable him to engage in the slightest enterprise, he needed a certain tranquillity on the part of the German princes, and, for this, peace with France.[5]

Thus it was that, in concluding this treaty, his son's advantage coincided well with his own.

It will scarcely have been by corruption that Louis contrived to keep the princes on his side; the power of the princes was also enhanced when the French gave the German King plenty of trouble; they needed not then fear him for themselves. However that might be, after the reconciliation between Louis and the House of Austria, in November, 1503, the electors excused themselves apologetically for their previous conduct, and resolved only to meet once every two years.[6] These meetings never took place

[1] Müller; Reichsstagstaat, book ii. p. 248, 260, and cap. iii. sec. 8.
[2] Müller, ii. cap. 5.
[3] Häberlin, Reichs historie, ix. 229, from the documents.
[4] Correspondence in Gudenus, Codex Diplomaticus Moguntinus, iv. 547, 551.
[5] Weiskunig, 278.
[6] Documents in Müller; Reichsstagstaat, ii. viii. pp. 276, 287.

again. This opposition was now virtually at an end. But at that very time Maximilian found an opportunity of destroying another older and more deeply rooted combination, which even foreigners class among the great factions of Europe, viz., the opposition of the Palatinate.

Forty years previously, Frederick, "Arrogator" of the Palatinate, in league with Bavaria-Landshut, victoriously resisted the grand attack of the Emperor and his whole party. We have seen the correspondence in which the then Elector of the Palatinate engaged with Charles VIII. and Louis XII. In the days when Louis concluded the Swiss treaty against Maximilian, the Elector married his son Ruprecht to the only daughter of George of Landshut. Those who forty years before had fought together were now dead; but the old hate and the old leanings still survived and lived on in their children.

It happened that Duke George of Landshut, when about to proceed in his carriage, accompanied by four physicians, to Wildbad, at Michaelmas, 1505, was suddenly taken so ill on the road that he could only reach his castle at Ingolstadt, so sick was he.[1] Should he allow his country to pass to Duke Albrecht of Munich, his old enemy, and Maximilian's brother-in-law, in spite of his being his rightful heir, according to the feudal law of descent? In order to pass it to Ruprecht, his sister's son, and his son-in-law, he committed to him his fortresses and his treasure, and called together the Estates for the 10th December. But he died before they convened; and this last scion of the House of Bavaria-Landshut, was borne to the grave by mere foreign knights, save one only, whom he had summoned to protect his son-in-law.[2]

The young Ruprecht was the first to appear before the Estates, with his knights and yeomen. "How," he exclaimed, "could anyone wish to defraud the grandchildren of Duke George, who were males, and of his own flesh and blood? The whole lineage of the House of Burgundy had descended through a woman, Bavarian blood also coursed through his veins." Then appeared Albrecht's envoys:

[1] Zayneri, de bello Bavarico liber Memorialis in Oefele, Rerum Boicarum, tom. ii. p. 350.
[2] Zayner, 363.

"The land was entailed upon a man, and, further, Albrecht was in the fourth, whilst Ruprecht was only in the eighth degree from George."[1] The Estates did not seem able to arrive at a solution, and so declared their readiness to submit to Maximilian's arbitration; yet this was also a decision, for the King had long since taken a side.[2]

The King thought first on his own advantage. He had three schemes. The first was for Albrecht, his sister's husband, in whose company he entered Augsburg, on the 30 January, 1504, to assist at the "Reichstag." His second was for certain districts of Landshut; and the third was the humiliation of the Palatinate, which he wished to deprive of the Landgraviate of Hagenau.[3] His mediatory proposal: "that that part of Bavaria lying across the Danube should be assigned to Ruprecht, and all the rest to belong to Albrecht," as well as others of a like nature, were rejected now by one party and now by the other. At last, on Easter Day, after the Dukes of Munich had held two hours' private conversation with him, he announced the same evening to the Estates of Landshut, in a garden at Augsburg, that "the war must unfortunately take its course."[4] His final decision gave the whole country to the Munich line. On the 29th of April, Ruprecht's consort took possession of the city and of a large portion of the Landshut territory.[5] Forthwith all the old enemies of 1461 rose up in arms. Wurtemberg, Veldenz, and Hessen against the Palatinate; the Munich House, with the assistance of Brandenburg, Saxony, and Suabia and the city of Nuremberg against Landshut. The war began.

But how about the French alliance of the old Count Palatine? His followers wore white crosses like the French; he sent his son repeatedly to Louis.[6] But all to no purpose; the new alliance with Maximilian prevented the

[1] "Handlung Zwischen Herzog Ruprecht und gemeine Landschaft," in Zayner, 370.
[2] Maximilian's Letter in Müller's Reichstagsstaat.
[3] "Der Echte Fugger" in Oefele's manuscript, ii. 471.
[4] "Handlung zu Augsburg von gemeine Landschaft wegen," in Zayner, 392. Especially p. 401.
[5] Proclamation when Landshut was taken, vide Zayner, 438.
[6] Zayner, Preface; and Zurita.

French King from listening to him. The Count Palatine resolved to only keep the fortress garrisoned, and to maintain two armies in the field, one in Heidelberg, and another in Landshut, with the view either to prevent or to requite pillage and plunder. The enemy, he reflected, was not so rich as he was, and would be first exhausted.[1]

The Palatinate itself was assailed on three sides. On the east of the Rhine, Ulrich von Würtemberg made the attack. He took Maulbronn, and 2,000 balls discharged from the Niederberg forced the cantons of Besigheim, Walheim, and Weinsberg to accept him in their sanctuary as their lord and master. Bretten alone was defended by the good pieces of ordnance that George Schwarzerd had cast, and by a company of Swiss from Thurgau.[2]

West of the Rhine, Alexander der Schwarze of Veldenz drove off herds of oxen and swine, levied contributions, and allowed his soldiers to cut up the silk altar-hangings to make jerkins, or to send them home to their wives. In Sonwald we find him lying in wait for the cattle to be driven out of a castle, so as to surprise the open gate. But now and again John Landschad would march against him from Kreuznach with better men, and deal with him likewise.[3]

William of Hessen with his fire wardens now ravaged the Bergstrasse lying to the right of the Rhine, and now the Alzheimer Gau, on the left; and it was only the peasantry of Ingelheim in their monastery, and the garrison of Caub, that offered him any formidable resistance.[5]

Whilst all this robbing, murdering, and pillaging was taking place—for we cannot call it regular warfare—the archives were ransacked for evidence of the King's claim to the "Landvogtei," and this, with Hagenau and Ortenau, passed into his hand.[5] Overjoyed at his success, which had been achieved without heeding the mediation

---

[1] Vendii Ephemerides belli Palatino-Boici, Ex Kölneri libris tribus concinnatæ in Oefele, ii. 480.
[2] Saltler, Eisenbach, Stettler. Crusii Annales Suevici, 525.
[3] Trithenius, Chronicon Hirsangiense, 608-613.
[4] Trithenius, 613-623. Münster, Kosmographie.
[5] Häberlins, note from a document in Lunig, ix. 278.

of any of the Electors,[1] by merely confirming the enemies of the Palatinate in the possession of what they had conquered, he proceeded to Bavaria, where some of his counsellors kept a vigilant watch over Kufstein, and others over Weissenhorn, to both of which he laid claim.

He arrived just in time. There also the war was being waged more with fire than with sword. Now it was the country about Munich itself, and anon the neighbourhood of Landshut, that was ravaged. The sentries of the towns and train-bands came into collision. One or the other fled. There were no deeds of valour worthy the name, and consequently no results were achieved.[2] Just as some Suabian and Brandenburg soldiery had retired before the Munichers, and the Landshut side now appeared to have gained the upper hand by dint of their 2,500 Bohemians, the King arrived on the scene. Four miles from the city of Regensburg, whence peals of bells, inviting to processions and prayers, accompanied him into the field, surrounded by his knights, he charged the Bohemians in person. He fell upon them, though entrenched behind a triple barricade and long stockades made of iron spikes driven into the ground, firmly bound together with chains, and although once unhorsed by a pike—his life was only saved by Erich von Braunschweig's devotion—at last succeeded in mastering them. This done, he marched into Regensburg, with music playing and drums beating, standards and the prisoners he had taken preceding him.[3] He had now gained the upper hand, and took for himself Weissenhorn, Mauerstätten, and Kufstein.

Now when the old Count Palatine looked about him, and saw both countries ravaged, and partly in the enemy's hand; when he found himself reft of his son Ruprecht, as well as of his daughter-in-law, both of whom had died during the war; when he saw too the Electoral Confederacy broken up, France leagued with Maximilian, his enemies unbroken, and no hope left, his courage sank, and he had recourse to entreaties. Maximilian, at length in possession

---

[1] Müller's, Reichstagsstaat, 406.
[2] Life of Götz von Berlichingen, published by Hagen, p. 41, f.
[3] "Die Regensburger Chronik," vol. iv. part i., Regensburg, 1822, p. 84.

of what he had coveted, able to boast that he had it in his power to utterly crush the Palatinate, and mindful that Munich also had not always favoured Austria, was prudent and forbearing enough not to desire its destruction, and so, in September, commanded a truce.¹ He then, in accordance with his original proposal, founded the younger Palatinate, on the other side the Danube, for the children of Ruprecht and George's grandchildren. After this triumphant victory, whom need the King fear in Germany?

Berthold von Mainz, the life and soul of all the opposition he had hitherto met with, died in December, 1504, and the King had long since taken into his service his chancellor, Stürzler.² In May, 1505, he again held a Reichstag at Cologne, where he had always wished it to meet, but the princes of his realm would never consent. We must especially lament that there was no one in those days who had either the opportunity to study, or the will and skill to chronicle, the active participation of the princes and their counsellors in public business. Such a one would tell us how the great ideas of a universal participation of the Estates in internal government, of the contribution of all Germans towards the common burdens, and of a real unity of the nation in opposition to the imperial power, were all born of the three attempts to frame a constitution by Estates, namely, the yearly Assembly, the Committee of the Realm, and the Confederation of the Electors, and how that, after attaining a certain development, they all perished at Cologne.

To live on in the memory of posterity is one half of life; but these attempts have almost been forgotten.³ In Cologne those ideas were relinquished, and the constitution began to return to its old groove. The Emperor was guaranteed for a year a force larger than ever before. This force was raised by a census of the Estates, and was no longer computed according to parishes and population; was fixed

---

¹ Hubertus, Thomas Leodius, Vita Friderici, Palatini ii., No. 42, No. 47, and Zurita.
² Häberlin, ii. 283. Tritbenius. Der Echte Fugger, i. 1.
³ (Note to new ed.) This remark is responsible for my later investigations, which I have published to the world in the first volume of my "Deutsche Geschichte."

at 1,000 horse and 3,000 foot soldiers, the pay of the former being reckoned at ten, and that of the latter at four guilders a month; this force was, moreover, to be equipped by the Estates.[1] No government cared how it was to be employed. The high Court of Justice, which was left to him to pay, thus passed into his hands. He was powerful enough to carry out his plans.

2. *Maximilian's Comprehensive Schemes. Philip of Castile.*

These successes were entirely due to the French alliance, and the same alliance was the basis of all new schemes and projects.

After negotiating in France during the whole Bavarian war, and after Ferdinand had appeared willing to assign Naples to the joint names of Charles and Claudia, and had ended in August by flatly refusing,[2] on the 22nd September, ten days after the battle of Regensburg, Maximilian, Philip, and Louis united in the most intimate league: "they would be one soul in three bodies, each be the friend of the other's friends, and the enemy of their enemies, and would intermarry their children. Louis would pledge his governors in Milan, Genoa, Asti, Bretagne, Blois, and Burgundy, all which provinces had been detached from the Crown, to deliver them all over into the hand of Charles and Claudia, in the event of his dying without male heirs of his body."[3] We do not find any having reference to Naples; but yet Ferdinand complained that it had been dealt with at Blois, as if it had been the Tyrol.[4]

Hereupon, in April, 1505, in Hagenau, that had just been taken, Amboise received not only for Louis but for Charles and Claudia as well, the fiefs of Milan, Pavia, and Anghiera, whilst Philip received for himself and his son

---

[1] Müller, Reichstagsstaat, ii. 441. Imperial decree in Müller, 509.
[2] Lettres du Roi Louis XII., vol. i. 1-7.
[3] In Dumont, iv. 1, 55.
[4] Zurita, 343.

the fiefs of Guelders.¹ In July, 1505, the Duke of Guelders, stripped of all French assistance, and forsaken of his barons, Wisch, Bronchorst, and Batenburg, actually threw himself at Philip's feet in Rosendaal, gave up the greatest part of his country, and entered into his suite.²

After this, greater enterprises were undertaken. In November, 1504, Isabella, Queen of Castile, and Philip's mother-in-law, died.³ Philip, without delay, took the royal sword and the royal title instead of the ducal hat, and was bent upon becoming her heir.⁴ But the old Ferdinand was no less determined to remain the real King of the Castilian kingdoms, under the title of a "Gobernador." Hence the schism in the Austro-Spanish house, and Philip made preparations to drive his father-in-law from Castile.

Maximilian turned his eyes towards Hungary, with a view of securing the disputed succession, and for this purpose the Empire had voted him supplies.

Immediately both these objects were attained, he could turn his attention to Italy. The treaty of Blois planned a general war upon Venice. Naples was demanded because it belonged to Castile. If we survey this general state of things, and reflect that, after Ferdinand's death, all the Aragon possessions, and, after Louis' death, all the rest of Italy together with a third of France would fall to the same great heir, these plans must be regarded as jeopardizing European liberty. But Maximilian dreamt of an universal monarchy over all the Latin-Teutonic nations. In the year 1505 he proposed to the King of France to repeal the Salic law, in order that Charles and Claudia might succeed him on the throne of France.⁵ In the year 1506, he declared Schwente Nielsen, Eric Johannsen, and other Commissioners of Sweden, who would not recognize the union nor the King of Denmark, under the ban of the Empire in the words: "their

---

¹ Acte de foi, in Dumont, 60. Pontus Heuterus.
² Barlandus, Duces Brabantiæ, 137. Teschenmacherus, Annales Geldriæ in Annal. Cliviæ, &c., p. 527. Heuterus, 274.
³ Luc. Marineus Siculus, 512. Petrus Martyr, Epist., 270.
⁴ Heuter., 270. Wagenaar, History of the Netherlands, ii. 281.
⁵ Zurita, ii. f. 152.

goods belonged to the first comer." [1] He declared that through his mother he had as good a claim to the kingdom of Portugal as King Manuel. He had the pretensions of a fugitive York to the crown of England transferred to himself.[2]

But God willed it that this should not happen. The development of the Romano-Germanic nation that had just begun, would have been interrupted and hindered thereby. When Louis XII., in the spring of 1505, fell dangerously sick, all patriots who desired to see the kingdom in a state of union, as well as all friends of the royal dynasty, which had been only consolidated by so much blood, began to dread that in a short time the realm would become divided, and the old domestic war revive.[3] It was primarily the partisans of Louisa of Savoy, the mother of the heir presumptive to the throne, Francis of Angoulême, who opposed it. The King himself repented his alliance of Blois. Did he not swear at his coronation at Reims never to suffer the realm to be diminished? It was Queen Anna who specially favoured the betrothal of Claudia and Charles, seeing, as she did, that the latter was destined to attain the highest dignity in our nations. She even did not spare a considerable sum of money, in order to degrade and dismiss from court Marshal Gie, who, during a former weakness of the King, had dared to counteract her schemes.[4] She was heart and soul in favour of the league. But the King being so sorely sick, the wife was fain to concede to the husband, what as Queen she refused to the King, and Anna at length gave way, forgot her difference with Louise,[5] and consented that Claudia should be betrothed to Francis of Angoulême, instead of to Charles. Amboise and the high dignitaries at court swore to further these ends. It was as yet kept a secret. But the league of Blois, and the schemes of the Austrian house had been broken in the chief point upon which they were based. Louis gradually recovered.

[1] Extract from Dalin, Swedish History, ii. 665.
[2] Zurita and Wagenaar, from the Chartr. van Brabant, Laye. Engleterre, ii. 269. Cf. Hormayr, Oesterrich, Plutarch. v. 178.
[3] Garnier, Histoire de France, xxi. 3-8. St. Gelais, 225 sq.
[4] Garnier, from Gie's trial, xxi. 463, 476.
[5] Fleuranges, Mémoires, 154.

Not long afterwards, the Inquisitor of Catalonia, Frater John Enquerra, repaired to the French court, in order to investigate the ground.[1] He was despatched thither by Ferdinand the Catholic, who was primarily threatened by Maximilian's plans, and was therefore desirous of entering into an alliance with France.

Should he cease to be King of Castile and the head of the European political world, and return to the insignificant position enjoyed by his ancestors? Isabella, by her last will, left him a few estates and rights in Castile. The succession she devised to her daughter Juana, decreeing at the same time that, "previous to her arrival, all Cortes should be prohibited, and only, should it be subsequently proved that she was either incapable or unwilling to conduct the government, a peaceful administration should be provided."[2] But Ferdinand was not content with this, but assumed the title of "Gobernador," and summoned the Cortes without delay. The Grandees, whose independence he had broken, were against him; notably Pacheco of Villena, who, at the beginning of Ferdinand's reign had lost his estates, his share of the Aragon plunder; and Manrique, of Najara, who saw his nephew prejudiced by Aguilar; their complaint was that, "he tempted the notables in the cities, and the Alcades in the castles, with presents, and was even bent upon reviving the long-forgotten case of Juana, Henry IV.'s daughter, thinking to marry her, only Manuel of Portugal would not give her to him; he was illegally striving to become lord of Castile." They did not appear in the Cortes.[3] The procurators of the seventeen cities, on the other hand—for Ferdinand had once, aided by the Hermandad of the cities, overcome the nobles, and the cities favoured him—appeared, declared themselves the representatives of the united kingdoms of Castile, recognized him as administrator in the room of his daughter, and received from him the oath.[4]

[1] Cf. also Nardi, Istorie Fiorent., p. 110.
[2] Zurita, i. 349. Gomez, Vita Ximenes, 981. Petrus Martyr, 279. Mariana, 278.
[3] Zurita, ii. 12. Carta in Zurita, ii. 22, 23.
[4] Zurita, ii. f. 6.

In spite of all this, Ferdinand could not possibly hold his ground, were Philip, strengthened by the league of Blois, to arrive in Castile, and the Grandees there were to declare for him. Nothing but a reconciliation with Louis promised him security.

Now that Isabella was dead, Ferdinand also could adopt Louis's maxim, a maxim which he used against every proposal advocating terms respecting Naples, and from which proceeded the intention to marry Charles and Claudia together, namely, that, " it was incompatible with his honour and conscience alike to sell his good rights to strangers." In October, 1505, Louis assigned his Neapolitan rights to his niece, Germana de Foix. Ferdinand promised to marry her, to pay a million of good gold within ten years, and to restore all the Angevins to their estates.[1] In addition to this, the two Kings promised each other mutual help against all enemies. Almazan, Ferdinand's other self, confided to some, that nothing would come of the prospective marriage between Charles and Claudia.[2]

The schemes of Maximilian and Philip, who after meeting in Brabant, in December, 1505, separated, the father to look after his Hungarian, and the son after his Castilian, affairs, were thwarted by the alliance Louis had contracted, not with them, as he had promised, but with their enemies. But the two former gained another in lieu thereof. When Aragon and Castile were at variance, it frequently had happened that England had allied itself with the one and France with the other. This natural state of things, and accident, procured an English alliance for the Austrian house.

In January, 1506, Philip had provided the expenses of his voyage by the sale of his desmesnes, and the enforced impost of the sixteenth pfennig. Four hundred nobles, with several thousand lansquenets, Flemings and Swiss,[3] embarked on board his fleet, fifty sail strong, and Philip himself on the ship of two brothers Huybert. The squadron steered through the Bay of Biscay, making for a Spanish

---

[1] Documents in Dumont, iv. i. 72. Extract in Guicciardini, iv. 357.
[2] Baco, Historia Henrici, vii. p. 369.
[3] Wagenaar, ii. 281. Ehrenspiegel, 1165. Nardi, Istorie Fiorent., iv. 111.

port, not far from Cordova, when the wind suddenly changed, and a storm arose. In the stress of weather, the Huyberts, though Philip vainly bade them "Watch,"[1] could devise no other means of safety than running for the English coast. At length, escaping through the race off Portland's chalk cliffs, they landed on the quay of Weymouth.[2] Here Philip was received as a most welcome guest, and not like a shipwrecked man, and was escorted with all pomp and ceremony to Windsor, a castle of the King Henry VII. Yet not for nought. Here in his most private chamber, Henry placed his hand upon his guest's shoulder, and said, "You have been saved on my coasts, and should then I suffer shipwreck on yours; I mean Suffolk, give him up to me." Philip had still a York, Edmund de la Pole of Suffolk, in his keeping, and much as he resisted: "for he would appear to be acting under compulsion," he was obliged at last to surrender him.[3] This done, Henry swore upon a portion of the true Cross, to come to the aid of his guest, in defence of his kingdoms, either such as he now possessed or should possess, against everyone who should attack him in them.[4] And thus strengthened, almost against his will, with a new ally, in April, 1506, Philip embarked for Corunna.

He arrived. "Now that he was come, the Galician and Castilian nobles should prove their promised allegiance." The Duke of Najara was already equipped: should he not receive the new prince in the same manner as the old? Not only Villena, but Benavente, who through the Aragons had lost his "messe" of Medina del Campo, Giron, of the oppressed house of Portugal, Garcilasso de la Wega, who hoped to be able to revive with Philip the influence he had enjoyed with Isabella, the Duke of Bejar, the Marquises of Astorga and Aquilar, and many others accompanied him.[5] They complained that, "the old Ferdinand wished to merge Castile into Aragon; the Jurado of

---

[1] Bayle, Dictionnaire, vide sub Huybert, from a "Mémoire Communiqué au libraire."
[2] Petrus Martyr, Epist. 296. Polydorus, Virgilius, Historia Anglica, 777.
[3] Baco, Vita Henrici Septimi, p. 336, 370.
[4] In Dumont, iv. 1, 77.   [5] Zurita, ii. 47-55.

Saragossa in his scarlet dress had already entered into Valadolid with his Mazza, and was now preparing for resistance; Philip should not trust in his assurances;[1] every noble who placed himself on his side was denaturalized, and forfeited, moreover, the protection of his suzerain."

On the other side, Ferdinand urged upon his party to ally itself with him, giving as his reason that its lady and true Queen was kept prisoner by her husband, so that none could serve her, and none address her. Philip was treating her as no yeoman ever treated his wife; they should, therefore, aid in liberating the Queen. In this endeavour he would stake his person and his life.[2] He retained on his side the cities, a few grandees and prelates, and the governors, who owed him what they were, and whom, as he said, Philip wished to displace. But, in a short time, all the grandees and prelates, and even his relatives, including the Condestable and the Almirante, had forsaken him,[3] and only a single man, the Duke of Alva, who never wavered, remained faithful to him. In the cities, the relatives of those imprisoned by the Inquisition looked towards the young King, and in still greater numbers, seeing that Luzero had by false witnesses incarcerated knights and dames, monasterial and secular clerics.[4] After this, a recourse to force was impossible. It could only be in an interview that Ferdinand could hope to assert his personal ascendency over his son-in-law. Fray Francis Ximenes of Cisneros arranged this meeting for him.

Upon a hill, in the midst of the mountain range of Gamoneda between Puebla de Sanabria and Rionegro, hard by the farm of Remessal, and close to a copse of oak trees, stands a chapel. Hither, on the 20th June, 1506, came Ferdinand from the one side with 200 light-armed troops seated on mules, all in mantles and red caps, with a sword hanging loosely from their belts, whilst from the other there approached 1,000 Germans with

---

[1] Petrus Martyr, 305.
[2] Carta, con que el Catholico se justifica, in Zurita, ii. 57, 58.
[3] Ferdinand's words, in Zurita, fol. 71.
[4] Llorente, Histoire de l'Inquisition de l'Espagne, i. 346. Zurita, 99, 116. Gonzalo Ayora's letter in Llorente.

muskets and spears, the finest and most stalwart men you could behold, and behind them, surrounded by his grandees, all wearing armour under their tunics, came Philip.[1] The old monarch, distinguished by his bald head and austere nose, rich in exploits; the youth white and ruddy of complexion and full of hope. The latter, on this occasion more serious than his wont; the former, brighter than usual. In the chapel, while Ximenes waited on the grassy slope before the door, they conferred with each other. Ximenes had already had negotiations with Philip, endeavouring to induce him to agree to a joint administration—urging that the shrewdness of age and the vigour of youth would then combine—and trying to persuade him, at all events, to leave Granada, which needed a practised eye, to the more experienced monarch.[2] And this is, probably, what Ferdinand also attempted on this occasion. In any case he pointed out to him the intentions and the character of his grandees. But all to no purpose. They departed as they came; yet, whilst journeying up the Duero, several miles apart, they continued their negotiations. Finally, Ferdinand was obliged to content himself with half the Indian revenue, and a limited control of the Grand Orders. He renounced all other share in the government.[3] But here his equivocation manifested itself. Whilst conceding this, after much resistance, he declared to the people, that: "he had had no other intention from the first but this; he had, it was true, formerly taken the government upon himself, yet he had only done this in order to display the greater grace towards his children.[4]

He went yet further. On the 28th June, after declaring with Philip, that, "it ought to be known that the gracious Queen must in no case interfere with the Government in any respect; otherwise, the complete ruin of these realms would be the result," he protested secretly to Almazan, that: "he made this confession only out of fear; in reality he was resolved to liberate his daughter."[5] On his way

[1] Jovii Gonsalvas, 278. Gomez, Vita Ximenes, 990. Mariana, 28, 252.
[2] Literæ Ximenes, in Gomez, 987.   [3] Zurita, ii. 63.
[4] Relacion del Catholico, in Zurita, 70.
[5] Concordia entre el Catholico, etc., and Protestacion del Catholico, in Zurita, 67, 68.

home he found the gates of several cities closed against him by the grandees; yet he comforted himself with the reflection that he had once been still more powerless, and yet had ruled them many long years. Full of other fresh cares and anxieties, he hurried back to Anjou.

No sooner was this over, than all cities opened their gates to the young King, and swore allegiance to him. Wherever there were governors of castles, who at first were not inclined to yield, they did so, as soon as a few companies of troops showed themselves. The grandees and prelates were besides in Philip's retinue.[1] The House of Austria succeeded in taking possession of Castile.

During this time Maximilian was in Hungary; fifteen years previously, the prelates, barons, and cities of this country had been obliged to swear to him that: "should Wladislaw die without male heirs, Maximilian, or, in case he was deceased, one of his sons should succeed; failing these, one of the heirs male of their body, begotten in direct descent, should succeed as a lawful heir to the crown."[2] Now Wladislaw, a monarch who never said anything but "Dober" to the Bohemians, and "Bene" to the Hungarians, was old and weak, and had only issue one daughter. Some said he would marry her to a grandson of Maximilian; others, that he was willing to give up his kingdom to the latter.[3] The Hungarians, however, and the Saxons, who dwelt amongst them, did not desire a German sovereign. The magnates assembled, and resolved that, whoever advocated the election of a foreign king, was a dead man; and Count John, of the house of Zapol, aspired to the crown for himself. Maximilian reminded them of their oath, and that their welfare, as also a successful resistance against Turkish encroachment, depended upon an alliance with Austria." But they gave a defiant answer; they summoned, as he himself expressed it, their power by the bloody sword.[4] He determined to attack

---

[1] All in Zurita.
[2] Bonfinius, Rerum Ungaricarum Decas, v. 2, 509, and the document in Sambucus, Rerum Ungaricarum, Appendix, 546.
[3] Linturius, Appendix ad Rolewinkiam, in Scriptt. Struvii, 600.
[4] Maximilian's proclamation in Datt, 568, and in Müller, 528.

this power, and, without ravaging the country—for otherwise it might become hostile to him—only to proceed against the magnates. On the right bank of the Danube he first compelled Oedenburg and the Count of Bozin, whose dominions extended a whole day's journey wide on these borders, to accept his terms. Next, during an eight days' truce, he passed over to the left bank and reduced Presburg. Having taken the island of Schütt, he thought he had conquered: for "it was the heart of Hungary." But a message from Wladislaw to the effect that "he must go to his wife, who was expecting her confinement," was followed shortly by another that, "on the 1st July she had been delivered of a child, who though very weakly, was yet a boy."[1] The magnates then gave his people 3,000 pieces of cloth, and 2,000 head of oxen, and recognized his rights.[2] How was it likely that a boy, who had had to be placed in the smoking skins of freshly slain beasts, in order to be kept alive, would eventually survive?[3] Maximilian left the country, but his prospects were saved.

Now that Castile had been taken, and the succession in Hungary assured, he turned his eyes towards Italy, in order to receive the Imperial Crown in Rome.

It was just about this time that he first heard for certain, that the betrothal between Charles and Claudia had been revoked by Louis XII. This was not publicly announced until May, 1506. The deputies of the cities, who, in the official account of this affair were, almost like the Cortes of Toro, simply styled Estates, appeared in Tours before the King, sitting with his prelates on his right, and his grandees on his left, and entreated him to agree to the betrothal of Claudia to Francis of Angoulême. This was ratified in their presence. Under their hands and seals, each and all, the counsellors of Bretagne with them, vowed to see that a marriage resulted therefrom.[4]

[1] *Idem*, in Müller, 531.
[2] Anton, Chroniques Annales, ii. p. 11.
[3] Michael Brutus' testimony in Struve, Corpus Historiæ Germanicæ.
[4] Récit de ce qui s'est passé, in Röderer's Mémoire pour servir, etc., in the Appendix, p. 425, and this Mémoire especially. St. Gelais, 181. Mémoires de Fleuranges.

Maximilian then learned that the road through his fief of Milan had been closed to him, whilst Philip received the tidings that Charles of Guelders, who had escaped from his retinue, had, by means of French and Aragon money, renewed the war in the Netherlands. Both were extremely indignant. Maximilian complained that "Louis had never really cared about the treaty; it was only the fiefs that he had coveted. He revoked the fiefs he had already granted in favour of his grandson Charles."[1] Philip was determined upon a general war. "My heart is not so cowardly, nor my relatives, and my worldly goods so insignificant," he wrote, "as that I could allow myself to be prejudiced in my good right. I would rather appeal to my whole party throughout Christendom, for, as I believe, it is stronger than that of my opponents."[2] But, firstly, Maximilian was resolved to break into Italy as best he could. His envoys, they and their attendants in full armour, went first to Venice, in order to entreat a peaceful passage.[3] But the Venetians would not allow a passage to the man who had so often and so publicly laid claim to their territory. Whilst his lansquenets were wandering about, they had time to occupy all their passes with infantry and cavalry.[4] Maximilian therefore hurried to the Carniolan ports, whither Gonzal had promised to send him ships; but the latter was dissuaded by the grand promises made by Ferdinand. Resolved upon daring the utmost, he went to the Karst in the Windish Mark, whence in four days the coast of Romagna could be reached, in confidence that the Pope would receive him with joy and would crown him.

But the most unexpected calamity befell him here. On the 16th September, his son Philip died at Burgos, of the Mazucco, an infectious fever.[5] He had never felt eager for this journey, nor looked forward to his Crown. He came not to live as king, but to die.

This death, which threw the Castilian and Netherland

---

[1] Proclamation, 533.
[2] Writing in the Lettres de Louis XII., i. 51.
[3] Lascari's letter in Macchiavelli, Legazioni, Opere, v. 127.
[4] Proclamation, and Bembus, Historia Veneta, 157a.
[5] The same proclamation, 540. Zurita, i. 389.

affairs into the greatest confusion, put an end to all Maximilian's further schemes and projects.

3. *Ferdinand, Lord in Naples and Castile.*

Ferdinand, on seeing Castile lost to him, was seized with anxious apprehensions regarding Naples.

In Naples where the kings had only swayed for short periods by means of their armies and the ascendency of their party, and where a paternal, ecclesiastical and hereditary monarchy was unknown, Gonzal, who had installed the captains of his army in rich possessions, and levied taxes as he thought right, enjoyed as much popularity as ever a king did.[1] He was dissatisfied with Ferdinand, who had refused to ratify his grants, and who in Spain had appointed a Neapolitan council, which forced him to dismiss his Germans.[2] Now the Castilians maintained that Naples belonged to them, in that it had been conquered by their money and their blood. Ferdinand rejoined that his were the rightful claims, and that the land appertained to him. As a matter of fact, all depended upon whom the General would make lord of the country. Gonzal inclined to the party of Philip and the Castilians; he refused to retain Philip's envoy to Julius, who was believed to be animated with the like feelings towards Austria. Maximilian sent a message to him to the effect that, "he should behave like a good knight of Castile, and then he should be assured of protection in Naples; he could then receive for himself Pisa and Piombino, which he was at that time supporting." At this time Gonzal, as we are aware, sent his ships to the Carniolan ports.[3]

These circumstances filled Ferdinand the Catholic with apprehension. At first he was for taking Gonzal prisoner; but reflected how disastrous such a step would be, were it to fail.[4] The day following his interview with Philip, on the 21st June, 1506, he took a different view of the state of

[1] Zurita, i. 320, 321, 330.
[2] Caracciolus, Vita Spinelli, in Muratori, xxiv. 52, 53.
[3] Zurita, ii. 30, 33, 46.
[4] Argensola, Annales de Aragon, from Almazan's papers, p. 75.

things, and drew up a document stating that, "he swore by his royal word of honour, by God, the Cross, and the Gospels, to confer upon Gonzal the dignity of Grand Master as soon as he should return to Spain."[1] Ferdinand's ambassador needed no more than ten days On the 2nd July Gonzal sent his reply to the King. "No one," he wrote, "was more anxious to live and die in his service than he was. For the rest of his life he desired to recognize no other King and master but him alone. This he swore by God, being a Christian, guaranteed it as a knight, confirmed it with his name, and set his seal thereunder."[2] He had now pledged himself, and Ferdinand took courage and, on the 4th September, set sail for Naples. But Maximilian arrived in vain at the Carniolan ports.

On his way, Ferdinand received the tidings of Philip's death, yet this event did not induce him to abandon the enterprise upon which he had embarked. On the 1st November, in company with his consort Germana, he rode through the five Saggi of Naples. The nobles and ladies came out of their houses to kiss his hand, Gonzal giving him their names.[3] He that was telling their names was none other than the man whom he had come to take away with him, whilst those who kissed his hand, were in great measure those whose old enemies, the Angevin barons, he was about to recall. Bent upon accomplishing his purpose, he was occupied so busily throughout the day, that he did not even allow himself time to once visit the castle garden.

When, in the previous year, the first news of his peace had been brought hither, everyone lamented that such a shrewd King was intent upon restoring those who had always proved so disloyal. Could his object perhaps be to make almost independent lords of the Sanseverini from Salerno to Reggio, of the Caraccioli in Apulia, of Bitonto in the Abruzzi, and of Trajetto on the Gariglian? His own party would thus become powerless, and the royal power sink into insignificance.[4] But all the same he adhered to

---

[1] Cedula del Maestrazzo, in Zurita, 65.
[2] Carta Satisfactoria, in Zurita, 67.
[3] Passero, Giornale, p. 147. Jovii Gonsalvus, 279.
[4] Zurita, ii. 34.

his intention. All that Don Cesar of Aragon had possessed, all that formerly belonged to the Borgia of Gandia, to Squillace and Don Juan, the portion of the dowager queens, all this he acquired, either by purchase or as feudal lord, and divided it among the injured parties. The knights who had conquered the country had now to retire from their new possessions and content themselves with compensation in money.[1] Dignities and incomes were not even spared. Difficult though the task was, he succeeded in carrying it through, thus satisfying among others also the plenipotentiary of France, who took part in the transaction. He restored all the exiles, princes, counts, and barons to their own, and reinstated among them Sannazar, Federigo's most faithful follower, in his country seat of Margolina, whose beauties, hill and slope, brook and dale, he had so often sung.

This settlement assured him the possession of Naples more securely than many victories would have done. The real object of contention between the rival parties was property, from which each was ever being ousted by the other: of this he made an end. He contrived to keep the Colonna in obedience and to win over the Orsini to his side again. It was, perchance, owing to the marriages which, as we have seen, were constantly taking place between the Anjou and Spanish families, between Sanseverini and Villahermosas, and between the Bisignans and Richesenzas,[2] that from this year forth the nobles of Naples remained loyal to a distant King. Henceforward the chronicles of Naples teem with accounts of the wonders done by a picture, to which pilgrimages were made barefooted and which was often presented with golden chains, with stories of murders and marriages, or it may be of an insurrection which broke out against a royal official, of a new law, or of a despotic landlord.[3]

With respect to Gonzal, Ferdinand issued a letter addressed to all princes and barons, and all men living and hereafter to come: "Through glorious deeds of bravery and generosity, Gonzal had regained for his crown the kingdom this side of the Faro; that he had governed it with un-

---

[1] Zurita, f. 112, 114.   [2] Passero, 163, 176
[3] Passero, 150, 155, 167 f.

wavering loyalty, and that he, the King, was his great debtor."[1] He then demanded of the Pope his sanction of the Grand Mastership he purposed to confer on him, but, "it must," he urged, "be kept secret, that the thirteen Electors do not oppose it."[2] To please him, he took from the faithful and reliable Spinello, who was an enemy of Gonzal, the office of accountant of the realm.[3] He gladly allowed Gonzal's retinue to outshine that of his own royal person. But, as soon as he had attained his object, when on the 4th June, 1507, he saw him take leave of all the nobles and ladies, who had accompanied him to the shore, and embark on one of his ships, he then felt himself recompensed for all his duplicity and deprivation, and he gradually laid aside the mask. Spinello received a letter with the superscription: "To the Count of Cariati," and with it a fuller share of administrative power than he had ever enjoyed. The Grand Mastership was never mentioned again.[4] Whenever Gonzal's friends said, "The great ship is running aground," he would reply, "The tide will raise it again."[5] On one occasion afterwards he had hope for it, but it never came to pass. The life of man is a long growth, a short bloom, a long decay; the first is full of hope, the last full of regrets. Gonzal had to content himself in Loxa with thinking on his daughter's marriage, and in keeping up communication with the world by letter. Then he often thought how he had once conducted Federigo's son and Cesar to Spain, and how he at last had returned home in the same manner. Both these actions he regretted, and a third that he did not mention.[6]

At length real Monarch of Naples, and Gonzal safe on his ships, Ferdinand hurried to Castile, which Philip's death had plunged into great confusion.

Before this occurrence, the old hereditary factions of the Nuñez and Gamboa, whose heads were Najara and the Condestable, had already again showed themselves among the grandees.[7] What was next to come depended chiefly

---

[1] Escritura, in Zurita, 139.   [2] Zurita, 128.
[3] Caracciolus, Vita Spinelli, 56.
[4] Jovii Gonsalvus, 282. Passero, 149.
[5] J. Ovonius, in Jovius, 286.   [6] Jovii Gonsalvus, 290, 291, 274.
[7] Petrus Martyr, epp. 317, 331.

upon the Queen's state of health. The disease from which she was suffering first declared itself on Philip's journey to Lyons, that is in the year 1503. After taking leave of him with many tears, she never more raised her eyes, or said a word, save that she wished to follow him.[1] When she learnt that he had obtained a safe conduct for her also, she heeded her mother no longer, but ordered her carriage to proceed to Bayonne; thence—for horses were refused her—she attempted to set out on foot; and, when the gate was closed, she remained, in spite of the entreaties of her attendant ladies and her father confessor, in her light attire sitting upon the barrier until late into the November night; it was only her mother who at length contrived to persuade her to seek her chamber.[2] At last she found her husband. She found him devoted to a beautiful girl with fair hair. In a momentary outburst of jealous passion, she had the girl's hair cut off. Philip did not conceal his vexation.[3] Here—who can fathom the unexplored depths of the soul, see where it unconsciously works, and where it unconsciously suffers, who can discover where the root of its health or sickness lies?—her mind became overshadowed. In Spain her love for Philip, and in the Netherlands her reverence for her father were her guiding passions: these two feelings possessed her whole being, alternately influenced her, and excluded the rest of the world. Since then, she still knew the affairs of ordinary life, and could portray vividly and accurately to her mind distant things; but she knew not how to suit herself to the varying circumstances of life.[4]

Whilst still in the Netherlands, she expressed the wish that her father should retain the government in his hands. On her return to Spain, she entered her capital in a black velvet tunic and with veiled face; she would frequently sit in a dark room, her cap drawn half over her face, wishing to be able only to speak for once with her father.[5] But it was not until after her husband's death that her disease became fully developed.[6] She caused his corpse to be brought

---

[1] Petrus Martyr, xv. p. 144. Gomez, 972.   [2] Zurita, i. 271.
[3] Petrus Martyr, Ep. 272.   [4] Gomez, 999. Zurita, ii. 28.
[5] Zurita, ii. 47, 73.
[6] In the year 1868 no little sensation was caused by an assertion put forward by a certain G. Bergenroth, who was employed by the English

into a hall, attired in half Flemish, half Spanish dress, and the obsequies celebrated over it. She never, the while, gave vent to a sob. She did not shed tears, but only sat and laid her hand to her chin. The plague drove her away

Calendar Commission to make researches among the records of Simancas, which assertion was diametrically opposed to the views here given by me, and which are generally accepted. In his work, "Supplement to vol. i. and vol. ii. of letters, despatches, and state papers relating to the negotiations between England and Spain" (cf. treatise in Sybel's Hist. Zeitschrift, xx. p. 231), he attempts to prove that Johanna's madness was a mere myth, invented in order to exclude her from the succession in Castile, either in favour of her father or her husband. Queen Isabella, he urges, had already intended this, induced by defects in the Catholic faith, of which Johanna had given proof. All this he attempted to prove by correspondence, which had been hitherto carefully concealed, but which had come at last into his hands in Simancas. In the first place he refers to the correspondence of the Sub-prior of Santa Cruz, Tomas de Matienzo, who was despatched to the Netherlands in 1498, in order to inform himself as to the state of the then Archduchess. A clerical question is here really involved. The Archduchess made her confession to certain brothers of a monasterial order, who did not belong to the strict ritual, but, being bound to no monastery, proceeded to the Netherlands, and thence back to Paris, whence they had come. The Archduchess had, under the circumstances, made them a considerable present. Now her old teacher and father confessor in Spain, who had remained there, reminded her that in this way she was not caring for the welfare of her soul. She should treat no one as her father confessor who even possessed or accepted property worth a pin's point; she ought only to make presents to the monasterial convents, who in return therefore would busy themselves with the welfare of her soul. Now that Sub-prior, as being a monk of the strictest observance, was destined for her confessor. In spite of a very cool reception, he succeeded all the same in ingratiating himself with the Archduchess. Following on his first reports, in which he describes himself as being severely offended, came others, in which he expresses himself as quite satisfied. He could find no fault with the religious bearing of the princess; her Court even, he declared, reminded him of monasterial discipline. What she was accused of was chiefly a want of strict surveillance over her household, under which the Spaniards had specially to suffer. First of all he was struck by the fact that the Archduchess never mentioned her relations. Later she said she did not care to mention her mother, Isabella, for that she pined so greatly for her that she could not avoid giving way to tears whenever she thought of her. We are very grateful to Bergenroth for the communication of this correspondence, which contains much welcome and reliable information. Only he ought not to have regarded the Sub-prior as an Inquisitor of faith; for there is nothing in the whole story but petty jealousies between monks. There is not a trace to be found therein of facts, which could cause the Queen to feel any scruples respecting the succession of her daughter in Spain. If Isabella later entertained any such scruples, from Burgos, but not away from her loved corpse. A monk had once told her that he knew of a king who awoke to life after being fourteen years dead. She took the corpse about with her. Four Frisian stallions drew the coffin, which was conveyed at night, surrounded by torches. Sometimes it halted, and the singers sang wailing songs.

they were due to Johanna's extraordinary behaviour in Spain which I have already alluded to, and which certainly awoke doubts as to her healthy condition. Yet her insanity was of a melancholic character, a sort of monomania as regarded her husband, a state of health which modern psychiatric investigations have proved never develops into madness. It was a matter of doubt whether she was insane at all or not. She is sometimes declared to have been so; whilst other observers never noticed anything of it. When the proposal was made in Castile to exclude her from the government and to pass it instead to her husband, one of the Grandees of the realm, the Almirante of Castile, was opposed to the plan. He had an audience of the Queen, in which she gave, though short, yet sensible replies, so that he contrived to defeat this proposal in the Cortes. She was always a subject of variance between the parties in Castile after the death of her husband, but still more so after her father's decease. From the correspondence which passed between the Marquis of Denia and the Emperor Charles V. touching her state, as well as from sundry other documents, it has been attempted to prove to satisfaction that the poor princess was subjected to the direst ill-treatment. Denia is said to have asserted that she had even been put to the rack by her mother. It is likewise said that her father, whenever she refused to take food because her will had not been performed, had her put to the rack. "She was to be put to the rack to preserve her life." But as a matter of fact the Spanish words of the text, p. 143, "Dar cuerda por conservarle la vida," have an opposite meaning. The King had given orders that in such cases she was to be humoured, in order to preserve her life. The word "dar cuerda" can still less bear the meaning attributed to it, as it has no pronoun attached to it. Just as little have the words "hazer premie," in the passage, the meaning attributed to them (cf. Bergenroth, 405 note), they signify a coercion, which may certainly have been employed upon her under certain circumstances, but in the manner previously recommended by Denia. In order to remove her from Tordesillas, which favoured the "Communeros," she was to be placed in a carriage at night and conveyed to Arevalo, which city was loyal to the Crown. For her state was such that the party of the Communeros endeavoured to oppose the mother to the son, who was now Emperor, and which involved danger for the latter. We may reject Bergenroth's conclusions with all possible certainty, prompted as they are by prejudice and a not unjustifiable hate of the Inquisition. This latter does not come here into question at all, but only that state of health of the Queen, which, in spite of long intervals, when she evinced interest in matters and shewed good sense, yet really rendered her incapable of governing. This opinion has come and gone like a meteor. (Note to 2nd Ed.)

Having thus come to Furnillos, a small place of fourteen or fifteen houses, she perceived there a pretty house with a fine view, and remained there: "For it was unseemly for a widow to live in a populous city." There she retained the members of the Government, who had been installed, the Grandees of her Court dwelling with her. Round the coffin she gave her audiences.[1]

After Philip's decease there existed as good as no sovereign power in Castile. At first the Grandees of both factions entered into an agreement under Ximenes, at all events for three months.[2] But as the Condestable and his party were desirous of inviting the King of Aragon, whilst Najara and his partisans were for appealing to the German King to undertake the administration of the kingdom in the name of the young Charles, seeing that the Cortes could not be constitutionally convened for deliberative purposes without the royal name, the result was that the whole country resolved itself into factions. One party actually did invite Ferdinand, and the other Maximilian. The first boasted that "the Catholic King would come and punish all his enemies;" the others, that "the father would be received like the son, and given an aid of 2,000 lances." Pimentel said: "I have two suits of armour, but I will use up both before I will tolerate the Aragon in Castile." Thereupon, throughout the whole country, the old feuds burst out afresh between the Ayalas and Sylvas at Toledo, the Arias and Lassos at Madrid, and the Benavides and Caravajals in Ubeda. Some seized strongholds, and exclaimed, "Castilla, Castilla for Queen Juana." These were Ferdinand's partisans. Galicia and Asturia both adhered to their princes, and hoped for Maximilian's coming. At court the heads of both these parties, the Condestable and Najara, were armed; their troops were constantly arrayed against each other.[3]

In this crisis the nation might well congratulate itself that it still possessed one powerful man, belonging to no party, the Archbishop Ximenes, of Toledo. His position

---

[1] Petrus Martyr, 316, 8; 320, 4, 8; 332, 5.
[2] Escritura in Zurita, ii. f. 81.
[3] Zurita, f. 88, 99, 107, 134. Llorente, Histoire de l'Inquisition, i. 348. Petrus Martyr, 343.

he had won for himself; and it, accordingly, merits a short review.

Ximenes, the son of a lawyer, versed in both theological and juristic science, and somewhile resident at Rome, had already received appointments at the hands of Mendoza and Cifuentes, two of Isabella's partisans. The former had made him vicar of his bishopric, and the latter governor of his county, when he bade adieu to his brilliant career, and retired into a Minorite monastery not far from Toledo. Here he went about barefooted, dressed in sackcloth, slept on a scanty layer of straw, and scourged himself frequently. In his happier hours he might be seen lying under some broad-spreading chestnut tree, in order to shield himself from the rays of the sun, which in those climes blazed so fiercely. He often reclined in the high grass, the Bible in hand, or else knelt and prayed. Here he experienced all the anguish and ecstasy of a solitary soul seeking God. But this was the way to his advancement. The Queen chose him for her father confessor; and then this man, tall of stature, pale and thin, with deep-set, piercing eyes, an aquiline nose, and a smooth forehead even in his old age, might be seen now and again visiting the court in his cowl, and hearing the Queen's confessions, after which he would retire again to the monastery. On one occasion, in the year 1495, he had just finished conducting the spiritual exercises of the Queen during Lent, and had just bidden his companion, Francis Ruyz to cook some vegetables, and saddle the asses to return,—for they intended to spend Good Friday in the monastery at Okanna—when he was a second time summoned to the Queen's presence, and received from her hands a letter with the Papal seal and the superscription: "To our brother Francis, the Archbishop of Toledo elect." Isabella, on the look-out for an archbishop, who had no illustrious relations, who would not entail property, nor spend his income in a way other than it was originally intended to be expended, viz., in the defence of Granada and the coasts, and in every Moorish war, had elected him. He exclaimed, "This is not intended for me," and rode away unperturbed to his monastery. A second command of the Pope at length forced him to accept the dignity; another advising him to comport himself accordingly. After that, he began to wear a silken outer dress, whilst his under covering remained monkish; to wear valuable fur, but of ashen grey colour, in order that it should remind him of his duties; to use soft and luxurious beds, and to keep a considerable staff of servants, and a fool—a sort of clever dwarf. But he himself often slept as he formerly did; and in the palace itself he maintained certain monks, to whom he spoke of nothing but of God and strict discipline, and for whose observance he drew up a table, teaching them how to abstain from worldly things.

In this union of spiritual and temporal things he lived his life. He spoke but very little, and scarcely ever laughed. His life was action and accomplishment: it forms a forcible contrast to the sufferings of the Queen. We read how, on one occasion, he came from the synod of his diocese, where he had been reading daily mass and directing all the ecclesiastical business, to the Aragon Cortes, and induced them to swear; this done, how he proceeded without delay to lay the foundation of the University of Alcala, which was all his doing, a work the King envied him; and how that thence he hied to Granada to convert the Moors, returned, and received (1502) the new Prince at Toledo. And then we are told how, instead of sitting at tournaments, he searched the manuscripts in his library, renewed the Mosarabic liturgy, discussed with seven learned men the plan of the Complutensian polyglot, and also helped to found a society which every night searched the streets to see if any deserving poor were in need of shelter. To-day he would draw up a plan for a campaign in Africa, and on the morrow one for founding a convent, and would carry both into execution. His letters, dealing with the affairs of State, were sealed with the image of St. Francis.[1]

This man, who, it is generally believed, induced Isabella to order in her will a mitigation of the Alcavala for the cities, and who was yet the first of all prelates and grandees, stood midway between the conflicting parties. He was not, as we have seen, successful in reconciling Philip and Ferdinand. But now, at least, he contrived to

[1] All from Ximenes' life by Alvar Gomez de Castro, of Toledo, in Schott's Hispania illustrata.

prevent an open civil war. He had also a guard, which was equipped in the Swiss style;[1] his horsemen might be seen riding out daily to exercise. New weapons continually arrived from the Asturian forges; and at last he brought it to pass that all other troops, save his own, quitted the court.

Now it was a matter of great import that Ximenes declared himself for Ferdinand. The Catholic King, probably, wished rather to reward him than gain him over by the dignity of Cardinal, which he had procured for him.[2] Maximilian's advent would beyond all doubt have resulted in the perfect disorganization of Castile, a war on all sides, and the most violent domestic strife. And when could or should Maximilian come, tied as he was by a Reichstag, weakened by revolt in the Netherlands, and fettered by an Italian campaign? Ximenes decided for Ferdinand. The most powerful men in the land listened to his advice. Villena, who had at first been almost heart and soul for Philip, came to him: "Is it right what the King demands? Swear to me that it is so." The Archbishop swore to him that it was right; thereupon whilst still clasping his hand, he vowed to serve King Ferdinand in his government.[3] The rest of the opposition of the Grandees Ferdinand contrived, in almost every case, to overcome by the grant of favours, so much so indeed, that his loyal supporters became quite jealous. Pimontel also gave in on receiving an "Encomienda" and a salary of 12,000 maravedi per annum.[4] Accordingly, in August, 1507, after having been absent a year, Ferdinand entered Castile without encountering any resistance, with Alcalds and Alquazils, his Mazzi and heralds; the Grandees hastened to kiss his hand. In the North there were still left several, whom neither he nor Ximenes had been able to gain over. They fled and lost their castles; Najara lost all save one. "And now," said Ferdinand, "we will open a new account together." In Andalusia, Priego and Giron were in open revolt. He deprived them also of their castles. The Inquisition abated its rigour somewhat, and Ximenes, whom the King had

[1] Zurita, f. 119, 120.   [2] Breve, in Gomez.
[3] Letter of the King to Villena, in Zurita, 110. Also in the same, 142.
[4] Zurita, ii. 133.

appointed Grand Inquisitor, acquitted all the accused Luzeros.[1]

In Tortoles the King met his daughter. As soon as they set eyes on each other, the father took off his hat, and the daughter her mourning veil. When she prostrated herself to kiss his feet, and he sank on one knee to recognize her royal dignity, they embraced and opened their hearts to each other. He shed tears. Tears she had none, but she granted his desire; only she would not consent to bury the corpse. "Why so soon?" she inquired. Nor would she go to Burgos where she had lost her husband. He took her to Tordesillas. Here the Queen of such vast realms lived for forty-seven years. She educated her youngest daughter, gazed from the window upon the grave of her dear departed, and prayed for his eternal happiness. Her soul never more disclosed itself to the world.[2]

These are the struggles engendered of the Neapolitan war through the pretensions of the house of Austria. Maximilian, owing chiefly to the opposition of Louis, who declared that he would consider everyone who recognized him his enemy, and, if he were a subject of his own, guilty of high treason, could at first not even obtain the guardianship over his grandchildren in the Netherlands.[3] At last, however, in 1507, he obtained it, when new dangers threatened from Guelders and from the French coast, and made his assistance desirable. But in Spain and Italy Ferdinand was triumphant. He at once turned his newly consolidated power against the outer world and foreign nations.

4. *Ferdinand's external Enterprises.*

Prior to the commencement of the Neapolitan war of 1501, the Xeque of Gerba had offered allegiance to the Spaniards, together with the whole coast line lying between Tripolis and Tunis. Isabella had often repented

---

[1] Zurita, 143, 148, 163. Moreover, Llorente, i. 352.
[2] Petrus Martyr, 359. Zurita, 144.
[3] Letter of Louis in the Lettres de Louis XII., i. 106, 107.

that Naples had at that time been preferred. Directly the first pause came between Ferdinand's reconciliation with France, in 1505, and Philip's arrival, Ximenes urged the renewal of the Moorish war, and himself subscribed the fourth part of the expense of fitting out a fleet, which attacked and took the great harbour of Maçarquivir, a splendid station of the African trade. His attention had first been drawn to this place by a Venetian; Lopez el Zagal was the first to spring on land.[1] But the great domestic disturbances, at all events in Andalusia, had not been completely suppressed, when the Moorish pirates were driven away from Velez and the rock lying before it. But as soon as tranquillity had been restored at home, and Ferdinand was no longer occupied by his Italian enmities, he again commenced greater operations in the interest of universal Christendom. To these belong also the colonization of America. Hitherto the Spaniards had been content to explore the islands and bays of the West Indies, to look for gold, to fish for pearls, and to preach Christianity peacefully. All these operations had been conducted by an admiral from a colony in St. Domingo. In the year 1509, Ferdinand having heard of the barbarous habits of the wild cannibals there, appointed two governors, Hoieda for the coast of Carthagena, and Niquesa for Veragua.[2] Their duties were: "to make the Indians his vassals and good Christians, but, should this be impossible, to reduce them to slavery or exterminate them." The governors themselves were not fortunate; but some of their companions founded a colony upon Darien, to which, in honour of the image of Maria Antigua at Seville, they gave the name of Antigua. Nuñez Balboa, a man who was reserved for great discoveries,[3] became its head.

But at the time of which we speak, the operations in Africa appeared to be of greater moment both for Spain and Europe: yet the other was greater both in respect of the

---

[1] Zurita, i. ii. 26.
[2] Sommario dell' Indie Occidentali di Don Pietro Martire, in Ramusio, Viaggi, iii. 18. Benzoni, Novæ novi orbis historiæ, a Calvetone latinæ factæ, p. 72.
[3] Pietro Martire, f. 21.

exertion expended upon it, as also of the successful results. On the eve of Ascension-day, 1509, Ximenes and Pedro Navarra set sail with their fleet and landed on the day following at Oran, before which city they found 12,000 Moorish knights gathered ready to defend it. "Shall we attack to-day?" asked Navarra. "Immediately," returned Ximenes. Before him the Cross was borne, and his monks, with swords over their cassocks, also advanced in line. The Galicians first stormed the heights, and maintained themselves there; then, strengthened by the other troops, they drove the enemy back upon the water reservoirs of the city. Here they awaited their artillery. They fought with this at a distance, and with their swords at close quarters. The enemy at length turned and fled. Whilst the enemy was being driven past its own city, other troops landed from the ships and took it. Thereupon the Spanish ensigns floated from the walls of Oran, and the troops shouted, "Africa! Africa for our lord, the King of Spain!" Ximenes, to whose prayers the victory was attributed, "owing to them the sun had stood still and had shone brightly over them, whilst gloom was spread over the Moors," consecrated the Grand Mosque as a Church of St. Maria de la Vitoria.[1]

Again, on the 1st January, 1510, in honour, as the Spaniards said, of the Saviour and His Mother, and of the Apostle St. James, and the knight, St. George, of blessed memory, Pedro Navarra, set sail from Ivica. On this occasion he was very successful. Bugia, a great and wealthy city, full of mosques, schools, hospitals, inns, and all manner of prosperity, was taken by him at the first assault. Xeque, Almoxarife, Alcadi, Musti, and all the Alfaquis of Algiers surrendered their city under the condition, that Ferdinand should not demand a single farthing more in contributions than the Moorish king had received, and would leave them their laws. Tedelitz surrendered. Muley Yahya, King of Tenez, promised to come as Ferdinand's vassal, as often as he should be summoned to the Cortes, or to the wars. At last Navarra, with brigantines, sloops, and barks, succeeded, one evening, in forcing his

---

[1] Zurita, ii. 180-182, whence Mariana, 275-287. Gomez, 1025.

way into the harbour of Tripolis, and on the following day, between nine and one, in taking this great city.[1]

But before all else it was now imperative to conquer Tremecen, Tunis, and the island of Gerba; then the African coast would be assured to the Spaniards. The King of Tremecen, a great potentate, swore with his Mezvar and Cadi, to pay an annual tribute of 13,000 Doblas in good gold. In Sicily, preparations were going on against Tunis. Garsia, Alba's eldest son, attacked Gerba. Garsia had to pay for his daring with his life on the burning sands.[2] But Ferdinand was for setting out in person to take over the command of the army. Only when the interior of the country was his, could he be certain of securing the harbours and coasts. This accomplished, his intention was to continue his holy campaign as far as Alexandria, the next city to Tripolis, and thence to the holy temple of Jerusalem. For this object, the Cortes of Aragon, Valencia, and Catalonia voted an aid of 500,000 pounds, which, considering their liberties, was a very considerable sum. A thousand English musketeers also joined in the expedition. The rupture between the Mores and Alarabs along the whole coast gave prospects of a great success, and they bethought themselves of an old prophecy, that ancient Carthage with its harbour would now fall into the hands of the Christians.[3]

With these hopes in his breast, Ferdinand set out for Malaga, in the year 1511, in order to begin the campaign. But on the way thither he was overtaken by ambassadors from Italy, who brought him such tidings from Romagna that his plans were turned into other channels.

[1] Zurita, ii. 211, 212, f.
[2] Zurita, 230. Fazellus, Historiæ Siculæ, 597.
[3] Zurita, 227. Senarega, Annales Genuenses, 608.

CHAPTER III.

OF VENICE AND JULIUS II.

THE development of the Romagnan question resulted in a general war. Once more Venice shows herself in the fulness of her might: independent, vigorous, and with comprehensive and grand ideas and aspirations. A general consideration of her position is accordingly indispensable.[1]

1. *Commerce, Conquest, the Venetian Constitution ; attack upon the Romagna.*

The lagoons were originally covered with low mud hovels, having scarcely an aperture to admit of light and air, and full of poor fugitives.[2] About the year 1500, there were to be seen there about seventy-two churches, built of stone, and glittering with gold, whilst three broad canals were flanked by palace on palace, all faced with variegated and white marble.[3] Even humble people slept on beds of walnut wood, behind green silk curtains, ate from silver, and went forth in golden chains and rings.[4] The West and East paid tribute here on their wares, before they were bartered and exchanged. Many large islands and splendid cities received hence their governors.

To this pitch of prosperity it had come through conquest and commerce; but its commerce was the original source

[1] I refrain from making any additions, acquired from recent research, to my original description. They will, I conceive, find a place in a later volume of my works. (Note to 2nd Ed.)
[2] Sansovino, Venetia, p. 140.
[3] Comines, Mémoires, 479.
[4] Sansovino. Hence Splendor Venetiarum clarissimus, in Grævii Thesaurus, v. 3, p. 282.

of its greatness. Just as those fishermen themselves originally belonged to the Greek, that is the Eastern, Empire, whilst the first territory they acquired for their sustenance belonged to the Lombard, *i.e.*, the Western Empire, and they were thus vassals to both, so now did the essence of their present trade lie in the connection of the distant East with the distant West. It was carried on in the following manner:—

As soon as the public galleys were ready for sea, and delivered over to those of the "Nobili," who, summoned by the cry of the heralds, had offered the best prices, some, according to primæval custom, sailed to Alexandria and the Black Sea, and others to Africa and the West.[1] The first were laden with copper and mercury from Hungary, with German steel, with alum from Italy, and velvet, camelot, cloth, mirrors, beads, and glass from their own city, each cargo worth 100,000 ducats.[2] In Alexandria, the watchmen on the tower looked out for their arrival, and signalled it to the toll-gatherer. The chief business was done in Cairo, in the Khan el Halili, the Persian merchants'-hall.[3] Thither, the caravans from Mecca brought the fine spices from the Moluccas, the silk of Bengal, cinnamon from Ceylon, pepper from Malabar, precious stones and stained wood from the Deccan, and pearls from Bahrein. In case the Indians preferred consigning their goods to the caravans through Cabul and Persia, to Derbend, the gate of gates, and to Azov, rather than to the sea,[4] or if the dwellers on the coast of Asia Minor produced anything rare or useful, like the goat's hair of Angora, this they fetched from Ayas or Azov. They conveyed all to the halls on the Rialto.

The Western galleys, on their part, did not export the same wares as the Eastern; these they left to the Western nations to fetch for themselves. Their cargoes were cloth

[1] Petrus Martyr, Legatio Babylonica (to Cairo), in 1502. Basil, 1533, p. 7.
[2] Sommario de' Regni, Città, etc. in Ramusio, Viaggi, i. 324.
[3] Petrus Martyr, Legatio Babylonica, 80. Leo, Descriptio Africæ, in Ramusio, 83.
[4] Pegoletti, Avvisamento del Viaggio and Aloigi di Giovanni, in Sprengel's Geschichte der Entdeckungen, 253, 257. Ritter's Geography, ii. 859.

and metal, gold chains for France, wax candles for the Spanish churches, fiddle-strings from Pacasto, and glass from Murano. In Gerba they owned a great house close to the castle, in Tunis they shared with Genoese and Catalans, a whole suburb of the town; in Oran and Temslan they did a great trade. Hence their goods found their way to the interior of the Soudan, to Timbuctoo, where the women wore veils of Venetian manufacture, and to Gago, where their most inferior cloth fetched one, and their scarlet forty, ducats the yard, and hither came the gold in return, which they sent back to the East.[1] In Malaga they loaded silk and grain, and wool also, though this latter they principally fetched from England. They even penetrated as far as Flanders and Denmark. It is computed that, besides these public vessels, nearly 3,000 private ships were engaged in trading with these same coasts, yet chiefly with other ports. Their trading capital, some considerable time previously, had amounted to 28,800,000 ducats.[2]

All this was controlled by the most rigorous laws. Save in the Fondaco, where the German cities had each their separate vaults, which they let to several business houses,[3] no one was allowed to trade with Germans, and only here such as were, as they expressed it, internal and external citizens. No vassal city was allowed to sell for export to, or buy from, foreign parts, except in Venice. No galley might stay away longer than a definite and precise time.[4] A law obtained that an emigrating manufacturer should at first be induced to return by persuasion, in case he did not obey, by the arrest of his relations, and, if he did not then return, he should be put to death.[5] By such measures their city was preserved as the source of trade and commerce.

It was necessity that prompted their first conquests. In

---

[1] Paruta, Storia Venetiana, iv. 117, whence all in Lebret, the history of the Venetian State, ii. 1046. Moreover, Leo, Africanus, Descriptio Africæ, in Ramusio, f. 70, 66, 58, 78, 79.
[2] Daru, Histoire de Venise, iii. 189, p. 51 from Filiasi.
[3] Document in the Records of Ratisbon, iv. ii. p. 141.
[4] Teutori, Saggio sopra l' historia Venetiana, i. 126; ii. 80, 85.
[5] Six-and-twentieth art. of the Inquisition Laws in Daru, iii. 90.

this province they were not always fortunate, and the war in 1379 left them little more than Negropont, Coron, Modon, and Candia. But, after that time, fortune and shrewdness opened to them a new way.

After the decease of Charles de la Pace, when one faction in Corfu did not desire to be reigned over by his son Ladislas, the people bethought themselves how frequently they had seen the victorious standard of Venice in their waters, and raised the ensign of the lion and founded a church to Michael, as an everlasting memorial. The same Ladislas, in the midst of the contention between the Horvaths and the Hungarian Queens, sold to them Zara, where he had been crowned.[1] For fear of the despot of Servia, Cattaro sent its Chancellor and begged for a Venetian magistrate who should judge according to the old laws. Filled with like apprehensions, Spalatro and Trau were delivered over to them by the citizens, Argos, Napoli di Romania, Patras, Lepanto, and ever so many other cities besides, were made over to them by their princes for money. Athens received a garrison from Venice; and, in consequence of a quarrel with his father, a prince of Constantinople delivered Saloniki into their keeping.[2]

And so it went on. Veglia refused to obey either a Frangipani, whether Nicolo or John, and preferred their rule. During a feud between the Queens Carlota and Catharina, they gained Cyprus.[3]

Their policy was as follows: whenever their neighbours became involved in differences or were in peril, they appeared on the scene, and offered the one protection and the other money; thus effecting their subjugation.

The same process they followed in Italy. To begin with, when the quarrel between Cividal d'Austria and Udine had convulsed the whole of Frioli, and the neighbouring States became likewise involved, it happened one day that the citizens of Treviso, and all the peasants, who had come into the city to defend it, shouted "San Marco!" and delivered themselves into the hand of the Venetian captain.

---

[1] Sanuto, Chronica Venetiana, 543, 844.
[2] Navagero, Chronicon Venetum, 1075, 1080. Daru, from MSS. ii. 99.
[3] Navagero, in detail, 1137-1198, 1203.

This incident brought about the subjection of the whole of Frioli. This enterprise was not without sufficient motive, for they needed a market in the vicinity for their daily supplies of food. But should they then, when the Visconti, in feud with the Carrara, offered them their cities of Verona, Feltre, and Belluno, implicate themselves in the general Italian movements, so full of storm, insecurity, and danger as they were? All who stood in any relation to the Carrara, must first be excluded from the Pregadi, before the Doge and Francis Foscari, the head of the Forty, could carry the day by the preponderating voice of a single ballot. Vicenza raised the standard of Venice. On the 12th July, 1405, there appeared on the square of St. Mark before the Doge and governing body twenty-two envoys from Verona on horseback, all dressed in white, bearing the seal of their country, the three keys of the city for the three estates, the white staff (the symbol of sovereignty), and two ensigns; and having delivered these insignia over, they took the oath of allegiance. The Doge answered them, " Ye are come from darkness into light," and gave them a gold embroidered standard of St. Mark. They shouted " San Marco," and rode back home. The Paduans, being in sore need, were allowed by Francis Carrara to do their wish, and they, having stipulated the maintenance of their liberties, surrendered to Venice.[1]

In Venice there was not entire satisfaction at this policy. Upon the mosaic floor of the Church of St. Mark, two lions may be seen depicted; one in the sea, great, strong, and courageous, the other on land, thin and weak; a picture symbolizing widespread views and opinions. The Doge Mocenigo was especially opposed to every new enterprise. " For whoever conquered," as he expressed himself, " sought evil and found it too. He, for his part, would not maintain people with great billhooks in order to ravage this beautiful garden of Milan, which brought them in some millions every year. Did the conquests they had already made, recoup the expenditure? He prayed God, our Lady, and St. Mark for peace." So long as he lived, but no longer, his opinion was wise.[2] A man of opposite views and ideas,

[1] Navagero, 1070. Sanuto, 794-831. Bilue's Historia Patriæ, 32.
[2] Arrenghi, in Sanuto, 949, 958. Sansovino, Venetia.

a man of whom he had warned his countrymen, Foscari, was chosen to succeed him. He made use of the misunderstanding between Philip of Milan and Carmagnuola, in order with the latter's help to acquire Brescia and Bergamo; he availed himself of the disturbances following on Philip's death to gain Crema, and utilized the tumults which had broken out between the nobles and the commons to gain possession of Ravenna, and subsequently of Cervia also. The income Venice derived from the mainland, as a result of this policy, rose to 800,000 ducats, and that accruing from the islands to 400,000 ducats.[1] Men said: "They have no rival on the seas, and are not minded to tolerate one on land."[2] How the internal machinery of this marvellous power worked, can easily be told if we look at the peculiar traditional forms of its constitution, but can only be explained with the greatest difficulty, if we look at the real moving and living principle animating the whole. If we reflect that the Doge could not say "Yes" or "No" to anybody without first taking counsel with his "Consiglieri,"[3] but that, on the other side, the three Inquisitors, without the interference of the "Avogatori," and laying aside all formality, had the right to condemn to death clergy and laity, nobles and commons, to make use of the public treasury, and to command the governors and generals,[4] we shall perceive that the counterpoise of Doge, Consiglieri, Pregadi, and the Consiglio was not worth much, but that the supreme power, which in other cities reposed in the hands of a Balia, here resided in the Inquisitors. It is certainly not at all clear from what families these were chosen, how the others tolerated it, and why there was here no trace of party feeling. Some remarks of Maximilian, that he was coming to liberate the old fathers from the violent oppression of the new aristocracy,[5] cast no real light, but only a glimmer upon this matter. Within this hall, no personality and no difference is marked, only some-

[1] Epitome proventuum Italiæ; also in Ludewig, Reliquiæ MSS. x. 445.
[2] Ferrante's letter in Fabroni, Vita Laurentii Medici, ii. 237.
[3] In Sanuto, 785.
[4] Daru, Histoire de Venice from the real documents, ii. 423.
[5] Maximilian's Manifestoes of the Years 1510 and 1511, in Hormayr's Archiv. für Historie, etc., A.D. 1810.

times hatred against secret renegades makes itself known, otherwise, there is only a common exertion and a common will. "They are very clever," says Comines, "they meet daily and hold Council; their neighbours will feel the effect."[1]

The disturbances which had taken place in Italy since Charles VIII.'s advent there, came very opportunely for their plans and policy. On every available occasion the Venetians spread their power all round about them. In the struggle between Charles and Ferrantino they acquired five fine cities in Apulia, excellently situated for their requirements, which they peopled by the reception of fugitive Jews from Spain.[2] Moreover, in the kingdom of Naples, one party had declared for them; we have, too, already seen how Tarento raised their standard. During the Florentine disorders, they were within an ace of becoming masters of Pisa. In the Milanese feuds they acquired Cremona and Ghiara d'Adda. Their power was all the more terrible, as they had never been known to lose again anything which they had once gotten. No one doubted that their aim was the complete sovereignty over the whole of Italy. Their historians always talked, as if Venice was the ancient Rome once more; therefore it was that the bones of Titus Livius were honoured at Padua, like those of a saint: "they should learn of him to avoid the faults of Rome."[3]

The Turkish war, which had kept them a while employed, now at an end, they next tried their fortune in Romagna, and endeavoured, availing themselves of the quarrels between the returning nobles and Cesar, to become, if not the sole, at all events the most powerful, vassals of the papal chair. Those nobles, who were often compelled to fly, and those who were accustomed to fly to them, were all, even including Guidubaldo, their head, so much bound to Venice, that "San Marco" had even been shouted in Guidubaldo's castles, with his approval and consent. The Venetians prepared to espouse the cause of those whom Cesar had suppressed. The cities re-

[1] Comines, Mémoires, 488.
[2] Leander Alberti, Descriptio Italiæ, p. 369.
[3] Comines, 483.

flected how genuine and substantial that peace was that the lion of Venice spread over all its dependencies. Having appeared in this country at the end of October, 1503, and having first promised the Malatesti other possessions in their own country, they took Rimini, with the concurrence of the prince and citizens. Without ado they attacked Faenza.[1] That city had recalled a natural scion of the Manfreddi, and for a good omen had called him Astorre; but the good omen proved an ill-starred one, when the governor of the castle surrendered. They were then also themselves obliged to surrender.[2] Men said: " Faenza is either a gate into Italy for the Venetians, or else their ruin." They continued their conquests, and, in the territories of Imola, Cesena, and Forli, took stronghold after stronghold. Cesena itself had already previously announced through Guidubaldo its subjection, and it was only the fear of Cesar's castles above their head that kept the cities still loyal. Then it was that the first minister of France stated his belief that, " had they only Romagna, they would forthwith attack Florence,[3] on account of a debt of 180,000 guilders owing them." If they were to make an inroad into Tuscany, Pisa would fall immediately on their arrival. Their object in calling the French into the Milanese territory was, that they considered them more fitted to make a conquest than to keep it; and, in the year 1504, they were negotiating how it were possible to wrest Milan again from them. Could they only succeed in this, nothing in Italy would be able longer to withstand them. " They wanted," as Macchiavelli said, "to make the Pope their chaplain."[4]

Julius II.'s First Exploits and Double Intentions.

But they met with the staunchest resistance in Julius, as in him they could discover no weak point[5] to attack.

[1] Bembus, Historia Veneta, 145-147. Baldi, Guidubaldo, ix. 127-141.
[2] Sansovino, Origine, 79.
[3] Macchiavelli, Legazione alla Corte di Roma, p. 331.
[4] His words in the same Legazione, p. 301.
[5] *Ibid.*, the forty-eighth letter, 391.

As pointedly as he could express himself, he declared to them, on the 9th November, 1503, that, " though hitherto their friend, he would now do his utmost against them, and would besides incite all the princes of Christendom against them;"[1] and once more, on the 10th January, he declared that: "he was, and always had been, firm and constant in his intention to regain the temporalities of the Church; and, further, that no terrorism, no treaty, nor conditions would prevent his carrying it out, for it was his duty."[2] But as no warning availed aught, "for their right was clear and plain, and they would satisfy his claims with their newly-coined gold," in September, 1504, he entered into the league with Louis, Maximilian, and Philip, which was not alone directed against Ferdinand, but against Venice as well. We have seen how this league became dissolved. The Venetians then retreated a step backwards. They restored all parts of the territories of Imola, Cesena, and Forli that they had occupied; until they had done so, Julius would not accept their obedience.[3] Yet he did not even then abandon his project of conquering the rest.

Julian was of a very impatient and violent character. When Michel Angelo painted the Sixtine chapel, and at last unveiled it, he could not wait until the dust raised by the fall of the scaffolding had cleared away.[4] Any thought that had once occurred to him possessed his mind unceasingly; it was visible in his features, he murmured it ever between his teeth; "he must die," he confessed, "did he not speak it out."[5] But this did not make him stubborn and inconsiderate. He once threatened Michel Angelo, requiring him to make haste and finish some work, and then on the following day sent him 500 scudi to pacify him.[6] In the same way, as he had always abided by his opinion in contradiction to his uncle Sixtus, to Innocent and Alexander, even when a fugitive and in peril, so did

---

[1] *Ibid.*, 304.
[2] Breve Julii Papæ, in Rainaldus, Annales Ecclesiastici, xx. p. 9.
[3] Bembus, Historia Veneta, vii. 155. Baldi, Guidubaldo, xi. 182.
[4] Vasari, Vita di Michel Angelo, p. 200.
[5] Zurita, ii. 28, explaining Paris di Grassis, Diarium, apud Hoffmannum, Collectio Nova, 450. [6] Vasari, *ibid.* 225.

he now act as Pope; he even unswervingly adhered to his resolve, mindful of his forefathers Nicholas and Gregory.[1] His temperament can be gathered from a portrait of him by Raphael. His boldly-chiselled features, closed mouth, his straight and fixed look, and long flowing beard, are graphically depicted, as he sits in an arm-chair, and thinks.[2] All his actions give evidence of his firmness. He aptly wore the oak on his coat-of-arms.

Now, as we have seen, Julius was resolved to tolerate princes in the Papal State, but only such as he could control. But it was not alone the Venetians who were capable of offering him resistance, but others also. John Bentivoglio, of Bologna, in particular, was almost independent. John ruled his city by a council of twenty, of whom ten conducted the "Imborsazione," the elections, and all public business for the first half of the year; and the other ten for the remaining half, yet both under his personal presidency. He was styled Prince, Governor, and permanent "Gonfaloniere" of justice; he could himself levy a tax.[3] He dwelt in a splendid palace, containing 370 rooms, among gardens, fountains, and fish ponds.[4] His sons, one of whom was designated to succeed him, built other palaces. He found a bell indispensable for calling his friends together; and a tower bears an inscription to the effect that, "he had built it, he, all whose wishes had abundantly been so realized by virtue and fortune, and whom they had so richly endowed with this world's goods."[5] On his shield were emblazoned a lily and an eagle; yet he trusted most in the lily and in French protection.

In the year 1506, when Louis XII. and Ferdinand the Catholic needed the papal sanction to their Neapolitan compact, Julius considered it practicable to compel the Bolognians to recognize their own dependence. The latter appealed to tradition and to the old treaties made with the papal chair. He, on his part, maintained the rights of a prince

[1] Bull to Louis XII., in Hottingeri Historia Ecclesiastica, vii. 45.
[2] A copy in the Guistinian collection in Berlin. *Vide* also Speth, Italien, i. 225.
[3] Hieronymus de Bursellis, Chronica Bononiensia in Muratori, xxiii. 881.
[4] Sansovino, Origine, 280, 289.   [5] Inscription in Bursellis, 909.

to alter a constitution even in the face of traditional custom; he announced that, he would come and see their mode of life for himself; if he was pleased, he would confirm it, otherwise he would alter it: the old treaties, he averred, were obtained by coercion, and now, at this time, an amelioration was possible.[1] The Venetians offered him their assistance in this enterprise, provided he would only ratify their possession of Faenza and Rimini. But he paid them no heed. With only a guard of twenty-five lances, a grey-haired man among grey-haired cardinals, on the 20th August, 1506, he took the field in order to conquer Bologna.[2] On the march thither he thought of reducing Perugia.

Now Giampaolo Baglione, who after Alexander's death ruled Perugia again in the customary manner by a Balia, the arbitrary ten (dell' Arbitrio), had always refused obedience.[3] He was now to be compelled to obey. What was there victorious in his mere advent? In Orvieto, Giampaolo, whom the Duke Guidubaldo had persuaded to subject himself, met him and promised to deliver his fortresses and gates into the Pope's power, and his troops into his pay. Before the capitulation had even been signed, before his troops, who had begun to collect, were on the scene, and in order to show that he trusted the honour of his enemy, the Pope entered Perugia, reinstated in their possessions those who had fled the city, left to Giampaolo his legal rights, and restored peace.[4]

In the case of Bentivoglio, the pride of his wife, Gineura Sforza, and his old confidential standing with Julius, with whom he had eaten and drank, prevented a similar subjection. Were his four sons, to whom he had committed the defence of the four quarters of the city, too weak to resist a Pope? He replied to Julius' demand that he should furnish quarters for him, his army, and 500 French lancers, that: "Only the Swiss guard could be admitted with the Pope's person," and further asked to be informed how

---

[1] Macchiavelli, Legazione al Papa, tom. v. p. 157.
[2] Macchiavelli, *ibid.* lett. iii. Hadriani Cardinalis Iter Iulii in Roscoe i. appendix, p. 519, in Hexameters.
[3] Macchiavelli, **Legaz.** v. 160.
[4] Macchiavelli, Legazione, v. 136, and Discorsi Sopra la prima Deca di Tito Livio, i. c. 27. Baldi, 192.

long he intended to remain?¹ "So," exclaimed Julius indignantly, "he prescribes laws for us, and will not receive us. Shall he dictate to us?"² Hereupon the Pope declared Bentivoglio and his adherents rebels against the Church, gathered to him his army and the aid Louis had promised him, and winding through the ravines and passes of the highest part of the Apennine range, carefully avoiding the positions occupied by the Venetians, and passing frequently by kneeling peasants, marched to Imola.³ At this juncture, the French, whose arrival Bentivoglio had never expected, actually advanced against him—for Julius and Louis were still friends—and, at the same time, his old adversaries in the city, who had so long kept silence, rose up in revolt, and with them many new opponents, all embittered by the cruelties perpetrated on the Marescotti (of whom shortly before nearly two hundred had been ruined on Cesar Borgia's accusation), and detesting him, too, for the arrogance of his sons.⁴ Then he likewise perceived that no one can be accounted happy before his death, and that he had falsely boasted that no one would ever expel him; accordingly, he entered into a compact with the French, which secured to him his private possessions, and then, after an uninterrupted prosperity of forty years' duration, quitted his palace, the pillar of his fortune, and his city. Julius, on the other hand, obeying the invitation of the now free people, was borne in through the gates of Bologna on an ivory chair, in his papal robes. He only deposed three members of the twenty, whilst adding twenty-three to their body. To this forty he committed a far more independent jurisdiction than that which they had enjoyed under the house of the Bentivogli, and released the people from all burdens. He desired to establish a truly free city, and one devoted to him for his protection and favour.⁵

Now whilst entertaining other plans and projects, as to which he was not reticent, and having delivered to the Mar-

[1] Macchiavelli, Legazione, 121, 165.
[2] Paris de Grassis, Itinerarium Iulii in Rainaldus, xx. 10.
[3] Hadriani Iter, v.s. 86. Baldi, Guidabaldo, 195.
[4] Georg. Florus, de bello Italico, p. 19. Arlieni, de bello Veneto, 24. Monstrelet, appendix, 239.
[5] Sansovino, Origine delle Case, 292. Nardi, History of Florence, iv. 114. Anton, Chronicques Annales, p. 40. Paris de Grassis, p. 13.

quis of Mantua the standard of the Church, bidding him under it wage just and victorious wars, and well pleasing to God,[1] it happened that affairs in Genoa were so far prejudicial to his objects as to divert his intentions into another channel.

In the years 1506 and 1507, Genoa passed through all the phases of a revolution. The first impetus was given by the leading democratic families, who, for a long time past, had been wont to see one of them, Fregosi or Adorni, at the head of affairs, and the old aristocracy doing service to them. Since the French occupation, however, both those leading families were in exile, and the supreme power resided in the nobles, and especially in the " Fiesci."[2] The " Popolares," having for a long time vainly demanded that two-thirds of the public offices should be again entrusted to them, were at length aided in their demands by the indignation of the proletariat at the conduct of some aristocratic youths, who, instead of paying, drew swords, showing on the hilts the inscription: " Chastise the peasant."[3] Accordingly, one day some of them placed themselves at the head of the people, and, with the cry of "People and King," organized an insurrection, and succeeded in wresting to them two-thirds of the offices.[4] The effect of this was to show the lower orders that the public peace only depended upon their good will. Rapidly following up their success, these latter next opposed the magistrates of the upper classes by appointing eight tribunes from their own midst, went even still further, and committed the supreme power to four men, and were then not content. At last, the " Cappetti "—plebs, whose sole wealth consisted in an old cap and a pair of woollen stockings—obtained the upper hand, and collecting daily in their societies, " The Peace," " The Concord," or whatever they were called, waxed greatly enthusiastic, chose a dyer for their chief, and made him an absolute Doge.[5]

The course of such revolutions often proceeds in the

[1] Breve in Dumont, iv. 1, 20.
[2] Senarega, Rerum Genuensium Annales, in many passages, and 576.
[3] Anton, Chronicques Annales, p. 47.
[4] Libertus Folieta, Historia Genuensis, 282.
[5] Principally in Senarega, 577-587. Georg. Florus, 24.

same way; from an ascendancy of the middle classes to the opposite extreme, next to the ascendancy of the proletariat, and, finally, to a monarchy from the plebs. These Genoese paid no heed to the King of France, until, in April, 1507, he advanced against them with his *hommes d'armes* and Swiss Guards. They then fortified a hill lying immediately before their walls, and occupied it with two masses of troops, the one posted on the summit, and the other on a lower point of vantage. But they lacked courage and discipline; and when Bayard, with 126 *hommes d'armes*, stormed up the hill from the one side, and the Obwald musketeers and the Bernese volunteers from the other, both divisions turned and fled, without even thinking of combining.[1] They had no other weapons left, but for all, aristocratic Anzians and plebeians, wives and maidens, to cry "Misericordia." Louis gave to all, with the exception of seventy-nine, their lives and property; but he burnt before their eyes the book of their compacts with him, and the letters of their imperial liberties, took their arms away, and built with their money a castle to hold them in awe. And so they went about, with shrugged shoulders and bowed heads; on their new coins they saw no longer the device of the griffin, but only that of the lily.[2]

But how could it be that the degradation of his country should not affect Julius II., who was proud to call himself, in his inscriptions, "Ligurian?" It might be that before Bologna, upon which, on Bentivoglio's flight, they had advanced, under an understanding with the nobles, and which they were only prevented by the people from occupying, he had found the French not so well disposed as he could have wished.[3] But Genoa was almost nearer to his heart. He was a kinsman of the house of the Fregosi, and perceived in their exclusion by the French a slight offered to himself. It was generally believed that he

---

[1] Bayard, 123. St. Gelais, 191. The Freiburger's letter in Fuch's Mailändischen Feldzügen, ii. 44, 45. Anselmus in Glutz. 202.

[2] Anton, 185. Louis' instruction for John de Cabellis, in Datt. de pace publica, 512. Senarega, 592 f.

[3] Maximilian's reply (to French allegations) in Goldast, Reichshandlung, 57.

had had a hand in the insurrection of the "Popolares;" and that it was with intention that Louis had brought three cardinals and thirty high prelates with him, planning, perhaps, to dispossess the Pope.[1] As a matter of fact, Louis had been in negotiation with Ferdinand to make Amboise Pope;[2] and certain overtures made to England appear to point to the same thing.[3] But Julius, instead, as had been his original plan, of awaiting the King's arrival in Bologna, returned in haste to Rome.

The result of this was, that the Pope's original plan, that of uniting the States of the Church, was supplemented by another, no less a one than to free Italy from the French. With respect to the first, he quarrelled with Venice; in carrying out the second, he might have assured himself of its support. Had both only been at one, and united with the greater part of the nation, which had a feeling of oppression,[4] they might, perhaps, together have achieved some result. But, just as in the whole nation itself, the feeling of faction entertained by certain confederations against each other was doubtless far stronger than the feeling of universal union—the first hereditary and deeply rooted, and the latter only existing in theory and in writings—so also did Julius and Venice prefer to fight out their own particular quarrel, to thinking of their common nationality and their common country. Both wished to possess Rimini and Faenza; otherwise no alliance between them. So did they confront each other, each looking beyond towards the same object, but, for the present, both hostile to each other.

[1] Folieta and Guicciardini, vii. 372.
[2] Mémoire, touchant les affaires de France in the Lettr. de Louis I., 62.
[3] Garnier, histoire de France, xxii. 84; sur la copie d'une negociation secrète.
[4] Instanæ Galateus, de situ Japygiæ, ap. Grævium.

3. *Discoveries of the Portuguese. Decay of the Venetian Commerce.*

It had now come about that Venice was incurring great danger on both sides of its existence; in its conquests and its commerce. To begin with, the Venetian trade had, in its real fountain spring, the East, suffered injury at the hands of those who had intended something quite different, and who were really engaged on a mission of universal utility.

In the year 1497, the trade on the coasts of Arabia, East Africa, and the Indian peninsula was in the hands of the Moors; naturally on the Arabian coast, at Aden, where the favourable monsoons were eagerly awaited, and at Ormuz, "the house of safety."[1] But scarcely less theirs was the fertile expanse of plain upon the other two coasts, which lay opposite each other, up to where the tableland begins. On the African coast, the Moors penetrated as far as the Uzige, whence they fetched gold and amber, and Cape St. Sebastian. The King of Quiloa, who was computed to receive annually 2,666,666 ducats of gold from Sofala, and the sheiks at Melinda and Mozambique were Moors.[2] On the Indian coast, lay the three kingdoms of Guzerat, Deccan, and Malabar. Over the two first-named, Moorish princes held sway, whilst in all their ports were Mongolian or Arabian governors. If a Banian wished to engage here in trade, he ventured not to embark without an Arabian convoy. The third, Malabar, had still an Indian, the Zamorin of Kolikod, for its chief; but he also was kept in no little dependence by 4,000 Mohammedans, who dwelt in his city, and often supplied him with money. Whoever was not minded to obey him, went into the mosque. One of his vassals, the Prince of Cranganore, even wore a beard, and entrusted the government to an Arabian.[3]

---

[1] Ritter's Geography, ii. 287. Especially Bartheme, Itinerario in Ramusio, i. 157.
[2] Barbosa in Ramusio, 289. Besides Corsali Fiorent., *ibid.* 178.
[3] Barbosa, 296. Sommario de' regni et città in Ramusio, p. 326. Barros, Asia, i, vi. 5, after Soltan.

Besides the three coasts, Malacca in further India was the most important emporium for the whole Eastern trade; thither China sent its silk twists, Bengal cotton fabrics, and the Thousand Isles real spices:[1] this place was the counterpart to Venice, sending to the latter the light, perfumed, and shining wares of the East, to receive in return the thick, heavy, martial or more artificial products of the West. Malacca likewise belonged to a Moorish king.

It is worthy of remark, that like Aden, lying as it does upon a promontory and severed by high mountains from the rest of the world, or like Ormuz, itself an island, Malacca, as well as the other emporia of this trade, have an insular position in common with Venice. Their wealth depended upon the Venetian traffic between West and East, which I have previously described, whilst the wealth of Venice depended upon the position of India and its connection with Europe.

It appeared quite impossible that this trade could ever be intercepted and ruined. The Indians were much too weak to rid themselves of the Moors, and no other nation had any access to these shores. But, even whilst it appeared so firmly established, it was in fact already seriously undermined. We must observe that many Europeans had by this time visited India, that a description by Edrisi of the African coast as far as Sofala was already extant,[2] and that, since Bartholomew Diaz had circumnavigated the Cape, there was only the small strip from its last promontory, near Santa Cruz, to Cape St. Sebastian that remained unexplored, unnavigated, and not drawn within the sphere of the world's intercourse. As soon as this small strip of coast was navigated, the Portuguese would find themselves again opposite their old enemies, the Moors, whom they had left in North Africa. Then it would be that India would become attached to Europe by a route other than that of the Moors and Venetians, and enter into an immediate connection with it. The Venetian trade must then necessarily decay.

We have already seen how Don Manuel became King of Portugal, a prince, who, whilst still a youth, had taken an

[1] Sommario de' regni et città.
[2] Sprengel, Geschichte der geographischen Entdeckungen, 155.

orb for a device, and one whom a bold and brave nobility were ready at any time to serve; a nobility bold not against him—for Manuel's forefathers had clipped its wings, and it was now its ambition to serve the King in the palace, and accept a small remuneration from him [1]—but bold against the Moors, and fearless on the sea. With a view to explore that unknown coast, and to discover India, Manuel, in July, 1497, fitted out three "Baloniere," and a "Ravetta," with a crew of 180 men. He gave them pillars, on which were inscribed a cross and his arms, ten prisoners who had been condemned to death, and who should explore the countries of barbarous nations, and letters for the priest John, and the Zamorin of Kolikod; he then hoisted his flag on the mast of the admiral's ship, and committed the whole expedition to the care of Vasco de Gama.[2]

Vasco, a man of a proud and great heart, as his poet describes him, and one who gladly offered his services in great enterprises, and who was always favoured by fortune, prayed, the previous night, with the monks of a church to Our Lady, and, on the morning of the 9th July, embarked on his cruise. The friends of the sailors, on seeing their sails disappear, commiserated them, saying, that they would never see any one of them again. The voyagers themselves really lost heart in the violent currents off the Cape, and would certainly have mutined had it not been for Vasco's brother.

Even when they had already passed it, and were cruising along the east coast of Africa, they considered themselves lost men, and their sole solace and common comfort was to pray. For many days, they saw nothing on the coast but Kaffirs, and could not comfort themselves by obtaining any intelligence. At last, having compassed Cape San Sebastian, they descried coloured men, and five days later, on the 1st of March, 1498, they were received with shouts of joy and music by other coloured men, wearing turbans, shields, and swords, in whom they recognized Moors, and who on their part considered them also Moors. From these they learnt that the island before them was Mosambique, and belonged to the Saracens, that voyages thence were

[1] Osorius, de rebus gestis Emanuelis, p. 364.
[2] Navigazione di Gama in Ramusio i. 116. Osorius, i. 26.

made to India and Arabia, and that Kolikod was no great distance away. On hearing this, they raised their hands to heaven and thanked God; the greater part of their work seemed now to have been accomplished. The actual discovery of the really unknown had been effected. They were again amidst their well-known enemies; but it was now for them to escape from these Moors and reach their destination.[1]

Now, their subsequent adventures, how they were threatened with death and destruction in Mosambique and Mombaz, how the good Prince of Melinda refreshed them with his sweet oranges and gave them a pilot, how they again caught sight of Orion, which had not shone upon them for a long period, is known to everyone from his early years. On the 29th of May, 1498, they, a remnant of about one hundred men, the first Christians of the Latino-Teutonic stock, lifted up their hands on the coast of Malabar, and poured out their thanks to the true God; they then liberated their prisoners, loaded their pilot with gifts, and cast anchor not far from Kolikod.[2]

The Moors instantly perceived the danger that threatened them, and resisted the intruders to their utmost. With great difficulty, and more as a proof that they had really been there, than as a commercial transaction, our Portuguese took some spices and precious stones away with them: they themselves were now reduced to two ships and sixty men; Vasco lost his brother Paul just before the goal; but fortune must always be dearly bought, and, as a result, the unknown coast had been explored, India had been discovered, and, on their return, their fame was noised abroad through Lisbon, Portugal, Spain, and the whole of Europe, and lives on even at this present day.[3]

After this exploit, Lisbon spoke of nothing else but of the wealth of Kolikod; how that a load of cinnamon, ginger, pepper, and cloves, which in Venice cost more than one hundred ducats, was to be had there for ten to twenty;

[1] Barros, Asio, i. iv. 1 and 2. Navigazione. Osorius, 24. Lichtenstein, Entdeckung des Vorgebirges, from Hormayr's Archiv für Geographie, &c., 1810, p. 636.
[2] Osorius, i. 33.
[3] Barros, i. iv. 5, 10. Osorius 40.

how that logwood grew there in bushes, and gumlac cost almost nothing; how pearls were fished for on an island near, and that the Arabians, in spite of all this wealth, were only badly equipped, and their ships easy to take. Nation and King were thus fired to energy. On the spot where Gama prayed previous to his departure, Don Manuel built a far finer church, dedicated to Our Lady, and called Belem, a monastery of the Hieronymites, and a mausoleum for the kings. He styled himself lord of the commerce, voyages, and future conquests in Ethiopia, Arabia, Persia, and India. He fitted out new ships without delay.[1]

These ships were not built alone for trade, but for war. For since Pedralvarez Cabral, of whose crew forty-five men had been killed at Kolikod, and Vasco de Gama, on his second voyage, had both been so much aggravated by the Moors and the Zamorin, that they were obliged to fire on the city,[2] it was palpable that nothing would be able to be effected here without war to the knife. It depended upon the issue of these wars, whether the old international intercourse should or should not exist longer. Even Manuel's counsellors sometimes doubted whether Portugal would be able to continue them, and the Venetians never conceived it possible; but those that undertook them were quite the men for the task, rendered brave as they were by chivalry, their detestation of the Moors, and their religion, and their achievements are truly marvellous.

The most celebrated is, perhaps, the first war undertaken by Pacheco Pereira, in the year 1503, in defence of the King of Cochin, against the whole power of the Zamorin; the former, although a vassal of the Zamorin, had allowed the Portuguese to land and take in cargo, and was, on account of this permission, driven from his throne, and had scarcely been restored to it again.[3] With four kings and the heir to the Crown, and with 75,000 infantry, and 160 ships, all furnished with good guns, cast by Christian refugees, the Zamorin advanced to battle. He came against

[1] Navigazione di Gama in Ramusio, 120 f.
[2] Pilotto Porteghese in Ramusio, 121. Thome Lopez, Navigazione, in Ramusio, 143.
[3] Giovanni da Empoli, Viaggio, in Ramusio.

three ships, bound together by ropes, which blocked the ford by which he had to cross, and against seventy-one Portuguese. He lashed twenty prames together with chains, in order to board one of the vessels, and then made a simultaneous attack upon the ford and the city; he planted artillery on the bank to bombard the enemy from afar, and had towers built on his ships, in order to destroy them from above. He himself showed dauntless courage. Even when some standing at his side were laid low by the enemy's bullets, he caused the laggards to be driven forward at the point of the sword, vowed to his gods, and selected his days. But Pacheco broke his chains with his guns, and contrived to surprise his cannon at the right moment and to spike them, whilst he kept off his towers with bowsprits and booms. Sometimes he would remain quietly on the defensive, until the enemy had come to close quarters; he would then signal his orders and fire his cannon; the result was the defeat of the enemy, and the ford red with blood. He also planted sharp stakes in the mud, on which the enemy spiked themselves. The struggle lasted five months. The enemy is said to have lost 19,000 men, whilst Pacheco's warriors scarcely lost a single one. It appeared to them a miracle. "God had fought for them: they had escaped unscathed from bullets, which rebounding from them even broke stones in pieces; when Pacheco's ship was stranded on the morass, and the enemy had already seized his rudder, at his prayer the flood had risen and floated the ship again. Nay more, when they were in peril of the enemy's floating towers, their guns were ineffectual, until Pacheco had prayed to God not to punish their sins that day, as the honour of the whole of Christendom was at stake." [1]

What was here conquered, however, was, although incited by the Moors, only an Indian power. From this time on both sides a greater war began. On the Sultan of Egypt declaring that, "Did they not cease warring, he would destroy the grave of Christ," the Indian Moors made preparations for a vigorous resistance. Don Manuel, on the other hand, in whose name Duarte Meneses was

---

[1] Osorius, iii. f. 101-116. Barros, i. vii. 8.

waging a rapid and glorious war against the Moors of Morocco, and who was also himself, on one occasion, on the point of joining personally in the campaign (for this war was none other than that which the forefathers of the nation had begun many centuries previously upon the Asturian mountains), replied to the Sultan's threat thus: "If he had hitherto injured him, he intended to inflict even more injury upon him in the future." He hoped one day to take Mahomet's house at Mecca.[1] Gama once said, "Moors and Christians have, since the foundation of the world, been in arms against each other."[2] Such were the feelings which animated King and nation; their war appeared to them a veritable crusade.

On the 25th of May, 1505, Manuel despatched twenty-two sail under Don Francisco d'Almeida; his object was to hold the Indian seas by a fleet permanently stationed there, and to secure the coasts by forts, such as had first been built in Cochin for the defence of the prince.

Beginning with the African coast, Francisco stormed and took Quiloa and Mombaz, both by nearly the same tactics. And when another, following in his footsteps, defying the hostility of the Sheik and the unhealthy climate, had established himself in Sofala, at the source of the gold trade, and when in Mosambique a fort had been built without opposition, the coast throughout its whole length was in their hands. The Prince of Melinda was devoted to their cause.[3]

Almeida's approaching visit caused joy and consternation in India; joy among the enemies of the Moors, and not only in the breast of the Prince of Cochin, who received a golden crown from Almeida's hands, but it also especially gladdened the heart of the great King of Narsinga, whose realm on the highlands of the Malabar peninsula extended as far as Coromandel, and from Comorin far northwards, who once had caused 10,000 Moors to be put to death on the same day, and who now offered one of his daughters to Manuel's son to wife;[4] but it filled Kolikod and the Moors with dismay and terror.

[1] Osorius, iv. 124. Emanuel's letter to the Pope in Osor.
[2] Thome Lopez, 138.
[3] Barros, i. viii. c. 4, 5, 6. [4] Barbosa and Osorius.

"Bad news," said two Persian merchants; "with our own eyes we have seen twelve ships, all full of Christians armed with white weapons." On receipt of these tidings, the Moslems were summoned from their minarets to prayer; after having prayed, they fitted out eighty-four large vessels with 104 prames.[1] Lourenzo, Francisco's son, was stationed with eleven sail not far from Cranganore, when they advanced to attack him; their masts were like a thick wood, their garments red, and with bows, swords, muskets, and cannon in sufficient numbers. Lourenzo addressed his men, saying, "Sirs, brothers, to-day is a day on which our Lord will receive many of us into His holy glory." He let them eat, until the Moors were there. He then said, "Now, my brethren, let us prove ourselves good knights." Thereupon he attacked the enemy's leading ship, grappled it, and sprang on board. His example was followed by others. Simon Martin sprang single-handed amongst fifteen Moors, and shouted, "Now, Christ, prove Thy faith;" he slew seven, and drove the remainder overboard. As soon as their two leading ships were taken, the Moors fled as one man. Lourenzo, seeing the great spoils that were his, and his ships undamaged, exclaimed, "Praised be Jesus Christ;" and built a chapel on the shore in honour of our Lady of the Victory.

Thus did the Portuguese fight, and thus their enemies. The Moors now, full of shame, hatred, and dismay, went about in great bands; they shaved their heads and chins, and bound themselves together under terrible oaths. "They would now either conquer or die." They awaited their enemy in the harbour of Panian, under the cover of their batteries. One morning, two hours before daybreak, the Christians under Francisco and Lourenzo were, before their very eyes, gathered, one and all, around the admiral's ship; a priest raised a great cross on high, and pronounced absolution and blessing upon all assembled. Many prayed to be permitted that day to enter into the glory of God. This scene lasted but a moment; the next, they had separated, and were on their way to the coast. The leaders were kept back. Then came Lourenzo, a youth who would

---

[1] Lodovico Barthema, Itinerario, iii. c. 34, 35, 37, fol. 107 f. Osorius, v. f. 166.

rather burn his booty than give it away under the price he demanded, but who, in spite of this obstinacy, was quite obedient to his father; tall, and splendid of stature, he was the first to spring on land. A conspirator wounded him in the arm; but Lourenzo replied by cleaving him asunder at one stroke, from the head to the breast. His father then, the royal ensign in his hand, came to his assistance. The victory was theirs. Francisco did not accede to the wishes of his soldiery to sack the city, for he knew that a strong enemy was in the vicinity, only waiting for them to begin the pillage. He himself threw the torches into the city to fire it.[1]

By this second battle of the Portuguese in India, the Moors also were vanquished. Their forts in Cranganore, Cochin, and for the present, at all events, upon the Angedives, as well as a victorious fleet cruising off the shore, kept the greater part of the coast of the Indian Peninsula in subjection to them.

The Arabian coast northwards and Eastern India still remained; they next turned their attention to them. In 1507, they took the Arabian fortress of Socotra, lying at the entrance of the Gulf of Aden; and there Albuquerque succeeded in building a castle at Ormuz, and in compelling the prince to pay 15,000 ducats tribute. The King of Columbo in Ceylon was forced to pay them 15,000 pounds of cinnamon, as an annual tribute.[2] The dismay spread by their bravery electrified the people. Before Cannanore, the inhabitants saw a Portuguese slay sixteen to eighteen of the enemy each day. They said, "Is it a Frank? Is it a god of the Franks? It is *the* god of the Franks, and he is stronger than our gods."[3]

Now, although these events had quite another aim and object than that of the advantage or detriment of Venice, yet it is certain that their effect upon the community of our nations was principally made important by the change in the scene of action.

It was not until 1503 that Portuguese merchants came to Antwerp, and offered their wares to German houses. Nicholas Rechtergem is said to have been the first to make

---

[1] Barthema, iii. 40. Barros, ii. i. c. 6.
[2] Barros, Dec. ii. i. cap. 3; cap. 1-4.   [3] Barthema, iii. c. 39.

an arrangement with them, and, after him, the Fugger, Welser, and Osterett.[1] The North Germans were much surprised at seeing the wares that they were otherwise in the habit of sending to the Netherlands now come to them from thence, for they were soon convinced that they were genuine. As a result, we find Augsburg now taking the lead among German cities.[2] Among German commercial houses, Fuggers', a house which in the year 1506, owing to Maximilian's good offices, sent three ships of its own to India,[3] took the lead, whilst Bruges was displaced by Antwerp in the Netherlands. The German trade with Venice decreased. In Italy itself, the Florentine houses, as that of the Marchioni, participated directly in the new voyages.[4] In Venice, the resulting reaction was at once felt.

Many other things also combined at this time. The Turkish war and the new ordinances of the Sultan of Cairo had already seriously damaged their commerce. In the year 1499, many houses on the Rialto went bankrupt, whilst others suffered in credit. A load of pepper, which in Kolikod cost about ten ducats, and was sold in Venice for forty, rose to one hundred and ten. How great was the panic then, when, in the year 1502, the news came that four barks had arrived at Lisbon bringing spices from Kolikod.[5] In a moment, the price of spices became depreciated, to the great detriment of the Venetians. They had comforted themselves for a long time with the hope that King Manuel would not be able to bear the expenses of the campaigns, and would at last succumb to his numerous foes. Whenever a bark was lost, the news was signalled from Cairo as though a victory had been won.[6]

When then, in the year 1507, after Almeida's brilliant victories, the Zamorin, the Zabai of Goa, and the Prince of Cambay all sent to the Sultan Khan Hassan of Cairo, im-

---

[1] Ludovicus Guicciardini, Descriptio Belgii, p. 164.
[2] Gasser, Augsberger Chronik, 259.
[3] Ehrenspiegel, 1269. Pentingeri, Sermones Conviviales ap. Schardium, i. 202.
[4] Giovanni da Empoli, Viaggio, p. 145.
[5] Diarium Ferrarense, p. 365, 380.
[6] Macchiavelli, Legazione al Duca Valentino, lett. 25. Opp. iv. 202 (Note to 2nd ed.). Sandi, Storia Civile, vii. 91.

ploring help, and when the latter, whose whole wealth consisted in the intermediate trade between Asia and Europe, determined to assist them, and when, at the same time, a great campaign of the Indians, and the Indian and Egyptian Moors was set on foot against the Portuguese, the Venetians took fresh courage and hoped that the Portuguese power would come to an end. Their own fortune, or misfortune, depended upon the issue of this undertaking, which would either for ever cut off the Portuguese voyages, or prevent both Moors and Indians from ever again molesting them. The Venetians themselves engaged in it. They sent metal smelters, as well as shipwrights, to the Sultan of Cairo, who was also their suzerain.[1] The fleet which the Sultan fitted out at Suez, and despatched under Mir Hossin, was manned in part by Venetians and Dalmatians.[2] His victory and his loss was their victory and loss also. Their maritime life and their sovereignty over the waves were alike dependent upon the issue that was to be fought out in India in the year 1508.[3]

4. *Maximilian's attack. Formation of the League of Cambray against the Venetian conquests.*

In a description of Italy dating from these times,[4] the Venetian possessions are never referred to, save under the name of the prince from whom they had been taken: "the city knows no superior; what she possesses she has robbed her neighbour of."

This was the sentiment animating Louis XII. and Maximilian, on the occasion of their first league at Trent, and on that of their second with Julius at Blois, when they resolved to conquer what belonged to them of the Venetian territory. And just now, when the existence or destruction of the Venetian trade in India was at stake, a third league was concluded with the same object in view, a league which really imperilled all their acquisitions.

[1] Tentori, Saggio, ii. 135.   [2] Zurita, i. f. 342.
[3] Osorius, vi. 196.
[4] Descriptio Italiæ, Ludwig, Reliquiæ MSS., tom. x. p. 426; according to p. 437, written between Charles VIII. and Louis XII.'s operations against Italy; translated into Latin, 1540.

In the summer of 1507, Maximilian held a Reichstag at Constance. His object was to obtain aid against Louis, and resources sufficient to enable him to invade Italy. "Seeing that Louis had broken all compacts, his enfeoffment with Milan was void; moreover, as he intended to depose the Pope and to endanger the imperial dignity of the German nation, the Empire was pledged to attack him."[1] After the King of France had allowed his party to fall to pieces through sheer negligence, he was unable to form another immediately, and, besides this, his envoy at Constance had been made prisoner. Maximilian made these concessions: that the supreme tribunal should be paid by the Estates—the origin of the sole permanent imperial tax that has ever existed[2]—and that a deputation of the realm should control the forces, money, and conquests of the realm; in return for these concessions, he obtained an aid of 12,000 men and 120,000 guilders for six months.[3]

Moreover, on this occasion he might expect from the Swiss not merely no resistance, but even support. Their envoys walked about at Constance in the mantles he had given them, were sometimes guests at his table, and received presents of silver goblets from him. The Council of Zurich voted him 6,000 men, and at once arranged what contingent each canton should furnish.[4] Towards the beginning of the year 1508, Maximilian arrived in Trent. At the first report of his arrival, the Ghibellines in Italy agitated so much, that it was deemed wise to send many of them to France. The Florentines, who were at a distance, and were besides not weak in themselves, were under French protection; yet they sent to conclude a prior compact with him.[5]

Fate willed it that Maximilian, whilst intending a

[1] Maximilian's Vindication in Goldast, Reichshandlung, 53. Short Summary of the Emperor's previous actions in the realm, published at this Reichstag; in Spalatin, Leben Friedrichs des Weisen, in the collections of Saxon History, at end.
[2] Pütter, Entwickelung der Reichsverfassung, i. 313.
[3] Müller's Reichstagsstaat, 643. Proceedings therein, 662.
[4] Report of the Reichstag at Constance in Ehrenspiegel, 1237; in Fuch's Mailänd. Feldzüge, 71, 79.
[5] Florus de bello Italico, 53. Vettori's Diplomatic Report in Macchiavelli's Legazione.

Milanese war, embarked upon one with Venice. The negotiations with the Venetian envoys at Constance led to no result. Was it likely that they would be willing to allow a man who had so often intended to rob them, and who had shortly before wrested Görz from them—the last count, their vassal, at whose decease it would have devolved upon them, had, in his old age, bartered it away to Maximilian—was it probable that they would be willing to permit him to march through their passes?[1] As Venice was leagued with France against him, he now, accordingly, resolved to attack that enemy which was less capable of resistance, and less dangerous to himself, in the event of his being attacked. On the 4th February, 1508,[2] at Trent, his heralds leading the way, and he himself following sword in hand, Maximilian held a great procession, and, with the Papal envoy's concurrence, adopted the new title of Roman Emperor elect, a title until then unknown. This he did, doubtless, in order to be able, as was actually done the same day, to arraign and condemn the Venetians, with all the greater show of right.[3] That very day, bread was baked for the army, and provisions were sent down the Etsch. In the evening, the soldiers were ordered to hold themselves in readiness. The next morning early, at three o' clock, the trumpets sounded, and the march began. The Emperor advanced with 4,000 infantry, and 1,500 horses, up the mountains of Asiago, in the direction of Vicenza. He had with him a Vicentine emigrant, Lionardo Trissino. He took the intrenchments of the Seven communes, and received the allegiance of half the mountain chain, where it sinks down to the Adriatic Sea from the chalk hills between Matajaur and St. Pelegrino. On his right, Frederick of Brandenberg marched down the Etsch with 2,500 men, and besieged Roveredo. On his left, the army of Eric of Brunswick-Calenberg descended from the hills, all iron shod, took Cadore, and

---

[1] Müller, Reichstagsstaat, 649. Chronicon Venetum in Muratori, 24, 155.

[2] Cf. Deutsche Geschichte (note to 2nd Ed.), vol. i. p. 348 (vide 2nd Ed.).

[3] Chief passage in Vettori's letter in the Legazioni of Macchiavelli, v. 212. Proclamation to the realm in Datt, De pace publica, 569.

advanced forty miles. All betokened a grand issue, and Loredano, Doge of Venice, no longer peremptorily prohibited the imperial envoys from passing through.[1] Yet, in spite of all this success, the Emperor was seen suddenly to stop, before he had even reached Vicenza, and then carefully closing the seven passes into his own country from the Isnitz to the Etsch,[2] to return to Innsbruck and Ulm.

The reason was this: the French party in Switzerland had contrived, through the mediation of two envoys from Louis, after many contradictory resolutions, in gaining the complete upper hand.[3] As to the means the French envoys adopted to attain their ends, we learn that one of them, Rocquebertin, once entertained all the guests in Baden, and, besides this, kept open house daily; the other, the Bishop of Roeux, once paid in Lucerne the reckonings of all the peasants that had come to market.[4] In the very midst of his operations against Venice, Maximilian heard the resolution of the Swiss, of the 25th January, which ran as follows: "if he injured the French king, he would force them to be mindful of their obligations to him," these words being a direct threat levelled at himself.[5] For how easily might not Louis turn an attack, directed against his allies, against himself, and how easily might he not again kindle a war against the Roman king, as he did in the year 1500! In March, the six months, for which period the realm had voted the supplies, had expired. Thus minded, he turned round and addressed himself first to the Suabian confederation: "An attack was to be feared upon the Tyrol, a member of their confederation, the perpetual estrangement of Allgau and Wallgau from the German nation to be apprehended, to be followed by the revolt of Flanders and Guelders, of Liege and Utrecht; the assistance of the confederation, if it would support the

---

[1] Vettori, 1-215. Second report to the realm in Datt, 571; and letter of 4th March, 1508. Bembus, p. 160.
[2] Göbel, Chronica von den Kriegsthaten Kaiser Maximilian's. From beginning.
[3] Passages from Anselm, Bullinger, Tschudi MSS. in Fuchs, 98 f.
[4] Various resolutions in Fuchs, 93, 102, 104, 106, 111.
[5] Resolution in Fuchs, Datt, Göbel, Damont, iv. 1, 90.

German confederates against the French with money and arms, might save everything.[1]

If danger threatened here, his advent averted it. The deputies of the Empire, at all events, voted him assistance for six months longer,[2] and although the aid was but irregularly paid—for the assessment, which in much later times was found to be irregularly made, and which represented "mediates" as being "immediates," must have been so at that time also—it was still considerable. With the Swiss he entered into fresh negotiations. Yet another danger threatened. Having intended a French war, and having undertaken a Venetian campaign, the danger threatening him did not come from France and Switzerland, as he had feared, but from Venice, which he did not fear.

The first move was made by Bartholomew d'Alvian, Captain of the Signorie, against Sixt Trautson, the Commander of Cadore. The Emperor had bidden him pull down the houses in the valley, and barricade himself. Trautson thought that mountains and snow were sufficient to protect him.[3] But through snow and defiles came Alvian, and found his enemy. Above, he was encircled by the peasants on the hills, who pelted him with stones; below, by Alvian's infantry, which attacked him with fire-arms, and was, at length, with his gallant band, who preferred death to surrender, overcome, and Cadore fell.[4] Then Alvian looked further afield. All the passes, with the exception of the Görz pass, were strongly defended. Then Hans Aursperg wrote to the Princes of Brandenburg and Brunswick, who were in the Pusterthal and at Trent, that, "with his Carniolans he was much too weak to hold this large broad road; but that, on the other hand, they were almost too well furnished with troopers and cannon for their passes: they should come to his assistance."[5]

The Princes, though warned, paid no attention to the summons. Alvian knew how to take advantage of his opportunity. He had 10,000 Venetians, French, and

[1] Letter in Datt, 572, f.
[2] Vettori, 230.
[3] Maximilian's instruction in Göbel, f. 1, and letter to Trent.
[4] Naugerii Oratio de Alviano, 3, 4; Vettori, 232.
[5] Aursperg to the princes in Göbel, f. 28 and 36.

Spaniards, took guns and scaling ladders with him, and on the 9th April, 1508, fell upon the Görz road, and first upon Kramaun, and stormed it. The country was unprotected, the inhabitants servile and discouraged, regarding the Signorie of Venice as their suzerain. The danger was imminent. Letters were hurriedly sent to all their neighbours: "Help, speed, haste, only haste! How can the poor walls of Görz withstand their cannon? Triest, Karst, and the whole of Austria will soon be lost. Let us not be destroyed by these Italians."[1] Forthwith a summons was sent through Carinthia, the Steyermark, and Carniola: "every man should present himself with armour and weapons, as soon as he heard the bells ring and shots fired, otherwise not only the houses but the churches would be in danger"—the solitary churches loved by the people.[2] But the Carinthians replied, "the 700 men in their passes, with the horses of the country, were their hope and defence, and these could not be dispensed with." The Styrians replied, "they were threatened by the Hungarians." The Carniolans, whose nobles were equipped with 700 horses, said that, "they required the help of disciplined troops; if the nobles were for compelling them, without bringing such troops into the field, they would rather strike them dead." Only Eric came with 1,400 men, but did not venture into the open field, "for he was too weak."[3]

Thus it happened that, on Easter Eve, after Andrew Lichtenstein had held out in the crumbling walls of Görz a day longer than he had promised, and had repulsed an assault, was obliged to surrender.

Immediately after, Wippach and Duino fell. When the people of Triest thrice saw with their own eyes a ship of the Venetian fleet approach with a white flag, and their garrison again open fire, they murmured together, "that was a bad business, for 100 years past they had lived under the ægis of Austria, and would still continue so to live; but they must have assistance." When now bombarded from the sea, they saw Bartholomew approach

---

[1] Three letters of Aursperg, 38, 43, 45.
[2] Two summonses of Eric of Brunswick, 45, 46.
[3] Replies of the Carinthians, 65; of Reichemburg, 76; and of Aursperg, 65, to Eric, and his Letter, f. 79.

from the land, and no help near, they surrendered, and bought themselves free from pillage. Hans Thur still held out for a while upon the almost inaccessible rocks of Mitterburg, and Hans Raüber in St. Veit am Pflaum; but they also called in vain for men and weapons and also they surrendered. Portenau had long since fallen, and the garrison was seen flying to Laybach. In this general disaster, only Bernhardt Reiniger on the Adelsberg showed real German courage. He scattered the first horse who approached for the sake of plunder. He took Savorgnano prisoner, shortly before the end of his victories. His castle fired and in ruins, he accepted safe conduct, and marched away.[1]

What Aursperg had said, was fulfilled to the letter. The Germans had lost forty-seven good towns.

Maximilian, the while, was journeying dejectedly up and down the Rhine.[2] Not enough that the attack upon Venice had proved so disastrous for him, on the other side of his realm, in the Netherlands, even Charles of Guelders was waging a successful campaign against him. This enemy was encamped in the strong Castle of Pouderoyen, at the confluence of the Waal and the Meuse, whence he had levied toll upon seventy-two villages and upon all the ships in the rivers. Sometimes he would ride through a rainy night upon bad roads and appear the next morning before a distant town, and fire it. In this way Weesp was burnt. The prophecy of their mermaid, "Muiden shall remain Muiden," availed the inhabitants of that city nought on this occasion, and it too was taken. In short, the Duke of Guelders kept the whole of the Netherlands in terror.[3] And, in addition to all this, Maximilian was filled with the gravest apprehensions of an insurrection in his realm.[4]

For one moment he must breathe. Whilst then the Prince of Anhalt succeeded at this crisis in seizing Pouderoyen,[5] he directed his military operations against

[1] Letter of the Kriegsräthe, 69; of the people of Triest, 71; and of Thur and Räuber, 72, 75. Bembus, 164-166.
[2] Diary of 1508, in Hormayr's Oesterreich: Plutarch, v.
[3] Hermannus, Bellum Gelricum in Matthaei Analectis Medii Ævi, i. 503-523.   [4] Letter of Maximilian in Datt, 575.
[5] Letter in Maxim. in Beckmann's Anhaltische Chronik. v. ii. 128.

Guelders alone, and ordered the Bishop of Trent to conclude a truce with Venice.

Some of the elders of the Venetian Senate had frequently, but vainly, warned their fellows that: "it would suffice, were they to act solely on the defensive; that offensive operations would only arouse new enemies." Not therein alone did the difficulty of their position consist, but in the entanglement of their relations with the Great Powers. Louis XII. who regarded the war in the Alps and in the Netherlands as one single affair, both parts being connected through his influence in Switzerland, demanded that Venice should include Guelders in the truce. The friends, who were advantageously situated, should protect him who was at a disadvantage. But to this the Venetians refused to agree. It is perhaps the grandest moment in their policy, that, after having overcome the Emperor, they refused to listen to the demands of France. They could not be prevailed upon to do more than restore Adelsberg to the Emperor: in all other respects, a truce was granted them for three years.[1] Maximilian, of course, felt himself terribly aggrieved, but Louis almost equally so, as the Venetians had refused him that consideration to which the services rendered them would appear to entitle him. And thus it came about, that Maximilian and Louis, between whom the struggle that had just burst forth principally lay, drew closer together. In July, 1508, Maximilian went to Bois le Duc, and then to his daughter and grandchildren. Negotiations were entered into between Cardinal Amboise and Maximilian's daughter, Margaret; they were, however, rendered difficult of a satisfactory issue, owing to Maximilian's refusal to desist from attacking Guelders, and by Louis' attitude, on the other hand, who would not be prevented from assailing Navarre. Margaret said, her head ached from the business.[2] But at last an understanding was arrived at. Muiden and Weesp were restored to the Emperor, whilst the King was guaranteed his Milanese investiture. Maximilian desisted from his schemes upon Guelders, and Louis from his against Navarre. But the

---

[1] Bembus, Histor. Venet., 167. Seissel, L'Excellence de la Victoire d'Aignadel in Godefroy's collection for Louis XII., p. 268.

[2] Margaret to Maximilian, in the Lettres de Louis, i. 134, f.

main outcome was this. They both resolved upon a joint attack upon Venice, by which they considered themselves aggrieved. Thus did the League of Cambray of the 10th December, 1508, originate. It was an alliance of the two powerful princes against a city, which had the audacity to take up an independent position between them. All princes who had any claims upon Venice, or rather upon its lands and possessions, were to be invited to join in the operations. The borders of Milan and Naples were to be readjusted in favour of Louis and Ferdinand, those of the Empire and Austria, in favour of Maximilian, and those of the State of the Church in favour of the Pope.[1] In this arrangement an erroneous, but as appears from the above-named description of Italy,[2] popular idea was followed, namely, that as Padua, Vicenza, and Verona primarily belonged to the Empire, they were given to it.

True, Maximilian could not possibly more easily exchange loss for compensation on the one side, and attain a victory on the other, than by entering into this league. He was the first to swear the compact of Cambray. Then did Louis, in the palace of Bourges, after sermon and mass, affix his seal to it; he showed himself very much delighted. An old plan had now ripened to accomplishment. Ferdinand dallied until March, 1509; he then laid his hand on the altar, and swore it by the Holy Eucharist.[3] The Pope unwillingly resorted to this extreme measure, often as he had threatened to do so, and although he had always incited Emperor and King to it. He went once more with the Venetian ambassador, George Pisani, to Civita Vecchia. The sea was tranquil, only a light cool wind filled the sails; he was lively and kindly disposed. He thought if only vassals were placed in his cities, like the Malatesti, he could endure this, and spare Italy this war. He proposed this course to the ambassador. Pisani coldly and proudly replied: "It is not our habit to make kings," and did not even announce the proposal to Venice. Then did Julius also confirm the league,

[1] Treaty in Dumont, iv. 110-115.
[2] Descriptio, 435.
[3] Gattinara's reports to the Austrian Court; Lettres de Louis, i. 167, and Petri Martyris Epistolæ, 410.

pronounced his ban upon Doge, senate, and the subjects of Venice; ordered his nephew, Francis Maria, the young Duke of Urbino—for Guidubaldo was dead—into the field, and prepared for the struggle.[1]

5. *The fall of the Military Power and of the Trade of Venice in* 1509.

Thus the very existence of Venice was in extreme jeopardy. Its trade depended upon the relations between Asia and Europe, and now, in India, Portuguese and Moors were engaged in a deadly struggle as to whether these should last longer or not. The acquisitions of Venice were due to the feuds of its neighbours, and thus it was that its neighbours had now leagued together more powerfully than ever to wrest from it the possessions obtained by conquest. The first struggle was, for the most part, in foreign lands, the second in their own, and to this latter they devoted their whole strength, and were self-confident enough not to fear for the issue.

As a matter of fact, the league was not as powerful as it appeared. Maximilian and Julius had both misgivings as to Louis, the first on account of Guelders, and the latter on account of Amboise's old schemes. Louis and Ferdinand, on the other hand, were afraid of Maximilian; the former for Milan, the latter for Naples.[2] They were negotiating, and had concluded alliances against each other, before ever their joint and common league became a "fait accompli."

Was it then impossible for the Venetians to detach one or other from this league? It must be confessed that, had they succeeded, they would have profited but little; besides which, Ferdinand never moved a finger until all was settled. At the beginning of April, Maximilian was in Xanten, instead of in Trent. The Venetians were undaunted at the Papal preparations: it was only Louis—the Louis whom

---

[1] Erklärung zum Bund, p. 116. Bembus, 173. Rainaldus, Annales Eccl., xx. 65.
[2] Lettres de Louis, i. 161. Zurita, ii. 178.

they themselves had invited to Italy—whom they really dreaded. To gain him over, appeared to them perhaps unfeasible, and, it might be, not even to their advantage. If we inquire what had really incited Louis against Venice, we shall at once perceive that it was not Julius's election to the Papal chair in the stead of Amboise; for the share Amboise himself had in this election is much more definite than that of Venice. He must have had other reasons, which declared themselves now and then. In the year 1501, he was impelled, as it appears, by nothing but his right, which he had from the Visconti; in the year 1504, by the open assistance the Venetians afforded the Spaniards, and, at present, the irritating factor was the truce they had concluded with Maximilian, without regard being paid to his demands. The hatred ever cherished by the prince and the nobles against the powerful communes was also a very powerful factor. "These fishermen," they said, "must be driven back again into their lagoons to catch fish." [1] And thus Montjoye, the first French king-at-arms, appeared in his "côtta," embroidered with golden lilies, on the threshold of the great hall in Venice, and there proclaimed war upon the Republic; war for life and death, with fire and sword, on land and sea, until the lands, which they had torn from others, were completely restored.[2]

"Father herald," replied Loredano to Montjoye, "God, whom no one can deceive, will decide between us." Their envoy in France said: "the world will see whether brute force or intellect will be triumphant."[3] It was sure to come to a struggle between them one day, and it may be in anticipation thereof, that they had summoned the French to Italy. Many entertained the hope that a glorious victory would be theirs, and Italy at last ridded of them.

With this thought they equipped and prepared for action. All the most tried knights of Italy—for the last glory of their country was at stake—took their money and formed their heavy cavalry.[4] From Apulia and Romagna came

---

[1] Chaumont's words in Macchiavelli, Legazione alla corte di Francia of the year 1504.

[2] Garnier, "Histoire de France," xxii. 163, and Darn. Hist. de Venose, iii.   [3] Fleuranges, Mémoires, 48.

[4] Senarega, De rebus Genuensibus, 596.

their infantry, the best being that formed by Dionigi di Naldi Berzighella, the head of a party in the Val di Lamone, from the inhabitants of this valley, and so well disciplined, that other companies also were organized after their pattern, all dressed in red and green, and called Brisignels.[1] For the peasants and citizens, a kind of Landwehr had been already organized. The coasts of Illyria, the Peloponnese, the Ægean sea and Hellespont sent light Greek horse. Half savage archers, the Sagdars, came from Crete.[2]

The supreme commander of this force was Pitigliano, a man who had never yet made a resolve, to say nothing of a deed, without a propitious constellation, and whom years—he was already over sixty—had made still more circumspect.[3] His lieutenant, Alviano, commanded the infantry. Of constellations the latter knew this much, that Mars was in the highest heaven when he was cut from his mother's body. He was small of stature and weakly in appearance, but yet had slain bears; his troops sometimes mocked at his figure, but he controlled them so rigorously, that not even a baggage boy would dare to desert the standard. His decisions sometimes looked like violence of temper, and his punishments seemed cruel; but afterwards, when he had cooled down, he was gentle and generous, and quite master of himself. By nature he was the boldest of the bold.[4] Seeing that many ascribed to him Gonzal's victory on the Gariglian, and, as he had conquered both Istria and Görz, his renown was fresher, and his fame greater than Pitigliano's was. Only in one thing did both agree together, that Pitigliano was justly proud of having never served a foreign potentate, and that Alvian conceived that he would now be able to defend Italy from the barbarians. He of the two had the boldest hopes. "If he might give reins to his horse and outrun the train and transport of his army, he would have Milan within three days. Had he not driven the French out of Naples? And the King was now approach-

---

[1] Bayard, 133. Note to Macchiavelli, Opp. iii. p. 6, from MSS.
[2] Bembus, 157. Mocenicus, Historia belli Cameriacensis, in Grævius, v. 4, 9.
[3] Alexander Benedictus, De rebus Caroli, p. 1617.
[4] Jovius, Elogium virorum bellica virtute illustrium, p. 219, from Alvian's Commentaries. Navagerus, Oratio de Alviano, p. 5, 6, &c.

ing: but he would bring him back, bound a prisoner, to Venice." He had with him an ensign emblazoned, upon which was a winged lion tearing an eagle. His cry was "Italy, freedom."[1]

But we must remember that all were not as sanguine as he was. Many thought that they ought to be satisfied, if, perhaps, Cesena and Imola were victorious over the Pope, and Genoa was roused by the Fregosi to revolt. The Signorie ordered that the attack be awaited behind intrenchments, and the campaign restricted to assistance afforded to places attacked. Amongst the people there was a presentiment that some disaster was approaching. A great conflagration, which at that time burnt down the arsenal, was regarded as a heaven-sent sign. But more still was said to have happened. The Virgin Mary was said to have been seen in the sea sitting on a log and saying, "Weep, country, weep."[2]

In April, 1509, the war commenced. The French soon crossed the Adda and cried "France," and then the Venetians crossed and cried "Libertà." Then the French, the Mantuans, who as well as the Ferrarians had joined the league, and the Papal troops simultaneously assaulted Treviglio, Casalmaggiore, and Berzighella respectively, and all three places fell. But, as they pushed on further, the first two were repulsed, and only the Papal troops succeeded in taking Russi. But the Venetians did not trouble themselves about the Papal army; they attacked the French with great fury. In Ripalta they drove out all who appeared to them to be suspicious, boys of fifteen and old men of seventy years; they then marched upon Treviglio for pillage, although situated in their own country.[3]

King Louis was in Milan, and intended remaining there two days, when, late in the night, Trivulzio came to him from the Adda with the tidings that: "Treviglio was being bombarded, and torches were being incessantly

[1] Arluni, De bello Veneto, ii. 57. Seissel, L'Excellence, &c., 308. Senarega, Ehrenspiegel.
[2] Joh. P. Vallerianus, Carmen ad Satellicum, in Roscoe, App. i. 586.
[3] Petrus Martyr, Epp. ep., 413. Principally Cœlius Rhodiginus, Lectiones antiquæ, v. 190.

waved from the walls, as a sign that it could barely hold out; but he felt himself too weak to save it." The King assembled his *hommes d'armes* in the morning, rode in full accoutrements through their lines, and set out.[1] On the way thither, he learned that the White Knight, his commander in Treviglio, had been made prisoner, and that the city was lost; the burghers of the city, who had been plundered and expelled by the Venetians, who spared neither the nuns nor the Holy Sacrament, and were looking for shelter in Milan, came to meet him. He pressed on; on the 6th of May, he transported his soldiers across the Adda, by two pontoon bridges, the one for the infantry and the other for the horse, and confronted the enemy;[2] he in the valley, they on the hills. He could thus either attack the foe in his camp or force him to come down into the valley. The camp, however, was too strong to be taken by assault, and in order, therefore, to compel him to come down, he irritated him for four days in vain with skirmishers; on the fifth day, the King went to attack cities in the rear of the enemy. He took Ripalta, and on Monday, the 14th of May, advanced upon Pandino. The roll of his army showed a strength of 28,232 men; the first division was commanded by Chaumont, the second by the King in person, and the third by Longueville.[3] Thus had come about what the Venetian Signorie had preconcerted, and Alviano's thirst for battle could no longer be restrained. "What use to a country is a soldier, if he allows it to be pillaged and plundered?" Therefore, whilst the French slowly advanced along the valley of the Adda, the Venetians, 33,000 men strong, hurried along the shorter road across the mountains, in order to anticipate them by arriving first at Pandino. Arms it is true rule the world, and the result of centuries of wisdom depends upon the issue of a single battle. Just where their two roads met, Alviano and the first French division caught sight of each other, and the French began the attack.

Alviano, eager for the fray, as soon as the first shots had been fired, being under the impression that the first

[1] Rosmini, Vita di Trivulzio, i. 392. Arluni, 63. Seissel, 299.
[2] Symphorian Champier, in Godefroy, 338. Bayard, 133.
[3] Bembus, 184-186. Champier's model roll, 344-354.

division formed the King's whole army, and wishing to protect his rear and flank from the attacking enemy, planted his thirty-six guns in the brushwood, and summoning Pitigliano to his assistance, hurled himself with his infantry through the vineyards and over the ditches at the enemy. The French gave way. Chaumont sent to the King, saying: "Sire, you must fight." Louis immediately sent Bourbon and Tremouille to his aid; behind them, sword in hand, and surrounded by princes and pensioners, came the King himself; then the standards waved and the rest of the army came up. It was in the midst of a thunderstorm, and the rain falling like hail appears to have concealed the arrival of the King from the Venetians. But as soon as they saw him — I can imagine that the lightnings burst through the gloom and gleamed on the steel armour, illuminating the field of battle—when they realized that the enemy was receiving assistance, their courage sank. Yet, for a while, the Brisignels gallantly and well withstood the charge of the King's Swiss and Gascons. Here lay the issue. It was upon peasants and shepherds from the high valleys of the Alps, from the Apennines and Pyrenees, that the fate of Venice lay. What did it matter to them? They were only bent on plunder. Now the Italians had their booty with them from Treviglio, and their sole care was to secure it, whether by victory or flight. The French and Germans had made no booty, and were, therefore, all the more eager to obtain it; and so the Brisignels were driven back. Alviano, in the thick of the fray, was wounded just as he was about to exchange his tired steed for a fresh one, and was almost immediately taken prisoner. All his troops fled precipitately; they in their wild career communicated their terror to Pitigliano's men, to whom they had not been able to communicate their courage, and they too fled. The day was completely lost. The King gazed on the great number of fallen and vowed a chapel to Maria Victoria for the repose of their souls.[1]

The story as told by most historians is to the effect, that of four divisions Alviano commanded the last, and that the

---

[1] St. Gelais, Histoire de Louis XII., 213-215. Champier, 340. Leferron, iv. 87. Fleuranges, Mémoires, 47. Bembus, 188.

others were too far ahead to come to his assistance.[1] Some will have it, that the first and attacking column was under Alviano's command, but that Pitigliano, who had quarrelled with him in Treviglio, looked on at the battle from the hills, and would not stir to come to his assistance.[2]

That Pitigliano was in the rear, seems to be confirmed by the retreat, which took the road to Caravaggio; had he gone before to Crema, he would not have gone back thither again, which would have been tantamount to throwing himself upon the victorious enemy's sword.[3] Pitigliano alone now endeavoured, though in vain, to rally his soldiers round the standard. They had lost their fame; but they would not lose their lives and booty as well. Some would not place their names again upon the rolls; some did so, received fresh pay, and then fled. The citizens of Brescia refused to be incommoded with an army such as this; they would only receive such of their men who were amongst them. In Peschiera, the army despaired of holding together; it found the gates of Verona closed against it, and, having for a while bivouacked upon the heath, took its way to Mestre, on the coast. Louis pursued the fugitives. The castle of Caravaggio held out three days; all other places surrendered at the first blast of the trumpet. In Brescia, the King rode up the steps into the upper court of the palace without meeting with resistance, and it was only Peschiera that needed to be stormed.[4] The inhabitants of Ferrara rang their bells, drove out the Visdomino, and restored the Polesin. The Pope proclaimed the victory in an Italian sermon, and occupied Rimini and Faenza. The Germans appeared on the Lago di Garda, in Frioli and beyond Vicenza. Many advised King Louis to press on to

---

[1] Bembus, Guicciardini, Petrus Martyr, 416. Many others.

[2] Nardi, iv. 23. Appendix to Monstrelet, 240. Arluni, 69. Especially Cœlius Rhodiginus, Lectiones antiquæ, 190, and Carpesanus, 1264.

[3] In the letters of Luigi da Porto (Lettere Storiche di Luigi da Porto Vicentino per aura di Bressau), which appeared in 1857, and which cannot properly be regarded as letters, but as a history in the form of letters, of the years 1509-13, all is ascribed to fate: "che avea disposto il cielo, che uno exercito possente a vincere, e combattendo anche con gran valore, dall' inimico cosi tosto e compiutamente battuto" (p. 36).

[4] Mocenicus, 16. Petrus Justinianus, Rerum Venetarum libri, p. 375.

the coast, and crown his triumph by utterly destroying Venice.[1]

In Venice itself, when, after Alviano's many letters, all promising victory, the news of this great disaster arrived, the Senate speedily assembled, the merchants closed their shops, the monks, mindful of the Pope's ban, fled, and the people, crying aloud, besieged the palace. The remnant of the army, 6,000 strong, had no inclination to fight more. Thereupon the Doge also invited Peter Barbo, an old, sick man, to the council; he had not attended the sittings of the Senate for a long time past, but he now put on his official dress, and was carried in a palanquin into the hall; yet he could give no other advice, but to trust in God's protection. Matteo Priuli was the first to propose that they should give up the subjected cities. This proposal was adopted: "Thus does a skipper throw cargo overboard to save his ship." Whilst twelve men examined the coast, to find where an attack would be least easy, whilst orders were despatched to Cyprus to open all stores, and all salt ships were commanded to load corn instead of salt, whilst the mills at Trevigi were grinding day and night, and preparations were being made to utilize the islands and the sea, whilst strangers who had no business connections were expelled, envoys were sent to Maximilian, assuring him that "the Venetians would retire from Verona, Vicenza, and Padua;" others were on their way to Naples, saying that: "the harbours and cities of Apulia were open to the King of Spain," others again repaired to the Pope, inviting him to occupy Rimini and Cervia.[2] These resolutions may perhaps be called heroic. The republic wished to get rid of all its conquests on the mainland, in order to be able to maintain itself, and perhaps compel its enemies to sign peace. The surrendered cities were ordered to subject themselves; how, otherwise, could the Paduan nobles have been enabled to boast that the Emperor, thanks to them, was lord of Padua?[3] Their former surrender to Venice had had the semblance of liberty, and so now,

---

[1] Paris de Grassis ap. Rainaldum, 68, and the quotations.
[2] Bembus, 196 f. Petrus Justinianus; Ehrenspiegel, 1260. Vettori, Sandi, whence Daru, iii. 347.
[3] Macchiavelli, Legazione of 1510.

Venice being unable to protect them, they received back of her, if not their oath of allegiance, at all events the liberty of choosing and electing their lord. As the Venetians later speak of criminal faithlessness, they must have expected that these cities would still hold out for them.[1] But the cities were dismayed as well as Venice, and so surrendered themselves, each to him whose claims the League had recognized.

Thus did the military power of Venice, and the hope of the Italian patriots, come to the dust. One single comfort yet remained, and a small comfort that; all Italians engaged in the battle who were wounded had been wounded in the head and breast, and not in the back.[2]

During these months of preparation and decision, the tidings reached Venice of the issue of the struggle in India. It was perhaps not less unexpected. For the operations of Mir Hossein and the Egyptian fleet at first were successful. Mir Hossein discovered Don Lourenzo in the harbour of Schaul, where the shallow water never allowed the Portuguese to come to close quarters, and board. Lourenzo, in attempting to gain the open sea, stuck fast between fishing poles, when Mir Hossein attacked him. The hero, covered with wounds, was laid under the mast, where he kept encouraging his men to the onslaught, until he was at last slain by a bullet in the breast.[3]

But the Mamelukes and Moors did not long rejoice over their triumph. Francisco, on hearing of the death of his only son, exclaimed, "Whoever loved him, let him not lament, but help me to avenge him;" and four days after the League of Cambray had been concluded, December, 1508, he sailed out to find Hossein. He burnt Dabul, a city of the Zambai, who had summoned Hossein to his assistance, and spared not a soul therein. On the 3rd February, 1509, he sailed against his enemy into the harbour of Diu; each of his ships singled out one of the enemy's, attacked, and boarded it. Whilst the struggle was going on on the ships, the prames of Kolikod, and the princes of Diu, anticipating

---

[1] Cœlius Rhodiginus, Lectiones ant., 191. Arluni, i. 86. Paul Jovius, Epitome, libri x., Histor., p. 89.
[2] Senarega, Res Genuens., 596.
[3] Barros, ii. 2-8. Osorius, 170.

what the issue would be, slipped away. Neither Dalmatians nor Venetians helped the Egyptians: they sank, or surrendered. Mir Hossein sprang on shore, mounted a horse, and escaped. Lourenzo was at length revenged. The coast cities of the Sultan thereafter could not pay him tribute more. The last hope of the Venetians was broken; and the Portuguese, without whose safe conduct no ship durst more enter the Indian Ocean, were completely masters of the situation. That was the time, Princess Helena of Abyssinia wrote, which Christ foretold to his blessed Mother: "In the land of the Franks a king would arise, who would destroy the whole race of the Moors and barbarians." [1]

From that time, Italy ceased to be the "inner court in the house of the world," as Ascanio Sforza expressed himself, and the centre of the European trade. The 3rd February, 1509, crushed the trade, and the 14th May, 1509, the military power of Venice.

What is it that exalts nations, and brings them low? Is it the course of their natural development, their growth and decay, as is the case with human beings? But external circumstances often marvellously co-operate to accomplish this end. Or is it, perhaps, a divine and predestined fatality for destruction or prosperity? The growing and flourishing state is girt round by other living forces, which prevent its expanding immeasurably. Venice had sprung up when its neighbours were weak; it now came into collision with stronger powers, and whilst developing itself widely, and occupying an independent position in their midst, it was attacked by them, and overcome. And simultaneously a new maritime power, which sought and found another centre, sapped those resources which had enabled it to rise so high. Venice could not become more than it now was; but, in its present state, it might still assert itself.

[1] Barros, ii. iii. 6. Osorius, 196. Literæ Helenæ, ap. Ramusium, i. 177.

6. *The War of the Venetians to save their City and a part of their territory.*

After these great blows had fallen upon it, and Venice was stripped of all save itself, and what it had once acquired in the oriental expeditions against the Turks, Julius and Ferdinand resolved to stay their hand, and to spare the rest. The former desired this course, for the city was an eye of Italy; the latter, because he was involved at that moment in his Moorish campaigns, and was mindful of his Catalonian claims to Neopatri and Athens: "Had he only 3,000 lansquenets, in addition to 20,000 Spaniards, he would even take Constantinople itself."[1] Louis and Maximilian, on the other hand, were for utterly annihilating Venice; and to this intent they joined hands, through the intervention of Amboise.[2] It was not until after the battle, that Louis received the Duke of Savoy into his camp, who demanded Cyprus. It was not until the 29th of May, that Maximilian, through many princes, counts, knights, and servants of the realm, proclaimed hostilities against Venice. He showed himself most energetic; he declared to the princes of the realm that the territory of Venice had been already won, and that he was now minded to take to the sea, and annihilate also the rest of their power. His plan was, with a Papal and a Spanish fleet, to attack the city from the sea, whilst a German and a French army, advancing down from the Brenta, invested the city on the land side, and reduced it. It could be divided up into four districts, and each prince could have a castle there.[3]

With these schemes in view, he made his preparations. Shortly before this, the three ships which the Fugger had despatched to Kolikod returned, and the instant gain of 175 per cent. made this house wealthy enough to pay him the money which Julius, Ferdinand, and Louis, each for different reasons, had promised him; namely, 300,000

---

[1] Paris de Grassis, in Rainaldus and Zurita, 185, 196.
[2] Zurita, 194, also Dumont, iv.1, 117.
[3] Fehdebrief (challenge), in Goldast, Reichshandlung, 92. Handellunge auf dem Wormser Reichstag, 96. Zurita, 182, 195.

ducats,[1] so that the profits of the Eastern trade were not merely withdrawn from Venice, but were even employed against her. But before he had finished preparing, his undertaking began to wear a different aspect.

On Louis' return to Milan, he was received with a triumphal arch, upon which were represented his achievements, his counsel, his march and his battle, the Nobili of Venice finding also a place thereon. In their flowing robes, with hand on breast, and faces serious and reflecting, they were to be seen looking as though it was not their sole purpose to defend themselves, but to repair the damage and to punish the faithless.[2] The facts are these. In the Venetian territories, both parties, rulers and subjects, appear at first to have believed that they could dispense each with the other. When the rulers saw that their enemies would not be satisfied with the possessions which they had renounced in their favour, but intended to subject even them themselves, and found that they needed a bulwark for their defence, and when now their subjects were by the rigour of the new government reminded of the clemency of the old, they both perceived that human unions are not as easily dissolved as cemented, but grow into a natural cohesion, the rending of which asunder is equivalent to jeopardizing life.

This was first realized in Trevigi, which lay amidst the estates of the Venetian nobles, and in Padua, whose daily traffic with Venice required at least eighty boats, and which yearly sold to Venice corn and the produce of its orchards and vineyards, to the value of 40,000 ducats.[3] When Leonardo Trissino appeared in Trevigi, to occupy that city in the name of the Emperor, it only required a shoemaker to raise the standard and the cry of "San Marco," for the whole of the people to join him. Had it not, 175 years previously, in similar distress, of its own accord thrown its fate in with that of Venice? It again received a Venetian garrison within its walls. The Imperialists were already in possession of Padua. Yet when,

[1] Ehrenspiegel, 1295.
[2] Arluni, De bello Veneto, 81.
[3] Savonarola, Commentarius de laudibus Patavii, in Muratori, 24, 1176, 1180.

in the early morning of the 27th of July, 1509, Andrea Gritti had surprised one of the gates—muffled musketeers behind hay waggons, each seizing one man of the guard, and 2,000 in reserve in a neighbouring thicket—and dashing through the streets raised the national cry, the people here also declared for Venice, and the lansquenets were forced to retire. The chiefs of the nobles were punished for having surrendered their city.[1]

But the war, owing to these circumstances, began to wear a changed aspect. Towards the autumn, Maximilian arrived on the scene with twenty-six princes and 12,000 horse— La Palice, Bayard, and French and Spanish auxiliaries with him—with more than one hundred cannon and so many lansquenets that his army was 50,000 men strong; like a true emperor, in the hope of a battle such as Louis had fought and won.[2] The peasants in the mountains surrendered themselves, those living nearer the plain fled with wife and child, with cattle and chattels, to the lagoons, behind banks and dykes; they drove 10,000 head of cattle to Cavarzere, 20,000 to Montalban, and thus we can see how the lagoons were peopled in bygone days; but no army appeared.[3] Only Padua opposed its triangular fortifications, with walls sixty feet in height, and five-fold escarpments, to the enemy's advance. Loredano, now convinced that the star of Venice depended upon the cities on the mainland being saved, set the Venetians a new example, and, though no noble had ever before served on land, now offered both his sons for the defence of Padua.[4] They were joined by 174 other young Nobili, each accompanied by ten men, bound to them for life and death. Thus they came, in all 10,000 men, to Padua. One day they were all assembled on the Pra della Valla, before the church of St. Justina, Padua's patron saint. Here an altar was raised, and upon it placed a copy of the Holy Gospels; after mass they one and all advanced to the table, and lay-

---

[1] Mocenicus, i. 21, 23. Coelius Rhodiginus, Lectiones ant., 191. Arluni, 86. Bembus, 203.

[2] Bayard, 144. Jovius, Vita Alfonsi Ducis Ferrar., 156. Weiskunig, 290.

[3] Petrus Justinianus, 372. Mocenicus, 30.

[4] Naugerii Oratio in funere Leonardi Lauretani, 1530, f. 31, 22, 36, 18. Savonarola, de laudibus, 1177. Carpesanus, 1269.

ing their hand on the Gospels swore to defend the city with true allegiance, and with their lives.[1]

Against this city Maximilian now advanced. His letters, which flew into the city attached to the points of arrows, were not heeded. The balls from his great mortars, which were placed on special carriages, and could only be fired off four times a day, terrified them not. Coelius Rhodiginus worked the while undismayed at his book "Lectiones antiquæ." The storm made by some Spanish companies of the Gonzal-school upon a bastion, which they scaled, turned to their own destruction, as the powder, concealed under dry faggots, caught fire and exploded. The lansquenets were ready to storm once more, if only some heavy-armed troops were joined with them. Maximilian really commanded the French *hommes d'armes*, who were with him, to help the others, but it was not agreeable to them. Bayard was wroth and said: "Shall we rush into danger at the side of mere tailors and cobblers? Let him send his German nobles with us." But these latter, on being appealed to, replied, "They were come to fight on horseback, and not to storm."[2] Maximilian, in the vexation of spirit which is aroused in every energetic man by the impediments of prejudice, gave orders to break up the camp, and throwing garrisons into the other fortresses, left Italy.

After this, the Venetian fortune was pre-eminently enhanced by the attachment of all the peasants to them. It would often happen, when the Germans were marching through the valleys between the vineyards, that, where the defile was narrow, peasants would come out from behind the vines and cry: "now they are going to avenge their fathers, children, and wives," and then attack them. They often concealed themselves behind the bushes, until a weak detachment came by, and they then would call upon the Venetians, who were also concealed hard by, to come and murder. The Marquis of Mantua was suddenly surprised, but escaped from the soldiers; but four peasants found him crouching in some Indian corn, and, in spite of

---

[1] Mocenicus, ii. 34. Petrus Justinianus, 384.
[2] Arluni, iii. 108. Ehrenspiegel, 1265. Zurita, 204. Chiefly Bayard, c. 37, p. 171.

his great promises, they consigned him to the tower of St. Mark.

The Bishop of Trent, whom the Emperor had left in Verona, caused a man who said he was Venetian to be apprehended; the bishop ordered him to execution; but he remained firm to the last.[1] Every day the situation grew worse. The Venetians then succeeded even in imperilling Verona, and actually in taking Vicenza, Monfelice, Montagnana, and many other places. Immediately they took a place, they erected a statue of Saint Mark there, but no longer, as formerly, with a book, but with a sword.[2]

Maximilian again commissioned his general, Rudolf von Anhalt, a man called by the neighbours at home "high crown of the lineage of Anhalt,"[3] famed for his allegiance—his army called him Anhalt, The True Blood—on the 7th April, 1510, to make incursions and ravage the land with fire and sword, with pillage and murder.[4] The most horrible deeds were done. In the Grotto of Masono, two thousand men, women, and children of good family had taken refuge; some of the French auxiliaries came to the grotto, and, making a fire at the entrance, cut off the ventilation, and all were smothered to death.[5] It was said that in Udine two angels with bloody swords had been seen upon the church top. In this war, in which sieges, stratagems, victories, counter-stratagems, defeats, and retreats interchanged in rapid succession, they appear to have fulfilled their omen throughout the whole of Frioli.[6] In Austria, some confessed that they had been hired by the Venetians to kindle and to burn.

Venice no longer waged this war in order to conquer or to liberate Italy—these plans were past and gone—but its aim now was to avail itself of the almost unexpected devotion of its people, and of the general state of affairs, to

---

[1] Especially Machiavelli, Legazione to Mantua of the year 1519, v. 319. Mocenicus, 40, 46. Bembus, 214.

[2] Machiavelli, *ibid.*, 10th letter, p. 324.

[3] Letter of Hieronymus, Bishop of Brindenburg, in Beckmann's Anh. Chronik, v. ii. 127.

[4] Commissoriale Maximiliani, in Beckmann, 130.

[5] Maximilian's letter to the Count Palatine Louis, in Goldast, Reichshandlung, 93. Bayard, 199-201.

[6] Petrus Martyr and Mocenicus, 55, 59.

regain, at all events in part, its territory and its land. Therefore, now that its Indian trade was ruined, it busied itself with a re-arrangement of commerce in the Mediterranean. Meanwhile new events took place.

7. *The Pope's Enterprises to effect the Liberation of Italy.*

"Your Holiness knows," the Venetians wrote, after their first disaster, to the Pope, "how we are situated: your Holiness will pity us. Blessed Father and Lord, our gracious master! If we have obeyed your precepts, as we have done, may the hand that inflicted the wound deign to heal it."[1]

The Pope thought he had humoured the League of Cambray long enough; "if the Emperor was not in possession of his cities, it was due to his own negligence;" and, on the 20th February, 1510, in St. Peter's hall, he released Venice from the ban of excommunication, and, stretching out his hand, pronounced his blessing over the envoy of the republic.[2] His noble soul was full of grand plans, urgently needed for the whole of Italy.

Amboise had supported the Emperor's expedition against Venice with French forces, in order that he should make him Pope; and in the manuscripts of Bethune is contained a whole list of favours, which Amboise would confer upon the Emperor, as soon as he had attained his aim.[3] His own danger, accordingly, confirmed Julius in his old intention of liberating his native land, Genoa, whence his relations, the Fregosi, had been exiled, and thus drive the French from Italian soil. Formerly this was quite as much the intention of the Venetians as his own; they had, however, first of all to fight out their quarrel together. This had now been done, and the power of Venice broken. Julius, then, now resolved to save the rest of the Venetian power, and to commence his work in league with the republic. The re-

[1] Epistolæ Venetorum, in Senarega, Annales Genuenses, Muratori, 23.
[2] Paris de Grassis, ap. Rainaldum, Annales Eccles., xx. 75; Bembus, 200; Daru from MSS., iii. 381.
[3] Garnier, from the MSS. xxii. 219, and Zurita.

solve was all the bolder, as this was sure to arouse his enemies to wage against him that war which they otherwise hesitated to begin. Although his scheme was so dangerous that the galleys had to be kept at Ostia ready for sea, in order, if necessary, to enable him to escape, he yet adhered to it: "It suited Louis to make the other princes his vassals, and him his chaplain; but he would not tolerate this tyranny any longer, drive the French from Italy he would, and if his sins were so grievous as to prevent his accomplishing his purpose, he would live no longer. He would shed his blood for the liberation of Italy."[1]

Without delay—hesitation he knew not—he proceeded to action, and first of all in Ferrara and Genoa.

Now in Ferrara, Alfonso d'Este swayed like his fathers did, independently of, and uncontrolled by, either his subjects, his relations, or his superiors. His subjects he ruled by tribunal and sword; he proclaimed his laws by sound of the trumpet, without asking any one, and punished the rebels with "corda" or sword.[2] He kept his brothers, Julius and Ferdinand, who had conspired against his life, in close confinement. As a result of the battle of Ghiara d'Adda, he had ridded himself of the Venetian Visdomino, who with his processions, and his drums and fifes, did not even spare his court; instead of cleaving to his suzerain, the pope, he adhered to emperor and king.

The Pope now demanded of this Alfonso that he should make peace with Venice. To make an attempt upon Genoa, in July, 1510, he dispatched Marc Antonio Colonna and the party of the Fregosi, who, in anticipation of his achievements, called him Julius Cæsar, and with the shout of "Liberty, Italy," came to the Riviera.[3]

But Alfonso, who, with cannon that he himself had cast, had shortly before, from his tower Pepos and the embankments on the river, annihilated a considerable Venetian fleet, which had advanced up the Po against him, would not assent to this peace.[4] Julius, wroth that he should have vassals whom he could not control, demanded yet

[1] Zurita, ii. 227, 235.
[2] Diarium Ferrarense, 229, 234, 290, everywhere.
[3] Lettres de Louis, i. 255.
[4] Bayard, 148. Coelius Rhodiginus, Lectiones ant., v. 194.

more: "Alfonso should not impose any fresh burthens upon his subjects, should moreover set free his brother Ferdinand, who was the Pope's godson, and should not, in defiance of his suzerain, send salt to Comacchio—for Augustin Ghisi, who had rented the saltworks in the newly acquired Cervia, complained of this [1]—this he would never have dared to do as long as Cervia was Venetian." But the only answer Alfonso returned was either a flat refusal or a subterfuge: he would not obey him.[2]

The Fregosi in Genoa were equally foiled. They hoped that their partisans would rise, as soon as they appeared. But the French had, on this occasion, a well-disciplined body of men both inside and outside the city, and kept every-one in terror. It is narrated that the peasants, when the heads of executed rebels were sent through their villages and stuck on stakes to strike terror into them, dared not, when they saw them blown down by the wind, to come close and touch them. If, then, the Fregosi expected a movement on the part of their adherents, their adherents, on the other side, first awaited a successful achievement on their part.[3]

This first misadventure aroused the Pope to fresh exertions. He put Alfonso under ban and fitted out a fleet against Genoa. But he conceived still greater schemes, namely, to conquer Ferrara at a single blow, to incite a revolution in Genoa, to drive the French from Milan, and to help the Venetians triumph over the Emperor. And in this he looked to the Swiss for assistance. The epoch arrived in which the Swiss attained the zenith of their renown, both in war and politics. Let us sketch in outline their situation at this time.

In February, 1509, Louis had abandoned the league with them,[4] and it is patent for what reason. In spite of his annual subsidies, he had on two occasions, the years 1501 and 1503, almost come to open war with them, had at last

---

[1] Leonardo da Porta, letter in the Lettere di Principi, i. 3.

[2] Jovius, Vita Alfonsi, 160. André del Burgo, in the Lettres de Louis I., 250.

[3] Senarega, 600-603. Machiavelli, Legazione alla Corte di Francia V., 347.

[4] Bullinger, in Fuchs, Mailänder Feldzüge, ii. 133. Garnier, 236.

been obliged to confirm the rights of the people of Uri to Bellinzona, and had never been able to satisfy the claims of certain mercenaries to payments long due. And as often as a campaign was in prospect, the parties rose up, after his league with them, the same as ever before. The negotiations of the year 1507 against Maximilian, cost him the very considerable sum of 230,000 guilders.[1] He thought he was bargaining for obedient mercenaries, but found them very refractory allies. Now Louis, who, be it remarked, had always a good estimate of money, will have thought that, even without annual subsidies, he had secured to him his true partisans by secret pensions, and an army by guaranteeing pay. Directly he had renounced the league, this supposition was confirmed. Without any annual subsidies, 6,000 Swiss joined his standard, and, taking part in the Venetian war, decided his victory on the very day that an alliance with Venice, which confidently promised success, was proposed in their own home. After the battle, nothing of course came of it.[2]

Whilst then the Swiss were now released of all obligations to any prince, the patriots among them hoped that, in the future, every Swiss would be restrained from accepting foreign pay, and would hereafter live in true liberty, without serving in the field, and accepting money for such service.

It must be confessed that this hope was not likely to be realized. To forego the money might not, perhaps, have been such a hardship either for the judges, who still sat in judgment beneath the fir at Lastorf, or for the people of quality, who appeared not to be able to afford to warm a separate room for their servants, or for the respectable householders, who were content with windows of cloth or, if of glass, of rough lattice-work, each square costing four pfennigs, or even for the simple cowherds and peasants.[3] But they could not live without war. As early in life as the boys were able, they dangled a sword over

---

[1] Stettler, in the J., 1507.
[2] Anshelm, in Glutz, 222 (iv. 122). Bembus, 177. Seyssel, 312.
[3] Glutz, from MSS., 456. Anshelm, in Fuchs, ii. 224. Also das Leben Johann Orelli's from his letters, though of somewhat later date, 478.

their left knee, stuck an ostrich feather in their caps, followed the drum call, and practised musket-shooting.[1] There was no fair held, no church festival, or even the appointment of a new magistrate celebrated, without reviews and musket-practice. Even the lame had to have coats of mail, and the priest in the pulpit was girded with a sword.[2] A wedding party was honoured when many uninvited guests followed, but only with halberts and swords, marching three and three.[3] Whenever these martial fellows were gathered together, families and guilds in separate rooms—yet all called each other "thou"— there would appear in their midst, perhaps, one who had just returned home from active service, and would clink the guilders that he had gotten as pay or booty, and fire the others to the wish that they also would be one day thought of in their homes as attired in fine helmets and with halberts. Amman Reding rightly remarks: "Their youth must spend itself somewhere."[4]

In the conviction that this people would, of all allies, be the least dangerous for Italy, Julius, who, first of all popes, had begun to surround his person with a Swiss guard, concluded with the Swiss, through the mediation of Matthew Schiner, Bishop of Valais, on the 26th February, 1510, an alliance for five years, in return for a subvention of 12,000 guilders; in return, they should furnish, in the pay of the Roman Church, 6,000 men against every enemy that would assail it.[5] With this alliance, Julius conceived that he would attain the consummation of his projects, without fail. In July, he sent 36,000 guilders to Martinach, and demanded the promised contingent.[6]

At the end of August, 1510, his comprehensive military scheme was developed. The Papal army occupied Modena and threatened Ferrara; and the Venetians (the Germans

[1] Wimphelingii Soliloquium, cap. xxviii. in Fuchs, 56.
[2] Instance in Glutz, 488.
[3] Wimphelingii Soliloquium, cap. 31, *ibid.* Glutz, from MSS. 492. Simler, Helvetia, ii. 50, in the Thesaurus Helveticus.
[4] Muller, Schweizer Geschichte, vol. v., cap. 2, nota 151.
[5] Article in Anshelm, iv. 100. Stettler, 444, and Fuchs, 151. Julius, Statement to the messengers. Extract in Fuchs, 216.
[6] Maximilian's letter to Ernest of Magdeburg, in Beckmann, Anhalt. Chronik, 135.

having departed) rose up against Verona. The fleet, which the Pope had entrusted with the ensign, the key, and the triple crown, had already put to sea for the purpose of attacking Genoa, and the Swiss, 8,000 men strong, appeared simultaneously on the Treisa, in order, advancing through Milanese territory, to fall upon the other side of Ferrara—as Chaumont had done upon Bologna—and thus decide the day. "The papal party was already in great strength at Ferrara, and Lucretia wished to fly. The city would be forced to surrender as Bologna did. And then—had not understandings with Brescia and Parma been arrived at, and was not the Ghibelline party in the whole of Milan on their side?"[1] The Pope now left Rome and went to Bologna. The cardinals of French sympathies forsook him; but he doubted not that he would succeed. In Loretto, he dedicated a great silver cross to the Virgin, with the superscription: "In this sign thou wilt conquer."[2]

It often happened, in Switzerland, that the negotiations which, before taking the field, did not promise to lead to any result, were immediately successful as soon as this had taken place, and when those who clamoured for the war had marched forth with the army. If we investigate, we find that this evil was often the real cause of much mischief, and finally occasioned the fall of the independent confederation.[3] On this occasion, the army had scarcely crossed the St. Gotthard, when the imperial and French parties began to bestir themselves. Maximilian's warning, that the Pope intended with their soldiers to attack Milan, and not Ferrara, and that, in the event of the army not returning, he would invade their territory with the collective might of the Empire, had some effect upon them.[4] Although the three old Waldstadts, which were always against Milan, were refractory, the majority resolved to

---

[1] Bembus, 256, 257. Ovelli, Leben, p. 75; Mocenicus, p. 60.
[2] Victorellus and Ciacconii vitas paparum. Vita Julii ii., Paris de Gr. 78.
[3] Mallet du Pan, Destruction of the Swiss Confederation, vol. ii. cap. 8, p. 111.
[4] From the letter in Fuchs, 178, and Tschudi, Continuat., *ibid.* Cf. Anshelm, iv. 125.

guarantee safe conduct to the French embassy; and, although Matthew Schiner reminded them: that the intention was to send troops to the Pope, and that, "if the King of France opposed the Pope, he became the Pope's enemy, and that they then by virtue of their compact with the Pope would be sworn foes of the King also," the majority still held to their resolve, to detain, until further advice, the army they had raised for the Pope.[1] Such an order always threw into confusion the troops already in the field, as they never believed it to be the command of a single party, but the outcome of an unanimous resolution. On this occasion, they had already left Varese and reached Chiasso on the lake of Como, but had become extremely discouraged through want of provisions—for they found nothing but chestnuts, grapes, and nuts, the mills having been stripped of their iron—and not this alone; their road was blocked by rivers without bridges, and they were surrounded on all sides by French horse, who did not exactly attack them—for they were afraid of rousing their vengeance—but kept harassing and threatening them.[2] In this plight, the order of the assembly found them, and, as some of their captains had been bribed, their general distress, confusion, and ignorance of the country determined them to retreat. On the 12th September, the first ships conveying the returning troops came across the lake to Lucerne,[3] and, on the same day, the French ambassador appeared before the assembly. The deputies of Uri, Schwyz, and Unterwalden indignantly quitted the meeting; the rest drew up a letter to the Pope, praying that: "the father of peace might deal gently and not subtilely with the Christians."[4]

Instead of the promised aid, the Pope, on arriving at Bologna, received this letter. The Venetians had already besieged Verona; but they were compelled to retreat by the French, who, now freed from all fear of the Swiss,

[1] Fuchs, from the resolution, 184. Testimony of M. Walters, 231.
[2] Mocenicus, 63. Bayard, 205. Bullinger, in Fuchs, 192.
[3] Breve Julii, in Fuchs, 239. Anshelm, in Glutz, 225.
[4] Glutz, from the resolution, 545. Walter's Zeugniss, 231. Simleri Vallesia.

hastened to the assistance of the city.[1] Moreover, the papal army had not been able to take Reggio, to say nothing of attacking Ferrara. The fleet despatched against Genoa showed itself in the harbour off Bado, and attempted to land, but it found itself confronted by another equally strong; and nowhere a friend. It exchanged a few stone shot from its mortars with the enemy, and returned.[2] All had failed. Here, where everything depended upon the ascendancy of the moment, and where the reputation of superiority must precede victory, the failure was doubtless due to the retreat of the Swiss.

And now, like the Picador in a bull-fight, when he has missed the deadly stroke, or like the hunter in the mountains, when the chamois that he has missed threatens to drag him into the abyss, did Julius perceive that instead of assailer and threatener he had become the assailed and the imperilled.

Louis hesitated long before meeting him. "The Pope intended devilish things against his honour and his states, of which he would lose nothing; but, unfortunately, war with him would rouse the whole of Christendom against him."[3] In the year 1510, Amboise died; and, as he left no one to inherit his position, as the King, in making his great plans, was in the habit of disregarding small ones, though these were the stepping-stones to his greater achievements, the government appeared less enterprising than formerly. "O my patron," cried Robertet, when a portrait of Amboise was brought to him, "wert thou alive, we were now with our army in Rome."[4] At last, after Louis, through the intervention of the Florentines, had vainly attempted negotiations, and when blow now followed blow, and attack attack, he also, at last, decided for the war. On the 16th of September, the clergy of the kingdom assembled at Tours, more for counsel than for action, and chiefly, in order to obtain the opinion of the nation, and there decided thus:

---

[1] Lettres de Louis, ii. 22. Maximilian, in Hormayr's Archid., 1812, p. 588.
[2] Mocenicus, Senarega, 604. Folieta, Historia Genusus, 262.
[3] Lettres, i. 270. Machiavelli, Legazione a. c. di Francia, lett. 6, v. 349.
[4] Macchiavelli, c. 383, 380.

"A prince might in any case return an attack made upon him by the Pope, provided it were only to weaken the Pope, and were not to his total destruction."[1] And this is exactly what the King proposed to do. In the same month, the imperial ambassador, Matthew Lang, bishop of Gurk, came down the Loire. The heir to the throne invited him to a banquet. The Queen sent him wine of Beaul and victuals from her table. The King promised a small contingent for a winter campaign, but, for the summer, a force of 1,200 lances, 10,000 men, and his own person to boot.[2] He boasted that: " he would in Italy create a new heaven and a new earth; the Pope should be deposed and the Emperor be as great as Charles the Great was." His looks showed how seriously he intended it. Day and night he pondered how to revenge himself.[3] In November, he sent his Milanese army into the field under Chaumont. The papal forces lay between Modena and Bologna, in order to protect both places. Chaumont marched up the Reno as if to threaten Modena. The papal troops at once retired thither, but thus cut themselves off from Bologna, and upon this city Chaumont threw himself without delay.[4] Julius himself was in the city.

Julius was cut off from his army, still without the assistance Ferdinand had promised him on account of the Neapolitan fiefs, without the stipulated help from Venice, and, withal, ill of a fever. In Bologna itself, his person was in peril. As the Bentivogli had sided with his enemy, the city was full of the mutterings of their friends and partisans, the Rinucceneti, the Fantuzzi, and the Caprara. Nothing but captivity seemed in store for him. In this sore distress, he evolved aid out of his inner self. He first of all promised the leading Bolognese, whom he had summoned to his bedside, that he would give them a Cardinal from among them. This was repeated to the people assembled on the market-place; many other favours

[1] Burgo à Marguerite, Lettres de Louis, ii. 33. Article in Gilles, Chroniques, p. 122.
[2] Burgo à Marguerite and Responsa Ludovici, Lettres de Louis, ii. 53, 78.
[3] Macchiavelli, Legaz., 365, 370.
[4] Mocenicus, 63. Maximilian, in Hormayr, 393.

were also promised, and thus it came to pass that they were quite won over to the Pope. And what influence has not the holy and august presence of a living pope always exercised upon the people! They all came together before his palace, 5,000 on horseback and 15,000 on foot, led by two Cardinals. He rose from his bed, showed himself upon the balcony, and spread out his hands to bless them; then, as though he would show them that, in his sore need, he committed himself into their hands, drew back his arms and laid them crossways on his breast.[1] This sign, which showed the people that their prince and the father of Christianity entrusted his person to their keeping and allegiance, moved their hearts more than any promises could do. They shouted for very joy. The Pope retired and said: " now we have triumphed." And in very truth so it was. The parties in the city at length silenced, the Spanish and Venetian horse riding into the city, and the English and Spanish envoys intervening with threats on the Pope's behalf, caused the French to beat a retreat. With joy he heard at an ever increasing distance their din and firing. Whilst still lying in bed, Julius raised his arm and cried: " Away, ye French, away from Italy." Gladness of heart made him well in a short time. He collected his army, and, in the month of December, despatched three generals against Mirandula and Ferrara.

These three were not, as it would seem, very excellent servants. The first, the Marquis of Mantua,[2] halted at a crossway, and said: "There is Mirandula and the enemy's country; here is Mantua and friendly country. Go ye thither, whilst I remain here: Do ye need me, fire your arms until I hear." This man had been liberated from the tower of St. Mark, principally owing to Julius' intervention.[3] The two others, the Cardinal of Pavia and the young Duke of Urbino, Julius' near relatives, were every day at feud together, and the Cardinal, at all events, was a man of such a notorious character that one day, on seeing a poor wretch

---

[1] Paris de Grassis, Diarium, in Rainald, 79. Sansovino, Origine, 299. Jovii Alfonsus, 166.
[2] Breve, in Dumont, iv. 1, 131. Also Macchiavelli, Legazione, 352.
[3] Mocenicus, 67.

who had been hanged, some one exclaimed: "well for thee, that thou hast not to do with a Cardinal of Pavia."[1]

Alfonso of Ferrara, whom they attacked, was a totally different man. He converted all his silver-plate into money, and pledged his wife's jewels with usurers. The earthenware plates and dishes still used at Court were celebrated as having been manufactured by the Prince's own hands. He always paid everybody at the appointed day. To this circumstance, he said, was due the obedience paid to him. The three hundred pieces of cannon, many of them cast from the metal which the citizens had delivered over to him, according to streets and guilds, ensured him the respect of friends and foes. The fortifications flanking his city were a model for many in the future.[2] The French whom Louis had sent to his assistance, were under ban, as he was, but kept in allegiance and obedience by nature and the laws of chivalry.

In this situation, the operations of the Pope did not seem likely to be crowned with success. Mirandula would scarcely have been wrested from its lady defender, the widow of Galeotto Pico, were it not that Julius, though a pope, and very old, had in the coldest winter season proceeded in person to besiege it.[3] It did not affect him at all, that, on one occasion, he only escaped from Bayard in a snow-storm, that he had once to spring out of his palanquin, in order that a drawbridge should be pulled up behind him, or that a cannon-ball fell into his tent before the city. The ball, as large as a child's head, he sent to Loretto, to be treasured as a keepsake and thank-offering. At last he succeeded in reducing the city, and marched into it over the frozen ditch, and through the breach in its walls, and restored the rightful lord.[4] But he alone of all his party showed this determined courage. Bastia del Genivolo taken, Ferrara was, in Alfonso's own opinion, lost to him. But his generals neglected to occupy a pass

---

[1] Paris, Bembus, Leoni, Castiglione, Cortegiano, 205.
[2] Jovii Alfonsus, 170, f. 197. Fleuranges, 78.
[3] Paris de Gr., 100, Bayard, 216, to compare with Benedictus Jovius, Hist. Novocom., p. 62.
[4] Fleuranges, 66, 72. Mariana, 301. Triulce au Roy, in Rosmini, Trivulzio, ii. 300. Alcyonius de Exil., ed Menken, p. 62.

that might have been defended by twenty men; through this Alfonso came, and saved his castle. Julius caused it to be proclaimed: "if he would dismiss the French he should not be again attacked;" but the man who brought this news was not reliable. Alfonso replied, "Julius will soon be in his grave; but a princely race rewards good services for ever." The man—his name was Augustin Gerlo —answered: "within six days he offered himself to kill the Pope, who received all his food from his hand." The Duke told it to Bayard as a fact. Bayard replied: "Sire, did I but know it for certain, I would communicate it to the Pope before nightfall." Alfonso shrugged his shoulders, and spat out: "For Bayard's sake he would not do it;" thus the enemies of the Pope and those whom he had placed under ban did him better service than his confidants.[1] When Julius, after the trifling war in the winter, in which the French and Papals only strove to keep open their connections, the former with Ferrara and the latter with the Venetians, as well as to cut off their enemies' correspondence, at length found himself, in April, again in the field with 9,000 foot, and 1,500 horse,[2] he no longer found Chaumont at the head of the enemy, but a man whom the disorganized state of the French army required. This man was none other than John Jacob Trivulzio, a captain, who often hanged or drowned his refractory soldiers; a man, who deducted from the pay of his Spaniards what they had stolen from a peasant; a man cursed by his soldiers—"this old man with the bald head had no strength nor life nor vigour in him, and was yet so stern;" but, all the same, he showed them how to retake fortresses.[3]

Thus did two septuagenarians, both grown grey in the turmoils of Italy, both brave and stern, oppose each other, and each desired battle. How could Julius be anxious to fight, he who was plainly so much weaker than his opponent? But he said: "Christ helps his warriors, and will find means to destroy the house of Este and the schis-

[1] Bayard, 223-231, 234-240.
[2] Leonardo da Porto, in the Lettere di Principe, 4. Paris de Grassis, 101.
[3] Rebucco, Andrea da Prato and Arluni, Historia Mediolanensis, in Rosmini, Trivulzio, i. 584. Arluni, Historia Veneta, iv. 55.

matical king." Trivulzio desired to make the way smooth for the King, for Louis was already on his way to Grenoble, in order to cross the hills, and fight out his cause himself. The issue was at hand, and the sword drawn.

At this moment, Matthew Lang appeared between the parties, and again an attempt was made to ratify a peace. A Venetian and a Ferrarian peace were to be concluded at the same time. All the ambassadors hurriedly met. The Scotch envoy, Murray, was specially energetic in his endeavours to bring about an understanding. The cardinals often deliberated.[1] But how was any arrangement with Venice possible, when Lang demanded Padua, Trevigi, and 700,000 ducats besides from Venice? He rejected all remonstrances and all promises whatsoever. His boast was that he always went straight like a candle.[2] Louis would not even agree to a formal truce. " Such a truce would break the heart of his people. He was now at an advantage, and might expect victory. First victory, then peace. He would enlist Grisons, would then take the field, and not return until he had both victory and peace, otherwise he would remain away altogether." He was all fire and flame, when Fregosian, who was taken in Ventimiglia, confessed that he had been sent by the Pope to stir up a revolution. Lang left the Pope.[3] Trivulzio crossed the Panaro, and drove back the Papal army, that needed not on this occasion defend Modena—for Julius had shrewdly delivered it into the hand of an imperial plenipotentiary—under the walls of Bologna. Here, on the 22nd of May, 1511, George Frundsberg joined him with 2,500 Germans.[4]

The cause of the Pope, who had gone to Ravenna, lay in the hands of the Cardinal of Pavia, who commanded in Bologna, and of the Duke of Urbino, who had charge of the army lying before that city.

Now the Cardinal, among his twenty constables to whom

---

[1] Coccinius, de bellis Italicis, ap. Freberum, Rerum Germanicorum, ii. 268. Marguerite à Henry, in the Lettres de Louis, ii. 96.

[2] Articles proposés, and Lang's letter in the Lettres, ii. 96, 139.

[3] Andrea del Burgo's letters, *ibid.*, 150, 170, 183, 190. Paris de Gr., 103.

[4] Andrea to Margreth. Reisner's Thaten der Frundsperge, f. 11.

he had entrusted the keeping of the city, had also committed one of the gates into the hands of the partisans of the Bentivogli, and, as often as he was warned of it, only replied: "It is all well, all is in good keeping." But in the night of that 21st of May, it came to pass, that the Bentivogli on the outside passed by the gates, whilst the Fantuzzi and Ariosti on the inside mounted the tower Degli Asinelli, and waved to them with a torch, and that, thereupon, those on the outside and those within both hurried to the gate San Felice, the one to open it and the others to rush in through it. Some of the faithful were already assembling to fall upon the Ariosti from behind, when the gate burst open, and with the shout of "Sega Popolo," the Bentivogli rushed into the city. The cry was taken up and resounded on all sides; the Cardinal instantly fled with 100 horse. The city was in the power of the Bentivogli.[1]

The noise and tumult, the shouts and the waving of torches was also observed by the Duke, who was lying before the gates. "What are they shouting?" he asked of an attendant, and they believed at first that it was "Chiesa" that they heard. But in a short time they could distinguish quite clearly the cry "Sega," and immediately afterwards heard from the sentinels all that had taken place.[2] The Duke perceived that he could not possibly hold his ground. Forthwith then, in the depth of night, abandoning his tents and baggage, but without further loss—he himself was with the rearguard—he withdrew with his army.[3] Only the Venetians who were with him were overtaken by the daylight and by the enemy in effecting their retreat. The French attacked them in the rear, and the peasants from the hills assailed their flank, whilst the Bentivogli threw themselves across their line of march. The last-named were cut through by some knights, to whom the urgency of their need gave courage. The peasants plundered the baggage; the French made prisoners

---

[1] Trivulzio's report in the Lettres, ii. 233. Nardi, 132. Especially Paris de Grassis.

[2] Leoni, Vita di Francesco Maria, duca d'Urbino, lib. i. p. 26.

[3] Leoni, Consideraz. Sopra l' histor. di Guicciardini, from the mouth of Ricardo Alidosi, iii. p. 41.

—one soldier, with a wooden leg, making three—and great booty. The same morning, the Bentivogli took the Pope's statue, a work of Michel Angelo, from its niche, and after dragging it through the city, broke off its head, and resolved to melt down the rest to make a cannon.[1]

Julius was still at Ravenna. Contradictory news reached him every hour. Sometimes hoping, and sometimes lamenting that, "he was betrayed by those whom he loved best," the tidings of the disaster at last reached him. The cup was not yet full. After a short time, the Cardinal of Pavia made his appearance with his horse. He threw all the blame upon the Duke, and effected that the command should be at once taken from him and entrusted to Altavilla of Capua. The Duke himself soon made his appearance, and only found his excuses but coldly received. In bitter rage at being both defeated and calumniated, and slandered to his uncle and before the whole of Italy, the young Italian, bent on vengeance, walked through the streets until his deadly enemy, seated on a mule, met him, and smiled a friendly greeting. In his wrath he threw himself upon him. Grasping the saddle with his left hand, and with the words, "Art thou guilty or I?" before he could even answer, with his right he plunged his spear into his side. The Cardinal's dying words were, "Punishment follows sin." The Duke rode away to Urbino.[2]

Now the Pope neither saw Ferrara conquered nor Italy liberated; what he did see was Bologna lost, his statue broken in pieces by a people whom he had loaded with favours, and a hostile army in his territory. Yet the heaviest stroke of all was the murder of his trusted friend by his nephew, whom he had brought up, and the consequent loss of them both. On the 28th May, he was brought in a palanquin from Ravenna to Rimini. He smote his breast, and wept bitterly, and that no one might see him, he was brought to Rimini by night.[3]

After this disaster, the Venetians could no longer resist. On the 1st of August, Maximilian declared to

---

[1] Leonardo da Porto, in the Lettere di Princ., 5. Coccinius, 271.

[2] Bembos, 274. Guicciardini, ix. 533. Ferry Carondell à Marguerite, Lettres, ii. 243. Leoni, Vita di Francesco Maria, 132.

[3] Paris de Gr., ap. Rainaldum, 89, 104.

them that he would set free the good old fathers and the people from the thraldom of the new and tyrannical nobility now reigning; he would give the city the freedom of the cities in his empire.[1] On the 2nd of August, his troops marched out from Verona. The Venetians were driven out of all Lombardy and Frioli back upon a few strongholds; but even these, Laniago and Soave, Kofel and Beitelstein, with many others, were taken, some under the personal superintendence of the Emperor. Then for the first time he marched upon Trevigi and Padua. Trevigi was besieged under favourable conditions as early as August.[2] Whilst the Germans scoured the country as far as Lido Maggiore and the lagoons, the Venetians, on their side, having no general worthy the name, were obliged again to avail themselves of the services of Lucio Malvezzi, with whom they were dissatisfied, and whom they had dismissed. They could not pay their troops, and these would have deserted in one body to the Emperor, could they have expected pay from him. But the greatest fatality was, that their good will did not continue. We see with astonishment, how the ruling body were ever and again obliged to order their Nobili to pay the imposts that were due. They adjured them by all that was holy, by their country and their children; but they did not merely threaten to eject the delinquents from the Pregadi, and to confiscate their estates, but they began by doing so. Yet all their adjurations, threats, and penalties were of none effect.[3] It suffices to say that Venice was in no less peril than Julius was.

How could they ever have conceived the idea of liberating Italy from its enemies? No pulse at that time beat for the idea of the unity and freedom of Italy. Only those States, which had become formed in the course of the few preceding centuries, and the Papacy boasted of life. Their union only lay in a common understanding, which might have repelled the attacks of foreign nations. But whilst each asserted and endeavoured to advance its own

---

[1] A letter of Maximilian, from the Italian in Hormayr's "Archiv. für Geographie," &c.
[2] Palice au Roy; Burgo à Marguerite, in the Lettres, iii. 15, 21, 10.
[3] Principally Bembus, 275-288. Mocenicus, 79.

cause, they became involved in feud with each other, appealed to foreign aid, and yet there was not one among all strong enough to place itself at their head and remove the invaders, who had still on their side justifiable claims and a strong body of adherents. Nothing remained for the determined Pope but to summon to his assistance, against the French and the King of France, the Spanish and the Swiss. But the result of this was doomed to be something other than the liberation of Italy.

Moral reflection.

It cannot be said that it was impossible, but it must be confessed that it was exceedingly difficult, for Italy to emancipate herself again from foreign nations. Far be it from me to pass judgment upon the temperament of a great nation, whence in those days learning and industrial impulses spread throughout Europe. No one can say that it was incurably sick; but certain it is that it suffered from serious diseases. Pederasty, extending even to the young soldiers in the army,[1] and which was regarded as venial because practised by the Greeks and Romans, whom all delighted to imitate, sapped all vital energy. Native and classical writers ascribe the misfortune of the nation to this evil practice.[2] A terrible rival of pederasty was the French syphilitic malady, which spread through all classes like the plague. How often did it not happen that generals were by it rendered incapable of service! The sons of Hercole of Este were once all suffering from it at once. Whole villages in the Venetian territory were affected by it and exterminated; we read of ships, if not of a whole fleet, that required to be remanned in Corfu, because the whole crew had been rendered unserviceable by this disease.[3] Precautions, such as we should perhaps take here in Germany against the spread of the disease, appear to be nothing but child's play.

It is, however, difficult not to identify this depravation,

[1] Ferronus, after the description of the battle of Pavia, 1525.
[2] Chronicon Venetum, in Muratori, xxiv. p. 12.
[3] Diarium Ferrarense. Chronicon Venetum, 73.

everywhere and always existent, although ever afresh denounced by preachers of morality, with the peculiar character of an epoch or a nation. We shall not, however, without fear of contradiction, be able to maintain that aspirations to fine language rather than to noble deeds, this imitation of antiquity in what it has achieved in the shade, rather than in what it has performed in the sun, as Macchiavelli says,[1] is mere luxury, and not healthy for a nation as such; for instance, the training of boys not merely in drawing and in composing prose and verse, but also in "fine hypocrisy," as their teachers expressed it,[2] which consisted in making dissembled speeches in public upon a worthless subject and with a worthless effect; sometimes raising and sometimes lowering the voice, and now in complaining and now in joyous tones, which they even affected in later years when grown up—in fact, this whole formal training, to which women, whom we find improvising Latin verses to the lyre, also aspired.[3] But no one can doubt that it is a weakness, when those who affect to be masters of life, recommend in the place of manliness, chastity, and strict self-determination, nought but acuteness and the semblance of such virtues.[4] Besides this, there were youths, who preferred to sit upon a mule than a horse, men who curled their hair, plucked out their eyebrows, and spoke as delicately to their superiors as though at their last breath; men who were afraid to move their heads lest they should disarrange their hair, men who carried a looking-glass in their hats and a comb in their sleeve. Many considered it the highest praise to be able to sing well in ladies' society, accompanying themselves on the violin.[5]

The motive for imitation is always to be found in weakness; foreign manners and customs forced their adoption upon the nation. And the misfortune was, that two nations strove for the mastery, and that whoever loathed French customs fell a victim to Spanish. He who did

[1] Macchiavelli, arte della guerra, i. beginning.
[2] Arluni, bellum Venetum, iv. 58.
[3] Gilles, Chroniques, 117. Sansovino, Venetia, 190.
[4] Macchiavelli, Principe and Discorsi. Castiglione, Cortegiano.
[5] Cortegiano, p. 43, p. 111, p. 125.

not speak French, learnt Spanish: he who disliked the loose dress of the French, chose the tighter-fitting garb of the Spanish and Germans. There were many who, in order to imitate the French, did nothing but shake their heads, or made bows and plied their feet so vigorously in the street, that their servants could not overtake them.[1] There were others, who took for their pattern the short and witty replies of the Spaniards, and their discreet and unpretentious appearance in every company and in every court, where they became each day more indispensable; these excellent chess players, who never appeared to take any trouble in the matter.[2] In any case they were captivated by one or the other custom.

The literature is also to a certain extent influenced by these conditions. Shortly previous to and during this period, there arose four important heroic poems, two at Florence, namely, Ciriffo and Morgante, and two at Ferrara, Orlandos, Bojardo's and Ariosto's. Ciriffo deals with St. Louis' crusade, the others treat of Charlemagne's knights. They mainly extol French heroes; they take for their subject rather the wars of the Spaniards against the Saracens than their own wars: if the matter of these poems had an effect upon the nation, it could only be against the national spirit.

[1] Cortegiano, 146, 147, 163.   [2] Cortegiano, 138, 169.

CHAPTER IV.

THE RISE OF THE AUSTRO-SPANISH HOUSE TO ALMOST THE HIGHEST POWER IN EUROPE.

1. *Julius II. in League with Spain.*

JULIUS was assailed not only in his temporal power, but also in his spiritual dignity. Those five cardinals, who had forsaken him and joined Louis, three French, a Borgia, for the sake of Lucretia Borgia of Ferrara, and a Caravajal, on the 19th of May, 1511, called a General Council of the Church—arguing, that contrary to his duty and his time the Pope was neglecting it—and invited the Pope himself to take part in it.[1] In the same manner as Charles VIII. opposed the Pope Alexander, in league with Savonarola, so now did Louis make use of these cardinals against Julius. The so-called ecclesiastical weapons were employed more by the Princes against the Pope, than by the Pope against the Princes. Julius knew how to meet the cardinals. "They ought to remember with what voice, what eye, and what countenance he had sworn to hold a council; they would say that he had done so in genuine simplicity of heart. Only the misfortunes and the restlessness of Italy had stood in his way. But now, whilst annulling their convocation, he himself called a Concilium, but not to Pisa (which a siege of fourteen years had rendered unsuitable for the purpose), and fixed it not for the following September, a much too short notice, but for April, 1512, and its meeting-place should be Rome."[2] The real danger did not lie in the Concilium, but

---

[1] Convocatio Concilii apud Pisam, in Goldast, Politica Imperial. 1194.
[2] Breve apud Rainaldum, Ann. Eccl., xx. 90-92. Paris de Gr., *ibid.*, 115.

in the superior powers of Louis, who intended to employ its resolutions to the destruction of the Pope. Like Alexander, who, on one occasion, when in dread of Charles, and in feud with Louis, concluded an alliance with Ferdinand, and, on another occasion, at all events intended it, so now did Julius, though hesitatingly and unwillingly, but under the compulsion of necessity, form an alliance with Spain.

Ferdinand was on the road to Malaga and the African war, when he received the Pope's missives complaining of Louis. He halted on his march. The Council of Castile considered that as there was already a domestic war, it was not necessary to seek an external one. Ximenes promised to contribute 400,000 ducats, and even to come in person.[1] Ferdinand, who, in the year 1510, owing to the Pope's investiture, which released him from all obligations to Louis, had become complete master of Naples,[2] knew well, that in league with the Church and by its sanction all could be attained; in feud with her, nothing. With these new great schemes in his head, he relinquished all idea of conquering Alexandria, and, in return for 40,000 ducats, their monthly pay, he offered the Pope 1,000 lances and 10,000 infantry.[3]

In August, 1511, the Pope secretly accepted his proposals at Ostia. On the 1st of October, they proclaimed their alliance. Its object was stated to be: "To conquer Bologna with its territory, and all the immediate possessions of the Roman Chair, and then to restore the unity of the Church." A further important stipulation was the following: "If any conquests should be made outside of Italy, the conqueror should be confirmed in their possession by the Pope."[4] Hereupon, after a grand procession through the city, the league was proclaimed from the "stone of decrees" in the grand square at Venice, which guaranteed half the pay. Ferdinand came from staghunting from the woods between Aranda and Lerma and swore it; declaring that, he moreover offered himself and

[1] Gomez, Vita Ximenis, ap. Schottum, 1057, 1058.
[2] Zurita, ii. 220. Passero, Giornale, 173.
[3] Zurita.
[4] Liga pro recussa Papæ, in Rymer, Fœdera, vi. 1, 23.

his goods, and all the goods and estates of his daughter to the service of the Church.¹

A fourth associate, with Pope, King, and Republic were the Swiss. The league was not proclaimed among them. Neither their pay nor their old treaty influenced them at all; but, of all the parties to the league, they were the soonest ready and the soonest equipped.

Through all the Swiss cantons there surged in this year a lively factious spirit. Especially was this the case in Valais and Freiburg. There Jürg uff der Flue and Matthew Schiner of Mühlibach strove against each other. Jürg, a strong hardy man, almost a hundred years of age, proud of his twelve sons and eleven daughters, all of whom his house-wife had borne him, living at Glis, on the Simplon, whither the people often went on a pilgrimage, and distinguished by reason of his family, who mainly were instrumental in conquering the Lower Valais.² Matthew Schiner worked his way up in the school at Como to be his teacher's deputy, as priest, gained the affections of the common people in an ascetic life—he slept on the bare boards—and, after studying zealously the law books, won over also the educated world, until a Bishop of Valais on his journey saw him, and promoted him to a higher dignity. Both were once friends: they had both together compassed the overthrow of the bishop, who had been Schiner's benefactor, and Matthäus, through Jürg's assistance, had himself now become a bishop.³ As long as Louis and Julius remained friends, they both served together; but as soon as war had broken out between these potentates, they also quarrelled. It is said that the bishop offered his services to the King for too great a price, and had on that account been rejected; but it suffices to say, that Jürg became the King's adherent, whilst Matthäus favoured the Pope. Since that time, they persecuted each other even to exile and imprisonment. They were obliged, alternately, to avoid Valais. In Freiburg, the bailiff, Francis Arsent, and Peter Falk, the Pope's partisan, strove to the

---

¹ Bembus, 290. Petrus Martyr, Epp., 467, 468.
² Simleri Vallesia, ii. p. 13, 33, in Thesaur. Helveticus.
³ Elogium Matthaei Schineri, in the Elogiis Jovi, 249-251. Simler, *ibid.* Stettler, 444.

bitter death. Falk triumphed; thereupon the old friendship between Freiburg and Berne was at an end; for, in the latter place, the Diesbach and the French party were in the ascendant.[1]

During these struggles, the assemblies presented a curious spectacle. The agreement with the Emperor, when an ally of Louis touching the inheritance, had been assented to by most, yet not by the Waldstadts.[2] Many cantons had already once taken home the draft of a new French alliance, and were disposed to accept it; but the three Waldstadts declared that, in the event of its being adopted, they would from that very moment, single-handed, march with their three standards against the King's land. Nothing was settled. Schiner also visited the assemblies in the various cantons, and, wherever he was, was a constant going and coming, writing, enlisting, and negotiating. Not a moment's repose. He showed himself so well informed, that it was believed that a privy demon told him everything;[3] but, in spite of all his exertions, he was not successful. A mere chance incident at length brought matters to a close.

A courier was despatched from Schwyz through the Milanese territory, in order to fetch the Pope's subsidy, but in Lugano was captured and taken—because he was carrying letters from Schiner to the Pope—and drowned in the lake. The person of a courier, in his distinctive dress, was considered to be as inviolable as that of a herald. But his dress, a coat with the arms of Schwyz, was made jest of, and his symbol—the wooden box— was even sold by auction. The bailiff may have done this, in order to insult the Ghibellines in Lugano, who were of Swiss sympathies, rather than the Schwyzers themselves; but, however this may be, this incident roused the Walstadts, who were already ill-disposed, to a perfect transport of frenzy. They complained that: "their honour had been wounded, and that they must devise a means of saving it;" accordingly, in September, 1511, they resolved, on their own initiative, to take the field

[1] History of Arsent's imprisonment and death in Glutz., 233-240.
[2] Document in Dumont, iv. 1, 133. Fuchs, 251.
[3] Fuchs, 262, 264. Bullinger MS. in Fuchs, 254.

against the King, and to call upon their confederates to join them.[1]

As, in the year 1500, the affront given to the Grisons aroused all the Swiss against the Emperor, in spite of the imperial party in their midst, so now, on this occasion, did even the French party obey this challenge, and prepare for war against France, yet not for pay or relying on their league with the Pope, but on their own initiative, and without pay.

When, then, in October, Schwyz in real earnest repeatedly called upon its confederate allies, by virtue of the eternal alliance subsisting between them, to take the field, the deputies of the others hurriedly presented themselves before the council of the land, in the hope of being able to appease it. But they were not successful. Schiner was not there; the very moment he had been made Cardinal by the Pope, he had been obliged to fly from his countrymen to Italy, where in disguise, and after many risks, he arrived, and passed through the midst of his enemies to Venice. Here, he received 20,000 guilders from the Signorie,[2] and found means to despatch a goodly portion of it to his friends in the confederacy. Instead of calming the excited feelings of the people, the deputies themselves were carried away. They promised to make the cause of the Schwyzers their cause, and to stake lives and property for their sake. But their masters at home who had sent them did not change their minds. The assembly was again reminded that the winter had arrived, the Gotthard was high and the passes narrow, and how was it possible to pay for provisions on the Italian side? The Emperor might meanwhile follow up his threat and attack. But all to no purpose. The assembled community declared for war: "they would find the King and punish him," and despatched their letters of summons to the other cantons. They then provided themselves with provisions and arms; one after another they all took the field.[3]

Thus began a new war, the central figure in which

[1] Fuchs from Schödeler, Silbereisen; Abschied, 255.
[2] Ciacconius, Vitæ Paparum et Cardinalium, 1383. Anshelm, in Glutz., 247. Bembus.
[3] Fuchs, 268 and 270.

was Julius. The dispatch of money through Schiner appears to have been his work; and it was also his plan that the Spaniards at the same time, 2nd of November, set out for Naples. As the French had retired from Treviso from fear of the Swiss, and the Germans were single-handed too weak to undertake the siege, the ruin of the Venetians was stayed; they were even enabled to show themselves again in the country.[1] It would perhaps have been better had the confederates awaited their advance and their arrival on the Po. But they could not be restrained.

On the 14th of November, 1,500 Schwyzers began the ascent of the St. Gotthard with the standard, under which they had vanquished Charles of Burgundy, and which they had never since unfolded. They were immediately followed by Peter Falk with 500 Freiburgers and some artillery. It was the first artillery that the St. Gotthard had yet seen. Lucerne gunners brought it over the lake, and Uri oxen along the pass from Flüelen; thence, with the assistance of the Ammaun of Urseren, they carried their ordnance with their arms across the heights! How the French on the Long Lake were terrified when they heard the first salvos![2]

Schwyzers and Freiburgers were the most zealous in the Papal cause, and now, without a moment's pause, they marched into the enemy's country. Four Freiburgers swam across the Treisa, in the face of a number of French arquebusiers, and threw a bridge across the river. It was not until Varese, where the plain begins, that they awaited the Uri, Unterwalden and Schaffhausen troops, and the rest only in Gallerat, where the French *hommes d'armes* were in force, and in advantage. They then pursued the enemy with their whole force as far as the hazel-trees of Milan, as the chroniclers express it.[3] Now was the time for the Spaniards and Venetians to make their onslaught. But the former were too far off, and the latter occupied in retaking their castles from the Imperials.[4] The Swiss with-

[1] Caracciolus, Vita Spinelli, 95. Coccinius, 273. Burgo, Lettres, iii. 82.
[2] Bembus, 294. Letter of Peter Falk in Fuchs, 272.
[3] Letters of the Constable and Councillors of Freiburg in Glutz. Appendix 18, p. 535. Schwytzer, Schödeler. Bullinger in Fuchs, 285 *sq.* Bayard, 252.
[4] Coccinius, 276. Reisner, Frundsperge, 113. Bembus, 205.

out horse and cannon in the face of a strongly fortified city, their first onslaught repulsed with severe loss, disheartened at the wet rather than the cold of the winter, which rained upon them for four whole days and nights, without provisions or money, and in a state of perplexity respecting Berne, were seized with, what the Italians called, the German mania, and which their chroniclers can only compare with a sudden rush of water from the hills—a cataract. It forces a channel for itself, and breaks its force against a rock, it then turns, perchance, and bursts away in an opposite direction, until by nature and circumstances it is restored to its right course. They now conceived the idea of turning homewards, and to return later with a still greater force. In their frenzy, they made their way home by fire and devastation; those from the country leading the way In the morning, they fired their bivouac; before them, behind them, and for miles on either side the villages were in flames. Thus they made their way from the hazel-bushes of Milan back to the mill of Bellenz: thence they rushed home across the mountains, still full of frenzy, saying that, it was owing to them that the French had come to Italy, and through them they should retire again.[1] They returned to their cottages and awaited the coming of the spring.

Then, and not till then, did the Spaniards and Venetians come.[2] They made their attacks simultaneously in different places. On the 25th January, 1512, the Venetians, summoned by Luigi Avogaro, made their appearance before Brescia, and, in the dusk of the evening of the 26th, the Spanish arquebusiers, with the Gozadines and Pepuli, the old enemies of the Bentivogli, made their appearance before Bologna.[3] But, on this occasion, neither one side nor the other were successful. They repeatedly renewed their attacks. On the 1st of February, Pedro Navarra sprung the mines, which he had bored under the houses of Bologna, and his Spaniards stormed. They were met by

[1] Benedictus Jovius, Historia Novocom., 63. Bayard, Stettler. Schödeler and Anshelm in Glutz., 256, 257. Petrus Martyr, Epist., 474. Appendix to Monstrelet, 241.
[2] Paulus de Laude in the Lettres de Louis, iii. 109. Jovius, Vita Alfonsi, 172. [3] Coccinius, 280. Zurita, ii. 264. Bembus.

the counter-mines of Gabriel von Sulz, and the overpowering fumes of kindled brushwood, so that Bologna was still safe. The Venetians, who bombarded Brescia with their whole force, were more successful on the 2nd. Some with ropes, and others by tunnelling, succeeded in effecting an entrance; the people then rose and Brescia fell. Crema, Cremona, and Bergamo declared for their old masters. France, on receiving the first intelligence of these doings, considered Milan lost.[1] Yet the army was not minded to give it up.

Gaston de Foix, the King's nephew, led the army. A stripling, in those years in which the youthful appearance gradually merges into manhood. He wore yet the first down on his face; his eye fired whenever he laid hand on his sword. He drew it, as he said, in love of his lady, whose colours, green and white, he wore round his arm.[2] In Reggio, he learnt the loss of Brescia, and heard of the peril of Bologna, and did not long hesitate, but sought the strongest enemy, and, on the 4th of February, advanced to the Felice gate.[3] The Spaniards, as soon as they heard of his arrival, fell back upon the Idice. After having strengthened the garrison, so as to be certain of success, he turned at once about, opened by surprise the passes of Mantua, drove the Venetians, who opposed him, into the hands of the Germans, who were advancing from Verona to meet him, and by the 17th of February was in the castle of Brescia—it is called the falcon of Lombardy, and is certainly high enough and menacing enough to deserve this name[4]—resolved with his French and Germans thence to take the city lying beneath him.

On the morning of the 18th, two companies of soldiers formed in the castle yard; in the gate the vanguard of volunteers, consisting of Germans under Fabian and Spet, Gascons, some *hommes d'armes* with short lances with long blades; further behind them the others, Germans, who, at

---

[1] Jean le Veau from Bologna, Lettres, iii. 132. Andrea del Burgo, p. 147. Carpesanus, 1273. Coccinius. Zurita, 266. Arluni, iv. 175.
[2] Elogium Foxeji in Jovius, Elogia, 225. Brantome, Capitaines, 142. Bayard.
[3] Jean de Veau, Lettres, iii. 153. Coccinius, 281. Zurita.
[4] Octavii Rubei Monumenta Brixiensia in Graev. Thesaur. iv. 2, 91.

the word, "to conquer the city or die," lifted up their hands as a sign of their good will, and cut notches in the spears which long usage had worn smooth, and French. When, then, the citizens below, declining to listen to the repeated summons to surrender, gathered together for resistance at the sound of the bell, Gaston led the attack upon them with the cry of, " Forward, in the name of God and St. Denis!" All the trumpets sounded.[1]

Whilst the Venetians, after their first ineffective fire, were again loading their muskets, the vanguard succeeded in descending the narrow path in single file; then uniting their force, they made an onslaught upon the Church of St. Florian and the Brisignels' intrenchments. Bayard, who had dashed amongst the Venetians, made the greatest impression. Gritti cried: "Let us vanquish this Bayard and the victory is ours," and he was severely wounded; but the assault was not thereby stayed. The church and the cannon were taken. The advance guard pursued the Brisignels through the citadel to the very gate of the city: they alone had decided the day. When the rest of their force arrived on the spot, and the gate of the city was opened, and the Venetians now saw the cannon directed against their close lines in the streets and were compelled to let down the drawbridge at the Nazaro gate—for flight, as they thought, whilst it was really destruction, for 500 lancers were concealed without and now rushed in—it became more like a massacre than a fight. In the narrow streets, their light horses availed the Stradiotti nothing, nor the heavy-armed their stout armour. They were all alike cut down. Only Avogaro, in spite of his throwing himself into the midst of the enemy, was not slain; his horse fell with him, he was made prisoner and saved for a bitterer death. Gritti was also taken. In all the houses the hideous scenes of war and pillage were enacted; the booty was carried off in 3,500 waggons.[2]

Thus were the attacks of the Swiss, Spaniards and Vene-

[1] Bayard, 261. Coccinius, 282. Epistola ad Episcopum Gurcensem in the Paralipomenis ad Chronicon Urspergense, 467. Mythical, in Appendix to Monstrelet.
[2] The foregoing and strangely enough also Carpesanus, 1276-1280. Louis to Margreth, Lettres, iii. 178. Arluni, iv. 179. Fleuranges, 87, 88.

tians successively repulsed, and Gaston triumphant: he next resolved to go in search of the Spanish knights, whom he had been told it was a pleasure to behold, all in gold and azure, and their horses completely covered with mail armour. These he now thought of challenging in a chivalrous contest of valour.

The Concilium especially furnished an opportunity for advancing against them. It had only been opened on the 5th of November in Pisa by the Cardinals; and on the 6th, Caravajal declared his readiness to remove it elsewhere.[1] After the first sittings, it was, in January, 1512, removed to Milan. Neither Maximilian nor Florence, and not even Flanders, which was subject to Louis' crown, sent any prelate. The Cardinals had been unwelcome in Pisa, and in Milan their presence was utterly ignored; but after Gaston's victories they were more courageous. They sneered at the Pope, released Bologna and Ferrara from his ban, and sent two envoys, one to Avignon, and the other to Bologna: "for it was seemly that the whole temporal possessions of the Church should be in their hands."[2] Now Louis, who most particularly avoided the appearance of waging war in his own name with the Church, in March availed himself of this pretext, and, in the name of the Concilium rather than in his own, dispatched his nephew accompanied by the legate, to the land of the Church, with 1,800 lancers, 900 light cavalry and 15,000 infantry; a goodly array considering the times.[3]

The Spaniards were not inclined to fight. Their King wrote to them: "Three things about which he was negotiating, must come about; the English invade France; the Swiss the Milanese territory once more; and the Emperor conclude peace with Venice; each one of which events were capable of annihilating the French. It would be better for the Pope to conquer late than to lose quickly."[4] Only they would not entirely abandon the country.

From the Apennines down to the sea there course six

[1] Macchiavelli's Legazione to the Concilium, v. 407.
[2] Petrus Martyr, ep. 470, *sq.* Nardi, 130, *sq.* Guicciardini, x. 559, 580.
[3] Andrea del Borgo, Lettres, iii. 197. Reports to Louis, 211.
[4] Zurita, ii. 279.

important streams, the Silaro, the Santerno, the Senio, the Lamone, the Montone, and the Ronco, all reaching Ravenna in the plain. They all intersect the country in the same direction. The Spaniards resolved to make use of these for the purposes of resistance. They could either be defended below, and this course was advised by Fabrizio Colonna, General of the Cavalry, but in that case the road *via* the Apennines to Toscana, and possibly to Rome itself, would be open to the enemy, or above; the latter plan found favour with Pedro Navarra, captain of the foot, an enemy of Colonna's, whose proud title angered him, but, Ravenna would in this latter case be in danger. Navarra gained his point here, as he always did. Their first encampment was at Castelpiero, on the first of those rivers. As soon as Navarra perceived that the French crossed lower down the stream, he set out; at Imola he found that the French pursued similar tactics; they crossed the second, third, and fourth rivers, and Navarra always entrenched himself ready to receive the enemy; finally, the French swerved to the left from the Montone towards Ravenna, and on Good Friday, the 9th of April, 1512, they stormed the city. In Ravenna, the Spaniards had their magazines, and they could not allow the city to be lost; on the same Good Friday, they advanced with their whole force between the Lamone and the Ronco down towards the city. The French storm was unsuccessful. On Easter Eve, the armies confronted each other.[1]

It was on Easter Sunday, at the hour when the rest of Christendom was waiting for the rising of the sun, before saluting each his fellow, when a herald of the Viceroy and Spanish Commander-in-Chief, Ramon de Cardona, had an interview with Gaston on the canal uniting the Montone and the Ronco, and now separated both the armies. "Shall we fight to-day?" asked Cardona; Gaston replied: "If ye will, we are ready." They both then broke asunder the white staves, which they held in their hands as a sign of peace, and rode back.[2] Gaston came to his captains; he said: "If fortune favours us, we will praise it, if not, God's will be done;" he shared with them the bread

[1] Report to Louis, Lettres, iii. x. 215, 216. Zurita, ii. 281.
[2] Coccinius, De bellis Italicis, apud Freherum, ii. 286.

and the bottle of wine, which he still had; they vowed to live and die with him.

Gaston sat on horseback, arrayed in the arms of Foix and Navarra; his coat of mail only extended as far as the elbow of his left arm; from it to the wrist he wore the colours of his lady.[1] The Bastard of Chimay warned him and said, that an old seer at Carpi had prophesied the death of one of the commanders; a blood-red sunrise meant death for either Gaston or Cardona; but the hero answered: "I will go into the battle."

Whilst they were thus riding along the canal, they perceived Pedro de Paz and some others of the enemy on the other side. "Ye appear to be amusing yourselves until this fine game begins," said Bayard. "Is it ye?" asked Pedro, "then your camp is fully 2,000 men stronger. If we could only amuse ourselves with you in peace! But who is the noble prince, whom I see among ye?" "It is the Prince of Foix." Gaston de Foix was the brother of Queen Germana. The Spaniards dismounted and saluted him. "My lord," said Pedro, "saving our master's service, we are at your disposal."[2]

Meanwhile, Jacob von Ems stood in the midst of the lansquenets, and addressed them thus: "My dear brothers, the French this day place their hopes upon you. You cannot, however, place your hopes in anyone except yourselves; for know this well, if you do not defeat the enemy, you will never escape from the peasants. Be steadfast in the fight! Think on victory or death!" And then he led them, after each had vowed to God to fast the ensuing Saturday on water and bread, across the bridge over the canal. "I would rather lose an eye," said the Captain of the French infantry, Molart, "than that they should go before us," and dashed with his soldiery through the water. They advanced against the enemy's centre, Alfonso of Ferrara with his cannon and Palice with 800 lancers supporting their flank. Behind them, at a short interval, came Gaston and the main body.

The Spanish camp on the right, where the cavalry were posted, was protected by the canal, and on the left, where the

[1] Senarega, Annales Genuenses, p. 613.
[2] L'histoire du bon chevalier Bayard, 310, 311.

infantry was drawn up, by a ditch, and a little further away by a dyke. Before his infantry, Navarra had moreover two ditches; some little distance in the rear of them, his two-wheeled carts were posted, and upon them were mounted iron contrivances, long and pointed, and curved on the sides like sickles, and close by, a goodly number of hooked arquebuses and cannon.[1]

It was for Gaston's army to drive the enemy from his strong position.

On their left, on the dyke, Alfonso planted his artillery, and on their right, on the other side of the canal, Ive d'Allegre mounted his cannon. Navarra's infantry having thrown themselves flat on the ground, it happened that the balls thrown by both fell entirely among Fabrizio's knights. Their stout armour did not protect them; they fell in thirties and forties; the foremost and hindmost closed up and spoke together; Fabrizio at last shouted, "Shall we all perish for the sake of a traitor?" The Spaniards cried, "God slays us, let us fight with men." With the shout, "España and St. Jago with the horse!" they advanced against the foe. On seeing this, Gaston said, "My Sirs, let us now see what ye will do for France and my lady," and closed up with Palice. All cried, "France, France," and the cavalry charge, their fine art, commenced.[2] The infantry, in obedience to Gaston's orders to halt until he gave the signal, stood the while still; but Navarra's hooked arquebuses and cannon wrought deadly havoc; two of the chief leaders, Molart and Freiberg, who were sitting together over a bottle, were both killed by one ball. Many distinguished captains, subaltern officers, and common soldiers fell; at last they would no longer endure to be exposed to this fire. In surmounting the first ditch, which Navarra had placed before him, Jacob von Ems fell mortally wounded. He exclaimed, "The King has been gracious to us, be

---

[1] Fleuranges, Mémoires, 89-93. Coccinius and Novæ e castris Gallorum in the Paralipomenis ad Chronicon Urspergense, 467. Also Ullrich Zwingli, Relatio de iis, etc., ap. Freherum, ii. 122. Reisner, Kriegsthaten, i. 114.

[2] L'histoire du bon chevalier, 312. Bayard à Laurens Alemand in Expilly's Supplement à l'histoire, 451. Also Daru, iii. 441.

firm," and died. On arriving at the second ditch, they were confronted by the Spaniards, who held their spears crossed to oppose them; whereupon Fabian von Schlaberndorf, the biggest and boldest man one could behold, clutching his spear by both ends, beat down six or eight of the enemy's spears, and opened a path. They forced their way to the open space between the ditch and the carts; here Fabian and Johann Spet placed green wreaths on their heads, and advancing, challenged the bravest of the Spaniards to mortal combat. Two came out to them. Spet was, before the fray, laid low by a bullet, but Fabian slew his opponent. At length, when they were close upon the arquebuses, the Spaniards sprang to their feet, and the infantry battle began. Spears broke and swords snapped; some fought with fists, with clods of earth, and teeth; sometimes one or other, fearing a cavalry attack on the flank, would cry, "Back, ye Germans!" but the first line never moved; then fell the powerful Fabian, Linser, the boldest man in the world, and many others. The Spaniards frequently cried, "Victoria, Julius," and it seemed probable that they would be victorious. But Navarra's hopes were always doomed to disappointment: the Germans remained unshaken.[1]

But at the same time, Fabrizio and his horse, after a cavalry engagement of three hours, felt that they were unequally matched with the French. Gaston himself ran an enemy through the body; the Bayards and Palices completed what the cannon had begun; the King's Guard used their iron firelocks with effect upon the helmets of the enemy; the attack of the light cavalry was repulsed by a short manœuvre. Ramon de Cardona fled. The young Marquis of Pescara did not forget his scutcheon and the words "with or upon" emblazoned on his standard; but his horse stumbled, and he was taken prisoner. The envoy of the Pope, John de Medici, was led before the legates of the Concilium. Fabrizio Colonna still defended himself, unknown, as he thought. "Roman," said one to him,

[1] Zurita, ii. 283. Guicciardini, x. 590. Petrus Martyr, Ep. 483. Especially Coccinius, 286, and Fleuranges, 94. *Vide* also Macchiavelli, Principe, c. 26, p. 63. Hatteni Epitaphia in Empserum in the Epigrammatibus; Opera, t. i. 184, 185, ed. Münch.

"yield to fate, and surrender to me." "Dost thou know me—who art thou?" "Alfonso of Este!" "It is well, no Frenchman;" he surrendered himself. The knights were completely disorganised.[1]

At this juncture, Pondormy also with cavalry careered across Navarra's ditches, and attacked the infantry in the flank. Ive d'Allegre broke into Ramazotto's company, in order to avenge the death of his son, whom they had killed in an insurrection. Others came to the assistance of the Germans, who were with the artillery. Navarra looked round, and saw that the battle was lost; he began to beat a retreat, though in good order. Yet once again he made a desperate onslaught upon the enemy, and was taken prisoner. This decided the day. Don Diego Chignones lay wounded on the ground, and saw the horsemen dashing past him. Half dead he raised himself, and inquired who had won the victory. He heard, "The French," and parted dissatisfied from the world.[2]

"Sire," said Bayard to Gaston, who was covered with blood and brains, "are ye wounded?" "No," replied Gaston, "but I have wounded." Bayard answered: "Thank God, now leave the pursuit to others." Whilst they spoke, Gaston perceived the Bastard of Chimay: "Well, Master, am I slain as you said?" "Sire, it is not yet over," was the answer. At that moment a musketeer came: "Look, Sire, two thousand Spaniards are on the height." These Spaniards had fought with some Gascons further away, and, after having defeated and pursued them, were now returning. Gaston again took up his helmet: "Who loves me follows me;" with twenty or thirty he rushed upon them; but found his death. It is, doubtless, sweet for a young man, after glorious achievements, and in the midst of great successes and hopes, to die, while yet free from the blame which later years bring only too easily. Memory immortalizes youth. Gaston's horse fell, and he defended himself on foot. Lautrec called to the Spaniards: "Spare him, he is the brother of your Queen;" but no quarter was given. He

---

[1] The foregoing and Jovius, Vita Alfonsi Ferrariensis, 176. Vita Leonis. Vita Davali Pescaræ, 280. Ferry Carondelet à Marguerite, Lettres, 228.

[2] The same and Passero, Giornale Napolitano, 180.

was slain, and thrown into the ditch: he had received fourteen wounds in his face.

When the French saw this, the joy of their victory was damped.

This conflict is remarkable as having been the only one in history, where Italians and Spanish, on the one side, opposed an alliance between Italians, Germans, and French on the other, since Italians and Germans were later always united with the Spaniards, and it is most especially remarkable for the co-operation of firearms with the spears of the infantry and the armour of the chivalry. The military discipline of the French *hommes d'armes*, and the stubborn resistance of the Germans bore off the victory.

The French came to the Germans, who were still drawn up in line, and said: " That is our ordnance that you took from us in Naples, now give it back to us. Will not ye also go out for booty?" They answered: "We have stood here, not for booty, but for glory and honour." They fell on their knees and thanked God.[1]

A Spanish knight was the first to bring the news of the battle to Rome. The Spanish ambassador at once shipped all his household goods on the Tiber; the populace, summoned by some of the barons to liberty, closed their shops and began to rise. Julius shut him up in the Castello St. Angelo, and was minded to leave Italy. Ferdinand, in anxiety for the peril of Naples, forgot his principles, and again appointed the great Captain commander-in-chief of the forces in Italy.[2] Thus the great war of the Pope, Venetians, Swiss, and Spaniards against the French and Germans completely failed. Other forces must needs be summoned to accomplish the end in view.

[1] After Fleuranges, Bayard's Letter, 453, and Cuccinius. Hatten, 183.
[2] Infessura in Rainaldus, 112. Petrus Martyr, 484. Jovius Vita Gonsalvi, 286.

2. Formation of a New League. The Situation and Coalition of England.

At this time, with perhaps the exception of the French, there was no nation more subject to its King than the English. The proud heads of the nation had become thinned in the struggle between the rival houses of York and Lancaster, and in the fresh rivalries which ensued between the members of that faction which finally triumphed. Comines computes that eighty scions of the blood royal were, as far as he could ascertain, slain in these wars. King Edward IV. in his battles cried: "Slay the lords; but spare the people!"[1] At length, Henry VII. was conveyed in a closed carriage to London to be crowned, and had either interned in the Tower, or put to death, the rest of the York faction;[2] not even sparing the man, whose secession at the decisive hour had alone procured him victory and the Crown. Hereupon he limited the clergy's right of asylum, and so far subjected the cities, that their liberties, without his Chancellor's confirmation, were a dead letter, and cowed the peasants after they had thrice risen in arms against him.[3] The organs of liberty— the tribunals and parliament—were subservient to him. His councillors in the Star Chamber dealt with murder, robbery, and every apparent attempt at insurrection. His financial justices, Empson and Dudley, made use of the conflicting laws of the realm, given by conflicting powers, to hold, by means of fines, payable for every transgression of the law, both the nation in obedience and the King in funds. But his Parliaments—following the precedent established in the civil wars, that each victor formed one of his own party, which was rather an organ of the supreme power, than an organ of the people —were from the first entirely subservient to him. The

---

[1] Comines, Memoires, pp. 41, 155.
[2] Polydonis Virgilius, Historia Anglica, 728.
[3] Baco, historia Henrici VII. Opus vere politicum, pp. 18, 360.

first consisted exclusively of men who had been excluded from former parliaments. Another parliament chose Dudley for its Speaker.[1]

This obedience was Henry VII.'s internal safeguard; the external lay in his relationships. We have already seen that he married his daughter to the King of Scotland and his son Arthur to Catherine. Arthur having died before, as is believed, he was able to consummate the marriage, Catherine, much as she wished to escape from these hard hearts, her father and father-in-law, was compelled to remain, because in her each thought himself surer of the other. But Henry was not yet contented. He united himself to the Austro-Spanish house through the marriage of Charles of Austria with his daughter Maria.[2]

This English prince, with his few hairs, few teeth, and a face that no painter would envy, parsimonious, and studying his own advantage more than his honour and glory, and whose servants were mere tools in his hand, left, in 1509, his realm to his son, who could wield the two-handed sword and the battle-axe as deftly as he could play the flute and spinet, lavish by nature, in want of a favourite, and eager for honour and glory.[3]

Yet being one flesh and blood they both went the same way. Although Henry VIII. bore a rose, half white and half red, on his scutcheon, he put to death Suffolk and Buckingham, the old servants of the Yorks, whose lives his father had spared. To put to death the fiscal judges was, at all events, as violent a deed on the part of the son as had been their employment by the father. His first favourite, Wolsey, who used the whole lustre of his archbishopric and his dignity as Papal emissary, to subject the clerics, and who, by virtue of his office of chancellor, subordinated all the bureaucracy to it, procured him all the essential advantages of supremacy, without the name. Parliament continued to vote what he wished, and, as he said to an opponent, "Man, to-morrow my bill or thy

[1] Baco, 113, 236, 350. Polydor. Virgilius, 775. Cf. also Hume.
[2] Polydor., xxvii, 2. Zurita, ii. 155. Vetturi in Macchiavelli, Legazione, v. 228.
[3] Baco and Polydor. Especially Edward Herbert of Cherbury, The Life and Reign of Henry VIIL, p. 4.

head passes." The whole manner and way of the father was his also; only he acted still more inconsiderately and more rapidly than the other.¹

He also based his foreign policy upon his relationships. His object was not merely to secure his own position, but to procure for the great league, to which he belonged, the ascendancy in Europe, and herein he proceeded with more energy and passion than his father had done.

At the very outset, immediately after his marriage with the Spanish Catharine, he found himself, through her, bound to Ferdinand, and, through his sister Maria, with Charles and Maximilian. In the year 1511, he sent aid to both; to the first against the Moors, and to the other against Guelders; and as long as they enjoyed it, he also had peace with France. In July, 1510, his envoys swore the old treaties with Louis.² But when, in 1511, Ferdinand entered into a league with the Pope, matters wore a different complexion.

One material success of the League of 1495 was, as we have seen, the formation of the grand Austro-Spanish alliance. At the present time, it was Ferdinand's plan to found in the same manner a new league, in name and aim in the interest of the Pope, but, in actual fact, having for its object the future greatness of his house.

But the foundation of all was the reconciliation between Ferdinand and Maximilian. After the long feud respecting Castile, Mercurin Gattinara was, of all Maximilian's counsellors, the first to arrive at the conviction that this reconciliation was the greatest need of his lord and master. How was it that the campaign against Padua had failed, was it not because Ferdinand had sent the Venetians supplies?³ In order to renew the old understanding, he betook himself to Spain; here, after at last abandoning Maximilian's claim for an immediate administration of Castile, which could never be obtained, and, by contenting himself with an arrangement, whereby Ferdinand as-

---

¹ Herbert, 14. Goodwinus, Annales Anglici, Henrico, Eduardo et Maria regnantibus, p. 17. Hume, Henry VIII., p. 117.

² Herbert, The Life, 15. Macchiavelli, Legazione, v. 348. Zurita, ii. 249.

³ Gattinara à Marguerite, Lettres de Louis, 194.

sured the succession in his realms to their common grandson Charles, he brought about the reconciliation, and restored the old alliance, and the natural friendship between both potentates. Since then, Ferdinand busied himself again with the Guelders affair, and the Emperor in his state papers devised war against the Moors.[1]

Ferdinand's next scheme was to draw the King of England and the Emperor, his nearest relatives, into his war.

He first succeeded with King Henry. When Louis invited the latter to take part in the Concilium of Pisa, the answer was given in the fact, that the monarch, whilst the French ambassador was speaking, leant on the shoulder of the Spanish envoy, Louis Carroz.[2] The league between Ferdinand and the Pope was concluded in the presupposition that Henry would join it. Henry hoped that the Pope would give him the title of "the most Christian monarch," and, on the 4th of February, 1512, he dispatched his plenipotentiaries to the Lateran Council. He hoped, if not to restore the greatness of the former English kings in France, at all events to unite Guyenne to his royal standard; and, for this purpose, his parliament, which assembled on the same day, voted him a. benevolence. He appointed privileges for faithful, and punishments for faithless, captains.[3] One of his motives, perhaps, was that his house, owing to Maria's marriage with Charles, had a claim to Naples, which Ferdinand represented as being in danger; and the five and a half millions which his father had left him gave him support and confidence. Suffice it to say, he entered into the league, and promised to rule the waves from the mouth of the Thames to le Trade. In the winter, he sent two messages to Louis, one about Guyenne, and one for the Pope. But as both were to no purpose, he declared war, and made common cause with Ferdinand; he agreed to supplement 8,000 Spanish infantry with 8,000 English arquebusiers, but to pay the cavalry jointly with him; whatever was con-

---

[1] Zurita, ii. 203. Letters of the Emperor of 1510 in Goldast, Hormayr, Beckmann. [2] Zurita, ii. 267.
[3] Herbert, The Life, 18, 19. Jean le Veau in the Lettres, iii. p. 150, of 10th February.

quered should belong to him whose forefathers had possessed it.[1]

Henry having now made his decision, both parties solicited the alliance of Maximilian. When, in August, 1511, Julius was lying sick unto death, Maximilian entertained a hope of becoming Pope himself. "He required 300,000 ducats to gain over the cardinals; and to raise this sum he would sacrifice his four chests full of jewels, and his feudal apparel. Nothing less was his due." Both parties entertained the same idea, even after Julius had recovered. The schismatic cardinals encouraged Maximilian, urging him only to come to Italy; there there were at his service 200 lances of Louis, the power of the Sanseverins of Mantua and Ferrara, as well as the prestige of the Concilium; the Pope could then be deposed, and he himself, if he desired it, be elected in his stead. Naples, they urged, was also open to him. On the other hand, Ferdinand reminded him that, "friendship with the present Pope, and not enmity, was essential, if he wished to become his successor."[2]

We do not precisely learn when and wherefore Maximilian abandoned this scheme, which looked far too complicated to be able to be realized; but, as he was allied with Ferdinand, there was no help for it as long as Julius was alive. Other matters were nearer his heart.

It had ever been his intention to conquer the Milanese and Venetian territory. But the one scheme really excluded the other, for he could not subdue the one without the assistance of the other. Ferdinand disclosed to him a way of attaining both objects successively: first of all, Milan to be conquered for Charles, their grandson, by coming to Maximilian's hands through the league; for this purpose, a truce to be made with Venice, then the assistance and co-operation of the latter; finally, an attack upon Venice itself.[3] Julius was already so

---

[1] Ratificatio Liga ap. Rymer, vi. 1, 25. Articul. 2, 7. Polydorus, lib. xxvii. p. 7.

[2] Maximilian's Letters of 18 Sept., probably 1511, to Margareth in the Lettres and to Lichtenstein in Goldast. Zurita, ii. 260.

[3] Zurita, ii. 262. Another proof are the negotiations at Mantua in the summer of 1512.

deeply entangled in the net of this family, that he agreed to whatever suited them. The Venetians declined to abandon Verona and Vicenza entirely, and refused the Emperor's demand, that they should recognize the Archduke Charles as their suzerain; the Pope, having gathered from a secret letter of Louis, which, though the words were crossed out, was still legible, that an alliance between the King and the Republic was to be apprehended, lost no time in bringing about a truce between the Emperor and Venice, which left to both parties what they possessed, and procured for the Emperor, to begin with, a sum of 40,000 ducats.[1]

This, and the disturbances in Guelders, which had recommenced, brought it about that the Emperor joined the league. At the very moment that he forsook Louis's side, his Germans had gained a victory for Louis. It is true that, shortly before the battle of Ravenna, a dim, uncertain, and mysterious intimation of this truce was made to them from the enemy's camp; but this news had no influence upon their courage and success. Venice also recognized the Lateran Council.

3. *Conquest of Milan.*

Three things had been foretold to his army by Ferdinand, and two had already happened: England was now involved in war with France, and the Emperor had made peace with Venice. In the days of the battle of Ravenna, the third was also realized: the invasion of Milan by the Swiss.

On that Good Friday, on which Gaston stormed Ravenna and the Spaniards went forth to battle, the bitterest foes of the French, coming from all the cantons of the Confederation, assembled in Baden, and resolved, even single-handed, to begin the war against the French. Each man of them was to announce the fact of their decision to his lords and superiors, and beg them for powder and muskets. The following Saturday week, they were to meet in Livinen

[1] Bembus. Document in the Lettres de Louis, iii. 217.

and, in God's name, advance against their enemies.[1] Neither the Diesbachs of Berne, who had mocked at the Cardinal Schiner in a Shrovetide play, nor yet those private individuals who had promised the French peace, in consideration of a sum of only 60,000 guilders, were able to cope with such a great rising of the people, and withstand the indignation of the cantons;[2] and even Jürg uff der Flue negotiated at Milan in vain. The papal party had been encouraged by new promises of temporal and spiritual favours, and the imperial party also had come over to them, in consequence of Maximilian's fresh attitude. On that Saturday after Easter, the 19th of April—it was inevitable—the Swiss, with the ensigns of their cities and provinces, and with armour, cannon, and weapons, sallied forth to aid the Pope.[3] Their envoys were despatched to the various courts; some, instructed, as it would seem, by the French party, repaired to Louis: "Why," they asked, "had he taken from them the subsidy which their poverty demanded, in return for which they had made France twice as great as it had been; but it often happened that God, through the instrumentality of despised creatures, broke the pride that was displeasing to him."[4] Others were sent to the Emperor. The Emperor said: "Both Italian and German Tyrol was open to them; the future prince of Milan should pay them 300,000 ducats immediately, and guarantee 30,000 ducats annually."[5] On the 6th of May, the Swiss set out, in greater numbers and better equipped than ordinarily. They were under the command of a field-marshal, one Jacob Stapfer, a master of ordnance, and a provost-marshal, to whom the soldiers from all the various cantons swore fealty. In all the taverns in the Tyrol, they found bread and wine; in Trent their captains, whilst seated at a meal in the bishop's garden, heard the intentions of the Emperor. In Verona, they received a hat and sword, a consecrated banner, and, moreover, each

---

[1] Letter in Fuchs, ii. 318.
[2] Anshelm and Glutz., 261. Lettres, iii.
[3] Report from embassy in Venice, in Stettler. Fuchs, 332.
[4] Petrus Martyr, and especially Garnier, from the MSS. of Bethane, p. 351.
[5] Fuchs, 321.

man, as first payment, a ducat, from the hand of their Cardinal.¹

They came just at the right moment for the Pope. Encouraged by the victory of Ravenna, Louis' Concilium had, in its eighth sitting, declared the Pope now and hereafter suspended from all Papal authority; but, after the loss of its commander-in-chief and so many brave men in the battle, the French army was not by any means strong enough to give effect to such a sentence.² La Palice, upon whom the command had devolved, was obliged to content himself with holding his strongholds in Romagna. But, on the 3rd of May, after passing the night in the Lateran Church, he also opened his Council in the midst of it, in order, as he said, to weed out the thorns from the acre of the Lord.³ On the 2nd, the Viceroy, Cardona, who, without halting, had fled from Ravenna to the Abruzzian mountains, again started from Naples, in order with fresh forces from Sicily to make a fresh attack upon the French.⁴ On this occasion, the plan was, to mass together in one camp the four armies, to wit, the Papal army, which had been organized under the Duke d'Urbino, the Spanish, the Venetian and the Swiss armies. At Vallegio, the Swiss actually joined forces with the Venetian cavalry and artillery; they were resolved, even if their way led through the midst of the enemy, to find the two other armies.⁵ How was La Palice to cope with such a hostile demonstration? For, as the English in the same month of May had sailed to Fuentarabia and, not content with throwing an army upon the Bidassoa were harassing the coast of Brest, and as, moreover, a great joint attack by English and Spanish upon Guyenne had also been announced, King Louis was more inclined to recall his *hommes d'armes* from Milan, than to send others thither.⁶ But it was still uncertain which of the two Concilia, that of the King of France, or that of the Pope, would retain the upper hand.

¹ Writings of Schweizer, Peter Falk, in Fuchs, 335 *sq.* Glutz., 266. Stettler.
² Acta Concilii Pisani, in Rainaldus, p. 113.
³ Historia Concilii Lateranensis, in Roscoe, Life of Leo I., App. 536.
⁴ Caracciolus, Vita Spinelli, 59. Zurita, ii. 285.
⁵ Mocenicus, 91. Lütener in Glutz., App. p. 538.
⁶ Andrea del Borgo, Lettres, iii. 256.

Two events caused matters to come to a speedier issue than could have been anticipated. Firstly, the Swiss intercepted a letter from La Palice, which was to the effect that he would scarcely be able to hold the field against a strong army. This letter, having been translated to his comrades by the Freiburg captain, they were unanimous in their decision, not, as they had originally intended, to advance to the Po to join their friends, but to march forthwith to the Oglio and attack the enemy, and to rest not a night on the way, save out of necessity, for in three or four days the battle must be fought.[1] The second event was really the decisive one. We remember that the King of France vanquished Lodovico Sforza by withdrawing his lansquenets, and sending the Swiss upon him. Curiously enough, he was overcome by the same means with which he had formerly conquered. The Swiss were in the field against him. On the 4th of June, strict orders were received from Maximilian, addressed to the lansquenets, their commanding captains, lieutenants, corporals, and privates to leave the French camp from that very moment. Now they were not in the Emperor's pay, but in the King's; but these lansquenets were either Tyrolese, and thus the immediate subjects of the Emperor, or related to the Suabian league, and, as such, also, more or less in subjection to him. Accordingly, when Burkhard von Ems, Jacob's nephew, and Rudolf Häl, the captains of this band, came into the council of war, which Palice had summoned to take counsel on the question of resistance, they declared in spite of all the fair promises of the general, that they must obey the Emperor's orders, and, on the 5th of June, begged the Confederation for safe conduct.[2] Some were for remaining six days longer, until the expiration of the term for which they had bound themselves; and about eight hundred, probably South Germans and such as had nothing at home to lose, resolved to try their fortune with the French still longer.

Hereupon Palice, seeing himself deprived of the faithful

[1] Peter Falk's Letter, in Fuchs, 357. The Solothurn Captains, in Glutz., 541.
[2] Missives and documents in Fuchs, 365. Roo. Especially Zurita, ii. *sq.* 289.

and victorious allies of Brescia and Ravenna, abandoned all idea of resistance, and retreated from place to place. For one moment, Trivulzio entertained the hope of being able to regain for Milan its old freedom, and he actually succeeded in winning over the leading Ghibellines. But what could be expected from these nobles, who only had a thought for their own immediate advantage? At the very first disturbance of the social order, they broke disguised into the houses of poor learned men and aged invalids, and forced them to give up their savings, the hope of their latter years. Trivulzio, like Palice, abandoned also all hope, and left the city.[1] Whilst, then, the French were retiring from Ravenna before the Papal army, and had in Bologna burnt the episcopal palace which they had occupied, and retired from the city—the Bentivogli never thereafter returned thither—Cremona surrendered to the Swiss, with the cry of "Julius, Church," and placed itself in the hands of the Liga. The Swiss advanced to Pavia.[2] Here they once more came upon a body of lansquenets. At first they met each other with their old jests of the Rhine and Gariglian, instead of with arms. But at last, when the French had retired, and the Swiss, invited by the citizens, entered the city, and the lansquenets, who also wished to retreat, were prevented by the breaking of a bridge, a desperate struggle ensued. The lansquenets saw that they were doomed to die at the hands of their old enemies; they accordingly first went and threw the money, which they carried in their sleeves, into the river, in order that their enemies should not profit by it; they then fought their fight, and were all slain.[3] Four days later, the French crossed the Mont Cenis; there was not a single city in the whole duchy that had not surrendered. Only the castles still held out.

Beyond all doubt it exceeded the expectations of the League, that Milan had so rapidly passed from the French hands, not into theirs, but into those of the Swiss.

[1] Arluni, de bello Veneto, ix. 195-201.
[2] Oath of Cremona in Daru, iii. 457. Falk's writings in Fuchs, 364.
[3] Principally Zwinglii, Relatio de rebus ad Paviam gestis, ap. Freherum, ii. 124. Falk's writings, 368, 378. Bayard, 328. Fleuranges, 104. Jovii vitæ virorum doctorum, p. 107. Leferron, iv. 102.

When Julius received the tidings, he read them through silently; he then drew himself up and said to his master of the ceremonies, "Victorious, Paris, we have been victorious." "May it be of service to your Holiness," replied the latter, and knelt down. The Pope: "May it profit you and all Italians, and all the faithful whom God hath deigned to deliver from the bondage of barbarians;" he unfolded the letter and read it through from beginning to end.[1] Shortly after, the news arrived from Genoa that his country was at last free; upon Jan Fregoso's arrival in Chiavia and upon receiving a letter from Matthew Lang, the French commander had fled to the Lanterna, his Swiss guard had disbanded, and Jan had thereupon entered the city.[2] Envoys from Bologna arrived, but without vestments and golden chains, to implore pardon of the Pope. Parma and Piacenza surrendered to him; he did not receive them as new, but as old subjects, whom an accident two hundred and fifty years previously had estranged from the Church.

Alfonso d'Este came under the protection of the Colonna to be liberated from his ban and to appease his anger.[3] Rome was ablaze with torches and *feux de joie*, the Pope presented an altar cloth with the inscription, "Julius II. after the liberation of Italy," to the church of St. Peter.[4] A great painting of Raphael immortalizes these events. In the Camera della Signatura, he represents Heliodor, as the horse with the rider in gold mail prepares to kick him as he is in the act of committing sacrilege, whilst two avenging angels hurl him down.[5]

These, beyond doubt, were the happiest days in the life of pope Julius; after so much exertion, danger, tribulation, and tears, his object was, as it appeared, attained, his plan had succeeded, and his name immortalized in the glory of his great deeds.

He owed the Swiss eternal gratitude, for it is patent to all eyes that it was they that rescued him at a single blow from his great spiritual and temporal danger. The other

---

[1] Paris de Grassis, ap. Rainaldum, 121.
[2] Senarega, incomplete, 615; Folieta, 294. Also Zurita.
[3] Carpesames, an Envoy of Parma, 1288. Jovii Alfonsus, 178 *seq.*
[4] Paris de Gr., 122.
[5] Speth, Kunst in Italien, ii. 294. Roscoe, Leo, iii. 393.

members of the League were not so happy; both Ferdinand and Maximilian had expected quite a different issue. Ferdinand only made use of the victory, to stay Gonzal's preparations. The army, which, in spite of this termination, and against the Pope's express desire, he sent across the Tronto,[1] seemed to be intended for somewhat else than to serve the Pope.

Conquest of Navarre.

At first, this same Ferdinand did not turn his eyes towards Italy as much as he did towards the French frontier—where the Marquis of Dorset had made his appearance with 8,000 English auxiliaries—that is towards Navarre.[2]

In those days, the kingdom of Navarre comprised the valleys and hills, fruitful and barren, which extend on both sides of the Pyrenees, on the one side from the Ebro, and on the other from the Nim, up to the snowy heights of the mountain chain. On both sides, the cattle were driven to the Alduidos to pasture: herds might be seen all the way from the Ebro valley as far as the church of St. Jago hard by St. Jean Pie de Port. Every loss caused by robbery was made good by the district in which it had happened, even across the hills.[3] Now this kingdom had for a long time been imperilled on both sides. In France, Louis defended the rights of Gaston de Foix, who was as much the grandson of the old Gaston, King of Navarre, as the possessor of the throne, Catharine, was his granddaughter.[4] She had made her husband, John d'Alibret, king of the country. On the Spanish side, Ferdinand, in opposition to this King and his adherents, the Agramonts, took the part of the Count Lerin, the head of the Beaumonts; the Count had once been one of the most powerful of vassals, a man, who had to be allowed to ignore the King's express invitation; but he had been driven out, and

---

[1] Zurita, ii. 307.
[2] Herbert, The Life of Henry VIII., p. 20.
[3] Garibay, Compendio universal de las Chronicas, tom. iii.; historia de Navarra. Barcel, 1628, p. 11.
[4] Polydorus, in extenso.

was now a fugitive in Andalusia. Moreover, King Louis was suzerain of one part of the land of Navarre; in the remaining portion, all Alcaldes had sworn allegiance to Ferdinand; he held five strongholds in the land, and had even the King's daughter in his keeping. Many years before this, there lived and reigned in Navarre a King, Sancho the Wise; this monarch had emblazoned on his coat of arms two lions, both pulling at a golden band, which they held in their teeth; this device represented Castile and Aragon struggling for Navarre. The relation of Spain and France to this country was analogous. At the commencement of the year 1512, Ferdinand, in order to secure himself against attack on the part of Louis XII. as a result of his concerted co-operation with the Pope against him in Italy, demanded of the Alcaldes that they should renew their oath of allegiance, requiring besides the surrender of the prince into his keeping, and three additional strongholds.[1] It was just at the time that Gaston attained every day to greater renown in Italy, and had additional claims to Louis's gratitude, which could only consist in his defence of his rights to Navarre. Gaston's death was the good fortune of the kings of Navarre. They immediately allied themselves with France, summoned the Estates of their realm from both sides the Puertos, obtained assistance, and prepared to resist the pretensions of Ferdinand and his English.[2]

Now it was either an idle tale that was spread abroad, or it was an actual fact, that a secretary of the King of Navarre had been stabbed in the house of his paramour, and that the priest, who was called in to offer consolation, found on him the copy of a treaty, by which Louis pledged himself to restore the old frontier of Navarre against Castile, and sent it to Ferdinand. This enabled the latter to gain over the Cardinal Ximenes and a part of the nation for his undertaking.[3] He declared, that he had long had in his possession a bull putting under ban the King of Navarre, who was as schismatic as the French sovereign,

---

[1] Zurita, i. 12. Garibay, 500.
[2] Zurita, i. 130; ii. 161; ii. 273-290. Garibay, 29, c. 25. Dumont, iv. 1, 147. Zurita, 294.
[3] Petri Martyris Epistolæ, ep. 491. Gomez, Vita Ximenis, 1060.

to whom he was lending his support; he commanded the Duke of Alba, who had gathered a great army in Vittoria, under the pretence of joining the English, not to combine with these latter, but, instead thereof, to advance upon Pampeluna.[1]

John was not yet ready, and no Frenchman was at hand, when the Duke of Alba appeared at the narrow gorge which divides the valleys of Biscay from those of Navarre. His muskets easily dispersed the 600 Roncalese who defended the pass. Don Luys, Count of Lerin, marched at the head of the Spaniards. The whole party of the Beamonts rose in his favour, and the cities, which had once belonged to him, received him with jubilation. On the fifth day, the army stood eight leagues from the city upon the heights which form the Cuenca, that is, the basin of Pampeluna. John d'Alibret was a king who went twice or three times daily to mass, and who would dance with a peasant woman and eat with a citizen, but not made for war and danger. He said, "Better be in the hills than a prisoner," and fled; two days later, his spouse also fled away. She said, "Ye were always John d'Alibret and wilt remain so. Were ye Queen and I King, this realm would not be lost." On the 25th July, 1512, Pampeluna surrendered to the Spaniards, and Alba guaranteed its general and special "Fueros" and all its rights; this done, with the exception of a few castles belonging to the Agramonts and the valleys of Roncal, the whole of the kingdom lying on this side was reduced. On the 10th of September, Alba proceeded into the land of Ultrapuertos, and on the same day took St. Jean.[2]

The English saw with astonishment how the French war, which they had come out to fight, resolved itself into a conquest of Navarre for Spain. Bayonne lies eight miles from St. Jean, and this former city they could, at all events, at once attack with combined forces. "But not to Bayonne," wrote Ferdinand, "where every pinnacle bristles with guns; before you there lies the open and unprotected country." The Marquis of Dorset, who was

[1] Antonius Nebrissensis, de bello Navarrensi, in Hisp. illustr., ii. 911.
[2] Garibay, 506. Antonius, 911, 912. Fleuranges, 115. Zurita, 302. Petrus Martyr, ep. 499.

annoyed at this constant hesitation and delay, replied that, "his orders were to go against Bayonne, and not against the open country; he would not approach the Spaniards by a single inch." His King was sooner over-persuaded than he himself. But before any other arrangement could be come to, a mutiny among his troops compelled the Marquis to retreat.[1]

Yet, without their assistance, Ferdinand understood how to defend his conquest. Alba was still in St. Jean, when, in November, 1512, d'Alibret succeeded, with French assistance, in penetrating into the kingdom through the defiles; closing them behind him, he began the siege of Pampeluna with every prospect of success. But Alba, making his way by paths little known, arrived at Pampeluna in the nick of time, and held out there, until fresh auxiliary forces from Spain showed themselves on the heights of Cuenca. Then d'Alibret retired, and the peasants, who had come with their waggons to buy and load the pillage and plunder of the city, returned dissatisfied homewards. And now Ferdinand brought the whole of Navarre this side the Pyrenees, 800 Pueblos, entirely into his power; the high chain of mountains formed an admirable frontier. Further, Navarre, lying on the other side, was never again united with the other, and, with but few traces left, the whole memory of the old brotherhood entirely disappeared. The conquered land desired the Aragon and Allodial law; but it only received the laws of Castile and vassal rights and customs. It retained its Cortes. The Procurators of the twenty-three cities held a sitting before the canopy of the throne, to settle the "Servicio," only under the canopy there sat, not their King, but a representative of the King of Spain. This also had become a piece of the great inheritance of Austria and Spain and of the great feud between this house and France.[2]

[1] Polydorus. Herbert, Life of Henry, 22.
[2] Antonius, 912-924. Zurita, 318-328. Garibay.

6. *Revolution in Florence. Other successes in Italy.*

In the July of 1512, Navarre was conquered, and, in the ensuing November, put into a state of defence; midway between both these events, in September, the Austro-Spanish house succeeded in an enterprise, which was perhaps of even greater influence upon international relations.

We have seen how the war, waged by Alexander's League some sixteen years previously, turned, after the French had been driven from Italy, against their principal supporters; to wit, the Popolares in Florence. During the time that Louis was in Italy, these same Popolares had enjoyed extended influence under the first man of the city, Peter Soderini, who had been raised to the position of perpetual Gonfaloniere; and, after Louis had been expelled, they still adhered to their old allegiance to him. For a second time, a League, none other than that of the Pope Julius, now turned against them.

Pisa, which, after indefatigable exertions, they had at length again subjected, was their destruction. After four campaigns, they came so far as to storm it; and killed one of their leaders, a certain Paolo Vitelli, because he did not take it. For three successive years, they came in May and ravaged the crops of the Pisanese as far as the walls of the city; they even attempted to divert the course of the Arno, and employed 80,000 labourers on the work; they spared no money in order to obtain the sanction of the Kings of France and Spain to their undertaking. From Podesteria to Podesteria, and from valley to valley, with the assistance of their citizen Macchiavelli,[2] they formed military stations of native soldiery. At length, in the year 1509, they succeeded in their object. They had invested the city by three camps, and had made the Arno inaccessible by building a strong bridge, and the Fiume Morto impregnable, with piles bound together under the water by iron bands.[3]

[1] Filippo Nerli, 89. Jacopo Nardi, 83.
[2] Guicciardini, vi. 343; viii. 418.
[3] Istruttione of Macchiavelli in the Legazione, iv. 106. His letters, 262, 264. Vasari, Vita di San Gallo, p. 133.

An intolerable famine broke out in the city, entailing a quarrel between the citizens, who were for holding out longer, and the country people, who violently demanded the surrender of the place. The latter obtained the upper hand. On the 8th June, 1509, the Florentines again entered Pisa.[1] But the reconquest of the place did not bring good fortune and prosperity to the Florentines. The name of Pisa, and the memory of an old Concilium in the place, incited both King and Cardinals to urge the summoning of a new Concilium there. The Florentines were under too deep an obligation to the King to be able to refuse; but the fact that they, although unwillingly, acceded to this demand, made the Pope their enemy.[2] This was, as far as could be seen, the principal reason for an attack upon them. In 1511, Julius appointed their great enemy, the Cardinal de Medici, legate at his army; and now that they had banished his Datario from their city, the Pope became all the greater supporter of this Cardinal, who intended to avail himself of the French reverse to make an attack upon Florence, and favoured his plans.[3]

Among Lorenzo de Medici's shrewd schemes, one of the shrewdest was the employment of the prestige, which he possessed as mediator of Italy, to obtain the least invidious and most certain enhancement of his house in the ecclesiastical preferment of his son John. When this family was driven from Florence, John's benefices, consisting in a prebendary, a priory, a provostship, four canonries, six benefices, fifteen abbeys, and an archbishopric, were one of its chief supports.[4] We do not find that John either grossly neglected or zealously administered the original offices of those benefices; it was his whole aim to live happily without being guilty of any striking faults, to make friends and gain prestige, and reinstate the lustre of his family. His face, as shown in Raphael's picture, if regarded but hastily, displays but the pleasure and satiety

---

[1] Macchiavelli's Reports, 267-290. Treischke, Geschichte der fünfzehnjährigen Freiheit von Pisa, p. 356.
[2] Jovius, Vita Leonis, ii. 35. Nerli, 104.
[3] Carondelet in the Lettres, iii. 78. Nardi, v. 144.
[4] Fabroni, Vita Leonis X. Adnotationes, p. 245.

seen in other ecclesiastics of high order; but if we regard it closer we are struck by an expression of deep thought, scheming, and firm will. He had a comfortable and pleasant way of living. It was also his wont to give way to other cardinals in the slightest matters of contention; he was serious or jesting, just as it suited them; he never dismissed their agents without their being able to tell their principals that the Cardinal de Medici was their obedient and humble servant.[1] He proved to the Orsini on the chase that he was of their blood. His palace was always full of music and song; it was a dépôt for the models, drawings, and works of the painters, sculptors, and goldsmiths of Rome. The literary world always found there a library open to their use. They were the books of his father Lorenzo; it gave him the greatest pleasure when he took up one and studied it page by page. He then imagined he was earning the approbation of his deceased father. His most subordinate servants only left him in the conviction of his mildness and goodness.[2]

His life was not pretence; but it availed him quite as much as if it had been most carefully studied. He won the hearts of all Florentines of his acquaintance. Men of quality did not fear from him Piero's arrogance. There were often assembled in Florence at that time, in the gardens of Cosimo Rucellai—a man more suited to scientific conversation and poetic essays than for the service of his country—young men of the Vettori, Albizzi, Valori families, whom high birth, youth, wealth, and the consciousness of an excellent education had made, one cannot say otherwise, somewhat overbearing. They had read in Roman history of the glories of the Optimates, and thus they styled themselves; they found out the weak points of the Gonfaloniere and the Consiglio, and mocked at them in masquerades. The good Soderini, meek and mild, did not interfere; but they joined the party of John Medici, through whom they hoped to attain greater influence.[3]

[1] Leonis X. Vita, autore anonymo conscripta, in Roscoe, Leo X., App. to 3rd vol., 581.
[2] Jovii, Vita Leonis, ii. 29, *sq*. Especially Alcyonius, de exilio. Edited by Menken, 1707, i. p. 12.
[3] Filippo Nerli, Commentarii, p. 106.

The Cardinal intended to make use of them to the advantage of his house, when he invited Ramon de Cardona to a campaign against Mantua.

Cardona came in August to Mantua, and negotiated there with Matthew Lang, touching the reorganization of Italy after the victory; the Medici promised to pay his Spaniards, whilst Soderini refused Matthew Lang the 100,000 ducats, which he demanded.[1] Soderini was blamed for his action in this matter; but how could Lang answer for the Spaniards? How could the Emperor, who, in 1509, had guaranteed the "status quo" of Florence in return for a money payment, and who was even then negotiating about it, be depended upon to alter it? Both Bishop and Viceroy resolved upon the undertaking, in favour of the Medici.

Soderini was a man who once demanded of the 300 priors, who had at various times been under him, to declare publicly, whether he had ever preferred a personal advantage to a public interest, and whether he had ever on any occasion recommended his friends for a judicial post.[2] He felt himself completely free from all the passions of Italian partisanship, and trusted the people under him.

When Cardona entered Tuscany, with the declaration that he was only coming against Soderini, the latter summoned the Grand Council and remonstrated with him, pointing out that he had gained his dignity by the will of the people, and not by force and deceit, and should all kings in the world, united, try to persuade him to lay down his dignity, he would not do so; he would only lay it down, when the people which had conferred it, demanded it back of him; he was in their hands, and into their hands he surrendered himself. He urged them to go amongst their Gonfaloniere and to decide the matter. They separated, and returned declaring their readiness to stake their lives and property for him.[3]

After this, Cardona found the Florentines more hostile than ever; their cities resisted him, especially Prato, which

---

[1] Nardi, Historie, 147; cf. Mémoire touching the meeting in Mantua, in the Lettres, iii. 289.

[2] From Ammirato and Cambi in Sismondi, Hist. d. républic ital., xiv. 130.

[3] Address by Nerli. Macchiavelli, in the Lettere a Una Signora, 7.

he besieged. On one occasion, being in straits, he declared his readiness to depart, provided the affairs of the Medici were left to the arbitration of his King Ferdinand, when all of a sudden everything was changed. Through a hole in the wall, which looked more like a window than a breach, the Spaniards succeeded in entering Prato.[1] They pillaged it, as Brescia had been pillaged, and by their doings filled all Florence with dismay. Rucellai's school made use of the first and greatest confusion. The youths, to the number of thirty, assembled under arms in the grand hall, and shouted at the door of the chamber where the Signori were assembled, that, "they would tolerate the Gonfaloniere no longer." As though they possessed the voice and the power of the people, they rushed forth, and bursting into Soderini's room, with the shout that, "his life should be safe, but that he must follow them," they tore him away with them. They opened the prisons, wherein sat some friends of the Medici, returned, forced from the Signori Soderini's deposition, and, of him himself, flight; and, before ever a treaty was signed, they opened the gates to the Viceroy and Juliano Medici, who was a brother of John.[2] A treaty was hereupon signed, the basis of which was the return of the Medici : between Ferdinand and Florence—and this is the vital point—there should be, in respect of Naples, an alliance for three and a half years, similar to that which had existed with Louis in regard to Milan, and, by virtue of which, the Florentines must, under the Medici, be as Spanish as, under the Popolares, they had been French.[3]

This arranged, Cardona left all internal matters to the Medici. At first, Julian permitted a limited Gonfaloniere, and, following the advice of Rucellai's friends, a council of the Optimates and much liberty. But this was not agreeable to John. Whilst yet outside the walls, he had determined with his followers on a different policy, and, after entering the city, arranged the like with the Condottiere there; when morning broke, both rushed to the palace to the cry of "Palle! Palle!" they first forced the Signori to summon the people to a parliament, and then, by the weak and servile voices

[1] Nardi, 147. Guicciardini, xi. ii. p. 13. Jovius, Leo, p. 53.
[2] The foregoing, and especially Nerli, 110, i.
[3] Document of the treaty in Fabroni, Vita Leonis X., adnot., 266-69.

of this forcibly collected assembly, to commit the supreme power to a Balia of fifty-five men. As soon as they were elected and assembled, a Medici carried the standard before the Signori up the steps of the council house. The fifty-five, together with 200 others whom they had joined with them, formed the Great Council; a council of seventy, and a council of a hundred was formed, following the example of the old Lorenzo. At the discretion of the Medici, new names were placed in the ballot boxes at all elections. Suffice it to say, the supreme power returned again to the Medici, John, Julian, and Lorenzo, Peter's son. The gaoler would often come up to two or three citizens and ask, "about what they were conversing;" among the first discontents and suspects, Macchiavelli was arrested and imprisoned.[1]

Now the Popolares, though thus humbled, were so little suppressed—as is shown by the fact that they afterwards regained their strength and seized the supreme power—that they were only awaiting the arrival of the French to rise again; and thus the Cardinal became bound to the Spanish cause against the French, not only out of gratitude, not only owing to Cardona's alliance, but owing to a constant and perpetual interest. It must be confessed that this part of mid-Italy had now come, beyond all question, into the power of the Austro-Spanish house. Lucca was forced to enter the League. Siena received a garrison of 100 Spanish lancers.[2]

In Mantua, after the Florentine undertaking, Cardona and Lang resolved to rearrange the Milanese and Venetian affairs.

In Milan, they wished to appoint as prince, not the young Maximilian Sforza, who had at length, after an exile of fourteen years in Regensburg[3] and the Netherlands, arrived at man's estate, but the Archduke Charles. This proposal was repeatedly brought before the Swiss during August and September; there should be paid them for their expenses 300,000 ducats and 50,000 ducats yearly

---

[1] Nardi, 156, *sq*. Nerli, 116. Macchiavelli, Lettere famigl., p. 11. Guicciardini, 17.
[2] Zurita, ii. 314.
[3] Order of the Regensburg Council in the Regensburger Chronik., iv.

subvention; for the present, that Sforza was not allowed to return to Italy.¹

The Venetian dispute was to be fought out as soon as the truce expired.² Cardona would not be kept back with his troops, and replied to all objections, that he was captain-general of the League. Brescia, before being taken by the French, had always belonged to Venice; but this did not prevent Cardona from taking this city, in October, 1512.³

How, then, if these plans were successfully carried out, would it then fare with the freedom of Italy, which the Pope thought he had achieved? The affairs of Ferrara compelled him to look to the interests at stake here.

He was not at one with Alfonso d'Este, although the latter had come to Rome for the purpose of coming to an understanding. One day, a page in the palace heard the Pope walking up and down his chamber, hissing between his teeth the words, "This Vulcan," and "Vengeance." Alfonso was called Vulcan, and he was immediately informed of this occurrence.⁴ It is possible that, at that moment, Julius was thinking of the Duke's plots against his life; suffice it, however, to say, that Alfonso, who had just been bidden to a banquet by the Pope, feared for his life if he accepted the invitation. With the aid of Fabrizio Colonna, who in this manner requited him for saving his life in the battle of Ravenna, he succeeded in effecting his escape. As a result of this, however, Cardona and Alfonso again became enemies. The Pope, who was determined to subject Ferrara, needed the Spaniards, as the Swiss had refused their assistance for this purpose.

Yet he did not go so far as to allow them, in return, to carry out their intentions upon Milan; Maximilian Sforza must, after all, be at last installed there; but he allowed them to have their freewill with regard to Venice. On the 25th November, he concluded an alliance with them, according to which the Venetians should leave Verona and Vicenza to the Emperor, retaining Padua and Trevigi in their hand, for an immediate payment of 250,000 ducats

---

¹ Fuch's, 444 (note to new edition). Anshelm, iv. 289.
² Especially Zurita.
³ Paul. Jovius, Vita l'escarœ, 382; and Zurita, ii. 338.
⁴ Curpesanus, Historiæ sui temporis up. Martène, v. 286.

and an annual tribute of 30,000.¹ This alliance promised him assistance against Ferrara.

This arrangement once carried out, and the greater part of Lombardy in the hands of the Emperor and the Spaniards, how could the remainder hold out for any length of time, seeing that the Swiss were venal and the young Sforza very weak, and, moreover, in the hands of Andrea del Burgo and other imperial councillors? Italy, instead of enjoying liberty, would thus come into greater subjection than ever. Were not Julius' intentions themselves praiseworthy? Were not the means he adopted bold and heroic? But all his exertions, instead of tending to the emancipation of Italy, merely enhanced the Austro-Spanish power. For ideal aspirations directed at attaining highest aims are subject to conditions having their own peculiar laws. Human actions are prompted by the first; their success, however, depends upon the second.

Before Julius saw the whole effect of his schemes, though he had an inkling of their issue, his death occurred, which took place in February, 1513.

There is credible evidence of the fact that his dissolution was hastened by anxiety as to the future of Italy.² It was fated that even his decease should further the intentions of the Austro-Spanish house.

Upon whom would it desire to confer the papal dignity, but upon that Cardinal, whom great favours had placed under an obligation, and whom, in consequence of the Florentine events and the danger with which it was threatened by the French and the popular party, it was able to call its own? To this Cardinal were devoted heart and soul as well the younger members of distinguished families in Florence as also the junior cardinals, especially Petrucci of Siena and Sauli of Genoa, for seeing how gentle and easy his nature was, they would share his power and authority. It was, perhaps, his abdominal complaint, for which he was operated in the Conclave itself, and which, in spite of his comparatively youthful years, held out no hope of old age, that contributed to his election; or per-

---

[1] Peter Bembus' Complaints, 310. Paris de Grassis, 125. Paolo Paruta. historia Veneziena, p. 9.
[2] In Bembus. Moreover, Zurita, ii. 336, 338, 341. Passero, 188.

haps his clever friend Bibbiena, who knew the weak
points of all the cardinals and how to make use of them.¹
At last the Cardinal Soderini, his natural enemy, also
gave way, and was followed by all the other cardinals.
He was elected. The people forthwith remembered his
generosity; the poets prophesied that Leo X.—he thus
styled himself out of respect for a dream his mother had
—would, like Numa following Romulus, also follow the
stormy Julius, to crown in times of peace every virtue,
every toil, and every art. His marvellous fortune was
the common theme, how he, but a year previously taken
prisoner at Ravenna, was miraculously liberated from
captivity, and had become lord of Florence and lord of
the world. All the inscriptions to be seen on the day of
his coronation, the anniversary of that battle—the Turkish
horse upon which he had ridden was also there—extolled
the "subduer of fortune." Of the treasure, which Julius
had so carefully hoarded up, 100,000 ducats were thrown
among the people. The cup of joy and hope was over-
flowing.²

For the outset, it was certain that his policy would
further the interests of the Spaniards, and that, among all
their many successes, his election was not the least.

6. *Struggle of the French and Swiss for Milan.*

Between the two great powers of Europe, the French and
the Austro-Spanish, both of which coveted Milan, stood
the Swiss, withholding it from either. They had themselves not merely gained in glory and prestige, but had
also acquired considerable tracts of land in the Milanese
territory. The valleys and defiles through which the Tosa,
Maggia, Osernone, and Malazza, flowing from the Alpine
chain, break their way through the rocky hills, not fruitful
—they supply only stone and men who know how to carry

---

[1] Pio from Carpi to Maximilian, Journal de Conclave, in the Lettres de Louis, iv., p. 72, p. 65. Paris de Grassis in Rainaldus, 133. Vita anonymi, 583.

[2] Poems in Roscoe, ii. 387. Jovius, Fabroni Vita, p. 65.

loads and sweep chimneys—but the highways of nations, had been occupied by them. Moreover, there had passed into their hands the pleasant shores of the Lago Maggiore, so far as they belong to Locarno, and the slope of the mountain chain where it sinks down towards Lake Como, a land full of tropical fruits and cornfields and vineyards: Lucano, Lugano, and Mendrisio, long since devoted to them, had come into their hands. The whole mountain chain from Monte Rosa to the Wormser Joch, with all the passes, for the possession of which nations had so often striven, had now, after passing from Italian into German hands, been brought to own obedience to the Confederation and the allied Cantons, through the instrumentality of the Grey League, which had not only appropriated the Mora and Lira valleys, but Veltlin also, as belonging to the monastery of Chur. Their cattle could now be driven in peace to the market at Varese, and the very first held, brought them extraordinary advantages; wine and corn came up to them from Italy without trouble.

It was now the Pope's care to install Maximilian Sforza as ruler of the rest of the Milanese territory, and this project was welcomed by the voice of the citizens of the capital, once more assembled on the green square before the Duomo;[1] but that it was carried out, was principally due to the staunch attitude of the Swiss. On the 30th December, 1512, he received the key of the capital from the hands of a Zurich citizen, and entered the city. The Swiss, whom he confirmed in the possession of their acquisitions, and promised a present payment of 200,000 ducats, and an annual subvention of 40,000, entered into an alliance with him, promising: "to defend him and his successors in the duchy by force of arms for all time."[2]

What a difference between the innocence of the early fraternities, who only designed defence, and this League, which amounted to an independent entrance into international disputes to defend a foreign land! what a difference between that night on the Rütli and these days, when all the princes of our nations vied with each other for the favour of the peasants! They felt it themselves. Marx Röust often

[1] Fuchs, 439. Arluni, de bello Veneto, 204.
[2] Article from the Act in Fuchs, 478. *Vide* also *ibid.*, 501.

narrated how, when he and the other deputies were sitting in the diet at Baden to cement and seal that League, three heavy blows were struck on the table by invisible hands.[1] There is a legend to the effect, that the three men who concluded the League in Rütli now rest in the Selisberg mountain, and keep watch over their people. To them the blows were attributed. Not only men, but nations also, have a zenith in their power and life; and never were the confederates more powerful than at this moment. In spite of this weird fright, they affixed their seals.

The war was there in a trice. Louis XII., who had always discerned the glory of his reign in the acquisition of Milan, was determined to reconquer it. He had already, in September, 1512, offered the Swiss, through the intervention of Savoy, both peace and alliance. In February, 1513, he made a second attempt. In order only to be able to send his envoys to the confederates, he overcame his scruples, and made over to them the strongholds which he still held in the district they had occupied.[2] But when Trivulzio urgently warned them not to increase the power of their own friends, adding, "That he had been present when proposals had been made to his King, to make common cause with others, and to join in conquering their possessions,"[3] he did not quite hit the mark. It was in no wise in the interest of Austria, but in their own, that they kept Maximilian Sforza at Milan, and this Prince was quite as dependent upon them, through their soldiers and their Cardinal, as he was upon the Emperor, through his councillors. Only a few in all, a son of Jürg uff der Flue, a son of Hetzel of Berne, and some captains from the Stein, gave the French envoys, Trivulzio and Tremouille, an audience on their passage through.

Louis was obliged to cast about for another league and other infantry for his undertaking.

---

[1] Bullinger in Fuchs, 481.
[2] Anshelm, iv. 311 (note to new edition).
[3] Trivulzio to King Louis—Lucerne, 5th February, 1512—in Rosmini, Trivulzio, ii. 209. *Ibid.* Sforza's letters to Stampa (note to new ed.). Anshelm, Berner Chronik., iv. 369.
[4] Gattinara to Margareth in Tremouille's letter; Lettres, iv. 99. Anshelm, iv. 409.

This league he found in the Venetians. Both he and they had again the same enemy to face, viz., the Austro-Spanish House; on the 13th March, 1513, they allied themselves, the King promising to restore Cremona and Ghiara d'Adda.[1] Infantry, bidding the Emperor defiance, came through all parts of the empire, some from Bohemia,[2] some from Suabia, the greater number from Lower Germany, and joined the French. The black troop under Thomas von Mittelburg, consisting of lansquenets, with great broadswords and armour, almost like knights, and were led by the young Fleuranges, who himself carried two standards, across the Meuse through Burgundy to Lyons;[3] other lansquenets were led by his brother, von Jamets. Their father, Robert von der Mark, who had inherited from his uncle William the name of "Boar of the Ardennes"—he had invented for the infantry a fence of iron chains, to rest the arquebuses upon—himself led 100 lancers. In May, the French army, 1,200 lancers and 8,000 foot, began their march across the mountains; on the 12th, it was received in Alessandria, and the Guelphs were all astir in the whole country.[4]

Now it lay in the nature of the interested parties, as well as in the situation, that neither the Spaniards, though with a strong army in the vicinity, and bound by various promises and obligations, bestirred themselves to protect the Duke,[5] nor that the Emperor ever sent the assistance he had promised. The 4,000 Swiss, who were in the country, retired from place to place. When thus the whole country rose up in the revolt—the French from the Castle of Milano again marched through the city as lords and masters—and the 4,000, with their Duke at their head, fled to Novara, the very city where Lodovico had been betrayed, all appeared to be at an end, and Trivulzio boasted that he had the Swiss like molten lead in a spoon.

But, on this occasion, he boasted prematurely. The Swiss

[1] Dumont, iv. 1, 182.
[2] Regensburger Chronik., iv. iii. 192, from the Emperor's letters.
[3] Fleuranges, Mémoires, 110.
[4] Bellay, Mémoires of Petrus Martyr, ep. 524. Morone in Rosmini, ii. 315.
[5] Contradictory correspondence in the Letters, iv. 118, *sq*.

replied to his attempts to persuade them: "With arms should he try them, and not with words." They all followed in this matter the advice of Benedict von Weingarten, a man, according to Anselm,[1] stout, upright, and wise, who, though he unwillingly took the command, led them bravely. The French attacks met with almost more contempt than resistance. The gates of Novara were left open, and the breach holes hung with sheets.[2] Whilst thus the Swiss, by this show of unanimous bravery, wiped out the shame of Novara, of fourteen years before, their confederates of the reserve crossed the mountains; the greater portion, the Waldstadts and Berne, came over the St. Gothard and down by the Lake Maggiore, whilst the smaller contingent, the Zurichers and Churwalden, crossed the little Bernhardin, and descended to the Lake Como.[3] A messenger soon arrived, asking, "Why they hurried? there was no danger," a priest shortly afterwards made the announcement that, "The Duke and all the Swiss had been slain."[4] But they collected, and resolved to find their comrades, dead or alive. Both forces hastened; the nearest road from the St. Gothard was chosen, and, on the 5th July, the greater part of the force had arrived close to Novara.[5]

On the same day, the French raised the siege. On the road to Trecas, Trivulzio selected a rising knoll, called Riotta, which, owing to ditches and marshes, was well suited for defence; they bivouacked here at night, mounted their guns, and intended the following morning to fix their iron palisade. Their good entrenchments emboldened them to await the coming of the 6,000 lansquenets, who, with 500 fresh lances, were already in the Susa valley.[6]

As soon as the Swiss appear in the field, their whole thought is battle. They have neither generals nor plans, nor yet any carefully considered strategy; the god of their

[1] Anshelm, Berner Chronik., iv. 385 (note to new ed.).
[2] Stettler and Anselm in Glutz., 323. Jovius, Historiarum sui temporis, i. 93.
[3] Stettler, Bullinger in Glutz., 315.
[4] Anshelm, iv. 383 (note to new ed.).
[5] Benedictus Jovius, Hist. Novocom., p. 66.
[6] Bouchet, Vie et gestes du cheval de la Tremouille, 184, and Trivulzio's Defence by Rosmini, i. 570.

fathers and St. Urs, their strong arm and the halberd are enough for them, and their bravery shows them the way. Those who had arrived at Novara on the 6th June, refreshed themselves with a draught, an hour's sleep and another draught, and then, without waiting for the Zurichers, they all, both those who had been there and the fresh arrivals, rushed in disorder, like a swarm of bees flying from the hive into the summer sun, as Anselm describes it,[1] through the gates and the breaches into the open. They were almost without guns, entirely without cavalry, and many were without armour; but, all the same, they rushed on the enemy, well entrenched as he was behind good artillery, and upon those knights, "without fear and blame," in full cuirass.

They stood face to face with the enemy; the first rays of the rising sun flashed from their breastplates; they seemed to them like a hill of gleaming steel.

They first attacked the lances and cannon of Robert von der Mark. Here were engaged the smaller body, in whose front ranks stood with their spears the bravest heroes, two Diesbachs, Aerni Winkelried, and Niklaus Conrad, all distinguished for their ancestry or the nobility of virtue;[2] the greater body, almost more by instinct than intention, made in the midst of the smoke and the first effect of the hostile artillery, a detour round a copse;[3] it sought and found the lansquenets. As these latter were reinforced by artillery, the Swiss again separated. Some fought against the black flags;[4] the greater part, however, threw themselves upon the guns. Thus they fought in three distinct places; the first against the knights, who often broke up their own ranks and appeared behind their flags; but they always rallied, and threw back their assailants. The next, 400 men, wielding the halberd in both hands, fought against a company of Fleuranges' black flags, dealing blow for blow, and thrust for thrust; whilst the third and greatest body were engaged with the lansquenets, who, besides cannon, had 800 arquebuses; but soon the rain of

[1] Anshelm, iv. 384 (note to new ed.).
[2] Nicolaus Konrad Hauptmann, Letter to his bailiff; *ibid.* 549.
[3] Captains of Solothurn home; *ibid.* 546.
[4] Fleuranges, Mémoires, 130, *sq.*

bullets ceased; only the clash of swords and the crash of pikes was audible. At length the flags of the lansquenets sank; their leaders were buried under a heap of slain; their cannon were lost, and employed against them.[1] Meanwhile the Blacks also gave way. Robert von der Mark looked about him; he saw his foot soldiery and his sons lost; in order to save these, he also retreated. He found them among the dead, among the victors, bleeding still from wounds, and rescued them.[2] In vain did Trivulzio appeal to St. Catherine and St. Mark; he, too, as well as Tremouille, who was wounded, was forced to retire.[3] The Swiss gave no quarter to the fugitives whom they overtook; they then returned, ordered their ranks for prayer, and knelt down to give thanks to God and their saints. They next set about dividing the spoil and burying the dead.[4]

It was the second hour in the morning, when the tidings of the issue of the battle reached Milan. The French, who, in anticipation of victory, had left the castle, immediately fled; some back thither, others to the churches and their friend's palaces; the Ghibelline faction at once rose, and city and country returned to their allegiance to Maximilian Sforza. The Swiss undertook to chastise those who had revolted. They compelled the Astesans who had left their houses to pay 100,000 ducats, Savoy, which had gone over to the enemy, 50,000, and Montferrat, which had insulted their ambassador, 100,000. This event enabled the Spaniards to hold their heads high. In Genoa, they restored the Fregosi, who had been expelled for twenty-one days, and Ottaviano among them; they reconquered Bergamo, Brescia, and Peschiera, which also had revolted.[5]

After this victory, the Swiss enjoyed far greater power in Milan than ever before. "What you have restored by your blood and your strength," wrote Maximilian Sforza, "shall belong for the future as much to you as to me," and these

[1] The foregoing and Paulus Jovius, Historiæ, s. t. i. 97. Carpesanus, 1291.
[2] Bellay, Mémoires, 4. Guicciardini, xi, 45.
[3] Rosmini, from Prato MS., and from " Un rozzo poema," i. 474.
[4] Anshelm, iv. 385 (note to new ed.).
[5] Stettler, Jovii Historiæ, 93. Vita Pescaræ, 285. Passero, 197, in detail.

were not empty words. The Swiss perceived that they were strong enough to attempt other achievements. "If we could only reckon upon obedience in our men," they were heard to say, "we would march through the whole of France, long and broad as it is."[1]

A General War Movement.

Two great combinations confronted each other: the Emperor, the Pope, Spain, England and Switzerland on the one side, and France, Venice, and Scotland on the other. The first group seemed to have in view an immediate attack upon France. Affairs in France, under Louis XII., developed in a similar way as under Charles VIII. The commencement, in both cases, rapid conquest; the turning point, a quarrel with the Pope; then a League; the final result, a loss of the conquests, and a jeopardising of the French position itself.

But as, on this occasion, all the factors were greater, the French exertions stronger, the Pope's enmity more violent and the achievements of the League in Italy more brilliant, it followed that the attack upon France, which at present was more supported by Maximilian's guidance than by his actual forces, was proportionately important and dangerous.

Julius, who on the 3rd of December, 1512, in his Council of 120 fathers, had pronounced the interdict against France, had prepared him for the coming storm. Ferdinand advised the taking of Burgundy, Normandy, and Guyenne from the French;[2] Maximilian and Henry VIII. also urged this course, as they had long-standing claims to these lands; the Swiss also agreed, in the hope of establishing their duke in Milan. The new Pope Leo was on account of the still prevailing schism obliged to cleave to the way of his predecessor. As a fact, in April, 1513, a general attack upon France from all four sides,

---

[1] Sforza's letter of 6th June in Glutz, appendix, 545. May in Glutz, 329.

[2] Paris de Gr. in Rainald. 126. Zurita, ii. 333.

the English, German, Italian, and Spanish, was determined upon in a formal alliance.[1]

But this scheme was not capable of being carried out on this scale, as the Venetians continued to side with the French, so that the arms of the league had also to be turned against them, added to which, Ferdinand never would have war on his frontier. Pursuing his tactics of 1497 and 1503, he concluded an unexpected truce for his frontier territory.[2] It thus came about, that the Spanish and Italian attack, that is Ferdinand's and Leo's armies, turned against Venice, whilst the attack upon France could only be left to the Swiss, who acted for the Germans, and to the English. Herein Maximilian showed himself once more very energetic and influential. He himself had, it is true, placed no large army in the field, but he had his hand in all the operations and was not slow to display his qualities of generalship.

On the 1st of August, 1513, the Spanish under Cardona, and 200 heavy and 2,000 light cavalry of the Pope, under Prospero Colonna, were arrayed before Padua against the Venetians. But the greatest strength of this force probably consisted in the Suabian and Tyrolese company, which the Emperor had sent them, under the command of the Count von Lupfen, and the captains, Frundsberg, Rogendorf, Landau, and Lichstenstein, who had been tried and proved in this war.[3]

On the same 1st of August, the Swiss promised him to make an attack upon Burgundy. In the Confederation, an extensive revolt of the peasants against the cities had just completely ruined the French party, and had even forced the Bernese to depose three new and two old magistrates, who were suspected of French leanings. This made the Emperor all the more certain of them; he promised them assistance, without which they could not undertake the expedition, artillery, horse and some money.[4]

At the beginning of August, the King of England joined

[1] Appunctuamentum of 5th April in Rymer, Fœdera, vi. i. 92.
[2] Zurita, ii. 352. Jacob de Bannissis, Lettres, iv. 114.
[3] Jean le Veau, Lettres, iv. 200. Ehrenspiegel, 1303. Reisner, Kriegsthaten, 16.
[4] Glutz., 332-340. From the Abschied of 1st of August, p. 343.

his army, which, since the 22nd of July, had been engaged in besieging Terouanne. This was, beyond doubt, the most important operation; it drew the attention of all eyes to it. The English were still quite the same in character as ever, not celebrating St. Martin's day because he was the patron saint of their enemies, calling the painted man, used for a mark at their bow-practice, "the Frenchman," and saying to their children: "hit the Frenchman in the heart;"[1] they had gladly offered themselves to the comites and vice-comites of their counties, both within and without their respective liberties, for selection for military service; they were mainly armed with bows and crossbows, leaden clubs and halberds; they arranged their march so that they could always barricade themselves at once behind their waggons, for they only cared to fight behind a strong position. Their King came with them, a true Lancaster that he was. Before setting out, almost in imitation of Henry V., he caused the last York who was in his power, Edmund Suffolk, to be put to death. He then took with him Charles Brandon, son of that Brandon who had carried the standard of Henry VII. in the battle of Bosworth Field, once the playmate and companion of his youth, a short time since created Viscount Lisle. In his suite were also Charles Somerset, all of whose ancestors had lived and died for the house of Lancaster, George Talbot, of the blood of the last hero in the struggle of the Lancasters against France, and many others whose names are connected with the same events.[2] The fame of his generosity, for exercising which his father's wealth furnished him the means, allured the knights and soldiery of Brabant, Hennegau, and Flanders, and even far into Germany, so much to him, that many sold all they possessed in order, well accoutred and equipped, to earn greater pay under him. He had splendid cannon, and amongst them probably those twelve large pieces of ordnance, called the twelve apostles, cast for him in the Netherlands.[3]

[1] Herbert, Life of Henry, 32. Hubert Thomas Leodius, Vita Frederici Palatini, 33.
[2] Martin du Bellay, Mémoires, 6. Goodwinus, p. 16. Herbert, p. 33.
[3] Marguerite à Henry, in December, 1513, in the Lettres, iv. 217. Hubert Leodius, iii. 1.

And in order to inspire as much confidence as the Swiss and the Spanish forces did, his army needed nothing further than an experienced general. Henry VIII., on begging the Emperor to lend him, for this purpose, the Duke Heinrich, the warrior of Brunswick, or the Marshal Vergy, the Emperor himself offered to lead the army of his friend.[1] He hoped with it to gain in open battle the bank of the Somme and, with the assistance of the Swiss, Burgundy, whereupon the two princes would unite and visit the French with a campaign, which would be as disastrous for them as ever an English war had been. On the 9th of August, he met the king near Aire. He himself wore Henry's red cross and the union rose; he was not annoyed that his two hundred horse, whose whole adornment lay in their golden chains, appeared insignificant in comparison with the brilliant accoutrements of the Royals, or that his servants stooped down to pick up the silver bells, which Henry's noble pages let purposely fall from their horses' trappings; he accepted from the king a tent, gorgeously fitted up inside with silk hangings, gilded trelliswork and golden vessels, and, if Bellay is to be trusted, 100 escus a day for his table, and came into his camp.[2]

Thirty-four years before, Maximilian had besieged the same town, and, on that occasion, gained his most brilliant victory over the French, who had come across the Lis to relieve it. Mindful of this former success—for on this occasion, also, Terouanne was only being besieged from one side—after having reconnoitred the camp and the walls with his master of the ordnance, he threw five bridges across the river. His luck would have it, that on the very same day that they crossed (17th August), the enemy, about eight thousand strong, made his appearance before him on the heights of Guinegat, descended, halted at the foot of the hill, and sent out light troops with provisions for the town. A simultaneous attack was planned by both the besieged and their friends outside upon both parts of the English camp. Thereupon Maximilian, sending his infantry to a brook in the rear of the enemy's

---

[1] Letters of Maximilian, first in June, iv. 157, and frequently.
[2] Paul Armestorf to Margreth in the Lettres, iv. 192. Ehrenspiegel, 1297 *sq.* Goodwin, 20. Herbert, 35.

camp, threw himself with 2,000 horse upon the advancing squadrons. These forthwith galloped back to their camp.[1] Here—it was four o'clock in the afternoon, and the knights had been in the saddle since two in the morning—many had exchanged their chargers for lighter horses, had thrown off their helmets, and were refreshing themselves with a draught. All at once, a general confusion and stampede ensued; the fugitives, coming from the one side, brought the news that "the enemy was at their heels," and dashed wildly on without stopping, and from the other side, came the tidings that the enemy's infantry was falling upon their rear. In vain the shout was raised of "Turn about, *Hommes d'Armes!*" Maximilian's flying artillery swept them before it; and this day was known hereafter by the name of the battle of the Spurs. And when at last, the bravest of them rallied on the bridge over the brook we have referred to, it was only to their destruction; the Burgundian cavalry found another way across the brook and cut them off. They were all obliged to surrender, one here and another there; La Palice, the Duke of Longueville, and a hundred others, all the flower of the army. Bayard, perceiving one of the enemy's knights all alone and careless, for the victory was theirs, rushed upon him sword in hand and cried, " Surrender to me, or thou art a dead man." The knight was wounded and surrendered himself. " But who art thou?" he asked. " I am Bayard, and surrender myself to thee again." Both the other attacks were likewise repulsed, and on the 22nd of August the town surrendered.[2]

At the same time—the 27th of August—the Swiss, about 30,000 men strong, united with the horse of Wurtemberg and Burgundy under Duke Ulrich and Vergy; they received the Emperor's siege guns from Landau, his

---

[1] Baptiste de Taxis in the Lettres, iv. 195. Polydorus, 27, 24. Herbert, Weiskunig, 303.

[2] Bellay, Mémoires, 6. Bayard, 345-350. Fleuranges, p. 145. Embellished in Jovius, 100. Heuterus, Birken. (Note to 2nd Ed.) A letter of an eye-witness in Brewer shows us the characteristic trait of Maximilian, that, though entreated to do so, he did not unfurl his standard, but declared his intention of fighting under the standard of St. George and the King of England. Thus the English ascribe the victory to their King. (Brewer, i. No. 4431.)

mortars from Breisach, his field cannon from Ensisheim, and a hundred arquebuses. Their captain had only power to make peace, in the event that the King would renounce all rights to Milan. On their march, they heard the news of the Emperor's victory. With all the greater courage they crossed the French frontier.[1]

This double attack could not but throw the French into great anxiety. Even before the English had arrived, Louis had found himself obliged to confess to the Court of Parliament that his pecuniary needs were so pressing, and his finances so much in arrear, that he must sell his demesnes to raise 400,000 livres, in order, without over-burdening his poor people, to resist the old enemies of his realm.[2] After the battle of Guinegat, he despatched his marshal to Paris in order to review the tradesmen and artizans. Once more, after a long pause, the banners of the trades unions were seen flying in the streets of the capital, and the same was probably the case in many other cities. The arrival of the Swiss horror-struck every soul. A murmur of despondency went through the whole nation; "the retribution for their misdeeds in Italy was now about to break over their heads."[3] In this crisis, France looked with a certain confidence to its old alliance with the Scotch.

It was the lot of King James IV., who once had been desirous of negotiating peace between the Pope and Louis, with a view of an expedition to Jerusalem, to be drawn into the whirlpool of this war. After a long peace, differences again arose with England, which threatened to end in a fresh breach. One of the chief disputes affected Andrew Barton. Barton was a bold pirate, who had also served King John of Denmark, James' nearest friend, against the Hanseatic League.[4] James had delivered to him letters of marque against the Portuguese, who had killed Barton's father; but he—as the Portuguese, English, and the Hanseatic League appear to have been united in a

[1] Solothurn and Zurich, captains, in Glutz., 345. Stettler.
[2] Garnier from the Parliamentary Records, MS. from Fontanieu, p. 470.
[3] Monstrelet, App. 246. Gilles, 124.
[4] Anonymi chronologia rerum Danicarum in Ludewig Reliq. MSS. ix. 52.

long-standing maritime alliance—employed them against the English also; for this he was sought for by the latter, and, in spite of a resistance, which has been immortalized even by his enemies in a long ballad, was at length killed.[1] James was still smarting from indignation at this, when he was implored by Queen Anna of France, his "lady" of chivalry, to come to her assistance: "for Henry's crossing to Calais threatened both her and Brittany." The King assembled his barons, in whom their many tournaments had awakened thirst for a real fray, and who were not a little influenced by the entreaties of the French ambassador, who, moreover, offered them 50,000 livres for their equipment. Having arranged matters with his nobles, James sent his herald, Lyon, to Terouanne to summon his neighbour to return, and when this had no effect—Henry reminded him of the fate of Navarre—he equipped himself in Edinburgh with 50,000 men.[2] The complicated situation became thus more complicated. From such a vigorous attack there could not but be expected some degree of success in England, which would oblige Henry to return to his realm. It would then be possible for the French, perhaps by an attack upon Italy, to compel the Swiss to retire, and at the same time to encourage the Venetians.

As soon as James crossed the Tweed, the shout of battle rang from village to village, and from town to town. Henry, who, in order to be more certain of the loyalty of his frontier provinces, had not compelled them to pay his benevolence, had entrusted them to the keeping of the Earl of Surrey, a scion of the famous house of the Howards. Round him the nobles gathered at Alnwick; his son, an admiral of the kingdom, landed in Newcastle with 5,000 men; the northern and southern shires all sent their contingents. James rested six days in Norham, and dallied for a while with Lady Ford; he was delighted to see the enemy assembling; for it was for battle that he had come: "he would fight," he said, "even though 100,000 English were arrayed against him." Thus minded, he entrenched himself upon the hill of Flodden, situated

[1] Goodwinus, Annales, p. 11.
[2] Buchananus, Rerum Scoticarum, l. xiii. p. 172 *sq*. Herbert.

between the river Till, where it flows at the foot of the Cheviots between high banks, and a swamp.

No less enthusiastic for the fray were the English; on Sunday, the 4th of September, they sent their herald Rougecroix up to the King, asking, "whether it was his intention to remain so long in England that they could fight on the ensuing Friday?" The King replied: "Were I in Edinburgh, I would haste to be there by that day." But was it likely that the English would attack him behind his entrenchments? In vain they begged of him to come down upon the plain of Milfield, which lay between them.[1] But when he saw that, following a report which had been spread, they made a detour, as though to invade Scotland—it was the 9th of September, and a Friday—he actually broke up his camp, burnt his tents, and, under cover of the smoke, marched, in order to anticipate them, along the heights, to a hill called Piperd. Here he halted. Towards the same place, through the low ground, came the English, and here the battle began.

Thomas Howard, who had killed Andrew Barton, stood, in order to answer for his conduct, as he said, in the very first line, and fought magnificently. Like valiantly, in another part, did James fight in the front ranks, and repeatedly threw back the enemy's standards. Now the one side, and now again the other, retired. But at last, owing to the English arrows hitting better up the hill than the Scotch guns did down, for they fired too high, the Scotch abandoned the offensive, and formed a square for defence; their king was here also to be seen fighting heroically. Whilst they were still fighting, and the flower of both armies falling, the night supervened. In this night, the Scotch sought their king, and found him not. Had he fallen, had he fled, or was he a prisoner? They retreated. The English, on visiting the battle-field the following morning, saw the guns abandoned, and knew that they were victorious. They found a dead body in royal dress, and brought it in triumph to Berwick. The Scotch maintained that, "it was Elphinstone, who on that

[1] Expostulations of the Earls, and answer in very words, in Herbert, 39.

day had worn royal apparel, in order to deceive the English; their king had been seen across the Tweed." But they themselves could not show him anywhere. Some said: " Alexander Hume, whose company alone remained almost intact, and who thereafter insulted both churches and monasteries, must have killed him ;" others, again, "that he had gone to Jerusalem to do penance for his sins;" the English accounts merely mention that King James IV. died in defending his banner.[1] The issue of this conflict upon the British isles was even more important than the events on the Continent. Henry VIII., whilst fighting against France, became master of Scotland.

Besides 8,000 others, twelve earls and seventeen barons fell in the battle. Margaret, Henry VIII.'s sister, had undertaken the government of the realm. The French, who could no longer avail themselves of the Scotch aid, had to fear the worst from the English and Swiss. On that fatal 9th of September, 30,000 Swiss crossed the Tille, which falls into the Saône, and formed three camps before the walls of Dijon. The fourth was formed by the Emperor's cavalry and artillery. On the self-same day, both Emperor and King were still at Terouanne, and were capable of making an inroad any day into French territory.

But on this occasion, France was not doomed to fresh devastation, and was saved. If it be asked how it came about, we may answer, that the turning point was their temporary yielding to the Swiss. Tremouille, on seeing his citadel at Dijon wrecked by bombardment, France undefended, and the Swiss ready for further operations, attempted to make arrangements with them, first through an agent, then by appearing in person, and finally through confidential persons, who went in and out of the camp at dusk.[2] To save France, he thought it to be the best policy to give up Milan. On the 13th of September, he had arranged terms of peace with them, according to which the

---

[1] Buchananus, Rerum Scoticarum, vol. xiii. p. 251-255. Goodwinus, p. 29. Especially Herbert. Polydorus, xxvii. p. 28. Jovius, Historiæ sui temporis, i. 102-106 (note to new ed.). Ruthal's English report to Wolsey : " The King fell near his banner," Brewer, i. 4461.

[2] Anshelm, iv. 470. (Note to new ed.)

King renounced his claims to Milan, Asti, and Cremona, paying the Swiss, moreover, 400,000 escus.[1] This is what they desired.[2] What did the conquest of Burgundy for the house of Austria interest them; besides, they had never bound themselves to assist in such conquest? Only it was a great mistake on their part to return home, without obtaining any security, or the King's word, for their peace. Meanwhile, the English also resolved to turn back within sight of the French frontier, which they were actually threatening, their object being to reduce a semi-free city, which lay at a distance from the sea. It is not very credible that this was done with the advice of Maximilian, who was especially interested in invading France, and we find, as a matter of fact, that immediately after this occurrence, he separated himself from Henry in a sort of quarrel.[3] Perhaps the latter was influenced by the example of Edward III., who had besieged this city at the beginning of his French campaigns; but the chief point, beyond all doubt, was, that he conceived this to be the easiest and most permanent conquest. For he had razed Terouanne to the ground, in answer to the entreaties of the Council of Flanders.

Suffice it to say, that, on the 15th—and it is impossible to know how far this is connected with the Swiss retreat—he made his appearance before the walls of Tournay, and, on the 23rd, he entered the city in his assumed quality of King of France.[4] This city of Tournay, which really belonged to the province of Flanders, had relations to the Crown of France similar to those subsisting between the German free cities and the Emperor. Henry likewise confirmed its liberties; but he did 'not suffer these liberties to prevent his building a castle there. And here his campaign ended. In his delight, that though he had not destroyed France, he had yet succeeded in his attack

[1] Bouchet, la Tremouille, 191-199. Ehrenspiegel, 1301. Especially Stettler (note to new ed.). Anshelm, iv. 471. In Glutz., p. 549, there is an extract from the document, which is preserved in the archives at Zurich.
[2] Jean le Veau, Lettres, iv. 192.
[3] Herbert, 36.
[4] (Note to new ed.) In Brewer, p. 676, de l'entrée du roi Henri comme roi de France et d'Angleterre.

upon her, and in taking two strongholds, he was amusing himself at Margaret's Court at Lille, or in his royal camp at Tournay with tournaments,[1] when the tidings reached him of the Venetian operations, operations to which we must turn our eyes; for the event, though a single one, was accomplished in various places.

In August, Cardona had left the walls of Padua behind him, resolved to compel the Venetians to accept his proffered peace. The Germans, Italians, and Spanish with him, had penetrated into Venetian territory beyond Bachiglione and Brenta as far as Mestre, in order, as they said, to see what the Venetians had reaped. The country people once more fled to the marshes by the sea; the inhabitants of Padua and Venice could plainly see the fine country houses on the shore one after the other in flames. Cardona rode up to the tower of Marghera, whence the streets and quarters of Venice were clearly discernible. From here George Frundsberg could not restrain himself from discharging a piece of ordnance against the city itself.[2]

To this pitch matters were allowed to come, before Alviano received permission to march out. What the allies had formerly desired, now that they had advanced so far, and were surrounded by rivers and difficult passes, turned out to be a source of no little peril to them. The discovery of a ford enabled them to escape across the Brenta; but, on the Bachiglione, when Alviano was posted in the pass of Olmo before them, Manfrone stationed in their rear on the road by which they had come, and when the peasants with their muskets crowned the heights on both sides of the defile, whilst they through the whole night had to shelter themselves behind the trunks of trees, they appeared to be lost, spoils and all. Alviano said that: "he had the remainder of the barbarian brutes between his scissors, and needed only now to close them." The next morning, the Imperials having retired a short distance to an open plain near Creazzo, he sent his flying artillery to the front, and made after them. An action took place. The Spaniards fought with desperate valour; Pescara

[1] Lodov. Guicciardini. Descriptio Belgii. Herbert.
[2] Specially Ehrenspiegel, 1304, and Carpesanus, 1293, Mocenicus, v. 110. Passero, 202. Reisner.

cried to his men: "If I die, let me not be trampled upon by the enemy," and led them, all athirst for the fray, against the enemy's centre. The Germans were protected by the strength of their arms: Frundsberg, who was in the front line, plied his sword right vigorously, and, taking breath like a woodman in a forest felling an oak, struck again and again. All fought in the certainty that they must either conquer, or die covered with disgrace; the Papal horse took Alviano's banner; the Venetian army was completely routed, and those who but just before thought themselves as good as lost, became all at once masters of the land.[1]

Such was the result of the attack upon Venice. This took place on the 7th October, 1513. About the same time, the Emperor, with Frangipani's help—more by treason than force of arms—contrived to effect the conquest of Marano, a Venetian city with a splendid commercial situation. Everywhere the League was in advantage. Three battles had been won, the Scotch nobility in great measure annihilated, and Venice so far humbled as to be compelled to accept the Pope, only just before its deadly enemy, as arbiter of its fortune; Milan, by a fourth great battle, and a peace, which only needed ratification, as well as by the actual occupation of the remaining strongholds, had been wrested from the French. Yet France as yet had only been attacked on her frontiers, and was not yet vanquished in the interior. To this end the next campaign was destined to lead. On the 17th October, 1513, it was agreed at Lille to begin the campaign of the ensuing year with three attacks upon France; from the German, English, and Spanish side, simultaneously.[2]

---

[1] Jovius, Historiæ, 111-114. Vita Pescaræ, 287. Paruta, 47-56. Guicciardini, ii. p. 55. Zurita, ii. 372.

[2] Herbert, 41 (note to new ed.). In Brewer, i. 4511, is to be found another extract from this compact, which displays some deviations, but which is yet even incomplete. According to it, Ferdinand pledged himself in express terms to surrender Guyenne to Henry VIII. "He shall give up his conquests to England." Moreover, both fleets were to be at sea before April: "Each power to send a fleet to sea before the end of April." No mention is therein made of the agreement, which we hear of in Margaret's letter. The records prove that the arrangement with Maximilian had been already concluded on the 16th of October; on the

Henry promised to procure from his parliament the assurance that, in the event of his dying without issue, the crown of England should pass to the Archduke Charles of Austria, who in the ensuing May was to wed his sister Maria.[1]

8. *Further schemes to ensure the enhancement of the Austro-Spanish House.*

In this perilous crisis, Louis XII. also felt himself obliged to approach the victor. He would not forego his claims to Milan, but he mooted another plan, which would be advantageous to the House of Austria.

One month after the treaty of Lille, on the 16th November, 1513, Louis XII. declared before lawyers that, "He did give and make over the Duchy of Milan to his younger daughter Renata, without revocation, without any exception."[2] It was soon seen what his object was in doing so. On the 1st December, he concluded a treaty with Ferdinand: "the same Renata should be married to one of Ferdinand's grandsons, who should then receive Milan, which should be taken from the Swiss." Ferdinand hoped by this marriage to unite the Guelphs and Ghibellines in Milan, as he had once, in Naples, succeeded in doing with the Anjous and Aragons.[3] In deep secrecy he despatched an envoy to Milan, to represent to the Duke Sforza how badly he was situated under the power of the Swiss, and, if possible, to detach him from their alliance.[4]

Anna of Bretagne, the old friend of the House of Austria, desiring to see her younger daughter well married, was the prime negotiator of these terms of alliance. When, on the

15th November it was confirmed by the Emperor. By it the Emperor also pledged himself to join in the attack upon France, for which purpose he promised to keep a certain number of troops in reserve in Artois and Hennegau. The marriage of Charles and Maria is therein mentioned with the greatest certainty. (Brewer, i. No. 4560). Some particulars have been modified thereby, but the main points remain the same.

[1] Margaret to Henry VIII. Lettres, iv. 239.
[2] Donatio de ducatu Mediolani, etc., in Dumont, iv. 1, 177.
[3] Treaty of Blois, in Dumont, 178.
[4] Fragment d'une lettre, in the Lettres de Louis, iv. 250.

2nd January, 1514, she died, one might have supposed that this incipient union would dissolve and disappear. But, on the contrary, this very occurrence gave it fresh life. For, as Louis still wished to have an heir of his body, he did not reject the proposal that he should take to wife Eleanor, the eldest of Ferdinand's grandchildren, and should enter into an hereditary league with the Austro-Spanish House. This done, Navarre also should remain to Castile. Fray Bernaldo de Trinopoli, a Dominican, remained behind for the negotiations, which lasted a considerable time.[1] Quintana, Almazan's confidant, was seen in February, 1514, to journey from Burgos to Blois, and from Blois to Innsbruck; on the 11th of March, he was for a long time closeted with King Louis; on the 12th, the King's council assembled once again, and finally, on the 13th, new treaties were signed. But the Great League had not as yet been arranged, but only a truce, to which, however, as Quintana assured, the Emperor, in Henry's name as well as his own, was a party, and in which, although Sforza was no party to it, Louis promised not to attack Milan.[2]

This truce was destined to lead to the grand alliance, and to universal peace. It can readily be perceived that this was in no wise in harmony with the compact of Lille, not merely, in that the war, then resolved on, lost its whole *raison d'être*, but, also, in that the prospective marriage of Charles with the English princess became very doubtful; for it was the interest of the House of Austria that the other of Maximilian's grandsons should be kept for the matrimonial alliance with Hungary, which, as the heir to the throne was a weakling, had every prospect of continuing the succession. But, on that account, no hostility was feared from Henry, who had moreover taken no steps, as yet, to obtain the sanction of his parliament: " he was Ferdinand's son-in-law; Maximilian, too, who had come into his camp, had shown him the greatest confidence that one man could show another. He would, accordingly, accept the truce, if he only did not hear of it too soon."

[1] Zurita, ii. 383.
[2] Treaty in Dumont, 179. Gattinara and Veau. Letters in the Lettres of March, iv. 289, 292, *sq.*

With the greatest secrecy then—the Spanish ambassador insisted that not even the King's daughter should be informed of it—the grand league was at length to be established.[1] In a contemporaneous French manuscript, the original draft of the league has been found: "Eleanor to marry Louis; Renata, the second grandson of the Emperor; Milan and Genoa to be delivered over into Ferdinand's hands, in favour of the two above-named; Louis to lay claim neither to Naples nor yet to the money he was to receive thence, and not to support Navarre; the Swiss to be jointly driven back within their borders. In return for this Tournay to be restored to France."[2] It almost looks as though Ferdinand, among other things, was bent upon preventing a new Philip rising up in the person of Charles. In any case, all this was admirably arranged for the enhancement of his house: on the 12th of August, he sent to Bernaldo de Trinopoli the authorization to arrange these marriages and to conclude this league.

In these days, the prestige of the Austro-Spanish house in Italy, Germany, and the whole of Europe, was greater than it had ever been. In May, 1514, Ferdinand concluded with Genoa a league, which has been the basis of all the later relations between the Genoese and the Kings of Spain, being almost those of vassal and suzerain.[3] They already began to anticipate how frightened Max Sforza would be, and how, under the pressure of his officials, who were quite devoted to the Emperor, he would surrender his citadels and his peoples in favour of the latter's grandson. The Swiss could be compensated with money.[4] Venice, that could not even retake Marano, was not a little weakened by a fresh disaster;[5] a conflagration, breaking out in the linen warehouses on the Rialto, spread on both sides the canal, and in one day and night destroyed property to the value of two millions. Leo was in alliance with this house; Naples was completely subservient. Thus much for Italy. In Switzerland, the people had ever risen afresh against the

---

[1] Gattinara to Marguerite, Lettres de Louis IV., 369, 371.
[2] Garnier, from the MSS. of Bethune, p. 509.
[3] Senarega, at end. Zurita, ii. 379.
[4] Francesco Vettori, in Macchiavelli, lettere famigl., p. 16.
[5] Guicciardini, ii. 69. Jovius, Historiæ, 115. Paruta, 45.

French faction, so that it appeared as if a King of France would never again be able to avail himself of their services. In Lucerne, six suspects were committed to prison, and two, who were found guilty, put to death. The country people of Baden seized the old Caspar Hetel, whose son had gone over to the French, and, paying no heed to the fact that his son had acted against his wishes, tortured and beheaded him.[1] "Hans Rudolf," the mother wrote to her son, "thou hast not acted as an honourable man, thou hast put thy father to death: never shalt thou again address thy mother: I will never own thee more as my son."[2] This conflict penetrated into the inmost secrets of filial love and affection; it redounded to the advantage of Spain and Austria over France; in the next following Swiss diets, there was no one to be found who would speak French. In Germany, the election of a bishop, even where the chapter was unfavourable to the candidate,[3] only cost the Emperor a word. For instance, a second Albrecht of the house of Brandenburg, that had always been devoted to the Austrian house, and from which, but shortly before this, another Albrecht had been appointed from the imperial camp in Padua to the office of Grandmaster in Prussia, received the Archbishoprics of Magdeburg and Mayence. A great tumult in Wurtemberg ended in the Estates advising their Duke to live rather at the Emperor's Court, or at all events, never to sever himself from Austria.[4] In Regensburg, that had long resisted an imperial administrator, there arrived at the commencement of the year 1514, Wolf von Wolfstall and the other Imperial Commissioners. Many of their opponents, "famous masters in their respective arts, old, honourable men with white hair," as the chronicles say, paid the penalty with their lives. Others were expelled and their wives sent after them. The Imperial Commissioners appointed a new council and made a new constitution at their discretion.[5] They boasted that the Emperor had, in the previous year, made a similar

[1] Letter of the father to the son, in Anshelm, iv. 410 (note to new ed.).
[2] Correspondence of the mother and son, in Stettler, 501.
[3] Hubert Thomas Leodius, Vita Frederici Palat., iii.
[4] Sattler, Württembergische Geschichte, etc., i. 180.
[5] Die Regensburgische Chronik., vol. iv. 3d part, 234-245.

example of more than one city.[1] At the same time, in the interest of Austria, George of Saxony vanquished the Frisians in the west, whilst in the east, Henry of Brunswick, the martial hero, overcame the Budjadins, and both united triumphed over Etzard Cirksena, Count of East Frisia, whom the Emperor had placed under his ban as being his enemy, for having supported these peoples. The Budjadins were undone by the winter of this year, which continued from October, 1513, to February, 1514, with such severity, that all their springs were frozen hard, so that the peasants for a long period counted their years from this great frost, and "Oevelgunne" was raised up over them. Etzard, in April of this year, offered George fealty in respect of East Frisia, and tribute for Gröningen and Ommeland. But this did not content George. In July, he devastated Damm with great cruelty. Gröningen was inclined for immediate submission. Etzard saw his enemy marauding as far as the gates of Emden.[2]

Among other motives, this great good fortune may have induced Christian II. of Denmark to sue for the hand of Isabella, Maximilian's second granddaughter. His father John had, in the year 1511, pledged himself to aid the French. After his death he also was prepared to support the Scots.[3] But he now severed himself from the Franco-Scottish alliance. In April, 1514, the matter was settled, and Christian promised to side with the Order of Prussia on behalf of the Empire, and to resist the pretensions of Sigismund of Poland.[4] In June, 1514, Maximilian's third granddaughter, Maria, journeyed through the Empire in order to wed Louis, the heir to the throne of Hungary.[5]

We see the position of affairs in Europe, how that the French had not merely lost Italy, but that their party had almost in every place either perished or become Spanish, and how the two great combinations threatened to merge into one, and Louis XII. was himself on the point of becoming a member of the Austro-Spanish family.

[1] Proclamation of the Commissioners, *ibid.*, p. 238
[2] Chytraci Chronicon Saxonicum, p. 207.
[3] Gebhardi, Geschichte von Danemark und Norwegen, ii. 55.
[4] Marguerite à l'Empereur, Lettres, iv. 325.
[5] Regensburgische Chronik., vol. iv. part 3, p. 243.

In July and August, it looked as though the Spanish monarchy would one day embrace the whole of Europe. At the same time, the same house was further advantaged by the second chief discovery in America. In September, 1513, that Nuñez Balbao, who had founded Veragua, sailed from Daria to find the South Sea. After much toil and exertion, outstripping his comrades, he climbed the peak of a high mountain and saw, first of all our races, before him the great ocean that separates both continents of the earth. He made a monument of stones and took possession of the mountain; he proceeded down the coast, called his notaries to him, and took possession of the sea for Ferdinand the Catholic. The Cazikan, who had shown him the way, he baptized, and gave him the name of his prince Charles, the heir to all this power in Europe and America.[1]

Concluding words to the new (second edition).

The narrative breaks off at the very moment of the crisis. A combination of dynasties and empires looms before us, a combination seemingly destined to combine the nations of Latin and Teutonic origin in a unity such as has never existed, and which certainly would have had a baneful influence upon their development. We perceive, at the very first glance, that the realization of such a scheme was confronted by the greatest difficulties; for both nations and countries were yet engaged in their own peculiar impulses and were represented therein by their several dynasties. To combine all these into one political system would in itself have been an utter impossibility. The idea of such a possibility was nothing but an expression of that defeat, which the most powerful nation of all, the French, had just suffered.

All had resulted from this, that the ever chivalrous France, superior in power to all other states, attempted, on the strength of old dynastic claims, to conquer Naples and

[1] Sommario dell' Indie Occidentali del S. D. Pietro Martyre, in Ramusio, Viaggi, 29.

Milan. As a rule, it has only been said that Italy would have been utterly ruined; but at the same time it is indisputable that such a conquest would have imperilled the independent development of Europe. But it happened that, through the dynastic union of Austrian Burgundy and Spain, in the struggles and vicissitudes I have here depicted, an opposing force arose which maintained the balance of power in Europe.

The generation whose acts and struggles have led to this result belongs, from an historical point of view, to the most remarkable that have ever existed; its political work was the founding of an European system of states; it brought the most heterogeneous elements of the north and south into a combination, wherein the unity of the Latino-Teutonic nations became more than ever conspicuous.

But such a state of things could not last, in the face of the ascendancy which the house of Austria had attained to, in the years 1513 and 1514. The life of Europe consists in the energy of great contrasts. In the year 1515, the most chivalrous of the French kings again began the struggle with brilliant success. But that at the same time serves to bring the Austro-Spanish combination to full reality. The antagonism which has since controlled the European world was becoming developed. The generation which appeared in the years next following represents it most clearly and vigorously. The times henceforward completely changed their course.

It would, perhaps, be an historian's task to describe successively the generations, as far as possible, in the order of their appearance on the stage of the world's history, showing how they belong together, and how they separate from each other. Full justice would have to be done to each one of them. It were possible to portray a series of the most brilliant forms and figures, all of which have the closest connection with each other, and in whose contrasts the development of the world makes further progress. Events are in harmony with their nature.

INDEX.

ABUAYAZID, 178, 180.
Alba, Duke of, 345, *seq.*
Albrecht, Duke of Munich, 217, *seq.*
Alexander VI., Pope, 41; alliance with Sforza, 42; league with Lodovico against Charles, *ib.*; places Savonarola under ban, 122; his character, 167; his power, 197; death, 201; supposed cause of his death, 205, *seq.*
Alfonso of Aragon gains possession of Naples, 29.
Alfonso II., son of Ferrante, marries daughter of Francis Sforza, 30; his character, 31; quarrels with Lodovico, 40; made king of Naples, 43; alliance with Pope Alexander VI., 44; preparations against Lodovico, 45; his overtures to Charles rejected, 56; renounces the realm in despair, 57; flees to a monastery at Mazzara, *ib.*
Alfonso d'Este, 298; refuses to obey the pope, 299; excommunicated, *ib.*; coins his silver plate, 307; at the battle of Ravenna, 327, *seq.*; liberated from his ban, 342; called " Vulcan," 353.
Alibret, John d', 343, 345.
Allegre, Ive d', 200, 328, 330.
Almeida, Don Francisco d', 269.
—— Don Laurenzo d', defeats the Moors, 270; his bravery at Panian, 270, *seq.*; his death, 290.

Alonso of Bisceglia, marries Lucretia Borgia, 169; murdered, 173.
Alvian, Bartholomew d', 277; takes Görz, 278; his character, 284; taken prisoner by Louis, 287; defeated by the Spaniards, 373.
Amboise, Cardinal, archbishop of Rouen, 134; made legate at the court of France, 183; aspires to the papacy, 208; receives the legation of Avignon, 209; his death, 304.
America, discovery of, 379.
Anhalt, Rudolf von, 296.
Anna, heiress of Bretagne, betrothed to Maximilian, 22; marries Charles VIII., 23; marries Louis XII., 135; negotiates alliance with Spain, 374; her death, 375.
Aragon, house of, its power, 29.
Ataülf, King of the Visigoths, 1.
Aubigny, 91, 189, 199.
Aursperg, Hans, 277, 279.

Baglione, Giampaolo, of Perugia, 258.
Bajazeth, fits out galleys at Constantinople, 56; letters to the pope, 74. *See* Abuayazid.
Balboa, 245, 379.
Barton, Andrew, 367.
Battles, Cambuskennet, 15; Cerignola, 200; Cranganore, 271; Cressy, 15; Dorneck, 148; Flodden, 369; Fornova, 80, *seq.*; Fraskenz, 145; Ganglian, 202; Ghiara d'Adda, 286, 298; Ha-

senbühel, 15; Mühldorf, 14; Navas de Tolosa, 8, *seq.*; Novara, 360; Ravenna, 328, *seq.*; Regensburg, 220; St. Aubin, 22; Sapienza, 179; Schwaderloch, 144, *seq.*; Spurs, 366.
Bayard, 189, *seq.*, 203, 261, 295, 307, *seq.*, 327, 330, 366.
Bentivoglio, John, of Bologna, resists Cesar, 172; 'treaty with him, 183; his power, 257; enters into a compact with the French, and leaves Bologna, 259.
Bibbiena, counsellor of Piero, 49.
Blanca, the lady of Savoy, receives Charles at Turin, 46.
Borgia, Cesar, his character, 168; made Duke of Valentinois, 169; marriage, *ib.*; makes war on Lodovico's sister, 170; takes Forli, 171, and Faenza, 172; murders his brother-in-law, 173; deceives Guidubaldo, 192; captures Urbino and Camerino, 193; alliance with Louis XII., *ib.*; treaty with the Orsini, 195; his treachery, 196; change of character after his father's death, 210; surrenders his castles to the pope, 212; is taken prisoner to Spain, 213; his death, *ib.*
—— Juan, marries Enrique Enriquez, 44.
—— Lucretia, marries John Sforza, 42; marries Alonso of Bisceglia, 169; marries the son of Ercole of Ferrara, 184.
—— Roderick. *See* Alexander VI.
Brandon, Charles, 364.

Cambray, League of, 281.
Cambuskennet, battle of, 15.
Capet, family of, and their descendants, 20.
Caracciolo, Jacob, surrenders Naples to the French, 59.
Cardona, Ramon de, Spanish commander-in-chief, 326, 329, 339, 350, *seq.*, 353, 363, 372.
Cerignola, battle of, 200.

Charlemagne, unites the Latino-Germanic nations, i. 5.
Charles VII. of Valois, subdues English in France, 20.
Charles VIII. assumes the government, 22; releases Louis of Orleans, *ib.*; marries Anne of Bretagne, 23; his character, 28; makes preparations for an expedition against Naples, *ib.*; starts for Italy, 46; his reception at Turin, 47; joined by Lodovico, *ib.*; his reception at Pisa, 52; is admitted into Florence, *ib.*; fears treachery, 53; issues a manifesto, 54; enters Siena, 54; and Rome, 55; treaty with the pope, 56; rejects the overtures of Alfonso, *ib.*; storms St. John, 58; conquers Capua, *ib.*; and Naples, 59, *seq.*; his retreat, 76, *seq.*; repulses Milanese and Venetians, 81, *seq.*; makes treaty with Lodovico, 85; the results of his expedition, 86; his death, 125.
—— Duke of Guelders, campaign in the Netherlands, 279. *See* Archduke Charles.
—— Archduke, marriage, 333; his succession to the crown of Spain assured, 335; refused as suzerain by Venice, 337; desired as prince by Milan, 352; succession to the crown of England assured, 374.
Chaumont, 287, 302, 305.
Christian II. of Denmark, 378.
Colon, Bartholomew and Christopher, their discoveries, 66, *seq.*
Colonization, arising from the crusade, 17, *seq.*
Colonna, Fabrizio, general of the Spanish cavalry, 326, 329.
—— Prospero, 363.
Coppola, Francis, counsellor of Ferrante, rebels against the house of Aragon, 32; is defeated, and put to death by Ferrante, 33.
Cranganore, battle of, 271.
Cressy, battle of, 15.
Crusades, the, 6, *seq.*

INDEX. 383

Davalos, Alfonso, 58.
Diaz, Bartholomew, 264.
Don Luys, Count of Lerin, 345.
Don Manuel, made king of Portugal, 126; marriage, 185; fits out ships for explorations, 265, 267.
Dorneck, battle of, 148.

Everhard the Elder, Count of Würtemberg, enters into compact with Maximilian, 97; his death, 130.
—— the Younger, his character, 97; renounces his kingdom, 130.
Empire, the, founded, 4, 6; constitution of, 99, *seq.*
Emperor, the, his position, 101.
Ercole of Ferrara, 183.
Etzard Cirksena, 378.
Europe, at the time of the Crusades, 7, *seq.*

Falk, Peter, 318, *seq.*, 321.
Federigo, Alphonso II.'s brother, commands fleet against Lodovico, 45; succeeds Ferrantino, 92; proceedings against him, 174, *seq.*; loses hope, 176; goes to Ischia, *ib.*
Ferdinand of Aragon, offers to help Charles, 56; his marriage, 62; and accession, 63; head of the clergy, 65; alliance with Maximilian, 98; alliance with Portugal, 126; league with Henry VII. and Maximilian, 128; treaty with Louis XII. about Naples, 175; forsaken by his relatives, 228; interview with Philip, 228, *seq.*; loses Castile, 230; goes to Naples, 234, *seq.*; returns to Castile, 236; gains the favour of Ximenes, and enters Castile, 243; operations in Africa, 245, *seq.*; joins the league of Cambray, 281; alliance with the pope, 317; reconciliation with Maximilian, 334; alliance with Henry VIII., 335; gains over Cardinal Ximenes, 344;

conquest of Navarre, 343, *seq.*; alliance with Florence, 351; with Louis, 374, 376; league with Genoa, 376.
Ferrante, king of Naples, marries his son to the daughter of Francis Sforza, 30; his alliances, *ib.*
Ferrantino, son of Alfonso II., leader of army against Lodovico, 45; is warded off by Aubigny, 46; forsaken by Florentines, turns to Rome, 54; loses Capua and Naples, 58, *seq.*; betrothed to Joana, 71; driven back by Charles, 77; gains possession of Naples, 83; repulses the French, 90; his return to Naples, and death, 91.
Flodden, battle of, 369.
Florence, surrenders to Charles, 52; war with Pisa, 106; power of, 110; the Consiglio, 115; burning of "Anathem" at, 118; compact with Maxmilian, 274; revolution in, 347, *seq.*
Foix, Gaston de, leader of the French army, 323, *seq.*; death, 330.
Fornova, battle of, 80, *seq.*
Franzipani, 373.
Fraskenz, battle of, 145.
Frundsberg, George, 309, 363, 372.

Gama, Vasco de, 265, *seq.*
Ganglian, battle of, 202.
Genoa, revolution of the "Popolares" at, 260; stormed by Louis, 261; league with Louis, 376.
George of Saxony, 378.
Gerlo, Augustin, offers to kill the pope, 308.
Germans, the, united with the Latins, 1, *seq.*; connected with the Crusades, 7, *seq.*; "German knights," 10, *seq.*; German auxiliaries decisive in European wars, 98.
Ghiara d'Adda, battle of, 286, 298.
Gonzaga, Marquis, 81, 201, 202.

384 INDEX.

Gonzal, advances from Reggio, 87, *seq.*; takes Taranto, 120; captures Cephalogna from the Turks, 180; his character, 190; reduces Rubo, 198; defeats the French at Cerignola, 200; enters Naples, 201; defeats the French on the Ganglian, 202; in Naples, 233; inclines to Ferdinand, 234; is deceived by him, 236.
Gossenbrod, George, 140, *seq.*
Granada, capture of, 66, *seq.*
Guidubaldo, of Urbino, deceived by Cesar, 192; his flight, 193; his return, 194, 207.

Hasenbühel, battle of, 15.
Henry VII., 127, 322, *seq.*
—— VIII., 333; alliance with Spain, 335; invades France, 364; wins the battle of the spurs, 366; enters Tournay, 371.
Hermandad, the, 64, *seq.*

India, discovered by Portuguese, 266.
Innocent VIII., Pope, his displeasure at Lorenzo's alliance with Ferrante, 37; is pacified by the marriage of his son with Lorenzo's daughter, *ib.*; his death, 40.
Inquisition, established in Castile, 63.
Isabella, daughter of Alfonso II., betrothed to John Galeazzo, 39; defends Bari, 188.
Isabella of Castile, refuses the crown, 61; appointed heiress to Henry IV., 62; marries Ferdinand, *ib.*; becomes Queen of Portugal, 185; death, *ib.*

James IV. of Scotland, 184; alliance with France, 367; death at Flodden, 370.
Jews, the, in Spain, 63, *seq.*
Joana, daughter of Henry IV., declared illegitimate by the nobles, 61; flees with Ferrantino to Naples, 71.

Jörg von Sargans, Count, 141.
Juana, wife of Philip, 185; her insanity, 237, *seq.*; meeting with Ferdinand, 244.
Julius II., Pope, 208; resists Venice, 255, *seq.*; his character, 256; marches against Bologna, 258; enters Perugia, *ib.*; and Bologna, 259; returns to Rome, 262; joins the League of Cambray, 281; pronounces his ban upon Venice, 282; removes the interdict, 297; quarrels with Alfonso of Ferrara, 299; fits out a fleet against Genoa, *ib.*; makes an alliance with the Swiss, 301; goes to Bologna, 302; wins over the Bolognese, 305, *seq.*; besieges and captures Mirandula, 307; calls a Concilium at Rome, 316; forms an alliance with Spain, 317; Parma and Piacenza surrender to him, 342; forms an alliance with Spain, 352; death, 354.
Jürg uff der Flue, 318, 338.

Khan Hassan, Sultan of Cairo, helps the Indians and Moors against the Portuguese, 273.

Lang, Matthew, Bishop of Gurk, 305, 309, 342, 350, 352.
La Palice, 189, 198, 294, 340, 366.
Leo X., Pope, 355.
Lerin, Count, 343, 345.
Liga, the, formation of, 73; ridiculed at Naples, 77; headed by the Pope, 119; victorious in Italy and France, 124; joined by Henry VII., 127.
Lille, treaty of, 373.
Lodovico the Moor, urges Charles to invade Italy, 26; is displeased at the Duchess Buona taking possession of Naples in the name of his nephew, John Galeazzo, 34; is driven out of Milan, *ib.*; stirs up the revolt against Florence, *ib.*; returns and takes on himself the con-

duct of affairs, *ib.*; his alliance with the Aragons and Pope Sixtus, *ib.*; helps John Galeazzo to the throne, thus acquiring the real power, 35; his character, *ib.*; his betrothal to Beatrice, 39; quarrel with Alfonso, 40; poisons Galeazzo, and is made Duke of Naples, 48; joins League against Charles, 73; makes treaty with him, 85; feud with Venice, 136; deserted by his allies, 149, *seq.*; goes to Germany, 153; again advances into Italy, 157; enters Milan, 159; is captured by Trivulzio, 164.

Louis XI.: His character, 21; gains possession of Burgundy and the cities of the Somme, *ib.*; gains Berry, Provence, and Anjou, *ib.*; wins battle of St. Aubin, and conquers Bretagne, 22.

Louis XII.: Accession and character, 133; divorces his wife and marries Charles VIII.'s heiress, 135; treaty with the Swiss, 143; goes into Italy, 154, *seq.*; league with the Pope, 166; advances against Naples, 174, *seq.*; his occupations and allies, 183; compact with Philip, 186; and with Maximilian, 215-222; illness, 224; revokes the betrothal between Charles and Claudia, 231; storms the Genoese, 261; joins Maximilian in an attack on Venice, 281; his hatred of Venice accounted for, 283; defeats Alvian, 287; his reception at Milan, 293; gives up the league with the Swiss, 299; decides for war, 304; fails in his attempt to make an alliance with the Swiss, 357; league with Venice, *ib.*; alliance with Ferdinand, 374, 376.

Louis of Orleans: Rebels, and is taken prisoner to Bourges, after the battle of St. Aubin, 22; released by Charles VIII., *ib.*; claims to Milan, 71; captured at Novara, 84; released, 85. *See* Louis XII.

Macchiavelli, 347, 352.

Malacca, emporium of Eastern trade, 264.

Mantua, Marquis of, 260; captured and imprisoned, 295, 296; liberated, 306.

Masono, grotto of, massacre in, 296.

Maximilian, Emperor of Austria, King of the Romans: Fails to uphold his wife's claim to Burgundy, 21; marries his daughter to the Dauphin, and assigns Artois and the free county to the French as her dowry, 21; recovers Artois and his daughter by peace of Senlis, 23; joins league against Charles, 73; his position and policy, 93; lord of the Netherlands, 94; his character and pursuits, 95, *seq.*; alliance with Spain through marriage of his sons, 98; his proposal at the Diet of Worms, 102; defeat of his plans, 105; prepares an expedition into Italy, 108, *seq.*; invests Livorno, 110; retreats to Germany, 118; makes a threefold attack on France, which is unsuccessful, 132; defeated by Swiss, 149; promises Milan to Louis, 177; treaty with France, 215; the Estates submit to his decision, 218; defeats the Bohemians, 220; league with Louis and Philip, 222; his doings in Hungary, 230, *seq.*; prepares to invade Italy, 274; adopts the title of Roman Emperor elect, 275; retreats to Innsbruck, 276; danger from Venice, 277; joins with Louis in an attack on Venice, 281; declares hostilities against

Venice, 292; storms Padua, 295; leaves Italy, *ib.*; reconciliation with Spain, 334; joins Henry VIII., 365.

Medici, John de, 329, 348, *seq.*; became Pope, 354. *See* Leo X.

—— Juliano, 351.

—— Lorenzo de: head of the Florentines, 36; enters into friendship with Milan and Naples, 37; his death, 40.

—— Piero de, son of Lorenzo, 40; devoted to the Aragons, *ib.*; his character, 41; his policy disapproved at Florence, 50; is forced to flee to Bologna, 51.

Melinda, Prince of, 266, 269.

Moors, the, trade of, 263; in Mozambique, 265; defeated by Lourenzo, 270.

Migration of nations, the, 2, *seq.*; 18.

Mühldorf, battle of, 14.

Naples, war in, 187, *seq.*; truce, 204.

Navarra, Pedro, conducts expedition to Africa, 246; takes Tripolis, 247; bores mines under Bologna, 322; captain of the foot, 326.

Navarre, conquest of, 343, *seq.*

Navas de Tolosa, battle of, 8, *seq.*

Novara, battle of, 360.

Oliveretto, 194.

Orsini, peace with Alexander, 120; treaty with Cesar, 195; destruction of, 197.

Orsino, Cardinal, 195.

—— Pagolo, 50.

Ostrogothic Empire, fall of, 4.

Pacteco, Pereira, 267, *seq.*

Papacy, the, founded, 4, 6; power of, not recognized before the seventh century, 4.

Pavia, Cardinal of, character of, 306; in command in Bologna, 309; flees, 310; his death, 311.

Petrucci, Antonello, counsellor of Ferrante, 30.

"Pfennig" tax, 105, 108, 131.

Philip, Archduke, 185, *seq.*, 214; league with Maximilian and Louis, 222; prepares to drive Ferdinand out of Castile, 223; alliance with Henry VIII., 227; interview with Ferdinand, 228, *seq.*; the cities of Castile open their gates to him, 230; his death, 232.

Pisa ceded to Charles by Piero, 50; gives itself up to the French, 52; war with Florence, 106; council of, 316, 325.

Pitigliano, 284, 288.

Pius III., Pope, 28; death, *ib.*

Portuguese, the, discoveries of, 263; their victories over the Moors, 267, *seq.*; bravery of, 271.

Rabot, Jean, Master of Petitions to Charles, 52.

Ravenna, battle of, 328, *seq.*

Regensburg, battle of, 220.

René of Anjou, 21.

Rienzi, Cola, 16.

Robert von der Mark, 358, 360.

Roger, king of Italy, 8.

Rovera, Julian della, Cardinal, urges Charles to invade Italy, 26; in disfavour with Innocent VIII., 37; resists Borgia, 41; elected Pope, 208. *See* Julius II.

Ruprecht, 217, *seq.*, 221.

St. Aubin, battle of, 22.

St. Jago, order of, 64.

Sancho the Wise, 344.

Sapienza, battle of, 179.

Savonarola, his prophecies, 51, 77; his doctrines, 112, *seq.*; his influence, 114, *seq.*; excites the hatred of the Pope, 120; placed under ban, 122; publishes the "Triumph of the Cross," 123; his death, 125.

Schiner, Matthew, Bishop of Valais, 301, 303, 318, 320.

Schwaderloch, battle of, 144, *seq.*

Senlis, peace of, 23.
Sforza, house of, 29.
——— Ascanio, resists Roderick Borgia, 41; with Lodovico in Italy, 138; besieges the castle at Milan, 160; imprisoned at Bourges, 165; released, 207.
——— Francis, gains possession of Milan, 29; becomes Lord of Milan, 36; the fates of his sons, 164.
——— John, of Pesaro, 42, 169, 171.
——— John Galeazzo, assumes dukedom of Milan, 35; betrothed to Isabella, 39; poisoned by Lodovico, 48.
——— Lodovico, the Moor. *See* Lodovico.
——— Maximilian, 352, 356, 361.
Slavs, the, 3, *seq.*, 9.
Soderini, 349, *seq.*, 355.
Spain connected with the Crusades, 7, *seq.*; its power, and the origin thereof, 61, *seq.*; royal marriages in, 185; war with France, 187, *seq.*; loses possessions in Italy, 189.
Spurs, battle of the, 366.
Suabian League, the, 100; cities of, called to the assistance of the Tyrol, 141.
Swiss, the, treaty with Louis, 143; win the battle of Schwaderloch, 144; drive back the Suabians, 145; defeat Maximilian, 149; their situation in 1510, 299; join Louis, 300; make an alliance with the pope, 301; cross the St. Gothard, 302; retreat, 303; associate with the pope, 318; rise up against the emperor, 320; advance into Italy, and are repulsed, 321; retreat, 322; again advance, 338, *seq.*; take Milan, 341; struggle with the French for Milan, 355, *seq.*; win battle of Novara, 360; cross the French frontier, 367.

Terouanne, siege of 365; destruction of, 371.

Tournay, siege of, 371.
Tremouille, 79, 160, 357, 361.
Trivulzio, John Jacob, 34; deserts Ferrantino, and goes over to Charles, 59; fortifies Asti, 107; arrayed against Lodovico, 149; occupies Milan with his Guelphs, 158; flees to the Tessin, 159; retires further, 160; takes Lodovico prisoner, 164; brings tidings to Louis, 285; at the head of the French, 308; drives back the papal army, 309; leaves Milan, 341; sent as envoy to the Swiss, 357; defeated at Novara, 361.
Turks, the, involved in the war in Italy, 178; gain a victory over the Venetians, 179; take Lepanto, *ib.*

Ulrich, of Würtemberg, 219, 366.
Urbino, duke of, 306; kills the cardinal of Pavia, 311; organizes the papal army, 339.

Valori, Francis, envoy to Charles, 50, *seq.*
Venice forms a league against Charles, 73; feud with Lodovico, 136; declares for the pope, 172; attacks the Romagna, 209, 254; its commerce, 248, *seq.*; its conquests, 251, *seq.*; its constitution, 253; its power, 254; war with Cesar, *ib.*; resisted by Julius II., 256; decay of its commerce, 263, 272; refuses to comply with the demands of France, 280; gives up the subjected cities, 289; its trade and military power crushed, 291.
Vinci, Leonardo da, summoned to Milan by Lodovico, 35.

Wladislaw, king of Hungary, 42, 230, *seq.*
Wolleb, Heini, 145.
Worms, diet of, 97, 102.

Ximenes, archbishop of Toledo, 180, 240; review of his life, 241, *seq.*; made cardinal, 243; declares for Ferdinand, *ib.*; urges the Moorish war, 245; sets sail for Africa, and takes Oran, 246; gained over by Ferdinand, 344.

Zamorin, the, of Kolikod, 263, *seq.*
Zjemi, 55, 60, 74.

ALPHABETICAL LIST
OF
BOHN'S LIBRARIES.
APRIL, 1893.

'I may say in regard to all manner of books, Bohn's Publication Series is the usefullest thing I know.'—THOMAS CARLYLE.

'The respectable and sometimes excellent translations of Bohn's Library have done for literature what railroads have done for internal intercourse.'—EMERSON.

'An important body of cheap literature, for which every living worker in this country who draws strength from the past has reason to be grateful.'
Professor HENRY MORLEY.

BOHN'S LIBRARIES.

STANDARD LIBRARY	345 VOLUMES.
HISTORICAL LIBRARY	23 VOLUMES.
PHILOSOPHICAL LIBRARY . . .	17 VOLUMES.
ECCLESIASTICAL LIBRARY . . .	15 VOLUMES.
ANTIQUARIAN LIBRARY . , . .	36 VOLUMES.
ILLUSTRATED LIBRARY	75 VOLUMES.
SPORTS AND GAMES	16 VOLUMES.
CLASSICAL LIBRARY	107 VOLUMES.
COLLEGIATE SERIES	10 VOLUMES.
SCIENTIFIC LIBRARY	46 VOLUMES.
ECONOMICS AND FINANCE . . .	5 VOLUMES.
REFERENCE LIBRARY	30 VOLUMES.
NOVELISTS' LIBRARY	13 VOLUMES.
ARTISTS' LIBRARY	9 VOLUMES.
CHEAP SERIES	55 VOLUMES.
SELECT LIBRARY OF STANDARD WORKS	31 VOLUMES.

'Messrs. Bell are determined to do more than maintain the reputation of "Bohn's Libraries."'—*Guardian.*

'The imprint of Bohn's Standard Library is a guaranty of good editing.'
Critic (N.Y.).

'This new and attractive form in which the volumes of Bohn's Standard Library are being issued is not meant to hide either indifference in the selection of books included in this well-known series, or carelessness in the editing.'
St. James's Gazette.

'Messrs. Bell & Sons are making constant additions of an eminently acceptable character to "Bohn's Libraries."'—*Athenæum.*

ALPHABETICAL LIST OF BOOKS

CONTAINED IN

BOHN'S LIBRARIES.

747 Vols., Small Post 8vo. cloth.

Complete Detailed Catalogue will be sent on application.

Addison's Works. 6 vols. 3s. 6d. each.

Aeschylus. Verse Trans. by Anna Swanwick. 5s.

—— Prose Trans. by T. A. Buckley. 3s. 6d.

Agassiz & Gould's Comparative Physiology. 5s.

Alfieri's Tragedies. Trans. by Bowring. 2 vols. 3s. 6d. each.

Alford's Queen's English. 1s. & 1s. 6d.

Allen's Battles of the British Navy. 2 vols. 5s. each.

Ammianus Marcellinus. Trans. by C. D. Yonge. 7s. 6d.

Andersen's Danish Tales. Trans. by Caroline Peachey. 5s.

Antoninus (Marcus Aurelius). Trans. by George Long. 3s. 6d.

Apollonius Rhodius. The Argonautica. Trans. by E. P. Coleridge. 5s.

Apuleius, The Works of. 5s.

Ariosto's Orlando Furioso. Trans. by W. S. Rose. 2 vols. 5s. each.

Aristophanes. Trans. by W. J. Hickie. 2 vols. 5s. each.

Aristotle's Works. 5 vols, 5s. each; 2 vols, 3s. 6d. each.

Arrian. Trans. by E. J. Chinnock. 5s.

Ascham's Scholemaster. (J. E. B. Mayor.) 1s.

Bacon's Essays and Historical Works, 3s. 6d.; Essays, 1s. and 1s. 6d.; Novum Organum, and Advancement of Learning, 5s.

Ballads and Songs of the Peasantry. By Robert Bell. 3s. 6d.

Bass's Lexicon to the Greek Test. 2s.

Bax's Manual of the History of Philosophy. 5s.

Beaumont & Fletcher. Leigh Hunt's Selections. 3s. 6d.

Bechstein's Cage and Chamber Birds. 5s.

Beckmann's History of Inventions. 2 vols. 3s. 6d. each.

Bede's Ecclesiastical History and the A. S. Chronicle. 5s.

Bell (Sir C.) On the Hand. 5s.

—— Anatomy of Expression. 5s.

Bentley's Phalaris. 5s.

Björnson's Arne and the Fisher Lassie. Trans. by W. H. Low. 3s. 6d.

Blair's Chronological Tables. 10s. Index of Dates. 2 vols. 5s. each.

Bleek's Introduction to the Old Testament. 2 vols. 5s. each.

Boethius' Consolation of Philosophy, &c. 5s.

Bohn's Dictionary of Poetical Quotations. 6s.

Bond's Handy-book for Verifying Dates, &c. 5s.

Bonomi's Nineveh. 5s.

Boswell's Life of Johnson. (Napier). 6 vols. 3s. 6d. each.

—— (Croker.) 5 vols. 20s.

Brand's Popular Antiquities. 3 vols. 5s. each.

Bremer's Works. Trans. by Mary Howitt. 4 vols. 3s. 6d. each.

Bridgewater Treatises. 9 vols. Various prices.

Brink (B. Ten). Early English Literature. 2 vols. 3s. 6d. each.

Browne's (Sir Thomas) Works. 3 vols. 3s. 6d. each.
Buchanan's Dictionary of Scientific Terms. 6s.
Buckland's Geology and Mineralogy. 2 vols. 15s.
Burke's Works and Speeches. 8 vols. 3s. 6d. each. The Sublime and Beautiful. 1s. & 1s. 6d. Reflections on the French Revolution. 1s.
—— Life, by Sir James Prior. 3s. 6d.
Burney's Evelina. 3s. 6d. Cecilia 2 vols. 3s. 6d. each.
Burns' Life by Lockhart. Revised by W. Scott Douglas. 3s. 6d.
Butler's Analogy of Religion, and Sermons. 3s. 6d.
Butler's Hudibras. 5s.; or 2 vols., 5s. each.
Caesar. Trans. by W. A. M'Devitte. 5s.
Camoens' Lusiad. Mickle's Translation, revised. 3s. 6d.
Carafas (The) of Maddaloni. By Alfred de Reumont. 3s. 6d.
Carpenter's Mechanical Philosophy 5s. Vegetable Physiology. 6s. Animal Physiology. 6s.
Carrel's Counter Revolution under Charles II. and James II. 3s. 6d.
Cattermole's Evenings at Haddon Hall. 5s.
Catullus and Tibullus. Trans. by W. K. Kelly. 5s.
Cellini's Memoirs. (Roscoe.) 3s. 6d.
Cervantes' Exemplary Novels. Trans. by W. K. Kelly. 3s. 6d.
—— Don Quixote. Motteux's Trans. revised. 2 vols. 3s. 6d. each.
—— Galatea. Trans. by G. W. J. Gyll. 3s. 6d.
Chalmers On Man. 5s.
Channing's The Perfect Life. 1s. and 1s. 6d.
Chaucer's Works. Bell's Edition, revised by Skeat. 4 vols. 3s. 6d. ea.
Chess Congress of 1862. By J. Löwenthal. 5s.
Chevreul on Colour. 5s. and 7s. 6d.
Chillingworth's The Religion of Protestants. 3s. 6d.
China: Pictorial, Descriptive, and Historical. 5s.

Chronicles of the Crusades. 5s.
Cicero's Works. 7 vols. 5s. each. 1 vol., 3s. 6d.
—— Friendship and Old Age. 1s. and 1s. 6d.
Clark's Heraldry. (Planché.) 5s. and 15s.
Classic Tales. 3s. 6d.
Coleridge's Prose Works. (Ashe.) 6 vols. 3s. 6d. each.
Comte's Philosophy of the Sciences. (G. H. Lewes.) 5s.
Condé's History of the Arabs in Spain. 3 vols. 3s. 6d. each.
Cooper's Biographical Dictionary. 2 vols. 5s. each.
Cowper's Works. (Southey.) 8 vols. 3s. 6d. each.
Coxe's House of Austria. 4 vols. 3s. 6d. each. Memoirs of Marlborough. 3 vols. 3s. 6d. each. Atlas to Marlborough's Campaigns. 10s. 6d.
Craik's Pursuit of Knowledge. 5s.
Craven's Young Sportsman's Manual. 5s.
Cruikshank's Punch and Judy. 5s. Three Courses and a Dessert. 5s.
Cunningham's Lives of British Painters. 3 vols. 3s. 6d. each.
Dante. Trans. by Rev. H. F. Cary. 3s. 6d. Inferno. Separate, 1s. and 1s. 6d. Purgatorio. 1s. and 1s. 6d. Paradiso. 1s. and 1s. 6d.
—— Trans. by I. C. Wright. (Flaxman's Illustrations.) 5s.
—— Inferno. Italian Text and Trans. by Dr. Carlyle. 5s.
—— Purgatorio. Italian Text and Trans. by W. S. Dugdale. 5s.
De Commines' Memoirs. Trans. by A. R. Scoble. 2 vols. 3s. 6d. each.
Defoe's Novels and Miscel. Works. 6 vols. 3s. 6d. each. Robinson Crusoe (Vol. VII). 3s. 6d. or 5s. The Plague in London. 1s. and 1s. 6d.
Delolme on the Constitution of England. 3s. 6d.
Demmins' Arms and Armour. Trans. by C. C. Black. 7s. 6d.
Demosthenes' Orations. Trans. by C. Rann Kennedy. 4 vols. 5s., and 1 vol. 3s. 6d.

Demosthenes' Orations On the Crown. 1s. and 1s. 6d.
De Stael's Corinne. Trans. by Emily Baldwin and Paulina Driver. 3s. 6d.
Devey's Logic. 5s.
Dictionary of Greek and Latin Quotations. 5s.
—— of Poetical Quotations (Bohn). 6s.
—— of Scientific Terms. (Buchanan.) 6s.
—— of Biography. (Cooper.) 2 vols. 5s. each.
—— of Noted Names of Fiction. (Wheeler.) 5s.
—— of Obsolete and Provincial English. (Wright.) 2 vols. 5s. each.
Didron's Christian Iconography. 2 vols. 5s. each.
Diogenes Laertius. Trans. by C. D. Yonge. 5s.
Dobree's Adversaria. (Wagner). 2 vols. 5s. each.
Dodd's Epigrammatists. 6s.
Donaldson's Theatre of the Greeks. 5s.
Draper's History of the Intellectual Development of Europe. 2 vols. 5s. each.
Dunlop's History of Fiction. 2 vols. 5s. each.
Dyer's History of Pompeii. 7s. 6d.
—— The City of Rome. 5s.
Dyer's British Popular Customs. 5s.
Early Travels in Palestine. (Wright.) 5s.
Eaton's Waterloo Days. 1s. and 1s. 6d.
Eber's Egyptian Princess. Trans. by E. S. Buchheim. 3s. 6d.
Edgeworth's Stories for Children. 3s. 6d.
Ellis' Specimens of Early English Metrical Romances. (Halliwell.) 5s.
Elze's Life of Shakespeare. Trans. by L. Dora Schmitz. 5s.
Emerson's Works. 3 vols. 3s. 6d. each, or 5 vols. 1s. each.
Ennemoser's History of Magic. 2 vols. 5s. each.
Epictetus. Trans. by George Long. 5s.
Euripides. Trans. by E. P. Coleridge. 2 vols. 5s. each.
Eusebius' Eccl. History. Trans. by C. F. Cruse. 5s.
Evelyn's Diary and Correspondence. (Bray.) 4 vols. 5s. each.

Fairholt's Costume in England. (Dillon.) 2 vols. 5s. each.
Fielding's Joseph Andrews. 3s. 6d. Tom Jones. 2 vols. 3s. 6d. each. Amelia. 5s.
Flaxman's Lectures on Sculpture. 6s.
Florence of Worcester's Chronicle. Trans. by T. Forester. 5s.
Foster's Works. 10 vols. 3s. 6d. each.
Franklin's Autobiography. 1s.
Gesta Romanorum. Trans. by Swan & Hooper. 5s.
Gibbon's Decline and Fall. 7 vols. 3s. 6d. each.
Gilbart's Banking. 2 vols. 5s. each.
Gil Blas. Trans. by Smollett. 6s.
Giraldus Cambrensis. 5s.
Goethe's Works and Correspondence, including Autobiography and Annals, Faust, Elective affinities, Werther, Wilhelm Meister, Poems and Ballads, Dramas, Reinecke Fox, Tour in Italy and Miscellaneous Travels, Early and Miscellaneous Letters, Correspondence with Eckermann and Soret, Zelter and Schiller, &c. &c. By various translators. 16 vols. 3s. 6d. each.
—— Faust. Text with Hayward's Translation. (Buchheim.) 5s.
—— Faust. Part I. Trans. by Anna Swanwick. 1s. and 1s. 6d.
—— Boyhood. (Part I. of the Autobiography.) Trans. by J. Oxenford. 1s. and 1s. 6d.
—— Reinecke Fox. Trans. by A. Rogers. 1s. and 1s. 6d.
Goldsmith's Works. (Gibbs.) 5 vols. 3s. 6d. each.
—— Plays. 1s. and 1s. 6d. Vicar of Wakefield. 1s. and 1s. 6d.
Grammont's Memoirs and Boscobel Tracts. 5s.
Gray's Letters. (D. C. Tovey.) [*In the press.*
Greek Anthology. Trans. by E. Burges. 5s.
Greek Romances. (Theagenes and Chariclea, Daphnis and Chloe, Clitopho and Leucippe.) Trans. by Rev. R. Smith. 5s.
Greek Testament. 5s.

Greene, Marlowe, and Ben Jonson's Poems. (Robert Bell.) 3s. 6d.

Gregory's Evidences of the Christian Religion. 3s. 6d.

Grimm's Gammer Grethel. Trans. by E. Taylor. 3s. 6d.

—— German Tales. Trans. by Mrs. Hunt. 2 vols. 3s. 6d. each.

Grossi's Marco Visconti. 3s. 6d.

Guizot's Origin of Representative Government in Europe. Trans. by A. R. Scoble. 3s. 6d.

—— The English Revolution of 1640. Trans. by W. Hazlitt. 3s. 6d.

—— History of Civilisation. Trans. by W. Hazlitt. 3 vols. 3s. 6d. each.

Hall (Robert). Miscellaneous Works. 3s. 6d.

Handbooks of Athletic Sports. 8 vols. 3s. 6d. each.

Handbook of Card and Table Games. 2 vols. 3s. 6d. each.

—— of Proverbs. By H. G. Bohn. 5s.

—— of Foreign Proverbs. 5s.

Hardwick's History of the Thirty-nine Articles. 5s.

Harvey's Circulation of the Blood. (Bowie.) 1s. and 1s. 6d.

Hauff's Tales. Trans. by S. Mendel. 3s. 6d.

—— The Caravan and Sheik of Alexandria. 1s. and 1s. 6d.

Hawthorne's Novels and Tales. 3 vols. 3s. 6d. each.

Hazlitt's Lectures and Essays. 7 vols. 3s. 6d. each.

Heaton's History of Painting. (Cosmo Monkhouse.) 5s.

Hegel's Philosophy of History. Trans. by J. Sibree. 5s.

Heine's Poems. Trans. by E. A. Bowring. 3s. 6d.

—— Travel Pictures. Trans. by Francis Storr. 3s. 6d.

Helps (Sir Arthur). Life of Thomas Brassey. 1s. and 1s. 6d.

Henderson's Historical Documents of the Middle Ages. 5s.

Henfrey's English Coins. (Keary.) 6s.

Henry (Matthew) On the Psalms. 5s.

Henry of Huntingdon's History. Trans. by T. Forester. 5s.

Herodotus. Trans. by H. F. Cary. 3s. 6d.

—— Wheeler's Analysis and Summary of. 5s. Turner's Notes on. 5s.

Hesiod, Callimachus and Theognis. Trans. by Rev. J. Banks. 5s.

Hoffmann's Tales. The Serapion Brethren. Trans. by Lieut.-Colonel Ewing. 2 vols. 3s. 6d.

Hogg's Experimental and Natural Philosophy. 5s.

Holbein's Dance of Death and Bible Cuts. 5s.

Homer. Trans. by T. A. Buckley. 2 vols. 5s. each.

—— Pope's Translation. With Flaxman's Illustrations. 2 vols. 5s. each.

—— Cowper's Translation. 2 vols. 3s. 6d. each.

Hooper's Waterloo. 3s. 6d.

Horace. Smart's Translation, revised, by Buckley. 3s. 6d.

Hugo's Dramatic Works. Trans. by Mrs. Crosland and F. L. Slous. 3s. 6d.

—— Hernani. Trans. by Mrs. Crosland. 1s.

—— Poems. Trans. by various writers. Collected by J. H. L. Williams. 3s. 6d.

Humboldt's Cosmos. Trans. by Otté, Paul, and Dallas. 4 vols. 3s. 6d. each, and 1 vol. 5s.

—— Personal Narrative of his Travels. Trans. by T. Ross. 3 vols. 5s. each.

—— Views of Nature. Trans. by Otté and Bohn. 5s.

Humphreys' Coin Collector's Manual. 2 vols. 5s. each.

Hungary, History of. 3s. 6d.

Hunt's Poetry of Science. 5s.

Hutchinson's Memoirs. 3s. 6d.

India before the Sepoy Mutiny. 5s.

Ingulph's Chronicles. 5s.

James' Life of Richard Cœur de Lion. 2 vols. 3s. 6d. each.

—— Life and Times of Louis XIV. 2 vols. 3s. 6d. each.

Irving (Washington). Complete Works. 15 vols. 3s. 6d. each; or in 18 vols. 1s. each, and 2 vols. 1s. 6d. each.

—— Life and Letters. By Pierre E. Irving. 2 vols. 3s. 6d. each.

Jameson (Mrs.) Shakespeare's Heroines. 3s. 6d.

Jesse (E.) Anecdotes of Dogs. 5s.

Jesse (J. H.) Memoirs of the Court of England under the Stuarts. 3 vols. 5s. each.

—— Memoirs of the Pretenders. 5s.

Johnson's Lives of the Poets. (Napier). 3 vols. 3s. 6d. each.

Josephus. Whiston's Translation, revised by Rev. A. R. Shilleto. 5 vols. 3s. 6d. each.

Joyce's Scientific Dialogues. 5s.

Jukes-Browne's Handbook of Physical Geology. 7s. 6d. Handbook of Historical Geology. 6s. The Building of the British Isles. 7s. 6d.

Julian the Emperor. Trans. by Rev. C. W. King. 5s.

Junius's Letters. Woodfall's Edition, revised. 2 vols. 3s. 6d. each.

Justin, Cornelius Nepos, and Eutropius. Trans. by Rev. J. S. Watson. 5s.

Juvenal, Persius, Sulpicia, and Lucilius. Trans. by L. Evans. 5s.

Kant's Critique of Pure Reason. Trans. by J. M. D. Meiklejohn. 5s.

—— Prolegomena, &c. Trans. by E. Belfort Bax. 5s.

Keightley's Fairy Mythology. 5s. Classical Mythology. Revised by Dr. L. Schmitz. 5s.

Kidd On Man. 3s. 6d.

Kirby On Animals. 2 vols. 5s. each.

Knight's Knowledge is Power. 5s.

La Fontaine's Fables. Trans. by E. Wright. 3s. 6d.

Lamartine's History of the Girondists. Trans. by H. T. Ryde. 3 vols. 3s. 6d. each.

—— Restoration of the Monarchy in France. Trans. by Capt. Rafter. 4 vols. 3s. 6d. each.

—— French Revolution of 1848. 3s. 6d.

Lamb's Essays of Elia and Eliana. 3s. 6d., or in 3 vols. 1s. each.

—— Memorials and Letters. Talfourd's Edition, revised by W. C. Hazlitt. 2 vols. 3s. 6d. each.

—— Specimens of the English Dramatic Poets of the Time of Elizabeth. 3s. 6d.

Lanzi's History of Painting in Italy. Trans. by T. Roscoe. 3 vols. 3s. 6d. each.

Lappenberg's England under the Anglo-Saxon Kings. Trans by B. Thorpe. 2 vols. 3s. 6d. each.

Lectures on Painting. By Barry, Opie and Fuseli. 5s.

Leonardo da Vinci's Treatise on Painting. Trans. by J. F. Rigaud. 5s.

Lepsius' Letters from Egypt, &c. Trans. by L. and J. B. Horner. 5s.

Lessing's Dramatic Works. Trans. by Ernest Bell. 2 vols. 3s. 6d. each. Nathan the Wise and Minna von Barnhelm. 1s. and 1s. 6d. Laokoon, Dramatic Notes, &c. Trans. by E. C. Beasley and Helen Zimmern. 3s. 6d. Laokoon separate. 1s. or 1s. 6d.

Lilly's Introduction to Astrology. (Zadkiel.) 5s.

Livy. Trans. by Dr. Spillan and others. 4 vols. 5s. each.

Locke's Philosophical Works. (J. A. St. John). 2 vols. 3s. 6d. each.

—— Life. By Lord King. 3s. 6d.

Lodge's Portraits. 8 vols. 5s. each.

Longfellow's Poetical and Prose Works. 2 vols. 5s. each.

Loudon's Natural History. 5s.

Lowndes' Bibliographer's Manual. 6 vols. 5s. each.

Lucan's Pharsalia. Trans. by H. T. Riley. 5s.

Lucian's Dialogues. Trans. by H. Williams. 5s.

Lucretius. Trans. by Rev. J. S. Watson. 5s.

Luther's Table Talk. Trans. by W. Hazlitt. 3s. 6d.

—— Autobiography. (Michelet). Trans. by W. Hazlitt. 3s. 6d.

Machiavelli's History of Florence, &c. Trans. 3s. 6d.

Mallet's Northern Antiquities. 5s.

Mantell's Geological Excursions through the Isle of Wight, &c. 5s. Petrifactions and their Teachings. 6s. Wonders of Geology. 2 vols. 7s. 6d. each.

Manzoni's The Betrothed. 5s.

Marco Polo's Travels. Marsden's Edition, revised by T. Wright. 5s.

Martial's Epigrams. Trans. 7s. 6d.
Martineau's History of England, 1800-15. 3s. 6d.
—— History of the Peace, 1816-46. 4 vols. 3s. 6d. each.
Matthew Paris. Trans. by Dr. Giles. 3 vols. 5s. each.
Matthew of Westminster. Trans. by C. D. Yonge. 2 vols. 5s. each.
Maxwell's Victories of Wellington. 5s.
Menzel's History of Germany. Trans. by Mrs. Horrocks. 3 vols. 3s. 6d. ea.
Michael Angelo and Raffaelle. By Duppa and Q. de Quincy. 5s.
Michelet's French Revolution. Trans by C. Cocks. 3s. 6d.
Mignet's French Revolution. 3s. 6d.
Miller's Philosophy of History. 4 vols. 3s. 6d. each.
Milton's Poetical Works. (J. Montgomery.) 2 vols. 3s. 6d. each.
—— Prose Works. (J. A. St. John.) 5 vols. 3s. 6d. each.
Mitford's Our Village. 2 vols. 3s. 6d. each.
Molière's Dramatic Works. Trans. by C. H. Wall. 3 vols. 3s. 6d. each.
—— The Miser, Tartuffe, The Shopkeeper turned Gentleman. 1s. & 1s. 6d.
Montagu's (Lady M. W.) Letters and Works. (Wharncliffe and Moy Thomas.) 2 vols. 5s. each.
Montaigne's Essays. Cotton's Trans. revised by W. C. Hazlitt. 3 vols. 3s. 6d. each.
Montesquieu's Spirit of Laws. Nugent's Trans. revised by J. V. Prichard. 2 vols. 3s. 6d. each.
Morphy's Games of Chess. (Löwenthal.) 5s.
Mudie's British Birds. (Martin.) 2 vols. 5s. each.
Naval and Military Heroes of Great Britain. 6s.
Neander's History of the Christian Religion and Church. 10 vols. Life of Christ. 1 vol. Planting and Training of the Church by the Apostles. 2 vols. History of Christian Dogma. 2 vols. Memorials of Christian Life in the Early and Middle Ages. 16 vols. 3s. 6d. each.
Nicolini's History of the Jesuits. 5s.

North's Lives of the Norths. (Jessopp.) 3 vols. 3s. 6d. each.
Nugent's Memorials of Hampden. 5s.
Ockley's History of the Saracens. 3s. 6d.
Ordericus Vitalis. Trans. by T. Forester. 4 vols. 5s. each.
Ovid. Trans. by H. T. Riley. 3 vols. 5s. each.
Pascal's Thoughts. Trans. by C. Kegan Paul. 3s. 6d.
Pauli's Life of Alfred the Great, &c. 5s.
—— Life of Cromwell. 1s. and 1s. 6d.
Pausanias' Description of Greece. Trans. by Rev. A. R. Shilleto. 2 vols. 5s. each.
Pearson on the Creed. (Walford.) 5s.
Pepys' Diary. (Braybrooke.) 4 vols. 5s. each.
Percy's Reliques of Ancient English Poetry. (Prichard.) 2 vols. 3s. 6d. ea.
Petrarch's Sonnets. 5s.
Pettigrew's Chronicles of the Tombs. 5s.
Philo-Judæus. Trans. by C. D. Yonge. 4 vols. 5s. each.
Pickering's Races of Man. 5s.
Pindar. Trans. by D. W. Turner. 5s.
Planché's History of British Costume. 5s.
Plato. Trans. by H. Cary, G. Burges, and H. Davis. 6 vols. 5s. each.
—— Apology, Crito, Phædo, Protagoras. 1s. and 1s. 6d.
—— Day's Analysis and Index to the Dialogues. 5s.
Plautus. Trans. by H. T. Riley. 2 vols. 5s. each.
—— Trinummus, Menæchmi, Aulularia, Captivi. 1s. and 1s. 6d.
Pliny's Natural History. Trans. by Dr. Bostock and H. T. Riley. 6 vols. 5s. each.
Pliny the Younger, Letters of. Melmoth's trans. revised by Rev. F. C. T. Bosanquet. 5s.
Plutarch's Lives. Trans. by Stewart and Long. 4 vols. 3s. 6d. each.
—— Moralia. Trans. by Rev. C. W. King and Rev. A. R. Shilleto. 2 vols. 5s. each.
Poetry of America. (W. J. Linton.) 3s. 6d.

Political Cyclopædia. 4 vols. 3s. 6d. ea.
Polyglot of Foreign Proverbs. 5s.
Pope's Poetical Works. (Carruthers.) 2 vols. 5s. each.
—— Homer. (J. S. Watson.) 2 vols. 5s. each.
—— Life and Letters. (Carruthers.) 5s.
Pottery and Porcelain. (H. G. Bohn.) 5s. and 10s. 6d.
Propertius. Trans. by Rev. P. J. F. Gantillon. 3s. 6d.
Prout (Father.) Reliques. 5s.
Quintilian's Institutes of Oratory. Trans. by Rev. J. S. Watson. 2 vols. 5s. each.
Racine's Tragedies. Trans. by R. B. Boswell. 2 vols. 3s. 6d. each.
Ranke's History of the Popes. Trans. by E. Foster. 3 vols. 3s. 6d. each.
—— Latin and Teutonic Nations. Trans. by P. A. Ashworth. 3s. 6d.
—— History of Servia. Trans. by Mrs. Kerr. 3s. 6d.
Rennie's Insect Architecture. (J. G. Wood.) 5s.
Reynold's Discourses and Essays. (Beechy.) 2 vols. 3s. 6d. each.
Ricardo's Political Economy. (Gonner.) 5s.
Richter's Levana. 3s. 6d.
—— Flower Fruit and Thorn Pieces. Trans. by Lieut.-Col. Ewing. 3s. 6d.
Roger de Hovenden's Annals. Trans. by Dr. Giles. 2 vols. 5s. each.
Roger of Wendover. Trans. by Dr. Giles. 2 vols. 5s. each.
Roget's Animal and Vegetable Physiology. 2 vols. 6s. each.
Rome in the Nineteenth Century. (C. A. Eaton.) 2 vols. 5s. each.
Roscoe's Leo X. 2 vols. 3s. 6d. each.
—— Lorenzo de Medici. 3s. 6d.
Russia, History of. By W. K. Kelly. 2 vols. 3s. 6d. each.
Sallust, Florus, and Velleius Paterculus. Trans. by Rev. J. S. Watson. 5s.
Schiller's Works. Including History of the Thirty Years' War, Revolt of the Netherlands, Wallenstein, William Tell, Don Carlos, Mary Stuart, Maid of Orleans, Bride of Messina, Robbers, Fiesco, Love and Intrigue, Demetrius, Ghost-Seer, Sport of Divinity, Poems, Aesthetical and Philosophical Essays, &c. By various translators. 7 vols. 3s. 6d. each.
—— Mary Stuart and The Maid of Orleans. Trans. by J. Mellish and Anna Swanwick. 1s. and 1s. 6d.
Schlegel (F.). Lectures and Miscellaneous Works. 5 vols. 3s. 6d. each.
—— (A. W.). Lectures on Dramatic Art and Literature. 3s. 6d.
Schopenhauer's Essays. Selected and Trans. by E. Belfort Bax. 5s.
—— On the Fourfold Root of the Principle of Sufficient Reason and on the Will in Nature. Trans. by Mdme. Hillebrand. 5s.
Schouw's Earth, Plants, and Man. Trans. by A. Henfrey. 5s.
Schumann's Early Letters. Trans. by May Herbert. 3s. 6d.
—— Reissmann's Life of. Trans. by A. L. Alger. 3s. 6d.
Seneca on Benefits. Trans. by Aubrey Stewart. 3s. 6d.
—— Minor Essays and On Clemency. Trans. by Aubrey Stewart. 5s.
Sharpe's History of Egypt. 2 vols. 5s. each.
Sheridan's Dramatic Works. 3s. 6d.
—— Plays. 1s. and 1s. 6d.
Sismondi's Literature of the South of Europe. Trans. by T. Roscoe. 2 vols. 3s. 6d. each.
Six Old English Chronicles. 5s.
Smith (Archdeacon). Synonyms and Antonyms. 5s.
Smith (Adam). Wealth of Nations. (Belfort Bax.) 2 vols. 3s. 6d. each.
—— Theory of Moral Sentiments. 3s. 6d.
Smith (Pye). Geology and Scripture. 5s.
Smyth's Lectures on Modern History. 2 vols. 3s. 6d. each.
Socrates' Ecclesiastical History. 5s.
Sophocles. Trans. by E. P. Coleridge, B.A. 5s.
Southey's Life of Nelson. 5s.
—— Life of Wesley. 5s.

Sozomen's Ecclesiastical History. 5s.
Spinoza's Chief Works. Trans. by R. H. M. Elwes. 2 vols. 5s. each.
Stanley's Dutch and Flemish Painters, 5s.
Starling's Noble Deeds of Women. 5s.
Staunton's Chess Players' Handbook. 5s. Chess Praxis. 5s. Chess Players' Companion. 5s. Chess Tournament of 1851. 5s.
Stöckhardt's Experimental Chemistry. (Heaton.) 5s.
Strabo's Geography. Trans. by Falconer and Hamilton. 3 vols. 5s. each.
Strickland's Queens of England. 6 vols. 5s. each. Mary Queen of Scots. 2 vols. 5s. each. Tudor and Stuart Princesses. 5s.
Stuart & Revett's Antiquities of Athens. 5s.
Suetonius' Lives of the Caesars and of the Grammarians. Thomson's trans. revised by T. Forester. 5s.
Sully's Memoirs. Mrs. Lennox's trans. revised. 4 vols. 3s. 6d. each.
Tacitus. The Oxford trans. revised. 2 vols. 5s. each.
Tales of the Genii. Trans. by Sir. Charles Morell. 5s.
Tasso's Jerusalem Delivered. Trans. by J. H. Wiffen. 5s.
Taylor's Holy Living and Holy Dying. 3s. 6d.
Terence and Phædrus. Trans. by H. T. Riley. 5s.
Theocritus, Bion, Moschus, and Tyrtæus. Trans. by Rev. J. Banks. 5s.
Theodoret and Evagrius. 5s.
Thierry's Norman Conquest. Trans. by W. Hazlitt. 2 vols. 3s. 6d. each.
Thucydides. Trans by Rev. H. Dale. 2 vols. 3s. 6d. each.
—— Wheeler's Analysis and Summary of. 5s.

Trevelyan's Ladies in Parliament. 1s. and 1s. 6d.
Ulrici's Shakespeare's Dramatic Art. Trans. by L. Dora Schmitz. 2 vols. 3s. 6d. each.
Uncle Tom's Cabin. 3s. 6d.
Ure's Cotton Manufacture of Great Britain. 2 vols. 5s. each.
—— Philosophy of Manufacture. 7s. 6d.
Vasari's Lives of the Painters. Trans. by Mrs. Foster. 6 vols. 3s. 6d. each.
Virgil. Davidson's Trans. revised by T. A. Buckley. 3s. 6d.
Voltaire's Tales. Trans. by R. B. Boswell. 3s. 6d.
Walton's Angler. 5s.
—— Lives. (A. H. Bullen.) 5s.
Waterloo Days By C. A. Eaton. 1s. and 1s. 6d.
Wellington, Life of. By 'An Old Soldier.' 5s.
Werner's Templars in Cyprus. Trans. by E. A. M. Lewis. 3s. 6d.
Westropp's Handbook of Archæology. 5s.
Wheatley. On the Book of Common Prayer. 3s. 6d.
Wheeler's Dictionary of Noted Names of Fiction. 5s.
White's Natural History of Selborne. 5s.
Wieseler's Synopsis of the Gospels. 5s.
William of Malmesbury's Chronicle. 5s.
Wright's Dictionary of Obsolete and Provincial English. 2 vols. 5s. each.
Xenophon. Trans. by Rev. J. S. Watson and Rev. H. Dale. 3 vols. 5s. ea.
Young's Travels in France, 1787-89. (M. Betham-Edwards.) 3s. 6d.
—— Tour in Ireland, 1776-9. (A. W. Hutton.) 2 vols. 3s. 6d. each.
Yule-Tide Stories. (B. Thorpe.) 5s.

New Editions, fcap. 8vo. 2s. 6d. each, net.

THE ALDINE EDITION
OF THE
BRITISH POETS.

'This excellent edition of the English classics, with their complete texts and scholarly introductions, are something very different from the cheap volumes of extracts which are just now so much too common.'—*St. James's Gazette.*

'An excellent series. Small, handy, and complete.'—*Saturday Review.*

Blake. Edited by W. M. Rossetti.

Keats. Edited by the late Lord Houghton.

Campbell. Edited by his son-in-law, the Rev. A. W. Hill. With Memoir by W. Allingham.

Coleridge. Edited by T. Ashe, B.A. 2 vols.

Vaughan. Sacred Poems and Pious Ejaculations. Edited by the Rev. H. Lyte.

Raleigh and Wotton. With Selections from the Writings of other COURTLY POETS from 1540 to 1650. Edited by Ven. Archdeacon Hannah, D.C.L.

Chatterton. Edited by the Rev. W. W. Skeat, M.A. 2 vols.

Rogers. Edited by Edward Bell, M.A.

Herbert. Edited by the Rev. A. B. Grosart.

Chaucer. Edited by Dr. R. Morris, with Memoir by Sir H. Nicolas. 6 vols.

Spenser. Edited by J. Payne Collier, 5 vols.

Dryden. Edited by the Rev. R. Hooper, M.A. 5 vols.

Gray. Edited by J. Bradshaw, LL.D.

Pope. Edited by G. R. Dennis. With Memoir by John Dennis. 3 vols.

Milton. Edited by Dr. Bradshaw. 3 vols.

Churchill. Edited by Jas. Hannay. 2 vols.

Scott. Edited by John Dennis. 5 vols.

Shelley. Edited by H. Buxton Forman. 5 vols.

Prior. Edited by R. B. Johnson. 2 vols.

Wordsworth. Edited by Prof. Dowden. 7 vols.

Burns. Edited by G. A. Aitken. 3 vols.

To be followed by

Herrick. Edited by George Saintsbury. 2 vols.

Goldsmith. Edited by Austin Dobson.

Butler. Edited by R. B. Johnson. 2 vols.

Thomson. Edited by the Rev. D. C. Tovey. 2 vols.

Collins. Edited by W. Moy Thomas.

Surrey. Edited by J. Gregory Foster.

Wyatt. Edited by J. Gregory Foster.

Swift. Edited by the Rev. R. Hooper, M.A. 3 vols.

Parnell. By G. A. Aitken.

Cowper. Edited by John Bruce, F.S.A. 3 vols.

Young. 2 vols.

Shakespeare's Poems.

THE ONLY AUTHORIZED AND COMPLETE 'WEBSTER.'

WEBSTER'S INTERNATIONAL DICTIONARY.

An entirely New Edition, thoroughly Revised, considerably Enlarged, and reset in New Type.

Medium 4to. 2118 pages, 3500 illustrations.

Prices: Cloth, £1 11s. 6d.; half-calf, £2 2s.; half-russia, £2 5s.; calf, £2 8s. Also in 2 vols. cloth, £1 14s.

In addition to the Dictionary of Words, with their pronunciation, etymology, alternative spellings, and various meanings, illustrated by quotations and numerous woodcuts, there are several valuable appendices, comprising a Pronouncing Gazetteer of the World; Vocabularies of Scripture, Greek, Latin, and English Proper Names; a Dictionary of the noted Names of Fiction; a Brief History of the English Language; a Dictionary of Foreign Quotations, Words, Phrases, Proverbs, &c.; a Biographical Dictionary with 10,000 Names, &c.

This last revision, comprising and superseding the issues of 1847, 1864, and 1880, is by far the most complete that the Work has undergone during the sixty-two years that it has been before the public. Every page has been treated as if the book were now published for the first time.

SOME PRESS OPINIONS ON THE NEW EDITION.

'We believe that, all things considered, this will be found to be the best existing English dictionary in one volume. We do not know of any work similar in size and price which can approach it in completeness of vocabulary, variety of information, and general usefulness.'—*Guardian.*

'The most comprehensive and the most useful of its kind.'—*National Observer.*

'A magnificent edition of Webster's immortal Dictionary.'—*Daily Telegraph.*

'A thoroughly practical and useful dictionary.'—*Standard.*

'A special feature of the present book is the lavish use of engravings, which at once illustrate the verbal explanations of technical and scientific terms, and permit them to remain readably brief. It may be enough to refer to the article on "Cross." By the use of the little numbered diagrams we are spared what would have become a treatise, and not a very clear one. . . . We recommend the new Webster to every man of business, every father of a family, every teacher, and almost every student—to everybody, in fact, who is likely to be posed at an unfamiliar or half-understood word or phrase.'—*St. James's Gazette.*

Prospectuses, with Specimen Pages, on application.

London: GEORGE BELL & SONS, York Street, Covent Garden.

www.ingramcontent.com/pod-product-compliance
Lightning Source LLC
Chambersburg PA
CBHW022118290426
44112CB00008B/719